Social Competence of Young Children with Disabilities

This book is printed on recycled paper.

Social Competence of Young Children with Disabilities

Issues and Strategies for Intervention

edited by

Samuel L. Odom, Ph.D.
Associate Professor
Department of Special Education
Vanderbilt University
Nashville, Tennessee

Scott R. McConnell, Ph.D.
Associate Professor
Department of Educational Psychology
University of Minnesota
Minneapolis, Minnesota

and

Mary A. McEvoy, Ph.D.
Assistant Professor
Department of Educational Psychology
University of Minnesota
Minneapolis, Minnesota

·P A U L·H·
BROOKES
PUBLISHING C⁰

Baltimore • London • Toronto • Sydney

Paul H. Brookes Publishing Co.
P.O. Box 10624
Baltimore, Maryland 21285-0624

Typeset by The Composing Room of Michigan, Inc., Grand Rapids, Michigan.
Manufactured in the United States of America by
The Maple Press Company, York, Pennsylvania.

Library of Congress Cataloging-in-Publication Data
Social competence of young children with disabilities : issues
    and strategies for intervention / edited by Samuel L.
    Odom, Scott R. McConnell, Mary A. McEvoy.
        p.   cm.
    Includes bibliographical references and index.
    ISBN 1-55766-085-9
        1. Handicapped children—United States.
2. Socialization.   3. Handicapped children—Education—
United States.   I. Odom, Samuel L.   II. McConnell, Scott R.
III. McEvoy, Mary A., 1953–
HQ773.6.S63   1992
371.9–dc20   91-33932
                                                   CIP

Contents

Contributors

Shirin D. Antia, Ph.D.
Associate Professor
Department of Special Education
and Rehabilitation
College of Education
University of Arizona
Tucson, Arizona 85721

Paula J. Beckman, Ph.D.
Associate Professor
Department of Special Education
College of Education
University of Maryland
College Park, Maryland 20742

Judith J. Carta, Ph.D.
Associate Scientist and Project
Director
Schiefelbusch Institute for Life Span
Studies
University of Kansas
Juniper Garden Children's Project
Kansas City, Kansas 66102

Lynette K. Chandler, Ph.D.
Assistant Professor
Department of Special Education
Southern Illinois University at
Carbondale
Carbondale, Illinois 62901

James J. Fox, Ph.D.
Research Director
Center for Early Childhood
Learning and Development
and
Associate Professor
Human Development and Learning
East Tennessee State University
Johnson City, Tennessee 37614

Tanya M. Gallagher, Ph.D.
Professor and Director
School of Human Communication
Disorders
McGill University
Montreal, PB
CANADA H3G 1A8

Howard Goldstein, Ph.D.
Associate Professor
Department of Communication
University of Pittsburgh
Pittsburgh, Pennsylvania 15260

Michael J. Guralnick, Ph.D.
Director
Child Development and Mental
Retardation Center
University of Washington
Seattle, Washington 98195

Thomas G. Haring, Ph.D.
Graduate School of Education
University of California-Santa
Barbara
Santa Barbara, California 93106

Everett Hill, Ed.D.
Associate Professor
Department of Special Education
George Peabody College for
Teachers
Vanderbilt University
Nashville, Tennessee 37203

Mary-Maureen Hill, Ed.D.
Research Assistant Professor
Department of Special Education
George Peabody College for
Teachers
Vanderbilt University
Nashville, Tennessee 37203

Kathryn H. Kreimeyer, Ph.D.
Adjunct Assistant Professor
Department of Special Education
   and Rehabilitation
College of Education
University of Arizona
Tucson, Arizona 85721

Joan Lieber, Ph.D.
Assistant Professor
Department of Special Education
College of Education
University of Maryland
College Park, Maryland 20742

Scott R. McConnell, Ph.D.
Associate Professor
Department of Educational
   Psychology
University of Minnesota
Minneapolis, Minnesota 55455

Mary A. McEvoy, Ph.D.
Assistant Professor
Department of Educational
   Psychology
University of Minnesota
Minneapolis, Minnesota 55455

Judith Niemeyer, Ph.D.
Assistant Professor
School of Education
University of North Carolina-
   Greensboro
Greensboro, North Carolina 27412

Samuel L. Odom, Ph.D.
Associate Professor
Department of Special Education
Vanderbilt University
Nashville, Tennessee 37203

Diane M. Sainato, Ph.D.
Assistant Professor
Department of Educational Services
   and Research
Ohio State University
Columbus, Ohio 43210

Sarah Savelle, M.Ed.
George Peabody College for
   Teachers
Vanderbilt University
Nashville, Tennessee 37203

Annette C. Skellenger, Ed.D.
Division of Special Education
Room 318 McKee
University of Northern Colorado
Greely, Colorado 80631

Preface

During the 1970s and 1980s, information about the social development of young children accumulated steadily. This information has allowed psychologists and child development specialists to draw a detailed picture of the development of social competence of preschool-age (Howes, 1988) and elementary school-age children (Dodge, Pettit, McClaskey, & Brown, 1986). This information depicts a clear, steady increase in the sophistication of children's abilities to engage in positive and productive social interactions with peers, emerging over the preschool and elementary school years.

This detailed picture of increases in social competence serves as a contrast to the developing social competence of young children with disabilities. Guralnick and Weinhouse (1984), among others, have found that preschool children with disabilities have delays in peer social competence that are in excess of those expected due to their cognitive delays alone. In his study of social behavior of children with disabilities in mainstreamed preschools, Strain (1983) found that a substantial number of these children had infrequent social interactions with peers and received very low peer sociometric ratings. Using a multimeasure assessment of social competence of matched groups of young children with and without disabilities, McConnell and Odom (1991) found substantial differences in the levels of social competence, with typically developing children obtaining consistently higher factor scores than children with disabilities.

In a national survey of preschool special education teachers, Odom, McConnell, and Chandler (1991) found that, on the average, teachers reported that 75% of the children with disabilities in their classes needed to learn more appropriate and positive ways of interacting with their peers. However, when these teachers were asked about the presence of materials to help them design programs for promoting social competence, 89.9% indicated that there was a moderate to great need for new materials. Taken together, these descriptive studies and survey results suggest that preschool-age children with disabilities have substantial and serious social competence impairments, yet few materials exist to guide teachers in designing programs for promoting social competence.

The purpose of this book is to provide a summary of both current knowledge about the social competence of young children with disabilities and intervention practices to promote social competence. Chapters in Section I of the book address theoretical and practical issues related to social competence.

ix

In the first chapter, Odom, McConnell, and McEvoy review the range of conceptualizations of social competence and examine the relevance of these conceptualizations for early intervention programs for young children with disabilities. Guralnick's chapter adds to our current understanding of social competence by proposing a hierarchical model that encompasses both social tasks that children encounter in their interactions with peers and strategies employed to accomplish those tasks. In their chapter, Beckman and Lieber provide an insightful examination of the relationship between parent-child social relationships and the development of peer-related social competence during the preschool years for children with disabilities. Fox's chapter extends this examination of family relationships by reviewing the literature on siblings' contributions to the development of social competence of young children with disabilities and, further, reviews the role of siblings in social competence interventions.

Many young children have their first consistent (i.e., daily) peer group experiences when they enter school. In fact, Guralnick (1990 and this volume) has pointed out that the development of peer-related social competence should be the focus of early intervention programs for young children with disabilities. In their chapter, Sainato and Carta examine the range of ways in which classroom variables affect the development of social competence of young children with disabilities. The implications of children's social competence extend beyond their current classroom and often affect placement in future settings. Chandler examines the ways in which social competence affects and is affected by transition to new classroom settings.

Researchers have developed a range of social interaction interventions for young children with disabilities. These are examined in Section II of the book. In their chapter, McEvoy, Odom, and McConnell describe the different types of interventions that have been developed for children with disabilities, primarily those with developmental delays, behavior disorders, and autism, and review evidence of the effectiveness of each type of intervention approach. However, other specific disabilities may affect uniquely the opportunity to develop social competence and to participate in social interaction with peers. Moreover, certain disabilities may have distinctive implications for the type of intervention strategy chosen. In their chapter, Antia and Kreimeyer review intervention strategies for young children with hearing impairments. Skellenger, Hill, and Hill examine the social functioning of young children with visual impairments and implications for planning their social competence interventions. Also, Goldstein and Gallagher examine the implication of specific language impairment for the development of social competence and propose intervention strategies for children with this disability. Although the research literature provides a range of interventions that could be employed for promoting social competence, little information exists about the actual use of these interventions in classroom settings. McConnell, McEvoy, and Odom review evidence for the use, or lack thereof, of social competence intervention by teachers.

In each of the chapters on intervention strategies noted above, authors review the current "state of the art." In the concluding chapter, Haring reflects on this current state of the art and proposes considerations for both the conceptualization of social competence and programming. His recommendations that interventions shift their focus from social interaction to the development of social relationships and that social networks of peers become integral components of intervention have important implications for practice.

In sum, this book covers the range of topics associated with social competence and related intervention approaches for young children with disabilities. The research literature on this topic is active and growing quickly. Yet, as we note in the McConnell et al. chapter, teachers' utilization of intervention procedures has not been as active. Our hope is that this book will stimulate researchers to further translate the research literature into effective but practical procedures for use in the classroom. We also hope the work presented here will stimulate teachers to use the research to program systematically for the acquisition of skills related to social competence. These skills will have life-long impact on the development of individuals with disabilities.

REFERENCES

Dodge, K.A., Pettit, G.S., McClaskey, C.L., & Brown, M.M. (1986). Social competence in children. *Monographs of the Society for Research in Child Development, 51* (2, Serial No. 213).

Guralnick, M.J. (1990). Social competence and early intervention. *Journal of Early Intervention, 14,* 3–14.

Guralnick, M.J., & Weinhouse, E.M. (1984). Peer-related social interactions of developmentally delayed young children: Development of characteristics. *Developmental Psychology, 20,* 815–827.

Howes, C. (1988). Peer interaction of young children. *Monographs of the Society for Research in Child Development, 53* (1, Serial No. 217).

McConnell, S., & Odom, S.L. (1991, April). *A performance-based assessment of social competence of young children with disabilities.* Paper presented at the Biennial Conference of the Society for Research in Child Development, Seattle, WA.

Odom, S.L., McConnell, S.R., & Chandler, L.K. (1991). *Acceptability and feasibility of classroom-based social interaction intervention for young children with disabilities.* Manuscript submitted for publication.

Strain, P.S. (1983). Identification of social skill curriculum targets for severely handicapped children in mainstreamed preschools. *Applied Research in Mental Retardation, 4,* 369–382.

We dedicate this book to the memory of our friend
and colleague, Robert Gaylord-Ross.
Robert's research on social competence expanded
our view of the concept and affected
positively the lives of many individuals with disabilities.
His work lives on through them.

I

Nature
and Development
of Social Competence

1

Peer-Related Social Competence and Its Significance for Young Children with Disabilities

Samuel L. Odom, Scott R. McConnell, and Mary A. McEvoy

As one watches Quenton, a minimally verbal 4-year-old boy enrolled in a preschool special education class, it is apparent that he is an active player. He runs the toy car along the taped road on the floor; he builds a block garage for the car; and he crashes the car off a bridge. However, during the entire play session, Quenton never gestures to another child or shares his toys. He moves his toys away from other children who are playing close to him and ignores the comments that peers make to him. When a peer sat his toys next to him and said, "Let's play cars," Quenton picked the peers' toys up and moved them away.

Martha is 5 years old and has autism; she is enrolled in an integrated special education class. Two peers without disabilities are seated on each side of her, and in front of all the children are small, plastic cowboys, horses, a covered wagon, and a set of small fences. When the activity begins the two peers scramble for the toys, while Martha watches their movements and rocks gently in the chair. The teacher redistributes the toys, giving Martha a horse and a cowboy. Martha puts the cowboy on the horse and bangs them on the table. Meanwhile, the two peers are talking about making a ranch and reaching across Martha to exchange toys. Martha moves back from the table as the peers brush against her during their play. She occasionally watches them but rocks in her chair during the rest of the period.

Allen, a 5-year-old boy with mild mental retardation, has a winning smile accentuated by the bright steel caps on his two front teeth. He has thick glasses and is shorter than the rest of the children in the

3

kindergarten class into which he is mainstreamed. He is watching two kindergartners jointly sorting buttons by colors and shapes in the "work jobs" center of the class and talking about what they have in their lunchboxes. After watching for a second, he says, "I sort too," and attempts to take some of the buttons to sort. The two peers first attempt to keep the buttons all to themselves, and then, when Allen persists, they go to another learning center.

Social competence is a central organizing theme for development and, essentially, for life. Humans enter a social world at birth and make their way through the world by successfully negotiating decades of social exchanges. Even in death, in most cultures, an individual is an indirect participant in a clearly social event (e.g., a funeral, wake) that recognizes or remembers her or his life.

Participation in this social world requires that individuals acquire at least a minimal level of competence in social interactions. Quenton, Martha, and Allen are young children with disabilities who experience difficulties in their interactions with peers. They rarely interact with peers, and when they do, their social behavior lacks the quality necessary to elicit ongoing social interaction or encourage interaction in the future. Although not all young children with disabilities display difficulties or delays in the acquisition of peer-related social competence, preschool special education teachers have reported that, on the average, 75% of the children in their classrooms need to learn to interact with their peers in a more positive and age-appropriate manner (Odom, McConnell, & Chandler, 1990). For professionals who work with young children with disabilities, the development of social competence, particularly as it relates to peers, should be a fundamental aspect of their intervention programs (Guralnick, 1989, 1990a; Strain, 1990).

The purpose of this chapter is to examine the concept of social competence, specifically as it relates to peer social interactions, peer relationships, and development in other domains. It reviews the historical significance and development of the construct of social competence, discusses the various conceptualizations of social competence, and suggests their implications for children with disabilities. This chapter then examines the relationship of social competence in the preschool years to later social development and development in other domains, and discusses the relationship of social competence to early intervention.

HISTORY OF THE CONSTRUCT OF SOCIAL COMPETENCE

The history of the construct of social competence parallels the history and development of psychology as a science. James Baldwin, an early psychologist, who some believe was a precursor to Piaget, was one of the first individuals to discuss the importance of social interactions for the development of children. He felt that through social interactions, children developed a sense of self and an understanding of moral reasoning (Baldwin, 1897, reported in Grusec & Lytton, 1988). Similarly, in his early theories, Piaget (1926) emphasized the importance of engaging in social interactions with peers for the development of cognitive abilities. In his early model of intelligence, E.L. Thorndike (1920) proposed that social intelligence was one of three forms of the intellect. Social intelligence, and its measurement, continued to receive much attention from psychologists through the 1940s, although interest waned after that time (Greenspan, 1979). Social intelligence appeared again in Guilford's structure of the intellect model, which was originally proposed in the the 1960s (Guilford & Hoepfner, 1971).

Current theories of intelligence also embody or acknowledge the importance of social competence. One of the seven forms of intelligence that Gardner and his colleagues (Gardner, 1987; Gardner & Hatch, 1989) proposed is labeled "interpersonal" and reflects skills related to competence in interpersonal interactions. Similarly, Sternberg (1985), in his triarchic theory of intelligence, embedded social competence in the concepts of both social and practical intelligence.

A major child development movement, begun in the late 1920s and particularly influential in the 1930s, resulted in increased interest by developmental psychologists and psychiatrists in children's social behavior (Renshaw, 1981). Research supported by the network of child welfare stations in this country, notably in Iowa and Minnesota, was a catalyst for this movement. During this period use of observational methodology began in earnest. Adoption of this methodology was reflected in the classic studies by Bott (1928), Challman (1932), Jack (1934), and, especially, Parten (1932), which have influenced substantially the work of investigators into the 1990s. During the same period, Moreno (1934) established the science of sociometry that, continues to be incorporated in many investigations of children's social competence.

World War II interrupted this rich and active area of research in the 1940s. Although important studies of children's social interactions and relations occurred in the intervening years (Chittenden, 1942; McCandless & Marshall, 1957), interest in and research on peer-related social competence did not return to its former level until the late 1960s. For example, Renshaw (1981) noted that in the 1940s and 1950s combined, researchers reported fewer than 40 studies, contrasted with 53 studies published in the 1930s. Today, observational studies of children's competence in peer interations are numerous. In their review of observational systems for coding peer social interactions, Odom and Ogawa (1991) employed two computer searches of the literature to find over 60 published studies across a range of journals dating from 1983 to 1989.

The original definition and diagnosis of mental retardation proved to be another historical event related to the study of social competence. Until the mid-1930s, the classification of children and adults as mentally retarded was based upon their performance on intelligence tests. Reacting, in part, to studies indicating that individuals who escaped from institutions for persons with mental retardation could survive well in the "real world," Doll (1941) and Tredgold (1937) proposed that measurements of social competence or adaptive behavior be incorporated into the criteria employed for diagnosing mental retardation. Doll's (1953) development of the Vineland Social Maturity Scale provided a standardized assessment for measuring such social abilities or competence. In the early 1960s (Heber, 1961), the American Association on Mental Deficiency incorporated measurements of social competence and adaptive behavior into their definition of mental retardation. Subsequent definitions of mental retardation have continued to include these measures (American Association on Mental Retardation, 1990; Grossman, 1973, 1983). Similarly, the ability to form social relationships (a dimension or outcome of social competence) is embedded in the *Diagnostic and Statistical Manual–III–Revised (DSM–III–R)* definition for the diagnosis of autism (American Psychiatric Association, 1987). These classification criteria suggest that social competence is a skill or ability that differs from general intelligence, and that certain disabilities, such as autism and mental retardation, are manifest, at least in part, through deficits in social competence.

CURRENT CONCEPTUALIZATIONS OF PEER-RELATED SOCIAL COMPETENCE OF YOUNG CHILDREN

Obtaining a consensus among contemporary researchers on the definition of social competence is a difficult task. Dodge (1985) noted that the number of definitions is nearly equal to the number of researchers interested in the topic. Definitions vary across and within theoretical orientations. In a review of the definition of social competence Odom and McConnell (1985) found definitions that represented "all-inclusive" (Anderson & Messick, 1974; Zigler & Trickett, 1978); behavioral (Foster & Ritchey 1979); cognitive (Shure, 1981); and performance-based (McFall, 1982) theoretical or conceptual frameworks. However, Guralnick (Chapter 2, this volume) points out that most definitions include elements of a child's *effectiveness* in influencing a peer's social behavior and *appropriateness* given a specific setting, context, and/or culture. Although social competence may imply more than these two dimensions, qualitative dimensions of social effectiveness and appropriateness of children's social behavior in their interactions with peers will serve as an organizational theme for examining social competence in this chapter.

It should be noted that this bipolar nature of social competence is implicit in most conceptualizations of social competence. Measures of social competence may reveal the absence of skills to interact with peers as well as overt behaviors that discourage interaction or alienate peers. From the discussion above, it follows, then, that socially incompetent behavior could be characterized by social ineffectiveness (literally the lack of a positive effect on a peers' behavior or near absolute absence of any peer-directed behavior) or inappropriate use of social behaviors (given the social context). The vignettes described at the beginning of this chapter are examples of these two types of social incompetence.

The units of analysis that researchers employ in their study of children's social competence represent well the different conceptualizations of the construct. This section examines the units of analysis (e.g., behavior, development of relationships) rather than describing more broadly differences in theoretical orientations (e.g., cognitive versus behavioral orientations). In their research, investigators have examined such indicators of children's social competence as singular social behaviors, accomplishments of social tasks, social status, and a performance-based measurement approach involving multiple measures.

Social Behavior

One, and perhaps the major, conceptualization of social competence is grounded in the specific social behavior of children during peer interactions. Social behaviors are the building blocks of interaction, and social interaction is the foundation upon which social competence is based. The behavioral aspects of peer social interaction of young children are a very visible and readily measurable aspect of peer social competence. Although the frequency of peer social interaction has served well as a screening indicator for children who are socially withdrawn (Greenwood, Walker, Todd, & Hops, 1979), some researchers have questioned the use of such measures as indicators of social competence, or incompetence (Asher, Markell, & Hymel, 1981; Rosen, Furman, & Hartup, 1988). For example, a global frequency measure might not identify a child who engages in ineffective or inappropriate interactions.

Social Reciprocity Social reciprocity is a behavioral dimension of social interaction that may reflect one aspect of social competence. Social reciprocity refers to the mutual exchange of interactions among peers. In their observations of preschoolers' social interaction, Hartup and colleagues (Hartup, Glazer, & Charlesworth, 1967) found that the children who used the most positive initiations were most likely to receive positive responses from peers. A similar but weaker relationship existed for using negative initiations. Other investigators have replicated this pattern of social reciprocity (Kohler & Fowler, 1985; Strayer, 1980). Hartup et al. (1967) also noted that children who directed social initiations to other children were also nominated most often as friends or preferred playmates. However, in their normative study of 461 preschoolers, Greenwood, Walker, Todd, and Hops (1981) found that low interactors tended to receive more initiations from peers than they directed to peers. The very low rate of initiations by this group was undoubtedly responsible for this effect.

One measure of the effectiveness of peer social behavior can be observed in the response that individual behaviors receive from peers. Social behaviors that receive a positive response from peers might be seen as more socially competent than behaviors that receive no response. Greenwood et al. (1981) found that positive social initiations with peers had a high probability of receiving a social response. However, the qualitative aspects of these initiations were not examined. In another study of preschool children's social initiations, Tremblay, Strain, Hendrickson, and Shores (1981) identified positive social initiations that peers used frequently and then calculated the probability of those behaviors obtaining a positive response from a peer. They found that sharing, play organization (i.e., suggesting a play idea), affection, assistance, and rough and tumble play had a higher probability than other initiations of eliciting a positive response from a peer. In a subsequent analysis in mainstreamed preschool classrooms, Strain (1983) found that children with disabilities who used these social initiations received higher sociometric ratings from their nondisabled peers than did children who did not engage in these behaviors.

In her investigation of social competence of Canadian preschool children, Wright (1980) found that three social behaviors, "seeking attention of peers," "using peers as an instrumental resource," and "leading peers," when they were positive and successful, related most closely to her criterion measures of social competence (e.g., cognitive problem-solving, perspective-taking). Again, each of these behaviors produced "effects" on the peers' behavior.

In one of the most comprehensive investigations of the development of peer social interaction, Howes (1988) observed toddlers and preschoolers to examine the increases in their complementary and reciprocal play (e.g., taking turns while engaged in the same play theme). For all the children, the proportion of time spent in peer interactions increased during the year. In addition, engaging in complementary and reciprocal play as young toddlers was related directly to the frequency of their cooperative, social pretend play (an advanced form of social interaction) in late "toddlerhood" and as preschoolers. Also, children's cooperative and social pretend play as toddlers was related to teacher and peer ratings of their social competence as preschoolers. Howes also examined children's social initiations (called peer entry, although other investigators use the term differently) and their effects upon peers (defined as either easy entry or rebuffs). She found that children rated higher on peer sociometrics and teacher ratings were more likely to show social initiations that allowed easy entry into social play with peers than were lower-rated children.

Social Behavior of Children with Disabilities   Preschool-age children with developmental delays often engage in fewer social interactions and less mature social behavior than same-age peers without disabilities. A myriad of studies on mainstreaming have documented differences in the frequencies of social interactions of young children with disabilities (see Odom & McEvoy [1988] for a review). In one of the more well-controlled studies of the peer social interaction of young children with disabilities, Guralnick and Weinhouse (1984) found that, although peer interactions of preschool children with disabilities increased across a 5-month period, the frequency of socially directed behavior toward peers was substantially below the level that would have been expected based upon the children's developmental level. Guralnick's later research (Guralnick & Groom, 1987, 1988) confirmed the existence of such delays in other groups of children with mild disabilities. Other investigators have noted delays or difficulties related to peer social interaction for preschool children with special needs, such as hearing impairment (Antia & Kreimeyer, Chapter 6, this volume; Higgenbotham & Baker, 1981; Levy-Shiff & Hoffman, 1985); spina bifida (Wallender, Feldman, & Varni, 1989); visual impairment (Skellenger, Hill, & Hill, Chapter 7, this volume); specific language impairment (Goldstein & Gallagher, Chapter 8, this volume; Rice, 1990); and psychiatric disorders (Strayer, 1980); as well as children who are gifted (Roedell, 1985).

Peer Group Entry Skills   The strategies that a child employs to join, or enter, an activity in which two or more peers are engaged has received much attention from researchers. In his ethnographic research on the peer relationships of preschool-age children, Corsaro (1981) found that over 50% of the attempts to enter peer groups were unsuccessful (i.e., the peer group members either rejected or ignored the children's attempts to enter the group). The social behavior that was most likely to be linked with success was producing a variant of the ongoing behavior (e.g., suggesting an extension of a dress-up activity that was already occurring). With kindergarten and elementary-age children, Putallaz and her colleagues (Putallaz, 1983; Putallaz & Gottman, 1981; Putallaz & Wasserman, 1990) have found that success in peer group entry requires that the child monitor the ongoing activity in order to obtain a frame of reference for, or understanding of the activity before making the initial approach to the peers. Such entry attempts differ somewhat from the social initiations noted above in that the setting for the skill is more circumscribed (i.e., making a social initiation into a preexisting activity in which two or more peers are interacting contrasts with making a social initiation in a variety of contexts with single peers who may or may not be engaged already). Corsaro's (1985) and Putallaz's (1983) work suggests that such group entry skills are important indicators of peer social competence for preschool and early elementary-age children. Similarly, Guralnick and Groom (1988) have noted the importance of such skills for young children with disabilities.

Peer Selection Choices   Being chosen as a preferred partner in social interactions and selectively choosing specific peers as partners in interactions are patterns of social behavior that may reflect social competence. Preschool children, and even toddlers, do not distribute their interactions indiscriminately; given the option, they purposefully choose the peers with whom they will interact. In fact, by 40 months of age, 80% of all children have at least one strong peer preference (Hartup, 1989). This selection, and its reciprocation from peers (i.e., selected peers also choosing the child as a partner in interaction), allows researchers to examine peer relationships rather than focusing solely on frequencies of social interactions or behaviors. It should be noted that often these reciprocal social interaction preferences have been called friendships (Guralnick & Groom, 1988).

Researchers have established different criteria for this peer selection preference. Howes (1983) defined reciprocal peer preferences (i.e., friendships) as dyads in which there was a 50% probability of a social initiation receiving a response, along with at least one unit of complementary play, and at least one positive exchange. However, the more common criteria involve children engaging in a certain percentage of their interactions with a specific peer or peers. For example, Hinde, Titmus, Easton, and Tamplin (1985), and Guralnick and Groom (1987) used a 30% criterion for identifying preferences: if 30% of a child's interactions involved a single specific peer, then that peer was identified as a preferred peer. In addition, a *reciprocal* preference would be established if that preferred peer directed 30%–33% of her or his interactions back to that child. Such reciprocal preferences may imply that children are establishing a positive relationship. Howes (1988) found that children who maintained reciprocal preferences throughout a 1-year period scored higher on general measures of social competence than children who did not maintain such preferences. In addition, interactions occurring with preferred peers involved less rejection and facilitated the acquisition of developmentally appropriate social skills.

The peer preferences of children with disabilities in integrated play groups also have been examined. Guralnick and Groom (1988) observed 4-year-old children with and without mild developmental delays, and 3-year-old children without delays (i.e., developmentally matched to the 4-year-old children with delays). The children with disabilities established *no* reciprocal interaction patterns, whereas the 4-year-old, nondisabled peers established the most reciprocal patterns. However, the preschoolers with disabilities did display unreciprocated preferences (i.e., they interacted with preferred peers but were not chosen as partners by those peers). Similarly to Howes, these authors noted that the interactions within reciprocally preferred dyads were much more positive and facilitative in nature (e.g., children were more likely to respond positively to a peer initiation, and conflicts or disruptions in the interaction were repaired more quickly).

Social Networks   A similar analysis of preschool children's social interaction that relates to social competence is the examination of social networks. From the 1970s into the 1990s ethologists have been interested in the examination of children's peer interactions (Blurton-Jones, 1972; La Freniere & Charlesworth, 1983; McGrew, 1972). In a relatively early study, Vaughn and Waters (1981) examined the peer positive interaction patterns, visual gaze, and dominance hierarchy within preschool peer groups and their relationship to social competence. Although they generally found that both positive interactions and dominance were related to sociometric measures of social competence, they also noted that visual gaze identified the latter (i.e., children directed their gaze toward children who were dominant). Also, in a study in an integrated classroom, Cavallaro and Porter (1980) found that children with and without disabilities tended to direct their gaze toward peers in the group without disabilities. During free play, children gazed more at children whom they sat next to during an indoor activity.

Using an ethological approach, Strayer and colleagues (Strayer, 1980; Strayer & Strayer, 1976) examined the formation of social networks as reflected by the proportion and style of interactions with specific peers in preschool classes. Although complex, such social network analyses reveal the preferences within and among social groups of preschool children. These patterns may provide a basis upon which to examine the development, stability, and competent use of social behavior (Strayer, 1989). Yan and his colleagues (Yan et al., in press) followed a similar approach in examining social cliques that develop among young adults with disabilities. Clique analysis has been applied with preschool children with disabilities since only the late 1980s (Storey, Smith, Wolper, & Strain, 1990). Thus, social network analysis provides a means for examining observationally a peer group's social structure, the relative competence of a child's interactions within that peer group, and the relationship of social competence to the peer group structure.

Summary of Behavioral Assessment of Social Competence   As shown above, behavioral measurement of social competence ranges from calculation of frequencies of global categories of social interaction to complex analyses of interactions that reveal social networks within peer groups. The advantage of many of these measurement strategies is that they usually occur in natural settings (e.g., classrooms) and contain information not only on the quality (i.e., appropriateness) of a child's behavior but also the effectiveness of the behavior during peer interactions. However, exclusive reliance upon behavioral measurement may provide a somewhat unidimensional view of children's social competence (i.e., provide information from only one source) and at times may limit the extent to which the competence of children's social behavior is examined within a social context.

Accomplishment of Social Tasks

Another conceptualization of social competence implies that the competent use of social skills can only be understood as it relates to a social task. Social behavior may be judged as competent or incompetent within the situational context (Dodge, 1985; McFall, 1982). Following a similar logic, Asher and his colleagues (Asher & Renshaw, 1981; Taylor & Asher, 1984) have proposed that competence may lie in the social goals that children choose and their strategies for achieving those goals. Similarly, Dodge, Petit, McLaskey, and Brown (1986) and Guralnick (Chapter 2, this volume) extended this notion by suggesting that the strategies children use in accomplishing a task (e.g., seeking help from a peer, beginning a playful interaction) and success in accomplishing the task are the bases for judging children's social competence.

Observational Study of Social Goals   Krasnor and Rubin (1983) developed a system for determining observationally the goals that children pursue through peer interaction and the strategies employed for accomplishing those goals in a social, problem-solving context. For example, a goal in an interactional sequence might be to gain a child's attention. To accomplish such a goal, the child might choose one of several strategies. She might issue a directive (e.g., "Mary, look at me"), only call the peer's name (e.g., "Mary"), or tap the peer on the shoulder and hold up an object for the peer to see. In Krasnor's (Rose-Krasnor, 1985) system, the strategies could be coded as successful if they accomplish the implied goal in the interaction.

From this social goals perspective, social competence would be reflected by the selection of goals for a given context, the selection of strategies to accomplish such goals, and the selection of alternative strategies when a single one fails (Krasnor, 1983; Krasnor & Rubin, 1983). The process of examining these aspects of social behavior is similar to the measurement of the pragmatics dimension of children's language, in which communication acts have both a function (i.e., goal, purpose, apparent outcome) and a form (Prutting, 1982). To date, the observational analysis of social goals of young children with disabilities has received little attention. It may be difficult to identify the social goals of the interactions of some of these children when they have unclear language or related interfering behaviors (Odom, McEvoy, Ostrosky, & Bishop, 1987). However, in one study employing qualitative methodology, Salisbury, Britzman, and Kang (1989) found that the six preschool children with disabilities in their study used different strategies (i.e., behaviors) to accomplish social goals, and when the initial strategies failed, the children often generated new strategies.

Social Tasks and Information Processing Like Krasnor and Rubin (1983), Dodge (1985) emphasized the importance of examining social goals or tasks (the two terms are used here synonymously) and the social behaviors used to accomplish those tasks. However, he also noted the importance of the link between cognitive processes and social behavior. Dodge and his colleagues developed an information processing model of social competence that includes five components: encoding, representation, response search, response decision, and enactment (Dodge, 1986). Convincing support for this model has been provided for aggressive school-age children who are rejected by their peers (Dodge, Petit, McLaskey, & Brown, 1986). However, many of the measurement strategies are quite verbal in nature and may be too sophisticated for use with preschool-age children with disabilities. Refinement of such measurement procedures for less developmentally mature children would be a necessary and important step in extending Dodge's work on social competence to preschool children with disabilities.

At the preschool level, Shure and Spivak (1979, 1981) developed a series of lessons to promote interpersonal problem-solving among at-risk, preschool-age children. Their presumption was that the ability to solve interpersonal social problems is the direct reflection of social competence (Shure, 1981), and, in fact, their interpersonal cognitive problem-solving training appeared to produce positive results in hypothetical situational tests and on teacher ratings of classroom behavior. For preschool children with mental retardation, Vaughn, Ridley, and Cox (1983) created a hypothetical behavioral task to measure children's interpersonal problem-solving abilities. However, the critical step of linking cognitive strategies or processes to the competent use of social behaviors to accomplish important social tasks awaits verification for preschool-age children with disabilities.

Social Status as a Measure of Social Competence

Researchers have proposed that peer relationships, as reflected by the child's social status within a peer group, may be another conceptualization of social competence (Gresham, 1986). That is, on the one hand, the development of positive relationships with peers will be based upon the competent use of social skills during peer interactions. On the other hand, an absence of positive ratings or nominations from peers or rejection by the peer group may indicate that a child lacks the social skills to establish positive social relationships or does not use those skills in a competent manner.

Sociometrics are the measures commonly used to assess peer relationships, although, as noted above, investigators sometimes use observational measures (Guralnick & Groom, 1988; Howes, 1983). Sociometric assessments may involve preschool children nominating specific children on positive (e.g., liked, a friend) and possibly negative (e.g., not liked, not a friend) dimensions (McCandless & Marshall, 1957), or rating each child in their class according to how much they like to play with the child identified in a picture or by name (Asher, Singleton, Tinsley, & Hymel, 1979). With preschool children, photographs often are used to identify the peers.

For preschool children, there does appear to be a relationship between social interaction among peers and both types of sociometric measures. Early studies suggested that children nominated most frequently as friends tended to engage in positive interactions with peers more frequently (Hartup et al., 1967). Later, Coie, Dodge, and Kupersmidt (1990) reported that social acceptance is related, at all ages, to helpfulness, rule conformity, friendliness, and prosocial interaction. However, children who are rejected by their peers (i.e., receive negative nominations or low peer ratings) tend to engage in aggressive or inappropriate interactions.

Researchers have used sociometrics to examine the peer relationships of preschool children with disabilities in integrated and mainstreamed settings. As mentioned above, Strain (1983) found a positive relationship between the social behavior of children with disabilities and the ratings they received from peers. To examine these differences further, Strain (1984) observed the social interactions occurring in friendship dyads (i.e., interactions with a peer that were rated as positive on the peer rating assessment) of children with disabilities and those of nondisabled children. Nondisabled children tended to select other nondisabled children or older, more cognitively mature children with disabilities as their partners in interaction. With other nondisabled friends, children tended to display more play organizing, share, reward-related, complimentary, and verbal interactions, while with friends with disabilities, more assistance, conflict resolution, and affection interactions occurred. In integrated play groups, Guralnick and Groom (1987) found that children with mild disabilities received significantly lower peer ratings than both same-age and younger, developmentally matched children without disabilities. When conducting a factor analysis of a multimethod assessment of social competence of children with disabilities in nonintegrated settings, McConnell and Odom (1991) found that peer rating scores loaded highly on one of four social competence factors.

Several concerns exist over using sociometrics as a single outcome measure of social competence in peer interactions. First, sociometrics provide only a summary score and thus provide little information about the nature or components of social competence for preschool children with disabilities. With elementary-age children, Coie, Dodge, and Coppotelli (1982); Dodge, Coie, and Brakke (1982); and Gottman (1977) have used positive and negative peer nominations to create "typologies" such as popular, neglected, rejected, ambivalent, and controversial groups of children. These typologies could have relevance for identifying children in need of intervention. However, such typologies require the use of peer nominations rather than peer ratings, which may be less reliable when used with preschool children.

Second, some investigators have questioned the reliability of sociometrics for preschool-age children (Hymel, 1983). For children without disabilities, there seems to be ample evidence that peer ratings are reliable and stable, at least for 4- and 5-year-old children (Howes, 1988; Poteat, Ironsmith, & Bullock, 1986). Similarly, Odom and Fewell (1988) found peer rating measures to be somewhat reliable and stable for one group of preschool children with mild disabilities. These authors also provided some evidence of behavioral correlates in the classroom.

A third concern about sociometrics is that they may be related to qualities or characteristics other than social behavior. Hymel, Wagner, and Butler (1990) noted that both nonbehavioral characteristics (e.g., physical appearance, names) and group processes (e.g., ethnic bias, gender bias, stereotyping) might influence peer acceptance and rejection. In his examination of nonbehavioral determinants of social status of children with disabilities, Strain (1985) found that such nonsocial variables as physical attractiveness, toy play skills, classroom disruption, and athletic skills contributed equally with social skills in predicting peer ratings. Similarly, in an intervention study that included sociometrics as an outcome measure, peers without disabilities were asked why they did not like to play as much with one child with disabilities to whom they had given low ratings. These peers gave reasons related to the child's physical appearance rather than his social behavior for the low ratings (Odom & Watts, 1991). For many children with disabilities, physical appearance may well be as powerful a factor in determining social status in the peer group as a child's social skills. For older children without disabilities, the relationship of physical appearance to sociometric status may be somewhat less clear (Hymel et al., 1990). In summary, although sociometrics provide a unique source of information related to social competence, their global nature and relationship to other nonsocial variables limit their use as a single indicator of social competence for young children with disabilities.

Performance-Based Assessment of Social Competence

In the previous discussion, behavioral, information processing/ problem-solving, or peer relationship/sociometric dimensions of social competence were described. These approaches to understanding social competence are unidimensional in nature in that they assess competence from a single perspective (e.g., social-cognitive abilities, peer acceptance). In the 1980s, unidimensional approaches to defining and assessing social competence were questioned. Hops (1983) and McFall (1982) proposed that social competence lies not in the behaviors that constitute interaction nor in the processes that underlie such behaviors, but, rather, in judgments about the competent performance of such behavior. In applying this conceptualization to social competence of preschool children with disabilities, Odom and McConnell (1985) defined social competence as "the interpersonal social performance of children with other children or adults as judged by significant social agents in the child's environment" (p. 9).

A performance-based assessment of social competence implies that single measures (e.g., direct observation, sociometrics) could provide useful but limited information about a child's social performance. Only in combination, through the use of multi-method assessments (Gresham, 1986), could a comprehensive picture of a child's social competence be obtained. Each source of information would be expected to provide both common, complementary information as well as unique information that represents the judge's opportunities to sample the child's behavior in other settings or from other perspectives. For example, a teacher could provide a rating of the child's peer interactions in school, the peers could provide sociometric information, the parents could provide information about the child's interactions with siblings at home or peers in the neighborhood, and a researcher could provide direct observation information about the child's interactions. One might expect these sources of information to agree at some level, but also that each source would contribute unique information about the child's social competence (e.g., the child might actually be acting differently in the home and at school). In a quantitative sense, this assessment approach employs the method of triangulation used frequently in qualitative research (Strauss & Corbin, 1990).

Several researchers have followed this performance-based approach. Gresham (1981) used a multimethod approach to investigate the validity of social skill measures for assessment of social status of elementary-age children. Among preschool children with developmental delays, Guralnick and Groom (1985) examined several dimensions of social behavior and found moderate correlations between direct observation of social play and teacher ratings of children's social competence. To examine further the application of this performance-based approach with young children with disabilities, McConnell and Odom (1991) collected peer ratings, teacher ratings, direct behavioral observations, and observers' summary ratings of social competence of young children with and without disabilities. A principal components analysis yielded a factor that accounted for 47% of the variance. General social competence factor scores differentiated significantly between groups of children with and without disabilities.

The advantage of a performance-based measurement approach to social competence is in the breadth of the information and perspectives sampled, and the opportunity to confirm information from one source with information from another. Moreover, when contradictory information does appear (e.g., between the home and school or between peer and teachers), the investigator may be led to examine whether there are differences in behavior occurring in different settings or with different individuals, or whether raters are using different standards for judging the child's behavior (e.g., from adult versus child perspectives). Although a performance-based approach emphasizes generating a summary measure or score, it can also provide an empirical standard against which to validate target behaviors for intervention.

PRESCHOOL SOCIAL COMPETENCE AND SUBSEQUENT DEVELOPMENT

Peer-related social competence has much relevance for early intervention and other child care services. Young children with or without other disabilities sometimes do not attain a level of social competence that is adequate for establishing positive relationships with peers. Such early impairments in social competence and the resulting reduction in opportunities to participate in peer group interactions have substantial implications for current and later development. This section examines the incidence of social competence problems among young children; the long-term implications of isolation from or rejection within the peer group at an early age; and the relationship of social competence to acquisition of other developmental skills.

Incidence of Social Competence Problems

It appears that a substantial number of children may not acquire the social interaction skills necessary for establishing positive peer relations or may use behaviors that could lead to peer rejection. Asher (1990) estimated that a many as 10% of all children may show social skills impairments or delays that could lead to peer rejection. He predicts, and others support this prediction (Hartup & Moore, 1990; Odom et al., 1990), that the incidence may be much higher for children with disabilities. As discussed above, across areas of disability or other special needs, many children use interaction skills with peers that are quantitatively and qualitatively different from the peer interaction skills of typically-developing children.

Relationship of Peer Rejection to Later Adjustment

From the 1960s into the 1990s, a large number of studies have documented the direct relationship between peer rejection or difficulties in establishing positive peer relationships and negative outcomes in adulthood. The studies have been cited repeatedly as a basis for developing intervention strategies for promoting social competence (Putallaz & Gottman, 1982). The convergence of these results leads many to the conviction that positive peer interaction is a necessary component for child development (McConnell & Odom, 1986), and that limited interaction with peers may deprive children of opportunities to learn more advanced social skills (Parker & Asher, 1987).

Several reviews examine the methodological integrity and conclusions of these studies (Asher & Parker, 1989; Kupersmidt, Coie, & Dodge, 1990; McConnell & Odom, 1986; Parker & Asher, 1987). Although many of the studies are open to criticism, and methodological improvements should occur in future research, Parker and Asher (1987) found that the studies generally supported the conclusion that early peer relationship difficulties predict later disturbances. Specifically, peer rejection, or behaviors that lead to peer rejection, such as aggression, appears to be related to withdrawal from school, certain forms of criminality, possibly to mental health problems (i.e., psychiatric referrals), and possibly to development of schizophrenia in females (Kupersmidt et al., 1990).

These results have direct relevance for early intervention. Although longitudinal studies generally have not incorporated data for preschool children, a variety of studies have demonstrated the stability of indicators of children's social competence across settings and from the early childhood to the middle childhood years (Asendorpf, 1989; Coie & Kupersmidt, 1983; Dodge, 1983; Howes, 1990; Ladd, Price, & Hart, 1990; Putallaz, 1983). The implications are that peer rejection or other indicators of social competence may well be related to difficulties in establishing peer relationships in the middle childhood years, which in turn appear to predict adjustment in adulthood.

Although studies of this type have not been conducted with children with disabilities, there is no reason to believe that such a relationship does not exist for these individuals as well. In fact, there is evidence that adolescents and adults with certain disabilities experience difficulties in developing social relationships (Chin-Perez et al., 1986; Haring, 1990; Mesibov, 1986). Moreover, there is some indication that successful integration into vocational placements may be related to the ability of adults with severe disabilities to initiate and respond to task- and nontask-related interactions with co-workers (Rusch, Chadsey-Rusch, & Johnson, 1990), and that dismissal from vocational settings may be related to difficulties in establishing positive interactions with co-workers (Greenspan & Shoultz, 1981). A similar relationship may well exist between successful integration into the community and social competence (Halpern, Close, & Nelson, 1986). The implication for early intervention programs is that peer social interaction skills may have long-term implications for adult functioning and should be a major focus for programming. In addition, such skills may well affect areas of development in childhood.

Relationship Between Peer Social
Competence and Other Developmental Skills

Social interactions with peers offer many natural learning opportunities for young children. Theorists and researchers have speculated that active and positive participation in peer interaction may affect the development of cognitive, language or communication, and even more advanced social interaction skills.

Cognitive Skills   As noted earlier, cognitive psychologists such as Piaget (1926) and Vygotsky (1978) identified the importance of social interaction for the development of more advanced and varied forms of cognition. From a Piagetian perspective, during interaction, peers may present alternative views or understandings of the world that, if they are not too different, create cognitive conflicts. Such conflicts may push the equilibration process, and result in establishing a more advanced understanding for the less mature child (Doise, 1990; Rubin & Pepler, 1980). The critical variable appears to be a child's ability to share the frame of reference or perspective of the peer, a cognitive skill that most children acquire by the time they are 4 years old (Tudge & Rogoff, 1989). From a Vygotskian perspective, advanced peers or adults may mediate acquisition of cognitive skills by their actions or communication of their thoughts, as long as such experiences are in the child's "zone of proximal development" (i.e., slightly more complex than what matches the child's current level of understanding).

For elementary-age children, a large number of studies in the United States and Europe have documented the acquisition of cognitive skills resulting from social interactions with peers within a problem-solving context (Doise, Mugny, & Perret-Clermont, 1976; Murray, 1972; Perret-Clermont, 1980; Tudge & Rogoff, 1989). In most cases, investigators have examined the acquisition of conservation skills or academic tasks. For young children with disabilities, the potential for nondisabled peers to give such a "cognitive push" has been one of the rationales commonly used for integration and mainstreaming (Bricker, 1978; Odom & McEvoy, 1988). Although such benefits may well exist for younger children with or without disabilities, particularly as they relate to social cognition and the cognitive underpinnings of sociodramatic play, research has yet to be conducted to demonstrate directly such a relationship.

Communication Skills   Social competence may provide a forum for acquiring communication skills. In fact, differences between social and communicative competence may be more a reflection of theoretical perspective than overt child behavior. In their discussions about the pragmatics movement in the language field, Prutting (1982) and Baudonniere, Garcia-Werebe, Michel, and Liegois (1989) have inferred that the two concepts are nearly identical. Guralnick (Chapter 2, this volume) and McFall (1982) noted the very direct and important relationship between children's and adolescents' ability to communicate and their competent performance in social interaction. Although the difference between these two areas may be more semantic than real, for the purposes of this brief discussion, receptive and expressive language will be treated as a domain separate from social interaction.

Social interaction and communication among peers differs from adult-child interaction in that it is more co-equal in nature (Hartup, 1983). In the context of positive interactions, especially if the participants are friends or preferred play partners, peers engage in "salient conversations" (e.g., talk about activities, coordinate play, escalate and de-escalate play) (Parker & Gottman, 1989); learn to use conversational turns (especially girls) (Black, 1989); clarify messages that are misunderstood (Gottman, 1983); and co-construct effective strategies for communicating (Strayer, 1989). When groups contain children of different developmental levels (i.e., either different ages or disabled and nondisabled), the more developmentally advanced children in those groups will reduce the complexity of their language to the level of the less mature children in the interaction (Guralnick & Paul-Brown, 1977, 1984, 1986; James, 1978; Masur, 1978; Shatz & Gelman, 1973). Guralnick (1981, 1990a) has proposed that these adjustments may facilitate the language acquisition of the less mature children. In their study of integration, Jenkins, Odom, and Speltz (1989) found that when social interactions between children with and without disabilities were increased, significant changes occurred in the language development of preschoolers with disabilities. Although language adjustment patterns were not examined in this study, increased opportunities to engage in social interaction with linguistically competent peers may have resulted in accelerated language development.

Advanced Forms of Social Competence   Participation in positive social interactions with peers is essential for the development of more mature levels of peer social competence. It appears that interactions, especially when they occur with friends or preferred playmates, provide a unique situation for learning social skills (Price & Ladd, 1986). Within these interactions, children may learn to gain access to materials and activities in a successful and appropriate manner (Black, 1989); build solidarity and mutual trust (Corsaro, 1981); coordinate play themes (Rubin & Pepler, 1980); reciprocate humor (Gottman, 1983); manage their emotional responses to play situations

(Parker & Gottman, 1989); engage in reciprocal interactions (Hartup, 1989); and learn the social norms of the peer group (Hartup, 1983). In addition, these interactions provide a relatively safe atmosphere for learning how to resolve conflicts effectively (Gottman, 1983); respond to aggression in an appropriate manner (Hartup, 1983); and engage in competition without aggression (Hartup, 1989). Howes (1983), Ladd et al. (1990), and Price and Ladd (1986) all emphasized that participating in sustained positive interactions, especially with a friend or preferred peer, may enhance social competence, which, in turn, makes the participants more attractive play partners.

Evidence for the support of this circular relationship between participating in social interaction and social competence comes primarily from the day-care literature. A variety of researchers have found that early and extended involvement in social peer groups enhances the later social skills of young children, in comparison with the lesser skills of children who do not have such experience in peer groups (Field, Masi, Goldstein, Perry, & Silke, 1988; Galluzzo, Matheson, Moore, & Howes, 1988; Harper & Huie, 1985; Lamb et al., 1988; Rubenstein & Howes, 1983). In addition, Field et al. (1988) found that this early day-care experience did not interfere with attachment formation with parents, as has been suggested by other researchers (Belsky, 1986). A concern with these studies is that they do not control experimentally the social experience variable. In an experimental study involving children with disabilities, Jenkins et al. (1989) found that increased participation in social interaction with nondisabled peers resulted in significant gains in social competence as measured by a teacher rating assessment.

Young children who lack the social skills to enter or maintain social interactions, including many young children with disabilities, are caught in a conundrum. They do not possess the skill for engaging in social interaction, yet peer social interaction is the primary medium through which they will learn more advanced forms of social competence. For children with disabilities, two other variables complicate this situation. There may be nonsocial variables, such as appearance or reputation, that prevent the child from establishing friendships or mutually preferred playmates in the classroom (Hymel et al., 1990; Strain, 1984). Also, if the child with disabilities is in a special educational setting in which there are only peers who also have limited social interaction skills, opportunities for social skill acquisition will be absent (Strain & Shores, 1983).

Mutual Influence Between Social Competence and Other Developmental Domains   The influence of social competence on other domains of development is not unidirectional. Guralnick (Chapter 2, this volume) illustrates how developmental domains may influence social competence as well as be influenced by social competence. In fact, cognitive or communication impairments may have a direct influence on a child's capacity to engage in peer social interaction, which, in turn, may inhibit the development of social competence. Hops and Finch (1985) found that the development of motor skills was related to their measurement of social competence for preschool children who were socially withdrawn. In a sense, cognitive, communication, and motor skills might be seen as prerequisite skills for at least a minimal level of social competence (McFall, 1982). Yet, to reiterate an earlier point, if a child can achieve a level of social competence that allows participation in interactions with mutually preferred playmates, such interactions have the potential for positive ramifications in other areas of development.

Family Influences and Social Competence

Although peer interaction exerts a powerful influence on the development of social competence, factors within the family may also influence the skill with which children engage in interactions with their peers. Beckman and Lieber (Chapter 3, this volume) describe many of the social tasks that serve as the bases for peer social competence and how they occur first in parent-child interaction; these tasks undoubtedly occur also in interactions with siblings (Fox, Chapter 9, this volume). Putallaz and Heflin (1990) have proposed that parents may directly (i.e., through classical and operant conditioning, modeling, and coaching) and indirectly (i.e., through arranging social contact and parent-child interaction) affect the development of their child's social competence (i.e., peer orientation or motivation, social skills or behavior, and understanding of social interactions of peers). In the 1980s, many studies linked variables in the home, such as attachment and emotional security (Attili, 1989; Lamb & Nash, 1989; Waters, Wippman, & Sroufe, 1979); maternal beliefs about competence (Rubin, Mills, & Rose-Krasnor, 1989); and family dysfunction (Ramsey, Patterson, & Walker, 1990), to social behaviors toward peers that would be judged to be competent and incompetent.

Given that the peer group and family members both appear to affect the development of social competence, a question remains about how these influences might interact. Hartup and Moore (1990) proposed a "conjunctive model" to explain this relationship. They cite evidence that some families may predispose children to interact in an antisocial or aggressive manner, which leads to rejection from the peer group. As these children are rejected by peers, they do not have access to the learning medium provided through peer interac-

tion. As they grow older, they "shop around" for social opportunities, tending to select unpopular or unskilled children as their
preferred peers, which further restricts their access to and social participation with positive peer models. Hartup and Moore (1990) and
Patterson and Bank (1989) propose that the social adjustment problem
seen in late childhood and adolescence may result from such peer
rejection in early and middle childhood. This model, although based
on the literature for children without clearly identified disabilities,
could apply as well to young children with disabilities.

IMPLICATIONS FOR INTERVENTION

Many chapters in this book are devoted to intervention strategies for
promoting peer-related social competence of preschool children with
disabilities. There is good reason to believe that the preschool years
are the time to begin such interventions. Mize, Ladd, and Price (1985)
noted that early childhood educational programs should incorporate
a fourth "R" in their curriculum, that is, a firm foundation for forming
and maintaining relationships with peers; Guralnick (1989, 1990b)
made similar recommendations for early intervention programs.

Given the stability of social competence from early to middle
childhood and adolescence, it would be very important to provide
intervention to promote positive peer interaction before behavior patterns become established and the child creates a reputation as an
unrewarding or antisocial playmate (Hartup & Moore, 1990). Howes
(1990) found that the peer group social structure becomes much more
rigid during the middle childhood years, in comparison to the early
childhood years. When conducting interventions in early childhood
education or early intervention programs, teachers or researchers
may find a somewhat more receptive (i.e., becoming involved directly in the intervention or serving as the basis for supporting newly
learned social skills) peer group than would be available in the middle
or late childhood years. From the meta-analysis that Schneider and
Byrne (1985) conducted for social skills training programs for young
children, it appeared that interventions occurring during preschool
years had considerably greater effects than those occurring in middle
or later childhood years.

Conceptualizations of peer-related social competence should
serve as the basis for determining the ultimate outcomes of intervention programs. Furman and Robbins (1985) examined the factors that
lead to intervention objectives for children, finally proposing that an
ultimate outcome should be to enhance children's relationships with
peers. Other researchers would recommend that an evaluation of

social competence should reflect the appraisal of the competence of the child's social participation with peers (McFall, 1982; Odom & Mc-Connell, 1985). For young children with disabilities, the development of friendships or social relationships, while a broad indicator of the child's social competence, also is influenced by a range of nonsocial factors that are outside the child's control (e.g., the child's appearance; access to a socially responsive peer group; and family variables, such as acceptance or adjustment that may differ from the norm).

The authors propose that interventions designed to promote peer social competence should address social behavioral dimensions, or their social learning and cognitive counterparts, that would allow children to participate in positive social interactions with a socially responsive and skilled peer group and to engage in more extended interactions with one or two preferred peers (i.e., friends). For children with disabilities, such interventions could entail creating programs that not only teach skills or social concepts, but also address nonsocial factors that relate to peer acceptance or friendship development.

Interventionists may agree with the proposal noted above, but divergence may occur when considering how to see it through and what strategies to employ. As seen in the chapters in this book, different disabilities create unique and challenging problems for teachers and researchers. The natures of these disabilities influence substantially the form of the intervention package. Also, the "state of the science" is in different stages of development, with interventions for children with certain disabilities having a long history of research (McEvoy, Odom, & McConnell, Chapter 5, this volume), whereas for children with other disabilities intervention, research, and development are just beginning (Skellenger, Hill, & Hill, Chapter 7, this volume).

CONCLUSION

Social competence in peer interactions is an organizing theme for development in the early childhood years. Although influenced by early and ongoing interactions with parents, peer social competence contributes uniquely to development in different domains and has implications for social functioning in later childhood, adolescence, and adulthood. Many children with disabilities experience difficulties in acquiring the skills necessary for interacting with peers in a competence and positive manner. Because of these difficulties, early childhood education and early intervention programs may, and indeed should, include social competence as a central emphasis for young children with disabilities. The following chapters examine the different dimensions of peer social competence and interventions to promote skills necessary for becoming a socially competent member of a peer group. These chapters should provide guidance for practitioners and researchers who wish to implement such interventions and examine their effects for young children with disabilities and their peers.

REFERENCES

American Association on Mental Retardation. (1990). AAMR takes the lead in defining mental retardation. *AAMR News & Notes, 3*(6), 1.

American Psychiatric Association. (1987). *Diagnostic and statistical manual* (3rd ed., revised). Washington, DC: American Psychiatric Press.

Anderson, S., & Messick, S. (1974). Social competency in young children. *Developmental Psychology, 15,* 443–444.

Asendorpf, J. (1989). Individual, differential, and aggregate stability of social competence. In B. Schneider, G. Attili, J. Nadel, & R. Weissberg (Eds.), *Social competence in developmental perspective* (pp. 17–86). Boston: Kluwer Academic Publishers.

Asher, S.R. (1990). Recent advances in the study of peer rejection. In S. Asher & J. Coie (Eds.), *Peer rejection in childhood* (pp. 3–14). New York: Cambridge University Press.

Asher, S.R., Markell, R.A., & Hymel, S. (1981). Identifying children at risk in peer relations: A critique of the rate-of-interaction approach to assessment. *Child Development, 52,* 1239–1245.

Asher, S.R., & Parker, J.G. (1989). Significance of peer relationship problems in childhood. In B. Schneider, G. Attile, J. Nadel, & R. Weissberg (Eds.), *Social competence in developmental perspective* (pp. 5–23). Norvell, MA: Kluwer Academic Publishers.

Asher, S.R., & Renshaw, P.D. (1981). Children without friends: Social knowledge and social skills training. In S. Asher & J. Gottman (Eds.), *The development of children's friendships* (pp. 273–296). New York: Cambridge University Press.

Asher, S.R., Singleton, L.C., Tinsley, B.R., & Hymel, S. (1979). A reliable sociometric measure for preschool children. *Developmental Psychology, 15,* 443–444.

Attili, G. (1989). Social competence versus emotional security: The link between home relationships and behavior problems in preschool. In B. Schneider, G. Attili, J. Nadel, & R. Weissberg (Eds.), *Social competence in developmental perspective* (pp. 293–311). Boston: Kluwer Academic Publishers.

Baudonniere, P.M., Garcia-Werebe, M.J., Michel, J., & Liegois, J. (1989). Development of communicative competencies in early childhood: A model and results. In B. Schneider, G. Attili, J. Nadel, & R. Weissberg (Eds.), *Social competence in developmental perspective* (pp. 175–195). Boston: Kluwer Academic Publishers.

Belsky, J. (1986). Infant day care: A cause for concern? *Zero to Three, 6,* 1–7.

Black, B. (1989). Interactive pretense: Social and symbolic skills in preschool play groups. *Merrill-Palmer Quarterly, 35,* 379–397.

Blurton-Jones, N. (1972). Categories of child-child interactions. In N. Blurton-Jones (Ed.), *Ethological studies of child behavior* (pp. 97–127). Cambridge: Cambridge University Press.

Bott, H. (1928). Observations of play activities in nursery school. *Genetic Psychology Monographs, 4*, 44–88.

Bricker, D.D. (1978). A rationale for the integration of handicapped and non-handicapped preschool children. In M. Guralnick (Ed.), *Early intervention and the integration of handicapped and nonhandicapped children* (pp. 3–26). Baltimore: University Park Press.

Cavallaro, S.A., & Porter, R.H. (1980). Peer preferences of at-risk and normally developing children in preschool mainstream classrooms. *American Journal of Mental Deficiency, 84*, 357–366.

Challman, R.C. (1932). Factors influencing friendships among preschool children. *Child Development, 3*, 146–158.

Chin-Perez, G., Hartman, D., Park, H.S., Sacks, S., Wershing, A., & Gaylord-Ross, R. (1986). Maximizing social contact for secondary students with severe handicaps. *Journal of The Association for Persons with Severe Handicaps, 11*, 118–124.

Chittenden, G.F. (1942). An experimental study in measuring and modifying assertive behavior in young children. *Monographs of the Society for Research in Child Development, 7*(Serial No. 31).

Coie, J.D., Dodge, K.A., & Copotelli, H. (1982). Dimensions and types of social status: A cross-aged perspective. *Developmental Psychology, 18*, 557–571.

Coie, J.D., Dodge, K.A., & Kupersmidt, J.B. (1990). Peer group behavior and social status. In S. Asher & J. Coie (Eds.), *Peer rejection in childhood* (pp. 17–59). New York: Cambridge University Press.

Coie, J.D., & Kupersmidt, J.B. (1983). A behavioral analysis of emerging social status in boys' groups. *Child Development, 54*, 1400–1417.

Corsaro, W.A. (1981). Friendship in nursery school. In S. Asher & J. Gottman (Eds.), *The development of children's friendships* (pp. 207–241). New York: Cambridge University Press.

Corsaro, W.A. (1985). *Friendship and peer culture in the early years.* Norwood, NJ: Ablex Publishing Co.

Dodge, K.A. (1983). Behavioral antecedents of peer social status. *Child Development, 54*, 1386–1399.

Dodge, K.A. (1985). Facets of social interaction and the assessment of social competence in children. In B. Schneider, K. Rubin, & J. Ledingham (Eds.), *Children's peer relations: Issues in assessment and intervention* (pp. 3–22). New York: Springer-Verlag.

Dodge, K.A. (1986). A social information processing model of social competence in children. In M. Permutter (Ed.), *Minnesota symposia on child psychology* (Vol. 18, pp. 107–135). New York: Academic Press.

Dodge, K.A., Coie, J.D., & Brakke, N.P. (1982). Behavior patterns of socially rejected and neglected preadolescents: The roles of social approach and aggression. *Journal of Abnormal Child Psychology, 10*, 620–635.

Dodge, K.A., Petit, G.S., McLaskey, C.L., & Brown, M.M. (1986). Social competence in children. *Monographs of the Society for Research in Child Development, 51*(2, Serial No. 213).

Doise, W. (1990). The development of individual competencies through social interaction. In H. Foot, M. Morgan, & R. Shure (Eds.), *Children helping children* (pp. 43–64). New York: John Wiley & Sons.

Doise, W., Mugny, G., & Perret-Clermont, A.N. (1976). Social interaction and cognitive development: Further evidence. *European Journal of Social Psychology, 6,* 245–247.

Doll, E.A. (1941). The essentials of an inclusive concept of mental deficiency. *American Journal of Mental Deficiency, 46,* 214–219.

Doll, E.A. (1953). *Measurement of social competence: A manual for the Vineland Social Maturity Scale.* Minneapolis: Educational Publishers.

Field, T., Masi, W., Goldstein, S., Perry, S., & Silke, P. (1988). Infant day care facilitates preschool social behavior. *Early Childhood Research Quarterly, 3,* 341–359.

Foster, S.L., & Ritchey, W.L. (1979). Issues in the assessment of social competence in children. *Journal of Applied Behavior Analysis, 12,* 625–638.

Furman, W., & Robbins, P. (1985). What's the point? Issues in the selection of treatment objectives. In B. Schneider, K. Rubin, & J. Ledingham (Eds.), *Children's peer relations: Issues in assessment and intervention* (pp. 41–54). New York: Springer-Verlag.

Galluzzo, D.C., Matheson, C.C., Moore, J.A., & Howes, C. (1988). Social orientation to adults and peers in infant child care. *Early Childhood Research Quarterly, 3,* 417–426.

Gardner, H. (1987). Developing the spectrum of human intelligence. *Harvard Educational Review, 57,* 187–193.

Gardner, H., & Hatch, T. (1989). Multiple intelligences go to school: Educational implications of the theory of multiple intelligences. *Educational Researcher, 18*(8), 4–10.

Gottman, J.M. (1977). Toward a definition of social isolation in children. *Child Development, 48,* 513–517.

Gottman, J.J. (1983). How children become friends. *Monographs of the Society for Research in Child Development, 48*(3, No. 201).

Greenspan, S. (1979). Social intelligence in the retarded. In N. Ellis (Ed.), *Handbook of mental deficiency: Psychological theory and research* (2nd ed., pp. 483–531). Hillsdale, NJ: Lawrence Erlbaum Associates.

Greenspan, S., & Shoultz, B. (1981). Why mentally retarded adults lose their jobs: Social competence as a factor in work adjustment. *Applied Research in Mental Retardation, 2*(1), 23–38.

Greenwood, C.R., Walker, H.M., Todd, N.M., & Hops, H. (1979). Selecting a cost-effective screening measure for the assessment of preschool social withdrawal. *Journal of Applied Behavior Analysis, 13,* 639–652.

Greenwood, C.R., Walker, H.M., Todd, N.M., & Hops, H. (1981). Normative and descriptive analysis of preschool freeplay social interaction rates. *Journal of Pediatric Psychology, 4,* 343–367.

Gresham, F.M. (1981). Validity of social skills measures for assessing the social competence in low status children: A multivariate investigation. *Developmental Psychology, 17,* 390–398.

Gresham, F.M. (1986). Conceptual issues in the assessment of social competence in children. In P. Strain, M. Guralnick, & H. Walker (Eds.), *Children's social behavior: Development, assessment, and modification* (pp. 143–179). New York: Academic Press.

Grossman, H.J. (Ed.). (1973). *Manual on terminology and classification in mental retardation.* Washington, DC: American Association on Mental Deficiency.

Grossman, H.J. (Ed.). (1983). *Classification of mental retardation.* Washington, DC: American Association on Mental Deficiency.

Grusec, J.E., & Lytton, H. (1988). *Social development: History, theory, and research.* New York: Springer-Verlag.

Guilford, J.P., & Hoepfner, R. (1971). *The analysis of intelligence.* New York: McGraw-Hill.

Guralnick, M.J. (1981). Peer influence on the development of communicative competence. In P. Strain (Ed.), *The utilization of classroom peers as behavior change agents* (pp. 31–68). New York: Plenum.

Guralnick, M.J. (1989). Social competence as a future direction for early intervention programs. *Journal of Mental Deficiency Research, 33,* 275–281.

Guralnick, M.J. (1990a). Peer interactions and the development of handicapped children's social and communicative competence. In H. Foot, M. Morgan, & R. Shute (Eds.), *Children helping children* (pp. 275–305). New York: John Wiley & Sons.

Guralnick, M.J. (1990b). Social competence and early intervention. *Journal of Early Intervention, 14,* 3–14.

Guralnick, M.J., & Groom, J.M. (1985). Correlates of peer-related social competence of developmentally delayed preschool children. *American Journal of Mental Deficiency, 90,* 140–150.

Guralnick, M.J., & Groom, J.M. (1987). The peer relations of mildly delayed and nonhandicapped preschool children in mainstreamed playgroups. *Child Development, 58,* 1556–1572.

Guralnick, M.J., & Groom, J.M. (1988). Friendships of preschool children in mainstreamed playgroups. *Developmental Psychology, 24,* 595–604.

Guralnick, M.J., & Paul-Brown, D. (1977). The nature of verbal interactions among handicapped and nonhandicapped preschool children. *Child Development, 48,* 254–260.

Guralnick, M.J., & Paul-Brown, D. (1984). Communicative adjustments during behavior-request episodes among children at different developmental levels. *Child Development, 55,* 911–919.

Guralnick, M.J., & Paul-Brown, D. (1986). Communicative interactions of mildly delayed and normally developing preschool children: Effects of listener's developmental level. *Journal of Speech and Hearing Research, 29,* 2–10.

Guralnick, M.J., & Weinhouse, E.M. (1984). Peer-related social interactions of developmentally delayed young children: Development and characteristics. *Developmental Psychology, 20,* 815–827.

Halpern, A.S., Close, D.W., & Nelson, D.J. (1986). *On my own: The impact of semi-independent living programs for adults with mental retardation.* Baltimore: Paul H. Brookes Publishing Co.

Haring, T.G. (1990). Social relationships. In L. Meyer, C. Peck, & L. Brown (Eds.), *Critical issues in the lives of people with severe disabilities* (pp. 195–217). Baltimore: Paul H. Brookes Publishing Co.

Harper, L.V., & Huie, K.S. (1985). The effects of prior group experience, age, and familiarity on the quality and organization of preschoolers' social relationships. *Child Development, 56,* 704–717.

Hartup, W.W. (1983). Peer relations. In M. Heatherington (Ed.), *Handbook of child psychology* (Vol. IV, pp. 103–196). New York: John Wiley & Sons.

Hartup, W.W. (1989). Behavioral manifestations of children's friendships. In T. Berndt & G. Ladd (Eds.), *Peer relationships in child development* (pp. 46–70), New York: John Wiley & Sons.

Hartup, W.W., Glazer, J., & Charlesworth, R. (1967). Peer reinforcement and sociometric status. *Child Development, 38,* 1017–1024.

Hartup, W.W., & Moore, S.G. (1990). Early peer relations: Developmental significance and prognostic implications. *Early Childhood Research Journal, 5,* 1–17.

Heber, R. (1961). *A manual on terminology and classification in mental retardation* (2nd ed.). Washington, DC: American Association on Mental Deficiency.

Higgenbotham, J., & Baker, B.M. (1981). Social participation and cognitive play differences in hearing-impaired and normally hearing preschoolers. *The Volta Review, 83,* 135–149.

Hinde, R.A., Titmus, G., Easton, D., & Tamplin, A. (1985). Incidence of friendship and behavior toward strong associates versus nonassociates in preschoolers. *Child Development, 56,* 234–245.

Hops, H. (1983). Children's social competence and skill: Current research practices and future directions. *Behavior Therapy, 14,* 3–18.

Hops, H., & Finch, M. (1985). Social competence and skill: A re-assessment. In B. Schneider, K. Rubin, & J. Ledingham (Eds.), *Children's peer relations: Issues in assessment and intervention* (pp. 23–54). New York: Springer-Verlag.

Howes, C. (1983). Patterns of friendship. *Child Development, 54,* 1041–1053.

Howes, C. (1988). Peer interactions of young children. *Monographs of the Society for Research in Child Development, 53*(1, Series No. 217).

Howes, C. (1990). Social status and friendship from kindergarten to third grade. *Journal of Applied Developmental Psychology, 11,* 321–330.

Hymel, S. (1983). Preschool children's peer relations: Issues in sociometric assessment. *Merrill-Palmer Quarterly, 29,* 237–260.

Hymel, S., Wagner, E., & Butler, L.J. (1990). Reputational bias: View from the peer group. In S. Asher & J. Coie (Eds.), *Peer rejection in childhood* (pp. 156–186). New York: Cambridge University Press.

Jack, L.M. (1934). An experimental study of ascendant behavior in preschool children. *University of Iowa Studies in Child Welfare, 9*(3), 9–65.

James, S.L. (1978). Effect of listener age and situation on the politeness of children's directives. *Journal of Psycholinguistic Research, 7,* 307–317.

Jenkins, J.R., Odom, S.L., & Speltz, M.L. (1989). Effects of social integration on preschool children with handicaps. *Exceptional Children, 55,* 420–428.

Kohler, F.W., & Fowler, S.A. (1985). Training prosocial behaviors to young children: An analysis of reciprocity with untrained peers. *Journal of Applied Behavior Analysis, 18,* 187–200.

Krasnor, L.R. (1983). An observational case study of failure in social problem-solving. *Journal of Applied Developmental Psychology, 4,* 81–98.

Krasnor, L.R., & Rubin, K.H. (1983). Preschool social problem solving: Attempts and outcomes in naturalistic interaction. *Child Development, 54,* 1545–1558.

Kupersmidt, J.B., Coie, J.D., & Dodge, K.A. (1990). The role of poor peer relationships in the development of disorder. In S. Asher & J. Coie (Eds.), *Peer rejection in childhood* (pp. 274–305). New York: Cambridge University Press.

La Freniere, P.J., & Charlesworth, W.R. (1983). Dominance, attention, and affiliation in a preschool group: A nine-month longitudinal study. *Tehology and Sociobiology, 4*(2), 55–67.

Ladd, G.W., Price, J.M., & Hart, C.H. (1990). Preschoolers' behavioral orientations and patterns of peer contact: Predictive of peer status? In S. Asher & J. Coie (Eds.), *Peer rejection in childhood* (pp. 90–118). New York: Cambridge University Press.

Lamb, M.E., Hwang, C.P., Bookstein, F.J., Broberg, A., Hult, G., & Frodi, M. (1988). Determinants of social competence in Swedish preschoolers. *Developmental Psychology, 24,* 58–70.

Lamb, M.E., & Nash, A. (1989). Infant-mother attachment, sociability, and peer competence. In T. Berndt & G. Ladd (Eds.), *Peer relationships in child development* (pp. 219–246). New York: John Wiley & Sons.

Levy-Shiff, R., & Hoffman, M.A. (1985). Social behavior of learning impaired and normally-hearing preschoolers. *British Journal of Educational Psychology, 55,* 111–118.

Masur, E.G. (1978). Preschool boys' speech modifications: The effect of listeners' linguistic levels and conversational responsiveness. *Child Development, 49,* 924–927.

McCandless, B.R., & Marshall, H.R. (1957). A picture sociometric technique for preschool children and its relationship to teacher judgements of friendship. *Child Development, 28,* 139–147.

McConnell, S.R., & Odom, S.L. (1986). Sociometric: Peer-referenced measures and the assessment of social competence. In P. Strain, M. Guralnick, & H. Walker (Eds.), *Children's social behavior: Development, assessment, and modification* (pp. 215–286). New York: Academic Press.

McConnell, S.R., & Odom, S.L. (1991). *Performance-based assessment of the social competence of young children with disabilities.* Unpublished manuscript.

McFall, R.M. (1982). A reformulation of the concept of social skill. *Behavioral Assessment, 4,* 1–33.

McGrew, W.C. (1972). *An ethological study of children's behavior.* New York: Academic Press.

Mesibov, G.B. (1986). A cognitive program for teaching social behaviors to verbal autistic adolescents and adults. In E. Schopler & G. Mesibov (Eds.), *Social behavior in autism* (pp. 265–284). New York: Plenum.

Mize, J., Ladd, G.W., & Price, J.M. (1985). Promoting positive peer relations with young children: Rationales and strategies. *Child Care Quarterly, 14,* 221–237.

Moreno, J.L. (1934). *Who shall survive?: A new approach to the problem of human relations.* Washington, DC: Nervous and Mental Disease Publishing Co.

Murray, F.B. (1972). Acquisition of conservation through social intervention. *Developmental Psychology, 6,* 1–6.

Odom, S.L., & Fewell, R.F. (1988). *Peer rating assessment of an integrated preschool class: Stability and concurrent validity of the measure.* Unpublished manuscript.

Odom, S.L., & McConnell, S.R. (1985). A performance-based conceptualization of social competence of handicapped preschool children: Implications for assessment. *Topics in Early Childhood Special Education, 4*(4), 1–19.

Odom, S.L., McConnell, S.R., & Chandler, L.K. (1990). *Acceptability, feasibility, and current use of social interaction interventions for preschool children with disabilities.* Manuscript submitted for publication.

Odom, S.L., & McEvoy, M.A. (1988). Integration of young children with handicaps and normally developing children. In S. Odom & M. Karnes (Eds.), *Early intervention for infants and children with handicaps: An empirical base* (pp. 241–267). Baltimore: Paul H. Brookes Publishing Co.

Odom, S.L., McEvoy, M.A., Ostrosky, M., & Bishop, L. (1987, May). *Observing the functional classes of social interaction of preschool children.* Paper presented at the national conference of the Association for Behavior Analysis, Nashville.

Odom, S.L., & Ogawa, I. (1991). *A methodological review of observational measurement systems of young children's social interactions with peers.* Unpublished manuscript.

Odom, S.L., & Watts, E. (1991). Reducing teacher prompts in peer-initiation interventions through visual feedback and correspondence training. *Journal of Special Education, 25,* 26–43.

Parker, J.G., & Asher, S.R. (1987). Peer relations and later personal adjustment. *Psychological Bulletin, 102,* 357–389.

Parker, J.G., & Gottman, J.M. (1989). Social and emotional development in a relational context: Friendship interactions from early childhood to adolescence. In T. Berndt & G. Ladd (Eds.), *Peer relationships in child development* (pp. 95–131). New York: John Wiley & Sons.

Parten, M.B. (1932). Social participation among preschool children. *Journal of Abnormal and Social Psychology, 27,* 243–269.

Patterson, G.R., & Bank, L. (1989). Some amplifier and dampening mechanisms for pathologic processes in families. In M. Gunnar & E. Thelen (Eds.), *Minnesota symposia on child psychology* (Vol. 22, pp. 167–209). Hillsdale, NJ: Lawrence Erlbaum Associates.

Perret-Clermont, A.N. (1980). *Social interaction and cognitive development in children.* London: Academic Press.

Piaget, J. (1926). *Language and thought of the child.* London: Kegan & Paul.

Poteat, G.M., Ironsmith, M., & Bullock, J. (1986). The classification of preschool sociometric status. *Early Childhood Research Quarterly, 1,* 349–360.

Price, J.M., & Ladd, G.W. (1986). Assessment of children's friendships: Implications for social competence and social adjustment. In R. Prinz (Ed.), *Advances in behavioral assessment of children and families* (Vol. 2, pp. 121–149). Greenwich, CT: JAI Press.

Prutting, C.A. (1982). Pragmatics as social competence. *Journal of Speech and Hearing Disorders, 47,* 123–134.

Putallaz, M. (1983). Predicting children's sociometric status from their behavior. *Child Development, 54,* 1417–1426.

Putallaz, M., & Gottman, J.M. (1981). An interactional model of children's entry into peer groups. *Child Development, 52,* 402–408.

Putallaz, M., & Gottman, J.M. (1982). Conceptualizing social competence in children. In P. Karoly & J. Steffin (Eds.), *Advances in child behavior analysis and therapy* (Vol. 1, pp. 1–37). Lexington, MA: DC Heath.

Puttallaz, M., & Heflin, A. H. (1990). Parent-child interaction. In S. Asher & J. Coie (Eds.), *Peer rejection in childhood* (pp. 189–216). New York: Cambridge University Press.

Putallaz, M., & Wasserman, A. (1990). Children's peer entry. In S. Asher & J. Coie (Eds.), *Peer rejection in childhood* (pp. 60–89). New York: Cambridge University Press.

Ramsey, E., Patterson, G.R., & Walker, H.M. (1990). Generalization of the antisocial trait from home to school. *Journal of Applied Developmental Psychology, 11,* 209–223.

Renshaw, P. (1981). The roots of current peer interaction research: A historical analysis of the 1930s. In S. Asher & J. Gottman (Eds.), *The development of children's friendships* (pp. 1–28). New York: Cambridge University Press.

Rice, M. (1990, June). *"Don't talk to him; he's weird": The role of language in early social interaction.* Paper presented at the Conference on the Social Use of Language: Pathways to Success, John F. Kennedy Center, Vanderbilt University, Nashville.

Roedell, W.C. (1985). Developing social competence in gifted preschool children. *Remedial and Special Education, 6*(4), 6–11.

Rose-Krasnor, L.R. (1985). Observational assessment of social problem solving. In B. Schneider, K. Rubin, & J. Ledingham (Eds.), *Children's peer relations: Issues in assessment and intervention* (pp. 58–74). New York: Springer-Verlag.

Rosen, L.A., Furman, W., & Hartup, W.W. (1988). Positive, negative, and neutral peer interactions as indicators of children's social competency: The issue of concurrent validity. *Journal of Genetic Psychology, 49,* 441–446.

Rubenstein, J., & Howes, C. (1983). Adaptations to infant daycare. In S. Kilmer (Ed.), *Advances in early education and daycare* (pp. 13–39). Greenwich, CT: JAI Press.

Rubin, K.H., Mills, R., & Rose-Krasnor, L. (1989). Maternal beliefs and children's competence. In B. Schneider, G. Attili, J. Nadel, & R. Weissberg (Eds.), *Social competence in developmental perspective* (pp. 313–334). Boston: Kluwer Academic Publishers.

Rubin, K.H., & Pepler, D.J. (1980). The relationship of children's play to social-cognitive growth and development. In H. Foot, A. Chapman, & J. Smith (Eds.), *Friendship and social relations in children*, (pp. 209–233). New York: John Wiley & Sons.

Rusch, F.R., Chadsey-Rusch, J., & Johnson, J.R. (1990). Supported employment: Emerging opportunities for employment integration. In L. Meyer, C. Peck, & L. Brown (Eds.), *Critical issues in the lives of people with severe disabilities* (pp. 145–169). Baltimore: Paul H. Brookes Publishing Co.

Salisbury, C., Britzman, D., & Kang, J. (1989). Using qualitative methods to assess the social-communication competence of young handicapped children. *Journal of Early Intervention, 13,* 153–164.

Schneider, B.H., & Byrne, B.M. (1985). Children's social skills training: A meta-analysis. In B. Schneider, K. Rubin, & J. Ledingham (Eds.), *Children's peer relations: Issues in assessment and intervention* (pp. 3–22). New York: Springer-Verlag.

Shatz, M., & Gelman, R. (1973). The development of communication skills: Modifications in the speech of young children as a function of the listener. *Monographs of the Society for Research in Child Development, 38*(Serial No. 152).

Shure, M.B. (1981). Social competence as problem-solving skill. In J. Wine & M. Syme (Eds.), *Social competence* (pp. 158–185). New York: Guilford Press.

Shure, M.B., & Spivak, G. (1979). Interpersonal cognitive problem-solving and primary prevention: Programming for preschool and kindergarten children. *Journal of Clinical Child Psychology, 2,* 89–94.

Shure, M.B., & Spivak, G. (1981). Interpersonal problem solving as a mediator of behavioral adjustment in preschool and kindergarten children. *Journal of Applied Developmental Psychology, 1,* 29–44.

Sternberg, R.J. (1985). *Beyond IQ: A triarchic theory of human intelligence.* New York: Cambridge University Press.

Storey, K., Smith, D., Wolper, N., & Strain, P.S. (1990, May). *The additive effects of treatment components in increasing integration in preschool settings.* Paper presented at the annual conference of the Association for Behavior Analysis, Nashville.

Strain, P.S. (1983). Identification of social skill curriculum targets for severely handicapped children in mainstreamed preschools. *Applied Research in Mental Retardation, 4,* 369–382.

Strain, P.S. (1984). Social behavior patterns of nonhandicapped and nonhandicapped-developmentally disabled friend pairs in mainstreamed preschools. *Analysis and Intervention in Developmental Disabilities, 4*, 15–28.

Strain, P.S. (1985). Social and nonsocial determinants of handicapped preschool children's social competence. *Topics in Early Childhood Special Education, 4*(4), 47–59.

Strain, P.S. (1990). LRE for preschool children with handicaps: What we know, what we should be doing. *Journal of Early Intervention, 14*, 291–296.

Strain, P.S., & Shores, R.E. (1983). A reply to "Misguided Mainstreaming," *Exceptional Children, 50*, 271–272.

Strauss, A., & Corbin, J. (1990). *Basics of qualitative research.* Newbury Park, CA: SAGE.

Strayer, F.F. (1989). Co-adaptation within the early peer group: A psychobiological study of competence. In B. Schneider, G. Attili, J. Nadel, & R. Weissberg (Eds.), *Social competence in developmental perspective* (pp. 145–174). Boston: Kluwer Academic Publishers.

Strayer, F.F. (1980). Child ethology and the study of preschool social relations. In H. Foot, A. Chapman, & J. Smith (Eds.), *Friendship and social relations in children* (pp. 235–265). New York: John Wiley & Sons.

Strayer, F.F., & Strayer, J. (1976). An ethological analysis of social agonism and dominance relations among preschool children. *Child Development, 47*, 980–988.

Taylor, A.R., & Asher, S.R. (1984). Children's goals and social competence: Individual differences in a game-playing context. In T. Field, J. Roopnarine, & M. Segal (Eds.), *Friendships in normal and handicapped children* (pp. 53–78). Norwood, NJ: Ablex Publishing.

Thorndike, E.L. (1920). Intelligence and its uses. *Harper's Magazine, 140*, 227–235.

Tredgold, A.F. (1937). *A textbook of mental deficiency.* Baltimore: William Wood.

Tremblay, A., Strain, P.S., Hendrickson, J.M., & Shores, R.E. (1981). Social interactions of normally developing preschool children: Using normative data for subject selection and target behavior selection. *Behavior Modification, 5*, 237–253.

Tudge, J., & Rogoff, B. (1989). Peer influences on cognitive development: Piagetian and Vygotskian perspectives. In M. Bornstein & J. Bruner (Eds.), *Interaction in human development* (pp. 17–40). Hillsdale, NJ: Lawrence Erlbaum Associates.

Vaughn, S.R., Ridley, C.A., & Cox, J. (1983). Evaluating the efficacy of an interpersonal skills training program with children who are mentally retarded. *Education and Training of the Mentally Retarded, 18*, 191–196.

Vaughn, B., & Waters, E. (1981). Attention structure, sociometric status, and dominance: Interrelations, behavioral correlates and relationships to social competence. *Developmental Psychology, 17*, 275–288.

Vygotsky, L.S. (1978). *Mind in society: The development of higher psychological processes.* Cambridge: MA: Harvard University Press.

Wallender, J.L., Feldman, W.S., & Varni, J.W. (1989). Physical status and psychosocial adjustment in children with spina bifida. *Journal of Pediatric Psychology, 14*, 89–102.

Waters, E., Wippman, J., & Sroufe, L.A. (1979). Attachment, positive affect, and competence in the peer group: Two studies in construct validation. *Child Development, 50*, 821–829.

Wright, M.J. (1980). Measuring the social competence of preschool children. *Canadian Journal of Behavioral Science, 12*, 17–32.

Yan, X., Storey, K., Rhodes, L., Sandow, D., Petherbridge, R., & Loewinger, H. (1990). Grouping patterns in supported employment work setting: Clique analysis of interpersonal interactions. *Behavioral Assessment, 12,* 337–354.

Zigler, E., & Trickett, P.K. (1978). IQ, social competence, and evaluation of early childhood intervention programs. *American Psychologist, 33,* 789–798.

2

A Hierarchical Model for Understanding Children's Peer-Related Social Competence

Michael J. Guralnick

Social competence emerged in recent years as a central construct in the fields of child development and early intervention (Guralnick, 1990d). Acceptance of the significance of this construct, however, has been a difficult process, as the term social competence has been used in so many different ways at so many different levels that it often has been in danger of losing its meaning and value entirely. Early attempts at a definitive consensus may have failed (Anderson & Messick, 1974), but the persistence of the construct gives testimony to its richness and potential for providing a framework for understanding a critical aspect of human development.

As emphasized throughout this chapter, perhaps the most demanding feature of social competence is that one is forced to attend to the dynamic and connected aspects of children's behavior patterns. In creating these behavior patterns, children must integrate, synthesize, and organize their knowledge and skills across sequences of social exchanges in order to solve the diverse problems of a social nature typically encountered in daily life.

Fortunately, since the 1980s, a number of methodological advances have occurred that have permitted analyses of these more dynamic aspects of interaction that characterize children's social competence, particularly peer-related social competence (Putallaz & Wasserman, 1990). First, improvements in technology have allowed high quality audio and video recordings to be made during social interactions. The use of split-screen technology and radiotelemetry devices for transmitting speech have permitted children to move about and interact freely while virtually all aspects of their social and communicative behavior are being recorded. Subsequent detailed analyses of these audiovisual records can provide the type of perspective necessary for understanding how behavior with peers unfolds within and across sequences of social exchanges.

Second, experimental paradigms have become increasingly sophisticated through the use of analogue settings. For example, rather than simply observing the interactions of children who happen to be available in existing nursery school settings, children are carefully selected from a variety of settings and brought together to participate in extended playgroups. In other situations a contrived task is arranged, as occurs when a "guest" child is presented with the problem of entering a play situation in which two "host" children are already engaged in play. This peer entry situation as well as the creation of specific playgroups have proven to be ecologically valid experimental situations, as the behavior patterns that develop appear to be similar to those that occur in more typical settings (Asher, 1983). These analogue settings are especially valuable because, if properly contrived, they can elicit behavior patterns that do not occur spontaneously very often yet have considerable developmental significance. Moreover, these settings allow control over variables not previously possible, such as the extent to which children are acquainted with one another, their chronological age, or their developmental status.

Third, advances in statistical techniques that permit analyses of social sequences are now beginning to contribute to the understanding of social competence. These methods have been used to detect precisely the dependencies in behavior that are so essential for understanding how children solve complex social problems (Bakeman & Gottman, 1986; Sackett, 1978). Although not extensively used as yet, their application to analyses of highly dynamic and complex events, such as the formation of friendships in young children, provides important examples of the power of these techniques (Gottman, 1983).

The purpose of this chapter is to present a model designed to capture the many levels at which socially competent functioning can be analyzed, with special emphasis on the integrative and dynamic aspects of young children's social competence with their peers. Although the model can be extended to other aspects of social competence, peer-related social competence has been chosen because of the now well-established significance of peer relationships and friendships to the development of young children (Ginsberg, Gottman, & Parker, 1986; Guralnick, 1986, 1990b; Hartup, 1983). The model itself is hierarchical, emphasizing the dependence of socially competent interactions upon more fundamental skills and abilities at different levels. However, one key to the model is the recognition that the peer-related social competence of children with similar skills and abilities at more fundamental levels can be vastly different at other levels. The implications of this model for assessment and intervention as well as its application to children with disabilities is presented.

THE NATURE OF PEER-RELATED SOCIAL COMPETENCE

The two features that have been part of virtually every attempt to define social competence are *effectiveness* and *appropriateness*. One working definition that encompasses these features suggests that peer-related social competence consists of "*. . . the ability of young children to successfully and appropriately select and carry out their interpersonal goals*" (Guralnick, 1990d, p.4). Competent behavior implies a high degree of successful outcomes, although success often includes some form of compromise or modification of a child's original goal. Successful outcomes are usually easy to identify, but even if success occurs, the manner in which children approach social problems, specifically the particular strategies they employ across sequences of social exchanges, will govern the degree to which children are considered to be socially competent. Ultimately, continued use of inappropriate strategies will affect not only access to groups and individual play partners but children's effectiveness as well.

Assuming that these two features are essential characteristics of socially competent functioning, a technique to assess and perhaps order children along some dimension of social competence is needed. Clearly, in recognition of the complexity of peer-related social competence, multidimensional assessments involving teachers, parents, observers, and peers would be appropriate (see Ladd & Mars, 1986). Nevertheless, the approach most frequently used to index overall peer-related social competence has been to utilize the perspective of peers. Specifically, peer sociometric techniques in which children are asked to evaluate one another in terms of liking, acceptance, popularity, or friendship have proved to be of great value (see Gresham, 1986). From a theoretical perspective, social knowledge of the peer group appears to be a developmentally critical feature of social competence during the preschool years (Howes, 1988). It should be noted, however, that considerable care must be taken in the selection of peer sociometric measures (McConnell & Odom, 1986; Musen-

Miller, 1990), and their reliability and validity for preschool-age children with disabilities have yet to be established. Nevertheless, carefully selected peer sociometric techniques have proved to be reliable measures (Asher, Singleton, Tinsley, & Hymel, 1979), and to exhibit concurrent (Gresham, 1986; Ladd & Mars, 1986) and predictive validity (Parker & Asher, 1987). Consequently, with this technique, an evaluation of a child's *social status* is obtained, usually indexed in terms of one's degree of *acceptance* within the peer group. This measure can serve as a reasonable criterion for ordering many groups of children in terms of peer-related social competence.

However reliable and valid they may be, assessments of children's social status provide only global perspectives of children's social competence with their peers. Presumably, judgments by peers summarized in sociometric measures reflect observations of, and direct experiences with playmates occurring in many different situations. It is assumed that with a sufficient number of peer contacts, assessments of success and appropriateness will result in a general impression of a playmate's competence.

But it is the specific interaction patterns themselves that distinguish children differing in terms of peer-related social competence. Comparisons of the social interaction patterns of children identified by peer sociometric techniques as accepted, rejected, or neglected have revealed that substantial differences do in fact exist among these groups in terms of their responsiveness, cooperativeness, positiveness, aggressiveness, and other similar characteristics (see Hartup, 1983). Nevertheless, as important as these descriptive correlates are, they do not easily capture the dynamic nature of peer relationships, the strategies involved, or the processes that are operating. It is suggested here that a more comprehensive approach is needed to characterize adequately behavioral patterns associated with an individual child's peer-related social competence. Accordingly, a model is proposed that recognizes the contributions of more static, nonsequential approaches, as well as those of the more dynamic, sequential aspects of peer-related social competence. Assessment implications for each level of the model is emphasized in this chapter, and the literature on the peer-related social competence of children with developmental delays is organized within this model.

OVERVIEW OF THE HIERARCHICAL MODEL OF PEER-RELATED SOCIAL COMPETENCE

The hierarchical model described in this section is an attempt to provide a comprehensive framework for understanding the factors that influence young children's peer-related social competence. To accomplish this, different levels of analysis are proposed. The model is hierarchical in that higher levels depend upon lower ones, and that specific processes transform elements from a lower level to achieve a different meaning in terms of peer-related social competence. Although important information can be obtained at each level, the main focus of the model is its emphasis on the more dynamic features of children's social exchanges, that is, the actual sequences of strategies that are used in a given context.

The model contains two major levels (see Figure 2.1). The first focuses on specific *social/communicative skills* that are essential for child-child interaction, and includes the influences of the more fundamental developmental domains of language, cognitive, affective, and motor development. These social/communicative skills (e.g., request-

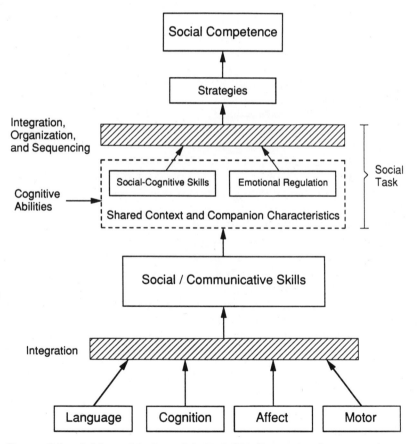

Figure 2.1. A hierarchical model depicting the major factors and processes contributing to children's social competence with their peers.

ing of or directing peers) emerge during the course of development and are dependent upon the integration of skills and abilities of the more fundamental domains. The second major level of the hierarchical model also reflects an integrative process. In this case, it is the transformation of social/communicative skills that are used to solve interpersonal problems in the context of *social tasks* that are of interest. This integration, organization, and sequencing of social/communicative skills at the second level of the model produces *strategies within a social task,* and it is these strategies that appear to be most closely associated with peer-related social competence.

Social tasks themselves (see Dodge, Pettit, McClaskey, & Brown, 1986) serve as a basis (context) for interpreting both the effectiveness and appropriateness of children's strategies. Children's efforts to enter an established playgroup is one social task that has received considerable attention. Other important social tasks include resolving various forms of conflict or establishing a friendship. Differences that may exist among children in accordance with their varying levels of peer-related social competence (as assessed by peer sociometrics) should be reflected in social interaction strategies employed during these social tasks. Presumably, it is the effectiveness and appropriateness of these strategies that constitute a primary basis for judgments of children's peer-related social competence.

In addition, the model incorporates possible *processes* that are associated with the selection of specific strategies (see dotted rectangular area in Figure 2.1). As a consequence, the identification of competent strategies and associated processes that occur during social tasks can provide a valuable framework for both assessment and intervention. In fact, it is argued in this chapter that future advances in assessment and intervention in the area of peer-related social competence for children, including those with developmental disabilities, will require an emphasis on more dynamic and comprehensive approaches that involve social tasks, social strategies, and associated processes.

It is important to note that many factors (e.g., physical attractiveness), other than how children employ strategies during social tasks, contribute to the judgments of children's social competence as assessed by sociometric status. Also, family influences, both direct and indirect (Fox, Niemeyer, & Savelle, Chapter 9, this volume; Puttalaz & Heflin, 1990), can have an important impact on the origins and maintenance of peer-related social competence. These and other related factors, however, are beyond the scope of this chapter (see Guralnick, 1990c). Nevertheless, it is *how* children go about solving social interaction problems that appears to be the primary contributor to judgments of peer-related social competence (e.g., Dodge, 1983). Accordingly, it is these interactional sequences and processes that are the focus of the hierarchical model.

LEVEL OF SOCIAL/COMMUNICATIVE SKILLS AND DEVELOPMENTAL DOMAINS

Social/Communicative Skills

The ability to communicate with other children for social purposes develops rapidly during the preschool period (Garvey, 1984). An array of social/communicative skills emerge that children use to direct others (usually in play sequences), to obtain information, to declare a position in a dispute, or to clarify a previous statement. The rather intricate conversations of young children and their various themes have also been analyzed carefully (see Schober-Peterson & Johnson, 1989), and a number of important coding schemes have been developed to capture these social/communicative skills. As might be expected, depending on the background of the developer of the coding scheme, taxonomies of social/communicative skills have emphasized either social factors or communicative ones. A common feature of these scales is that assessments of social/communicative skills consist of important but static, primarily nonsequential characteristics of peer interactions.

From a communicative perspective, Dore (1986), for example, has organized "conversational acts" into major categories such as questions; requests (including requests for action, permission, attention, or suggestions or invitations); providing information (including facts about the external world, feelings, evaluations, and/or claims); and responses to the questions or actions of others. It is important to note at this point that the grammatical forms used to convey these conversational acts can vary widely since children are capable of making suggestions or asking questions in a number of different ways. Directives can be quite explicit (e.g., "Do it!"), or they can be presented in ways that place less of a demand on the companion to respond (e.g., "Would you do this for me?"). The various forms of communicative acts are discussed later in this chapter in the context of social tasks, and relate more closely to analyses at the level of strategies children use than to analyses at the level of social/communicative skills.

Alternatively, from a social development perspective, White and Watts (1973), for example, have developed a scale (subsequently modified by Doyle, Connolly, & Rivest, 1980, and Guralnick & Groom, 1987) with categories that include the use of peers as resources or leading peers in activities. The actual definitions of these categories closely correspond to communicative acts involving questions addressed to peers (using as a resource) and requesting others to carry out an action (directing others). These and other scales derived from communicative or social development frameworks do differ in many respects, but it is their similarities that are, perhaps, most interesting. That is, these scales appear to be tapping similar features of peer interactions. Although investigators from different fields have tended to work in parallel with one another, it is likely that a complete understanding of peer-related social competence will benefit from the convergence of knowledge and methods derived from many disciplines. The close association between social and communicative skills further highlights the integrative nature of the processes associated with children's peer relationships (see Gallagher & Prutting, 1983).

Developmental Domains

As indicated in Figure 2.1, social/communicative skills depend upon more fundamental processes associated with a child's major developmental accomplishments. Skills and abilities associated with these developmental domains are integrated to enable children to understand and use specific social/communicative acts. First, the emergence of language is perhaps most salient during the preschool period as children achieve an extraordinary command of its structural aspects (see Wells, 1985). Both receptive and expressive elements are important, as control over both obvious and subtle aspects of language are mastered. Second, cognitive abilities not only provide the primary basis for establishing a child's developmental level but also serve as a framework for considering the more specific aspects of cognitive development, including an array of information processing events (e.g., integrating information), as well as the more basic skills associated with memory and categorization of objects and events. Third, the ability to recognize and display affect is, of course, another critical domain that must be considered in the context of social/communicative skills. Both of these abilities have been linked to social competence with peers (Walden & Field, 1990). Fourth, the child's general level of motor development, particularly mobility and skills associated with gesturing, will affect how effectively social/communicative skills can be performed.

The contribution of each of these developmental domains to a child's social/communicative skills should not be underestimated. Limitations in one or more areas or subdomains can have a substantial influence on the understanding and expression of social/communicative skills. This is, of course, of special concern for children with disabilities, not only because of the possibility of substantial developmental delays or deficits in these domains, but also because of the unevenness in development that results. Yet at the same time, it must be recognized that children are remarkably resilient, capable of compensating for delays or deficits in specific developmental areas, and can integrate available abilities in developmental domains to create an impressive array of social/communicative skills.

Implications for Assessment

Within the framework of the level of social/communicative skills, what information should be included in an assessment instrument that can be meaningful to educators and clinicians? Typically, clinicians have tended to rely more on global measures that provide minimal information (Guralnick & Weinhouse, 1983). Yet, despite the fact that assessments derived from analyses at the level of social/communicative skills are primarily nonsequential and are based on observations obtained from numerous contexts, they nevertheless can provide potentially important characterizations of children's interactions with their peers. Accordingly, in the following sections brief descriptions of areas that warrant assessment at the level of social/communicative skills are presented. The intent here is to identify domains to be included in a comprehensive approach to assessment at the level of social/communicative skills that could be used for *clinical purposes.* Moreover, an effort is made to firmly ground these domains in existing research, particularly where it has been demonstrated that these assessments are sensitive to children's social status. These assessment domains are based in part on the *Assessment of Peer Relations* (Guralnick, 1990a), an instrument that considers both the level of social/communicative skills and the level of social strategies and social tasks.

Purpose, Frequency, and Success of Initiations An assessment of peer-related social competence at the level of social/communicative skills must include measures of the extent to which children engage in interactions with their peers. Although simple frequencies of interacting tell us little about peer-related social competence (Asher, Markell, & Hymel, 1981), the tendency to initiate social bids and the purposes of those social bids can provide useful indices of a child's orientation to and involvement with peers. The goals or purposes of an initiation are especially important and, as noted earlier, the *selection* of an interpersonal goal has been included as a component of the definition of peer-related social competence. Children who continually elect to pursue goals that are associated with acquiring the toys and materials of companions or those whose major social involvement with peers is designed to prevent them from carrying out an action will certainly create an atmosphere of acrimony, ultimately affecting both the appropriateness and effectiveness of their interpersonal goals. Accordingly, assessments of the purposes of social initiations and related characteristics provide insight into what interests and motivates children to interact and the general tendency to initiate social interactions. Of interest as well is the extent to which children use diverse forms of expression to initiate interactions. If efforts to acquire objects are cast repeatedly in the form of imperatives, without any type of mitigation or embedding, potential difficulties in adapting initiations to context factors may well exist.

Krasnor and Rubin (1983) conducted a comprehensive analysis of the goals or purposes of children's initiations, in which over 6000 interactive attempts by 3- and 4-year-old children were coded into the following eight goal categories: 1) efforts to stop another child's action; 2) action on the part of the self, such as obtaining permission from another child to participate in an activity; 3) acquiring objects; 4) directing the attention of another child; 5) eliciting affection; 6) gaining specific information or clarification; 7) general initiations to engage in social contact; and 8) eliciting from another an active response not coded in any of the other categories. Similar goal categories have been used in other investigations (e.g., Guralnick & Paul-Brown, 1984; Levin & Rubin, 1983). Most goals tended to be associated with directing others in play (i.e., behavior requests) or obtaining the assistance of peers (i.e., information requests). Nonspecific initiations, apparently designed to establish social contact, also occurred frequently.

Of further importance is the fact that related studies have found that the degree to which children are successful in gaining an *immediate* response to their initiations (social/communicative interactions) is closely associated with general measures of peer-related social competence (Wright, 1980). Often, however, responses by peers to these initiations are obligatory or perfunctory. Nevertheless, a positive response in any appropriate form provides an index of the timing, clarity, and other aspects of the initiation as well as reflecting the willingness of a peer to interact positively. Consequently, an immediate indication of success (e.g., achieving a reasonable response to a question or an acknowledgement of or compliance to a directive) should be included as part of an assessment at the level of social/communicative skills. Also to be considered are peers' responses to diverse grammatical forms of directives or questions.

Responsiveness   Interest in initiating interactions with others provides a reliable assessment of the extent to which children are socially oriented toward their peers. Yet, some children may have considerable difficulty initiating but may be highly responsive to the social bids of others. Responsiveness, a key characteristic of peer-related social competence (Asher, 1983), provides another theoretically independent measure of interest in peer relationships. As important as this measure may be, responsiveness at the level of social/communicative skills consists only of immediate, positive, and reasonable responses to one's peers. Accordingly, this measure may, as in the case of immediate success of initiations, reflect primarily obligatory or perfunctory reactions.

Forms of Expression   Verbal forms of communication begin to supplement rather than supplant various aspects of nonverbal interactions with peers from the toddler to the preschool years (Finkelstein, Dent, Gallacher, & Ramey, 1978). Despite the fact that much can be accomplished in terms of social exchange among peers at the nonverbal level, reliance on primarily nonverbal modes of communication may limit more complex aspects of thematic play development involving planning and long-term strategies. Accordingly, even for children who are verbal, an evaluation of the child's use of verbal abilities with peers and his or her intelligibility would seem essential. Given the potential importance of verbal interactions to peer relationships during the preschool years, and the fact that the quality and quantity of verbal exchanges are highly sensitive to problems in virtually any developmental domain, an assessment of the status of a child's forms of expression seems essential.

Settings and Play Themes   Even at the level of social/ communicative skills, children's willingness to respond as well as the purposes, frequency, and success of their initiations will vary substantially across different settings, play partners, and play themes (see e.g., Rogers-Warren & Wedel, 1980; Vandenberg, 1981). Play themes in which children become involved, along with associated toys and materials, are particularly important to identify because both reveal an interest in certain play activities, and the toys and materials facilitate social exchanges within the broad structure of the theme (Guralnick, 1986). Consequently, assessments of the circumstances that are associated with varying levels of social interactions with peers provide additional information that may be especially valuable in designing intervention strategies.

Developmental Domains   Finally, as noted in Figure 2.1, information concerning a child's developmental status in each of the main developmental domains is needed to provide a framework for intervention. A child's cognitive level is especially important because it provides the developmental basis for expectations of the level of the child's peer relations. Much of this information can be obtained from multidisciplinary assessments that are usually administered to children with disabilities. Often, this information must be supplemented by probes that focus on aspects of development that are most relevant to peer-related social competence. Issues concerning attention, specific abilities in information processing, or perhaps special problems in receptive language should be included as background information to be considered in designing intervention programs.

LEVEL OF SOCIAL STRATEGIES AND SOCIAL TASKS

Until recently, the vast majority of efforts to assess and improve children's peer-related social competence have taken place at the level of social/communicative skills. Designing more stimulating environments or emphasizing specific intervention techniques to increase the frequency of initiations, to encourage children to be more responsive, to select goals that are more positive, and to improve a child's intelligibility may well produce valuable changes in children's peer interactions.

Nevertheless, interventions guided by assessments at the level of social/communicative interactions are likely to be limited. Although the various assessments of this type do provide a useful descriptive profile of a child's peer interaction patterns and can perhaps suggest general directions for intervention, they reveal little about the specific nature of the problems or the processes that are producing a particular pattern of social interactions. As a consequence, in many instances only the surface features of peer interactions (e.g., frequency and purpose of social initiations) may be affected by intervention. In fact, even substantial changes at the level of social/communicative skills are no guarantee that improvements in socially competent functioning will result. For example, one intervention approach frequently used is to change systematically a child's available play partners to include those with characteristics likely to foster peer interactions (e.g., involving younger peers for less assertive children [Furman, Rahe, & Hartup, 1979] or including children who do not have disabilities in an effort to provide a more stimulating and responsive environment for children with developmental delays [Guralnick & Groom, 1988]). Of importance is the fact that these interventions do not necessarily result in improvements in general peer-related social competence, despite substantial and potentially important changes in social/communicative skills, such as a greater frequency of positive social interactions (see Asher et al., 1981). Consequently, as significant as these changes in general social activity are at the level of social/communicative skills, they may not alter in any meaningful way the appropriateness or effectiveness of children's social behavior. It is argued here that in order to accomplish meaningful changes in peer-related social competence, social strategies in the context of social tasks must be considered.

The Importance of Social Strategies and Social Tasks

As the hierarchical model presented in Figure 2.1 suggests, through various processes to be discussed below, social/communicative skills are integrated, organized, and sequenced during the course of a specific social task in order for strategies to be created. In the context of a social task, social/communicative skills take on new meanings and are transformed into strategies that consist of constructs such as insistence, intrusiveness, negotiation, threat, compromise, justification, behavior synchronous with the group, or deescalation of play. In essence, strategies reveal how social/communicative skills are used in a manner that allows others to make judgments of both appropriateness and effectiveness. The importance of a shared context can be seen in this model as well, for, in order to select appropriate strategies, young children must be responsive to the generally understood conditions that may exist in different settings (e.g., rules regarding the ownership of toys). A sensitivity to the characteristics of their companions (e.g., chronological age) is also important, as children must make adjustments as needed. Chronological age is a particularly salient characteristic, and it has been demonstrated that young children are indeed capable of making reasonable and appropriate adjustments in accordance with a companion's age (Gelman & Shatz, 1977; Lederberg, 1982; Masur, 1978; Sachs & Devin, 1976; Shatz & Gelman, 1973).

Interestingly, linguists studying conversational or speech acts in the area of pragmatics also have recognized the importance of appropriateness, incorporating this construct into the conditions that underlie an utterance's ability to be transmitted successfully (Searle, 1969). Issues of relative status or ownership of toys, for example (see Newman, 1978), must be recognized at some level by both partners in an exchange for an appropriate utterance to result. Along the same lines, Garvey (1975) has identified what she has called "meaning factors" that help in understanding the appropriateness of children's requests for action. Such factors include a child's recognition that the peer is obligated or willing to carry out a request or has rights that might conflict with what one is being asked to do. Often children anticipate the need to form appropriate utterances by providing required information related to these meaning factors in advance of a request or by justifying or otherwise explaining the basis for the request. Similarly, companions recognize the importance of these conditions by questioning when a child appears to make a request that violates the underlying but unstated understanding of what is and what is not appropriate.

At the social strategy/social task level of analysis, a number of important social tasks have been identified, including obtaining compliance to a request, resolving conflicts during play, gaining entry into peer groups, and maintaining play with companions for sustained periods of time. As can be seen, some tasks have a longer-term goal and may even subsume other social tasks as events unfold. However widely or narrowly defined, as long as tasks can be identified adequately, assessments of effectiveness and appropriateness can be obtained. In the discussion that follows, the peer group entry task is used to illustrate the hierarchical model and how assessments could be carried out at the social strategy/social task level of analysis.

Peer Group Entry

One of the most difficult and critical tasks facing young children is to figure out how to become involved in play with peers who are already participating in an ongoing play activity. Failure to accomplish this social task clearly will prevent children from becoming integrated into playgroups. Moreover, peer group entry has been found to be highly diagnostic of general problems in peer-related social competence (Putallaz & Wasserman, 1990). Unfortunately, it appears that about 50% of all initial attempts to enter a group are rejected or ignored. Consequently, for those children who persist, and most do, they must select a series of strategies that will persuade their companions to allow them to participate in the group's activities. In many instances, this persistence creates conflicts, thereby requiring children to be skillful in managing the social task of dealing with conflict in the context of group entry as well.

One way to identify strategies that are appropriate and effective is to compare the group entry techniques used by children varying in terms of social status. As expected, children judged by their peers to be more socially competent (assessed through peer sociometric measures) enter groups more easily or successfully than those judged to be lower in sociometric status (Black & Hazen, 1990; Howes, 1988). Often comparisons of the strategies children use are carried out in analogue situations in which two children (hosts) are asked to play a particular game together and a third child (entry child) is then introduced into the setting. As noted earlier, this analogue situation permits control over the characteristics of all children, especially the entry child, whose sociometric status can be determined through ratings obtained at the child's regular preschool or day-care program. Detailed videotaped records are often obtained of the child's attempts to gain entry.

A number of studies have now utilized this approach, and it is possible to make some generalizations about the appropriateness and effectiveness of specific strategies that occur during the peer entry situation (Black & Hazen, 1990; Corsaro, 1981; Dodge, Schlundt, Schocken, & Delugach, 1983; Hazen & Black, 1989; Putallaz, 1983; Putallaz & Gottman, 1981; Putallaz & Wasserman, 1989). First, it has been well established that children seeking entry into an existing group must initially understand the group's "frame of reference" by accurately perceiving the particular play themes or events. This is ascertained through observations of children focusing on (i.e., watching) the ongoing play activities. In turn, this frame of reference allows children to become "connected" to the host children by making comments relevant to the play activities. Relevance is a construct that appears repeatedly in the group entry literature and has general significance for children's peer-related social competence (Asher, 1983). Particularly damaging to children's likelihood of entry success are self-statements or comments that tend to redirect the host children's play activities. But beyond relevance is the fact that children's understanding of the frame of reference also permits them to demonstrate a synchrony or harmony with the group and their activities. For this to occur, the strategies that are selected will tend to be nonintrusive ones, particularly nonverbal behaviors, such as imitating aspects of play or engaging in play in proximity to the hosts that constitutes a variation of the hosts' activities. Once this occurs, and indications from the hosts suggest at least tentative acceptance, more directive, intrusive strategies can be employed effectively.

But what happens when children do not immediately succeed? As just noted, there are so many factors that can influence the success of initial overtures that failure is a frequent occurrence. Children might misjudge the type of play activities or the interest of their hosts in having them involved, or their initial attempts may be too disruptive. To overcome rejection in all of its subtle and obvious forms, children must first learn to persist in their tasks. The ability to solve problems in the context of social tasks requires a longer-term view, and, unless children are willing to pursue alternative strategies in the face of initial failure, successful group entry rarely will be realized.

Independent evidence that this is an important characteristic for children during interactions with peers was obtained by Guralnick and Groom (1990), who found that children rated by their mothers as being generally more persistent engaged in more extensive interactions with their peers.

However, when children do persist in the face of initial failure, they immediately find themselves in a conflict situation (see Shantz, 1987). Social bids may be ignored or rejected or other attempts at entry resisted. As a consequence, how appropriately and effectively children resolve conflicts likely will determine the ultimate outcome of their efforts to enter peer groups. In fact, children who employ strategies during entry that are associated with more successful resolution of conflicts, such as negotiation, compromise, and making alternative suggestions (e.g., Eisenberg & Garvey, 1981; Phinney, 1986), are far more effective and are judged to be highly socially competent (e.g., Hazen & Black, 1989). Of special note was the finding that less socially competent children seeking to enter groups respond negatively to hosts' alternative or temporizing suggestions to their entry bids without providing any further explanations for their behavior (Hazen & Black, 1989). Clearly these flat rejections following a disagreement are not likely to lead to a productive continuation of social exchange.

Implications for Assessment

These studies provide a clear sense of the strategies employed by socially competent children during peer entry situations and also suggest behavioral patterns that lead peers to judge others as less competent. Any assessment of children's strategies during the entry social task must consider these findings, and may require arranging an analogue setting if attempts are not frequent enough in the typical play setting.

Strategies   First, an assessment should be made of how children approach the initial attempt to gain entry and, most important, whether they try to understand the frame of reference. As noted, unless a shared understanding of the activities of the participants is achieved, connected and relevant social exchanges will not result. This frame of reference must not only include a recognition of the social task at hand and existing play activities, but also consider as well the specific context and characteristics of the hosts. That is, appropriate strategies will require comments that are relevant, as well as those that recognize issues related to ownership, general classroom rules, and other social obligations of the participants. These assessments of whether entry children try to establish a shared frame of reference can be determined by the degree to which they wait and observe the hosts' activities. Evaluations of the content of their comments provide an additional measure. Furthermore, it is important that children seeking entry continue monitoring the activities of the hosts if the initial entry attempt is not successful. Unless evidence of monitoring is found in the assessment, it is unlikely that the child's subsequent entry attempts will succeed.

The degree of intrusiveness constitutes the second major dimension of peer entry skills. Typically, less intrusive strategies, such as encirclement or producing a variant of the ongoing behavior (see Corsaro, 1979), are the strategies chosen initially by socially competent children. These may be repeated over the course of an entry sequence if no response or a rejection is received, but eventually they will be followed by more direct requests for participation. Assessments of the specific strategies and degree of intrusiveness can be obtained readily during subsequent turns in the peer entry sequence.

A third area to be assessed in the peer entry situation relates to the strategies children employ to resolve conflicts. How children select and organize strategies to insist, mitigate a request, threaten, offer counter proposals or compromises, or provide reasons for their actions, provides insight into the ways in which conflict is managed. Given the ubiquitous nature of conflict for social tasks in general, children's ability to manage conflict in different situations is central to the understanding of peer-related social competence. The Assessment of Peer Relations (Guralnick, 1990a) instrument attempts to capture these events.

Processes   Within the hierarchical model, it has been suggested that social interactions with peers are based upon more fundamental, social/communicative skills that are transformed into strategies within the framework of social tasks. The model also suggests that the specific strategies that are selected depend upon many other factors, most important, the context and the characteristics of one's companions. What remains unclear, however, is how children actually go about processing information as part of the social task in order to arrive at the selection of a particular strategy (represented by the dotted lines in Figure 2.1). Insight into how children think about problems that involve relationships with peers can be extremely valuable for designing intervention programs. In particular, for children who are less competent, it must be determined what it is they do that results in the selection of strategies that are responsible for judgments of low social competence. If these processes can be understood, perhaps they can be altered.

This is precisely the reasoning that led Dodge and his colleagues (Dodge et al., 1986) to propose and test a model of social-cognitive processing applicable to social tasks. These investigators suggested that children process social information in five sequential steps: 1) encoding social cues in the present situation, 2) mentally representing and interpreting those cues, 3) generating possible behavioral responses (strategies), 4) evaluating the consequences of possible responses and selecting a specific strategy, and 5) enacting a behavioral response. Problems could occur at one or more of these steps, and a novel procedure was developed to establish the connection between each of these processing steps and children's peer-related social competence (see Dodge et al., 1986).

Preliminary support for this model, particularly for the peer entry task, was obtained, and each step in the complex social-cognitive process appears to be consistent with what are known to be important aspects of social competence with peers. The first step, encoding social cues in the present situation, is most critical because it requires children to engage attentional and perceptual processes. Emotional expressions of peers, their tones of voice, and the types of play themes that exist are the kinds of cues to be encoded at this stage, although there is as yet no higher order cognitive interpretation as to their meaning. It is apparent that children who fail to attend to cues appropriately at this step cannot possibly generate strategies that are relevant or connected. As Walden and Field (1990) observed, the ability of preschool children to encode affective expressions is strongly associated with peer-related social competence.

Even social cues that are accurately encoded are somewhat ambiguous by their very nature. Consequently, in the second step, the interpretation of the cues, bias due to past experiences may result in children interpreting cues inaccurately, thereby failing to appreciate the intent of a companion's social interactions. For example, an unusual sensitivity to rejection may lead to the interpretation of a cue that was intended to communicate postponement of involvement in a peer group as a final rejection, ultimately resulting in a highly negative emotional reaction. In this example, the influence of children's abilities to regulate their emotions can be seen as a critical factor during the course of a social task. Although Dodge et al. (1986) emphasize the more cognitive components associated with social information processing, it is apparent that children's abilities to regulate emotions, especially during conflict episodes, must be considered also (Gottman, 1983; Gottman & Katz, 1989). A complete model will require an understanding of both the social-cognitive and emotional aspects of peer-related social competence.

It should be noted that the third and fourth steps of the Dodge et al. (1986) model require a recognition of the importance of the availability of a range of possible strategies as well as an understanding of the context and companion characteristics needed to select a strategy that is appropriate. Awareness, at some level, of the relationships between strategy selection and the broader context of events is highly demanding from a cognitive perspective and requires extensive experience. Moreover, for those children who tend to make rapid or impulsive decisions, the fourth step may easily be overlooked, resulting in a lower likelihood of selecting an appropriate strategy.

As might be expected, these processes are extremely difficult to assess in preschool or disabled children. The methods used by Dodge et al. (1986), as creative as they may be, may not be applicable to these children since they depend on sometimes complex verbal reports. Nevertheless, to the extent that these processes reflect how children approach social tasks, the model may be useful in establishing hypotheses about the source or sources of children's peer interaction problems. In essence, any model guides the development of hypotheses. For complex and multidimensional domains such as peer relations, intervention consists of a trial-and-error process based upon a series of hypotheses or clinical judgments. Appropriate assessments of social-cognitive processes consistent with models such as that proposed by Dodge et al. (1986), as well as indicators of children's ability to regulate their emotions during social tasks, can provide better information about how children approach social tasks.

Cognitive Abilities   As can be seen from the descriptions of the skills needed to be socially competent, children's success in adapting to the rapidly shifting nature of social exchanges clearly contains a strong general cognitive component. The ability to grasp play themes, to remember and execute sequences of social behavior, and to retrieve past information are only a few of the cognitive abilities that are part of this complex process. In the hierarchical model, cognitive abilities exert influence at two levels. At the level of social/communicative skills, cognitive abilities contribute, for example, to recognizing the various intentions of companions and integrating events involving objects and peers. At the level of strategies and social tasks, cognitive abilities play a similar role, although higher order cognitive processes related to planning or the evaluation of consequences are of more significance.

As might be expected, general cognitive development is associated both with children's ability to achieve their interpersonal goals and with social status (see Wright, 1980). Putallaz (1983) observed that even in the peer entry situation, a substantial positive correlation existed between cognitive ability and sociometric ratings received by children. Other investigators have found similar relationships (Krasnor & Rubin, 1983; Quay & Jarrett, 1984).

Despite this correlation, general cognitive development accounts for only a relatively small proportion of the variability found in children's peer-related social competence. Of course, many noncognitive factors such as a child's ability to produce intelligible speech or having sufficient motor skills to engage in rough and tumble play can have an important impact on children's peer-related social competence. But, as seen earlier, other processes, including those associated with social-cognitive information processing and the ability to regulate one's emotions during social tasks, extend beyond general cognitive abilities and appear to be most closely associated with peer-related social competence.

APPLICATION OF THE HIERARCHICAL
MODEL FOR CHILDREN WITH DEVELOPMENTAL DELAYS

Since the 1980s interest in the peer-related social competence of children who do not have disabilities has promoted a similar interest in various groups of young children with disabilities. Moreover, research in this area has intensified as a consequence of the movement to mainstream preschool-age disabled children (Guralnick, 1990b). It has been well recognized that the ability of children with disabilities to establish and maintain social relationships with peers is central to their social integration and social acceptance in mainstreamed settings.

Unfortunately, existing research has revealed that, overall, children with disabilities have a peer interaction deficit; that is, their degree of involvement in peer interactions falls substantially below expectations based on their developmental levels (Darbyshire, 1977; Guralnick & Groom, 1985, 1987; Guralnick & Weinhouse, 1984; Higgenbotham & Baker, 1981; Markovits & Strayer, 1982; Siegel, Cunningham, & van der Spuy, 1985; Vandell & George, 1981). This finding appears to be quite robust, occurring in numerous contexts with a range of assessment techniques and for children with differing disabilities. The primary characteristic of this deficit is less involvement in group play in conjunction with a correspondingly greater involvement in solitary play.

By examining the patterns of social interactions of peers at both the level of social/communicative skills and of social strategies and tasks, the hierarchical model and corresponding assessment domains presented in this chapter may be useful in understanding the nature of this deficit as well as suggesting areas for future research. Similarly, the model can perhaps serve as a framework for approaching the difficult problems related to intervention to improve children's peer-related social competence, especially when social-cognitive and emotional regulation processes are considered.

It is beyond the scope of this chapter to present a detailed analysis of the hierarchical model (see Guralnick, in preparation); however, in this section, a brief summary of how this model can be applied to existing data for children who have mild to moderate (cognitive) developmental delays is presented (see Guralnick & Bricker, 1987 for a description of these children). The deficit for this group of children has been well documented as delayed children engage in extensive amounts of solitary play and limited amounts of group play, and have low social status as assessed by peer sociometric measures (Guralnick, 1990c).

Social/Communicative Skills

It would be reasonable to expect that delays in cognitive development as well as associated difficulties for children with disabilities would have a major impact at the level of social/communicative skills. However, this does not appear to be the case. Social interactions with peers appear to occur with reasonable frequency and are organized in a reciprocal fashion (Dunlop, Stoneman, & Cantrell, 1980; Guralnick & Weinhouse, 1984). The willingness of children with developmental delays to interact and their responsiveness to the social bids of others have not been investigated extensively, although available evidence does suggest that children with mild delays are sufficiently responsive to the social bids of peers (Guralnick & Paul-Brown, 1986). Children with developmental delays are also able to communicate their intent (especially directives and questions) as well as developmentally matched groups of children who do not have disabilities and are as effective in obtaining an initial and immediate response to their social bids (Guralnick & Groom, 1985, 1987; Guralnick & Paul-Brown, 1986). The distribution of social/communicative skills that occurs during the course of social exchanges with peers, even including mitigated and unmitigated directives, is also similar to that of an appropriately matched group of children who do not have disabilities (Guralnick & Groom, 1987; Guralnick & Paul-Brown, 1989). It is not known whether the purposes of the initiations of children with delays differ, although preliminary analyses have not revealed any differences (Guralnick, Paul-Brown, Booth, & Groom, in preparation).

Despite overall similarities of the peer interactions of children with delays to developmentally matched children who do not have disabilities at the level of social/communicative skills, some differences have been observed. Specifically, there is a strong tendency for social/communicative interactions to occur less frequently in children with delays (Guralnick & Paul-Brown, 1989), although overall frequency is highly sensitive to settings and to the characteristics of a child's companions (see Guralnick & Groom, 1988). This is especially apparent for those skills associated with directing others in play (Guralnick & Groom, 1985, 1987). As just noted, for children with delays the success rate in social bids is similar to that of nondisabled children, but there is a strong tendency for success to decrease with increasing experience with peers (Guralnick & Groom, 1987). Although the complexity of the speech of children with delays that is directed to peers is less than that of nondisabled children (Guralnick & Paul-Brown, 1989), expressive language is not a strong correlate of peer-related social competence (Guralnick & Groom, 1985). Of greatest concern, however, has been the unusually high level of disagreements (i.e., statements of disapproval, criticisms, refusals to comply, minor struggles) observed during peer interaction of children with delays (Guralnick & Paul-Brown, 1989).

In general, then, assessments of peer interactions of children with delays at the level of social/communicative skills have revealed many similarities to appropriately matched groups of children who do not have disabilities, in conjunction with some concerns regarding the frequency, quality, and perhaps success of social exchange with peers. Taken together, however, it is the similarities rather than the differences that emerge as the primary pattern of interactions at the level of social/communicative skills. Even with the differences that have been identified, it is difficult to see their contribution to understanding the substantial peer interaction deficit that is characteristic of children with delays. The natural next step would be to examine children's interactions at the level of social strategies and social tasks. Although overall measures that are summed across all social situations and social tasks at the level of social/communicative skills do not appear to be correlated strongly with the special problems of children with delays, it is reasonable to anticipate that difficulties may become apparent when children with delays are challenged to solve complex social problems within social tasks. They may have difficulty with the requirements of integrating, organizing, and sequencing social/communicative skills, while remaining sensitive to the context and the characteristics of their companions.

Social Strategies and Social Tasks

Unfortunately, analyses at the level of social strategies and social tasks for children with developmental delays have not been carried out in any systematic fashion, and constitute a major barrier not only to the understanding of the peer-related social competence of this group of children but for children with disabilities in general. That problems are likely to be evident at the level of social strategies is suggested by the finding that unusually high levels of disagreements occur during peer interactions of children with delays (Guralnick & Paul-Brown, 1989). It may well be that the strategies employed by these children during disputes that arise during the peer entry situation or surrounding the ownership of toys are not appropriate or effective. Given the central role that conflict management plays in peer relations (Gottman, 1983), it would not be surprising that problems in this area would have a pervasive influence on peer interactions, thereby substantially contributing to the peer interaction deficit. These and related hypotheses are being evaluated in current analyses of the conflict resolution strategies of children with delays during directive episodes (Guralnick et al., in preparation) and in the direct assessment of peer entry behavior as part of the University of Washington's component of the Research Institute on Preschool Mainstreaming.

Further speculating within the hierarchical model suggests that the ability of children with delays to regulate their emotions during typical exchanges with peers should be evaluated carefully. Moreover, given that attentional problems commonly are revealed in studies of children with delays (Krakow & Kopp, 1983), it is likely that their ability to encode appropriate social cues is impaired, which would cause distortion of the remaining steps of the social-cognitive processes suggested by Dodge et al. (1986) that are necessary for producing appropriate strategies. The importance of establishing a shared understanding or frame of reference and its association to issues concerned with the relevance and connectedness of social exchanges has been emphasized in this chapter, and difficulties in this domain due to encoding problems may well turn out to be one of the most critical factors in understanding the peer-interaction deficit of young children with developmental delays.

CONCLUSION

In this chapter, a hierarchical model has been presented in order to provide a framework for understanding young children's peer-related social competence. Critical features of the model are its reliance upon a developmental perspective and a recognition that the contributions of many disciplines are necessary for a complete understanding of the peer interactions of both nondisabled and disabled children. In fact, the study of peer relationships, because of its fundamental integrative, sequential, and dynamic nature has served as a catalyst for bridging the often disparate areas of linguistics, clinical child psychology, developmental psychology, and early childhood special education.

The hierarchical model contains two major levels of analysis: social/communicative skills, and social tasks and social strategies. It appears that the latter is most relevant to understanding the construct of peer-related social competence. This level of analysis provides an opportunity to examine systematically the unfolding of social events over time and helps focus on the processes that are associated with solving complex social interaction problems with peers. Assessments of peer interactions during defined social tasks is an emerging area of research for children who do not have disabilities but remains largely unexplored for children with disabilities. Once assessments of social strategies and processes within social tasks are carried out, a more thoughtful approach to intervention may well emerge.

REFERENCES

Anderson, S., & Messick, S. (1974). Social competency in young children. *Developmental Psychology, 10,* 282–293.

Asher, S.R. (1983). Social competence and peer status: Recent advances and future directions. *Child Development, 54,* 1427–1434.

Asher, S.R., Markell, R.A., & Hymel, S. (1981). Identifying children at risk in peer relations: A critique of the rate-of-interaction approach to assessment. *Child Development, 52,* 1239–1245.

Asher, S.R., Singleton, L.C., Tinsley, B.R., & Hymel, S. (1979). A reliable sociometric measure for preschool children. *Developmental Psychology, 15,* 443–444.

Bakeman, R., & Gottman, J.M. (1986). *Observing interaction: An introduction to sequential analysis.* Cambridge: Cambridge University Press.

Black, B., & Hazen, N.L. (1990). Social status and patterns of communication in acquainted and unacquainted preschool children. *Developmental Psychology, 26,* 379–387.

Corsaro, W.A. (1979). "We're friends, right?": Children's use of access rituals in a nursery school. *Language in Society, 8,* 315–336.

Corsaro, W.A. (1981). Friendship in the nursery school: Social organization in a peer environment. In S.R. Asher & J.M. Gottman (Eds.), *The development of children's friendships* (pp. 207–241). New York: Cambridge University Press.

Darbyshire, J.O. (1977). Play patterns in young children with impaired hearing. *The Volta Review, 79,* 19–26.

Dodge, K.A. (1983). Behavioral antecedents of peer social status. *Child Development, 54,* 1386–1399.

Dodge, K.A., Pettit, G.S., McClaskey, C.L., & Brown, M.M. (1986). Social competence in children. *Monographs of the Society for Research in Child Development, 51*(2, Serial No. 213).

Dodge, K.A., Schlundt, D.C., Schocken, I., & Delugach, J.D. (1983). Social competence and children's sociometric status: The role of peer group entry strategies. *Merrill-Palmer Quarterly, 29*(3), 309–336.

Dore, J. (1986). The development of conversational competence. In R. Schiefelbusch (Ed.), *Language competence: Assessment and intervention* (pp. 3–60). San Diego: College-Hill.

Doyle, A., Connolly, J., & Rivest, L. (1980). The effect of playmate familiarity on the social interactions of young children. *Child Development, 51,* 217–223.

Dunlop, K.H., Stoneman, Z., & Cantrell, M.L. (1980). Social interaction of exceptional and other children in a mainstreamed preschool classroom. *Exceptional Children, 47,* 132–141.

Eisenberg, A.R., & Garvey, C. (1981). Children's use of verbal strategies in resolving conflicts. *Discourse Processes, 4,* 149–170.

Finkelstein, N.W., Dent, C., Gallacher, K., & Ramey, C.T. (1978). Social behavior of infants and toddlers in a day-care environment. *Developmental Psychology, 14,* 257–262.

Furman, W., Rahe, D.F., & Hartup, W.W. (1979). Rehabilitation of socially-withdrawn preschool children through mixed-age and same-age socialization. *Child Development, 50,* 915–922.

Gallagher, T.M., & Prutting, C.A. (Eds.). (1983). *Pragmatic assessment and intervention issues in language.* San Diego: College-Hill.

Garvey, C. (1975). Requests and responses in children's speech. *Journal of Child Language, 2,* 41–63.

Garvey, C. (1984). *Children's talk.* Cambridge, MA: Harvard University Press.

Gelman, R., & Shatz, M. (1977). Appropriate speech adjustments: The operation of conversational constraints on talk to two-year-olds. In M. Lewis & L.A. Rosenblum (Eds.), *The origins of behavior: Vol. 5. Interaction, conversation, and the development of language* (pp. 27–61). New York: John Wiley & Sons.

Ginsberg, D., Gottman, J., & Parker, J. (1986). The importance of friendship. In J.M. Gottman & J.G. Parker (Eds.), *Conversations of friends: Speculations on affective development* (pp. 3–48). New York: Cambridge University Press.

Gottman, J.M. (1983). How children become friends. *Monographs of the Society for Research in Child Development, 48*(3, Serial No. 201).

Gottman, J.M., & Katz, L. (1989). Effects of marital discord on young children's peer interaction and health. *Developmental Psychology, 25,* 373–381.

Gresham, F.M. (1986). Conceptual issues in the assessment of social competence in children. In P.S. Strain, M.J. Guralnick, & H.M. Walker (Eds.), *Children's social behavior: Development, assessment, and modification* (pp. 143–179). Orlando: Academic Press.

Guralnick, M.J. (1986). The peer relations of young handicapped and nonhandicapped children. In P.S. Strain, M.J. Guralnick, & H.M. Walker (Eds.), *Children's social behavior: Development, assessment, and modification* (pp. 93–140). New York: Academic Press.

Guralnick, M.J. (1990a). *Assessment of peer relations* (draft version). Research Institute on Preschool Mainstreaming. Child Development and Mental Retardation Center, University of Washington, Seattle.

Guralnick, M.J. (1990b). Major accomplishments and future directions in early childhood mainstreaming. *Topics in Early Childhood Special Education, 10*(2), 1–17.

Guralnick, M.J. (1990c). Peer interactions and the development of handicapped children's social and communicative competence. In H. Foot, M.

Morgan, & R. Shute (Eds.), *Children helping children* (pp. 275–305). Sussex, England: John Wiley & Sons.

Guralnick, M.J. (1990d). Social competence and early intervention. *Journal of Early Intervention, 14,* 3–14.

Guralnick, M.J. (in preparation). *Early childhood mainstreaming: A developmental and systems approach.*

Guralnick, M.J., & Bricker, D. (1987). The effectiveness of early intervention for children with cognitive and general developmental delays. In M.J. Guralnick & F.C. Bennett (Eds.), *The effectiveness of early intervention for at-risk and handicapped children* (pp. 115–173). New York: Academic Press.

Guralnick, M.J., & Groom, J.M. (1985). Correlates of peer-related social competence of developmentally delayed preschool children. *American Journal of Mental Deficiency, 90,* 140–150.

Guralnick, M.J., & Groom, J.M. (1987). The peer relations of mildly delayed and nonhandicapped preschool children in mainstreamed playgroups. *Child Development, 58,* 1556–1572.

Guralnick, M.J., & Groom, J.M. (1988). Peer interactions in mainstreamed and specialized classrooms: A comparative analysis. *Exceptional Children, 54,* 415–425.

Guralnick, M.J., & Groom, J.M. (1990). The correspondence between temperament and peer interactions for normally developing and mildly delayed preschool children. *Child: Care, Health and Development, 16,* 165–175.

Guralnick, M.J., & Paul-Brown, D. (1984). Communicative adjustments during behavior-request episodes among children at different developmental levels. *Child Development, 55,* 911–919.

Guralnick, M.J., & Paul-Brown, D. (1986). Communicative interactions of mildly delayed and normally developing preschool children: Effects of listener's developmental level. *Journal of Speech and Hearing Research, 29,* 2–10.

Guralnick, M.J., & Paul-Brown, D. (1989). Peer-related communicative competence of preschool children: Developmental and adaptive characteristics. *Journal of Speech and Hearing Research, 32,* 930–943.

Guralnick, M.J., Paul-Brown, D., Booth, C., & Groom, J.M. (in press). *Sequential analysis of behavior request episodes.*

Guralnick, M.J., & Weinhouse, E.M. (1983). Child-child social interactions: An analysis of assessment instruments for young children. *Exceptional Children, 50,* 268–271.

Guralnick, M.J., & Weinhouse, E.M. (1984). Peer-related social interactions of developmentally delayed young children: Development and characteristics. *Developmental Psychology, 20,* 815–827.

Hartup, W.W. (1983). Peer relations. In E.M. Hetherington (Ed.), P.H. Mussen (Series Ed.), *Handbook of child psychology: Vol. 4. Socialization, personality, and social development* (pp. 103–196). New York: John Wiley & Sons.

Hazen, N.L., & Black, B. (1989). Preschool peer communication skills: The role of social status and interaction context. *Child Development, 60,* 867–876.

Higgenbotham, J., & Baker, B.M. (1981). Social participation and cognitive play differences in hearing-impaired and normally hearing preschoolers. *The Volta Review, 83,* 135–149.

Howes, C. (1988). Peer interaction of young children. *Monographs of the Society for Research in Child Development, 53*(1, Serial No. 217).

Krakow, J.B., & Kopp, C.B. (1983). The effects of developmental delay on sustained attention in young children. *Child Development, 54,* 1143–1155.

Krasnor, L.R., & Rubin, K.H. (1983). Preschool social problem solving: Attempts and outcomes in naturalistic interaction. *Child Development, 54,* 1545–1558.

Ladd, G.W., & Mars, K.T. (1986). Reliability and validity of preschoolers' perceptions of peer behavior. *Journal of Clinical Child Psychology, 15,* 16–25.

Lederberg, A.R. (1982). A framework for research on preschool children's speech modifications. In S. Kuczaj (Ed.), *Language development: Vol. 2. Language, thought, and culture* (pp. 37–73). Hillsdale, NJ: Lawrence Erlbaum Associates.

Levin, E.A., & Rubin, K.H. (1983). Getting others to do what you want them to do: The development of children's requestive strategies. In K.E. Nelson (Ed.), *Children's language* (Vol. 4, pp. 157–186). Hillsdale, NJ: Lawrence Erlbaum Associates.

Markovits, H., & Strayer, F.F. (1982). Toward an applied social ethology: A case study of social skills among blind children. In K.H. Rubin & H.S. Ross (Eds.), *Peer relationships and social skills in childhood* (pp. 301–322). New York: Springer-Verlag.

Masur, E.F. (1978). Preschool boys' speech modifications: The effect of listener's linguistic levels and conversational responsiveness. *Child Development, 49,* 924–927.

McConnell, S.R., & Odom, S.L. (1986). Sociometrics: Peer-referenced measures and the assessment of social competence. In P.S. Strain, M.J. Guralnick, & H.M. Walker (Eds.), *Children's social behavior: Development, assessment, and modification* (pp. 215–284). Orlando, FL: Academic Press.

Musen-Miller, L. (1990). Sociometrics with preschool children: Agreement between different strategies. *Journal of Applied Developmental Psychology, 11,* 195–207.

Newman, D. (1978). Ownership and permission among nursery school children. In J. Glick & K.A. Clarke-Stewart (Eds.), *The development of social understanding* (pp. 213–249). New York: Gardner Press.

Parker, J.G., & Asher, S.R. (1987). Peer relations and later personal adjustment: Are low-accepted children at risk? *Psychological Bulletin, 102,* 357–389.

Phinney, J.S. (1986). The structure of 5-year-olds' verbal quarrels with peers and siblings. *Journal of Genetic Psychology, 147*(1), 47–60.

Putallaz, M. (1983). Predicting children's sociometric status from their behavior. *Child Development, 54,* 1417–1426.

Putallaz, M., & Gottman, J.M. (1981). Social skills and group acceptance. In S.R. Asher & J.M. Gottman (Eds.), *The development of children's friendships* (pp. 116–149). Cambridge: Cambridge University Press.

Putallaz, M., & Heflin, A.H. (1990). Parent-child interaction. In S.R. Asher & J.D. Coie (Eds.), *Peer rejection in childhood* (pp. 189–216). Cambridge: Cambridge University Press.

Putallaz, M., & Wasserman, A. (1989). Children's naturalistic entry behavior and sociometric status: A developmental perspective. *Developmental Psychology, 25,* 297–305.

Putallaz, M., & Wasserman, A. (1990). Children's entry behavior. In S.R. Asher & J.D. Coie (Eds.), *Peer rejection in childhood* (pp. 60–89). Cambridge: Cambridge University Press.

Quay, L.C., & Jarrett, O.S. (1984). Predictors of social acceptance in preschool children. *Developmental Psychology, 20,* 793–796.

Rogers-Warren, A., & Wedel, J.W. (1980). The ecology of preschool classrooms for the handicapped. In J.J. Gallagher (Ed.), *New directions for exceptional children: No. 1. Ecology of exceptional children* (pp. 1–24). San Francisco: Jossey-Bass.

Sachs, J., & Devin, J. (1976). Young children's use of age-appropriate speech styles. *Journal of Child Language, 3,* 81–98.

Sackett, G.P. (1978). Measurement in observational research. In G.P. Sackett (Ed.), *Observing behavior: Data collection and analysis methods* (Vol. 2, pp. 25–43). Baltimore: University Park Press.

Schober-Peterson, D., & Johnson, C.J. (1989). Conversational topics of 4-year-olds. *Journal of Speech and Hearing Research, 32,* 857–870.

Searle, J.R. (1969). *Speech acts: An essay in the philosophy of language.* Cambridge: Cambridge University Press.

Shantz, C.U. (1987). Conflicts between children. *Child Development, 58,* 283–305.

Shatz, M., & Gelman, R. (1973). The development of communication skills: Modifications in the speech of young children as a function of listener. *Monographs of the Society for Research in Child Development, 38*(5, Serial No. 152).

Siegel, L.S., Cunningham, C.E., & van der Spuy, H.I.J. (1985). Interactions of language-delayed and normal preschool boys with their peers. *Journal of Child Psychology and Psychiatry, 26,* 77–83.

Vandell, D.L., & George, L.B. (1981). Social interaction in hearing and deaf preschoolers: Successes and failures in initiations. *Child Development, 52,* 627–635.

Vandenberg, B. (1981). Environmental and cognitive factors in social play. *Journal of Experimental Child Psychology, 31,* 169–175.

Walden, T.A., & Field, T.M. (1990). Preschool children's social competence and production and discrimination of affective expressions. *British Journal of Developmental Psychology, 8,* 65–76.

Wells, G. (Ed.). (1985). *Language at home and at school: Vol. 2. Language development in the pre-school years.* Cambridge: Cambridge University Press.

White, B.L., & Watts, J.C. (1973). *Experience and environment* (Vol. 1). Englewood Cliffs, NJ: Prentice-Hall.

Wright, M.J. (1980). Measuring the social competence of preschool children. *Canadian Journal of Behavioural Science, 12,* 17–32.

3

Parent-Child Social Relationships and Peer Social Competence of Preschool Children with Disabilities

Paula J. Beckman and Joan Lieber

An important question about the social development of young children concerns the association between children's social competence with peers and their social relationships with adults. For many years, researchers in child development assumed that social relationships between children were simply by-products of relationships with parents (especially mothers). Since the 1980s, however, peer relations have been viewed as much more unique and critical to the overall social development of the child. In many ways, exchanges between children appear to have unique qualities that differentiate them from children's exchanges with adults. Guralnick (1986) has noted that peer interactions involve much more equal participation and balance between partners. Interactions with adults are frequently led by the adult, who tends to initiate more of the interaction and who provides a responsive and anticipatory social environment. Additionally, Guralnick noted that interactions between children tend to take on different forms and have different themes than do interactions with adults.

Despite the contrasts that can be drawn between patterns of adult-child interaction and patterns of interaction between peers, there is evidence suggesting a relationship between these two behavioral systems (Vandell & Wilson, 1987). However, there is relatively little research investigating the relationship between these two behavioral systems for children with disabilities. This is unfortunate since impaired peer interactions may reflect a more general impairment of social abilities that permeates many types of social exchanges (Guralnick, 1986). Moreover, if investigators are able to identify difficulties that are consistent regardless of the interaction partner, intervention strategies may be devised that can begin earlier and that can be used in a variety of contexts.

This chapter examines the relationship between children's interactions with parents and their interactions with peers. Specifically, first the existing evidence concerning the relationship between these behavioral systems is reviewed. The limited information regarding sibling interaction is discussed briefly. Then a number of social strategies that seem to be critical components of social competence are identified and their potential importance across a variety of social contexts, described. Finally, the implications of these findings for future research and intervention is discussed.

THE RELATIONSHIP BETWEEN
PARENT-CHILD AND PEER INTERACTIONS

Families are thought to influence a child's ability to interact with peers (Parke, MacDonald, Beitel, & Bhavnagri, 1988). Among studies concerning children who do not have disabilities, two distinct research perspectives exist (Hay, 1985). One group of researchers has investigated primarily the influence of attachment (i.e., primarily mother-child attachment) on children's interactions with peers. A second group of researchers initially was interested only in the development of peer interaction (Vandell, 1980). Only later did these researchers extend their investigations to other relationships (i.e., primarily mother-infant) to determine the origins of child-child interaction. Although both bodies of literature have focused on the relationship between the two behavioral systems, they rest on fundamentally different assumptions and offer differing contributions to the understanding of social competence in young children. Both bodies of literature are discussed briefly below to identify features that are most relevant to an understanding of social competence in young children. Literature concerned with children who do not have disabilities is reviewed first, and a review of studies focused on children with disabilities follows.

Attachment to Parents and
Children's Social Competence with Peers

The interface between attachment to parents and later peer interaction has been conceptualized in two ways (Jacobson, Tianen, Wille, &

Aytch, 1986). In one view, securely attached children are seen as having more opportunity to develop interpersonal skills because the mother is viewed as a "secure base" from which the infant can explore (Ross & Goldman, 1977). It is through exploration that children acquire competence with their peers. In the other view (Jacobson et al., 1986), the securely attached child is not necessarily more skillful, but is friendlier, more enthusiastic, and, thus, is considered a more attractive playmate.

Lieberman (1977) considered the relationship both of mother-child attachment and of experience with peers to competence in preschool peer relationships. After partialling out the relationship between attachment and peer experience, Lieberman concluded that secure attachment was related to nonverbal interactions such as sharing and showing objects. In another study that considered the effects of prior peer experience, Easterbrooks and Lamb (1979) related the quality of infants' attachment to frequency and quality of interaction with an unacquainted partner. Infants who were more willing to explore following separation from their mothers had the most frequent and positive interchanges with their peers.

The previous studies provide support for the notion that securely attached infants, particularly those who engage in more exploration and less proximity-seeking behavior, are also children who show social competence with their peers. However, Jacobson et al. (1986) argued that the behaviors of both members of the dyad must be considered in social competence assessment. They suggested that attachment may influence children's responsiveness to peers as well as their ability to initiate social interactions. In observing a group of 2-year-olds in a free-play situation, Jacobson et al. (1986) found that securely attached toddlers were distinguished from those who were avoidant or ambivalent by their responsiveness. Securely attached toddlers were sensitive social partners who matched their behavior to that of their partners.

When a sample of these children was followed through age 3, Jacobson and Wille (1986) found that securely attached target children who were matched with securely attached partners showed the highest level of positive interactions. Ambivalent and avoidant children were as likely as securely attached children to initiate interactions, and as likely to respond to initiations in a positive way; however, partners were less responsive to ambivalent and avoidant children. Jacobson and Wille attribute this difference to the content of their play, which was less interesting than that of the securely attached preschoolers. They concluded that there is a link between attachment and later peer interaction because there is a qualitatively different pattern of response for children with different attachment patterns.

There is virtually no information about how attachment to fathers is linked with children's ability to interact with peers. There are several reasons for this lack of information. First, the study of the attachment/peer interaction link regarding relationships with *mothers* does not have an extensive history, and the theoretical basis for the mother-infant link is stronger than that for the link with fathers. Second, the extent of involvement of fathers with their children is significantly less than that of involvement of mothers (Lamb & Oppenheim, 1989). In spite of the relatively small amount of time that fathers spend with their children, the quality of their attachment has been investigated (e.g., Cohen & Campos, 1974; Lamb, 1977). Evidence indicates that children form attachments to both parents; however, when both parents are available, infants prefer mothers when distressed (Lamb, 1981). In contrast, Lamb found that children show more affiliative behaviors (e.g., smiling, vocalizing) toward fathers. Bridges, Connell, and Belsky (1988) argue that mothers and fathers may have relationships with children that are independent and distinct.

Given the potential association between attachment and later peer competence, it is important to understand how attachment in children with disabilities influences peer relationships. Unfortunately, knowledge in this area is particularly limited. There is some information, however, about attachment formation itself in children with disabilities (Blacher & Meyers, 1983; Spieker, 1986). These studies indicate that, while children with disabilities certainly show evidence of attachment, traditional markers of attachment are often delayed.

One group of researchers (Goldberg, Lojkasek, Gartner, & Corter, 1989), however, studied a group of premature infants to examine the influence of the security of attachment on social development at age 4. Goldberg et al. found that children who were more securely attached as infants showed more prosocial, flexible, and diverse strategies with peers. However, several factors limit the contribution of this investigation to knowledge about the attachment/peer interaction link. First, all children were preterm infants; no children with other disabling conditions were considered. Second, children who had IQ scores below 80 at age 4 were excluded from the study. Third, peer interaction was not actually observed at age 4; children were given a social problem-solving task, and asked to indicate which peer interaction strategy they would use.

In sum, for children who do not have disabilities, there appears to be conflicting information about the influence of attachment on later social competence with peers. There is some consensus that securely attached children who are eager to explore their environment make competent social partners. Existing evidence indicates that securely attached infants are responsive to peers and tend to match their behaviors to those of their partners. There is less convincing evidence the securely attached children show more willingness to initiate social encounters.

The relationship between attachment for children with disabilities and later social competence with peers is unknown. However, given the potential importance of attachment to peer social competence for children who do not have disabilities, it is possible to speculate that the social competence of children with disabilities might be influenced if attachment processes are disrupted. It is not clear how information from relevant studies of children with disabilities could be used by interventionists if they were available. A more fruitful approach might be to examine directly the relationship between children's social behavior with adults and their social behavior with peers.

Interaction with Other Partners and Social Competence with Peers

Mother-Child Interaction

Children Who Do Not Have Disabilities   In an effort to explain the relationship, for children who do not have disabilities, between early interactions with parents and later sociability with peers, Vandell (1980) considered the relative merits of three competing hypotheses. The first hypothesis is that the parent-child and the peer interaction systems are basically different (difference hypothesis). The second hypothesis is that the two behavioral systems are characterized by underlying similarities (similarity hypothesis). The third is that the mother-infant interaction system acts as a precursor to the peer social system and that the child's social competence is shaped by experience with the mother (precursor hypothesis).

In order to test the three hypotheses, Vandell (1980) compared interactions of first-born infants at 6, 9, and 12 months as they interacted with their mothers and with a same-sex peer. Results supported both the difference and the similarity hypotheses. In support of the difference hypothesis, Vandell reported that infants vocalized to and looked at other infants more frequently than at mothers; they touched the mothers more frequently than the infant peers. The systems were similar in that infants who smiled at their mothers also smiled at peers, and infants who vocalized to their mothers also vocalized to peers. No support was obtained for the precursor hypothesis since no behaviors that appeared first with the mothers were then transferred to peers.

Expanding on this work, Vandell and Wilson (1982) further described similarities and differences in the two systems. They found that mothers were sensitive partners who were likely to respond to infant initiations. In addition, mothers acted as if the infants' nonsocial activities were social and called for a response. Thus, when mothers interacted with their infants, longer and more complex interactions occurred because mothers scaffolded the interaction (Bruner, 1983). In contrast, infants were less likely to vary the complexity of their behavior based on the skillfulness of their partner. Vandell and Wilson (1982) found no difference in the proportion of simple versus complex socially directed behaviors with mothers or with peers.

In a subsequent study, Vandell and Wilson (1987) observed the social interactions of second-born infants with three different partners (i.e., mother, preschool-age sibling, and peer) at 6 and 9 months of age. In contrast to Vandell's (1980) earlier results, they found that the interactions that occurred between mother and infant at 6 months influenced the interactions that occurred between infant and peer at 9 months. It is not clear why results from the two studies were different; however, these results provided support for the precursor hypothesis.

Bakeman and Adamson (1984) also compared children's interactions with mothers and peers over time. Infants were observed with their mothers and a peer at ages 6, 9, 12, 15, and 18 months. Results showed both similarities and differences in the infants' interactions with peers and with mothers and, similarly to the Vandell and Wilson (1987) study, noted that these interactions changed over time. In addition, there was evidence that infants' ability to coordinate their attention to both an object and a partner was facilitated by the mother.

Children with Disabilities   Less information is available concerning the relationship between the mother-child system and the child-child system for children with disabilities. One investigation (Lieber & Beckman, 1990) directly compared the interactions of young children with disabilities both with their mothers and with peers in an early intervention center to determine the extent to which child behavior was similar across partners. Toddlers with a variety of disabling conditions were observed. Results indicated that toddlers directed more social behaviors (e.g., smiles, gestures, vocalizations) to mothers than to peers. Furthermore, toddlers used more complex socially directed behaviors (i.e., those involving a look plus two or more social behaviors) to mothers than to peers. The exchanges that occurred within dyads were different for mother-child dyads compared with child-child dyads as well. For example, with mothers, the number of turns per exchange was significantly greater than with peers. For individual children, there was some indication that social skills were stable across partners. For example, those toddlers who used simple or complex socially directed behaviors with their mothers, also used them with peers. Additionally, children who used vocalizations and object-related social acts with their mothers, used them with peers as well.

Father-Child Interactions

Children Who Do Not Have Disabilities   Although fathers spend less time with their children than do mothers, there is evidence that when they do interact with their children, the types of roles they fulfill and the types of play that occur are different from these interactions with mothers (see Parke & Tinsley, 1981 for a review). Regarding children who do not have disabilities, an example is Stevenson, Leavitt, Thompson, and Roach's (1988) findings that, during a child's first year, fathers engaged in more functional play (i.e., play involving manipulating objects), while mothers engaged in more instructive play with their infants. During the preschool years, fathers were more likely to initiate rough play, and mothers were more likely to initiate fantasy play for both boys and girls (Roopnarine & Mounts, 1985).

The relationship between fathers' (as well as mothers') play with their children and peer competence was tested by Parke et al. (1988). In this investigation, both mothers and fathers played for 20 minutes with their 3- to 4-year-old children under two conditions: typical play and physical play. These parent behaviors were then related to two measures of social skill with peers. Popularity in boys was associated with mothers who provided verbal stimulation and with physically playful fathers. Popularity in girls was also associated with physical playfulness in fathers, but with directive mothers. These parental behaviors were also associated with positive child characteristics as rated by teachers. Parke et al. concluded that physically playful interaction may help children use and interpret social signals. This is particularly interesting as a new conclusion, and it needs to be tested directly to validate its role in the development of social competence in children.

Children with Disabilities   Little is known about the relationship between fathers' interactions with children who have disabilities and the children's peer relationships. This is unfortunate because fathers may play a significant role in contributing to social competence with peers. For example, fathers have been found to be more playful in their interactions with children than mothers, and this playfulness occurs with fathers of children with disabilities as well (Field, 1981; Levy-Shiff, 1986; Levy-Shiff, Sharir, & Mogilner, 1989). Although there have been no direct empirical tests, it is possible that fathers have a potentially stronger role as social partners than mothers. Because the content of fathers' interactions appears to be more closely linked to the content of children's interaction with each other (i.e., physical play), children may be more likely to generalize specific skills gained in interaction with fathers to interaction with peers.

Sibling-Child Interaction

Children Who Do Not Have Disabilities   One additional family relationship that has been associated with peer interaction is the relationship between young children and their older siblings (see also Fox, Niemeyer, & Savelle, Chapter 9, this volume). Siblings may play an intermediate role between those of parents and peers in facilitating social competence in young children. Vandell and Mueller (1980) suggested that interactions with older siblings might maximize the advantages associated with the other types of interactions. Older siblings are more competent than the child's peers and may be more responsive than the peers to the initiations of their younger siblings. In contrast, since older siblings are less dominant than parents, interactions with them may be more equal. A number of studies have supported this hypothesis (e.g., Dunn, 1988; Dunn & Kendrick, 1979; Lamb, 1978; Pepler, Corter, & Abramovitch, 1982). For example, Pepler et al. (1982) found that roles were more distinct in sibling relationships than in peer relationships. Older children showed leadership and directed the interaction, while younger children imitated their siblings, submitted to aggressive behavior, and responded positively to prosocial behavior. Their high frequency of imitation and marked affective tone (both positive and negative) was confirmed by Dunn (1983) in her study of sibling relationships.

Furthermore, in an extensive longitudinal study, Dunn (1988) found distinct changes in social understanding within sibling relationships over time. She provided some evidence that this social understanding occurs earlier in sibling relationships than in peer relationships. For example, complementary role-taking occurred at about 18 months of age for some siblings when it was suggested by the older sibling. It was only later (toward the end of the 2nd year) that the younger child took the initiative for this activity. This can be compared with the developmental progression suggested by Howes, Unger, and Seidner (1989) who found that complementary role-taking occurred with peers at the end of the 2nd year. In addition, joint pretend play occurred with siblings at an earlier age than with peers. Dunn (1988) observed the beginnings of joint pretend play at as early as 18 months with some sibling pairs; by 24 months, 32 of the 40 younger siblings engaged in this activity. Once again, it was the older sibling who initially took responsibility for setting up the activity and assigning the roles to be taken. It must be noted that not all sibling peers interacted frequently, nor did they all have positive interactions when they were together (Dunn & Kendrick, 1979). So that, while siblings may provide the opportunity for the development of skill in social interchange for younger children, it does not always occur.

There have been few studies that have directly examined the influence of sibling relationships on peer interaction. Vandell and Wilson (1987), however, did compare the impact of the two systems on each other with very young children. Interactions of infants with their older siblings (i.e., ages 3–6 years) and with peers were compared at ages 6.5 and 9.5 months. Descriptions of the forms of interactions with different partners indicated that infants behaved differently with peers than with siblings. For example, there was more time spent in turn-taking exchanges with siblings than with peers, as well as a higher proportion of longer exchanges. It seems clear that older siblings played the dominant role in these exchanges, ensuring that they continued. There was some generalization from experiences with siblings to experiences with peers. Infants who initiated more exchanges with their siblings at 6 months, initiated more with peers at 9 months. In addition, those infants who used more coordinated socially directed behaviors at 6 months with siblings, used more at 9 months with peers.

Children with Disabilities   It is evident that little is known about the links between relationships that occur with siblings and their impact on peer relationships for children who do not have disabilities. There is even more limited information about children with disabilities. In a review of sibling relationships in which one of the siblings has a disability, Gallagher and Powell (1989) summarized findings for interactional patterns. Most of the literature related to siblings focused on the adjustment of the nondisabled child. Investigations of interaction *per se* have concluded that the nondisabled sibling frequently assumed the role of teacher or helper. This finding is not unexpected, given that many of the nondisabled siblings in the studies reviewed were considerably older than the brother or sister with a disability.

No studies were found that investigated the influence of sibling relationships on the peer relationships of children with disabilities. One study, however, provides some information related to this issue. Lieber and Beckman (1990) compared the interaction of toddlers with peers in early intervention centers to the interaction of those toddlers with familiar playmates. Eleven out of the 17 familiar playmate dyads observed included siblings (others were either other relatives or friends); thus, data can be considered only suggestive. Results indicated that interactions in which the partner was a familiar playmate were more sophisticated than those in which the partners were peers. This relative complexity was found whether the partner was older or within 1 year of the age of the target child. Thus, similar to Dunn's (1988) findings, this comparison shows that interactions with a sibling may allow children with disabilities to use more complex and coordinated behavior before they are capable of that behavior with a peer.

Summary   In summary, there appears to be some generalization of social skills across partners. For very young children, initial interactions with mothers are dominated by the mother, who ensures that the interaction continues. While infants use some skills learned with their mothers across partners, there is indication that the content of that interaction varies. What seems to generalize to a greater extent across partners is an approach to social interaction, a desire to be involved socially, in addition to several strategies for making that happen. Children may initially learn some of these strategies with their mothers, and these strategies may then be used in a number of contexts.

It is interesting to note that even more effective strategies may be learned from engagement with partners other than the mother. Although mothers are largely engaged in caretaking activities with their children, many fathers spend time with the children in physical play. There is no information, however, about whether children are able specifically to generalize skills learned with fathers into contexts with peers. Similarly, strategies developed in interchanges with siblings may generalize directly into other contexts. Again, however, there is only suggestive evidence which awaits direct testing.

Thus, evidence is emerging about the relationship between the way in which children interact with their parents and the way in which they interact with peers. This is a particularly critical link for early interventionists who deal with young children with disabilities. One of the difficulties that early interventionists have in promoting social competence in young children with disabilities is that frequently social competence has been conceptualized as a variety of isolated skills. The impact of other relationships on the social competence of young children suggests that promoting isolated skills within only one type of social relationship may limit the interventions that are developed. It might be more productive to explore the development of social strategies that could be used in a variety of contexts (see Guralnick, Chapter 2, this volume). These issues will be explored in detail later in this chapter.

KEY SOCIAL STRATEGIES WITH PEERS

One possibility for explaining the concept of social competence is to focus on social strategies that might be used over time in different social contexts. These strategies appear to develop over the first few years of life. Some occur with a variety of social partners, while others may be specific to certain contexts. First, the strategies that children use with peers will be described, and then the extent to which similar strategies have been observed with other partners will be considered.

Orienting and Maintaining Attention

Carlson and Bricker (1982) identified several strategies that are important to the child's ability to participate in dyadic exchanges. For example, the ability to orient and maintain attention to social stimuli is basic to social exchanges with any partner. Children must be able to focus on a social stimulus and maintain attention. For children who do not have disabilities, this ability to regulate attention typically develops early in the first year of life and is seen as a critical component of the more complex skills that emerge later, such as coordinating actions with those of a partner (Eckerman, Davis, & Didow, 1989).

Children seem to orient to peers early in the first year of life. For example, Field (1979) found that the heart rate of 3-month-old infants increased when they saw peers. In addition, in comparison with seeing their own reflection in a mirror, it was more likely that infants would smile, reach, and vocalize when they saw a peer. Fogel (1979) found that infants between 5 and 14 weeks showed general arousal with peers, which was characterized by generalized gross motor actions using the arms and body. These movements were different from those observed in the mother's presence, which were characterized as smoother, more varied, and involving expressive movements in the face and fingers.

Children with disabilities may have particular problems in this area. For example, children with neurological and/or sensory impairments may have difficulty discriminating social stimuli and maintaining attention (Campbell, Leib, Vollman, & Gibson, 1989). No direct studies were found concerning the ability of children with disabilities to orient and maintain attention to peers. However, to the extent that a particular disability interferes with these abilities, it is reasonable to hypothesize that interaction with peers would be influenced.

Initiation

The ability to initiate social exchanges has been widely studied among researchers. For children who do not have disabilities, in the first year of life social overtures typically involve a peer-directed activity that is accompanied by visual gaze. Examples of peer-directed activities include smiling, vocalizing, and reaching (Hartup, 1983). However, Hartup argues that even when babies are deliberately brought together, social contacts occur infrequently.

There is a steady increase in initiations between 12 and 42 months of age (Holmberg, 1980). Holmberg found that children used more positive initiations including verbal behavior, gestures, and physical contact as they got older. There was a change in the relative frequency of negative initiations, as well. For 12-month-old children, negative initiations made up 51% of the initiations; by 42 months they accounted for only 21%.

Some literature suggests that children with disabilities may have difficulty initiating social exchanges. Lieber and Beckman (1990) found that toddlers with disabilities showed about five initiations per 15-minute session. This rate is similar to the initiation rates of younger, nondisabled children in other studies (Holmberg, 1980; Mueller & Brenner, 1977). However, Lieber and Beckman found that when toddlers with disabilities did initiate, they were relatively successful, with a success rate of over 75%. In fact, they were more successful than nondisabled toddlers in Holmberg's (1980) study who, at 30 months, were successful in their initiations about 63% of the time. Thus, although young children with disabilities may initiate less than children who do not have disabilities, they seem to be at least as successful in their attempts.

Other research describing the social initiations of toddlers with disabilities has focused on investigations of the behavior of disabled children with friends (Field, 1984). Field found that, with friends, toddlers were more assertive in initiating play. They approached, vocalized, laughed, and took toys more frequently. In contrast, children without friends wandered and watched other children more. Difficulty with initiations continues into the preschool years for children with disabilities. In a study of social interaction among preschoolers, Beckman (1983) found that nondisabled children initiated more social contact than children with disabilities.

The ability to initiate requires not only social interest, but other skills as well. Certain basic skills (e.g., the ability to crawl, reach and touch, and vocalize) are all mechanisms available to the developing child that allow social contact. Some children may have difficulty initiating contact due to the presence of disabling conditions that limit these abilities (Walker, 1982). Special arrangements and modification of the physical environment, appropriate positioning techniques, and similar strategies may facilitate the child's ability to initiate social contacts.

Responsiveness

In addition to initiating social exchanges, young children must also be able to respond to the overtures of others. Frye (1981) noted that even when infants who do not have disabilities make overtures toward a peer, they are unlikely to obtain a reaction. Even when a peer does respond, the exchange is unlikely to continue. A number of investigators (Frye, 1981; Hartup, 1983) have reported that interactions between infants from 6 to 12 months of age most often consist of a single overture followed by a response. However, exchanges begin to increase by the end of the 1st year. Vandell and Wilson (1987) found that at 6 months, 85% of babies' interactions (e.g., two contingent behaviors) took the form of simple act/react sequences. By 9 months, 76% of the exchanges were of this form and there were more longer exchanges. Elaborated interchanges account for increasingly more of children's social interactions over time. Holmberg (1980) documented increases, which continued through 42 months.

Despite evidence that children with disabilities are able to respond to overtures by others, they appear to develop this ability more slowly than their nondisabled counterparts. In one sample of toddlers with disabilities, Lieber and Beckman (1990) found that 23% of the social exchanges between these children in an early intervention program involved act/react sequences; 35% involved elaborated interchanges. Thus, toddlers with disabilities were capable of engaging in longer social exchanges. However, there was virtually no change over time in the relative proportion of these exchanges.

Other authors have reported that preschoolers with disabilities may have difficulty engaging in reciprocal exchanges. For example, Beckman (1983) found that preschoolers with disabilities engaged in fewer and shorter behavior chains relative to their nondisabled peers. The length of the interactions was shortest for preschoolers with the most severe disabilities. Similarly, Guralnick and Weinhouse (1984) found few changes in responsivity over time in two groups of preschool children with cognitive disabilities. Younger children with more severe disabilities did interact socially; however, the exchanges consisted primarily of short interchanges (initiation/response). While a second group of older children with mild impairments were more social than the younger, more severely disabled children, they still showed marked impairments in peer interactions. Two-unit exchanges were still the predominant form of interaction.

Further description of the social behaviors of preschoolers with disabilities in dyadic situations is provided by Quay and Jarrett (1986). These authors examined the social reciprocity of preschool children with a variety of mild disabilities who were paired with both disabled and nondisabled peers. Although both groups initiated interactions, children with disabilities were unable to match their responses to the initiations of their partners. For example, in response to friendly initiations by partners, children with disabilities were less likely to respond in a friendly way, more likely to respond in a negative way, and more likely to ignore initiations than nondisabled children. This study suggested that the extent to which the child responds appropriately to an initiation is an important feature of social behavior. Unfortunately, the appropriateness of a response often is not addressed in studies of children's social responses.

Coordination of Attention to Persons and Things

By the beginning of the 2nd year, most infants who do not have disabilities become increasingly able to coordinate attention to persons and things (Eckerman et al., 1989). They are capable of joint attention with another person on a common object and can manipulate something that their partner is manipulating. Most evidence suggests that this ability is not present in the first year of life.

Hay, Pederson, and Nash (1982) found that, although infants in the first year showed more distress when toys were absent, they also directed more social behaviors toward peers during toy-absent than during toy-present conditions. Vandell, Wilson, and Buchanan (1980) reported that during the first year, interactions were both more frequent and longer in the absence of toys. Likewise, Jacobson (1981) reported that social interaction at 10 months was more frequent when toys were absent. These findings are interesting in light of the Mueller and Lucas (1975) hypothesis that early social contact tends to emerge out of object contact. However, it should be noted that both studies found some evidence for shifts toward more object-centered social behavior at the end of the first year and the beginning of the second. This suggests that the role of objects in social interaction may change around this time. No studies were found that directly considered the ability of children with disabilities to coordinate their attention to both peers and objects.

Imitation

Imitation is yet another critical social skill. Eckerman et al. (1989) view imitation as important for several reasons. First, imitation is one way that young children achieve social coordination with partners. Second, imitation can be used whether or not the partner is behaving in a way that invites participation. Third, imitation can be used in response to both conventional and idiosyncratic behaviors. Fourth, imitation is one of the clearest ways through which partners can relate to each other's behavior in the absence of verbal skills.

In studying the role of imitation in social exchanges among nondisabled children from 16 to 32 months of age, Eckerman et al. (1989) found that imitation was the predominant behavioral strategy enabling children to coordinate their social behavior with that of a partner. Imitation becomes increasingly important as a social strategy in the 2nd year of life. While relatively few of the interactions of infants between 6 and 12 months involve imitation (Vandell & Wilson, 1982), it becomes a more important social strategy as children become toddlers. However, young children with disabilities often have difficulty with imitation and must be taught specifically to imitate (Cooke, Apolloni, & Cooke, 1977).

Complementary Play

Howes (1987) describes complementary and reciprocal play as play in which partners exchange roles in action as well as take turns. Thus, at a given point, the play of two partners is different, but complementary. Examples of complementary play include hide and seek and playing catch with a ball.

Mueller and Lucas (1975) suggested that complementary play is more sophisticated than imitative exchanges because it involves both role reversal and reciprocally dependent actions. Thus, in complementary play both participants have their roles to play. If one child initiates a social interchange, the partner is constrained in responding and must reciprocate with an act that is matched to the act of the initiator. For example, one child runs to the middle of the room; the other child chases him; then they reverse roles. There is some disagreement (Eckerman et al., 1989) about whether complementary play is developmentally more advanced than imitative play; however, resolution of that issue awaits further investigation. No studies were found that directly examined the complementary play of children with disabilities.

Games

Another strategy that can be observed in the more complex interactions of toddlers and preschoolers is the ability to engage in games with peers. Eckerman et al. (1989) define games as lasting for at least two turns of action for each child, agreeable to both children, and having a common topic. A common topic or theme appears to be an especially important feature of children's games. Brenner and Mueller (1982) identified a number of games that commonly emerged across different toddler play groups for nondisabled children. Examples included run and chase, peek-a-boo, and object exchanges. They found that longer exchanges were more likely to be centered around common topics than were shorter exchanges and that common topics were more frequently observed with older than with younger toddlers. Similarly, Eckerman et al. (1989) found that the frequency and duration of games increased over time for dyads, with imitative or imitative and complementary games being largely responsible for the growth. Additionally, Ross (1982) noted that from 15 to 24 months of age, the frequency and structural complexity of games increases. Once again, however, no information was found that focused on the ability of young children with disabilities to use games in their play with peers.

Integrating Pretend Play and Social Play

A social process that is typically observed in children who do not have disabilities some time during the 2nd or 3rd year of life is the ability to integrate pretense and social play (Howes, 1985). Children of this age frequently integrate social roles into their play (e.g., doctor and patient). Howes et al. (1989) and Fein, Moorin, and Enslein (1982) have shown that coordinating pretend play with another child is more difficult and occurs later for children who do not have disabilities than engaging in solitary pretend play. Social pretend play is considered more complex than other forms of social play because the child must coordinate nonliteral play with social contact.

Lieber and Beckman (1991) have demonstrated similar findings for children with disabilities. In a study of 17 preschool children with a range of disabilities, children demonstrated more sophisticated pretend play when alone than when engaged with a peer. For example, more time was spent in manipulative play when children were in dyads than when they played alone. In contrast, when children were alone they were able to plan before carrying out pretend play—which was the highest level in the observation system used—significantly more than when they were with a partner. In all dyads, there was only one instance of coordinated pretend play (e.g., Child A: "I go work"; Child B: "Bye"), and that instance clearly was fleeting.

Directing and Organizing Play

Another strategy that characterizes the play of socially competent children is the ability to direct and organize play. During the preschool years, the interaction that occurs between peers taps an increasing ability to collaborate in the mutual construction of play.

Goncu (1987) described different phases of social play and the ways children maintain their play activity through the different phases. The first phase involves entering the play group. A child can accomplish this indirectly through a nonverbal approach, by producing a variation of the group's activity or simply by nonverbally occupying the play area. Corsaro (1979) found that these strategies were successful for 3- and 4-year-olds. Interestingly, when children made explicit requests for entrance or disrupted the group, they were unsuccessful. The second phase is the initiation of pretend play. Peers must agree to change from nonplay to play and agree that actions no longer will be interpreted literally. A child accomplishes this simply by beginning to play rather than negotiating the roles in advance. Play is differentiated from nonplay by exaggerated facial expressions, movements, and intonation patterns. In the third phase there is joint construction and maintenance of play. In order for play to continue smoothly, partners must express and negotiate a shared plan. This collaboration is evident for children between the ages of 3 and 5; however, typically, only older children compromise their plans based on their partners. The fourth phase is termination. Typically, children accomplish this simply by leaving the play area. Goncu and Kessel (cited in Goncu, 1987) found that for 3- to 5-year-old children, less than 1% of their utterances terminated the play.

It is evident from the preceding descriptions of social strategies that increases in complexity and sophistication from the toddler period are extensive. Episodes of social interaction become elaborate and progress from the simple act-react interchanges of the early toddler period to an entire play activity in the preschool period consisting of entry into a playgroup, initiation of play, reaching agreement to construct and maintain play by expanding and extending it through negotiation, and termination of play.

Guralnick and Groom (1987a, 1987b) argue that children with disabilities often have particular problems with group play. They speculate that one reason may be a lack of entry skills that permit joining an on-going playgroup. Additional support is provided by van den Pol, Crow, Rider, and Offner (1985) for the inability of preschool children with disabilities to participate fully in sophisticated group play with nondisabled peers. While children with and without disabilities did interact socially, during more elaborate, cooperative play, nondisabled children preferred other nondisabled children as partners.

Guralnick and Groom (1987a) confirmed that play sophistication was indeed affected by characteristics of the partner. When children with mild impairments were paired with agemates who did not have disabilities, the frequency and quality of social play improved. However, it was not the children with disabilities who directed the play. That responsibility was taken by nondisabled children; they took an active role in organizing and generating social interactions.

KEY SOCIAL STRATEGIES WITH OTHER PARTNERS

The social strategies just identified are clearly important to social competence with peers. There is also evidence that at least some of these strategies may be important with other partners as well. This section considers evidence for use of social strategies described above in social exchanges with partners other than peers.

The first strategy identified previously was the ability to orient and maintain attention. The ability to focus attention on a social stimulus begins early in the first year of life for children who do not have disabilities. The mother is typically the primary object of this early attention and many early interactions center on feeding. The father and other involved family members are also stimuli for the developing infant's attention (Brazelton, 1982; Carlson & Bricker, 1982). There is considerable evidence that young children with disabilities (or who are at risk for developing disabilities) show some delays in producing these behaviors. For example, Field (1981) found that high-risk infants observed at 4 months of age smiled less, vocalized less, and averted their gaze more than a comparison group of typically developing infants. There were similar findings for infants with Down syndrome (Richard, 1986).

The second strategy identified previously was the ability to initiate social exchanges. As infants develop a larger repertoire of motor, communication, and social skills, they are increasingly able to initiate interactions with their caregivers. There is evidence, however, that children with disabilities may have more difficulty initiating such exchanges. Mundy, Sigman, Kasari, and Yirmiya (1988) found that young children with Down syndrome made fewer requests for objects or requests for assistance with objects than children without Down syndrome. Similarly, Levy-Shiff (1986) found that there were fewer initiations in general for preschoolers with mental retardation than for a developmentally-matched nondisabled comparison group.

The third strategy described previously was the ability to be responsive to social stimulation. Early signals, including facial expressions, smiling, and vocalizing, are among the tools infants use to respond to their parents' overtures. By 3 months of age, most infants are participating in contingent, mutually rewarding exchanges with their caregivers (Brazelton, 1982; Carlson & Bricker, 1982). However, a number of authors have noted that children with disabilities often have problems engaging in behaviors that are typically considered responsive. For example, Stone and Chesney (1978) noted that, in their sample of infants with delays, over half of the mothers reported delays in, or infrequency of smiling and late onset of vocalizing. Seven out of 15 reported that their infants seldom looked at them. Hanzlik and Stevenson (1986) compared toddlers with mental retardation and with cerebral palsy to toddlers who did not have disabilities, matched on mental age and matched on chronological age. They found the toddlers with mental retardation were less positively responsive than either children with cerebral palsy or children of the same age who did not have disabilities. These differences were not evident when children were matched for mental age. Additionally, Stoneman, Brody, and Abbott (1983) showed that children with Down syndrome were less contingently responsive to both parents than a control group of children without disabilities.

The fourth strategy identified as important to peer interactions was the ability to coordinate attention to people and things. This strategy can also be observed during interactions between infants and their caregivers. Mothers frequently present objects to infants to look at or reach out to and touch or hold. Mothers also may point and talk to infants about interesting objects or events in the environment. In the study described earlier by Bakeman and Adamson (1984), infants' ability to coordinate attention to both persons and objects was facilitated by the mother. Several researchers (Landry & Chapieski, 1989, 1990; Lieber & Beckman, 1990; McCollum & Stayton, 1988) have described difficulties for children with disabilities in achieving joint attention during interaction with mothers. Neurological problems can interfere with a child's ability to direct attention or action toward the focus of the mother's attention. Landry and Chapieski (1989) observed that when new toys were introduced, 12-month-old infants with Down syndrome manipulated the toys less, or did not respond to the toys at all. These difficulties were not evident for a high-risk, preterm group of children matched for degree of developmental delay.

As children develop social competence with peers, their interchanges revolve around play, with symbolic and fantasy play predominating in the preschool years. The specific social strategies involved in this type of play, including entering play groups, directing play, and coordinating social and pretend play, have been investigated primarily in the instance of peers being the play partners. There is some evidence (Roopnarine & Mounts, 1985) that mothers do engage in fantasy play with their children and that children are capable of more sophisticated pretend play when the mother is involved than when the child plays alone (Slade, 1987). However, there is less information related to the use of processes needed in pretend play for disabled children with their mothers. Dunst and Trivette (1988) found that pretend play was more likely to occur with mothers in higher functioning children and children developmentally at risk than in children with either mental disabilities or physical impairments.

SUMMARY

In summary, investigating the development and use of social strategies with a variety of partners seems to be a promising way to explore how social competence develops in young children with disabilities. Most evidence to date relates to the relatively simple strategies of initiating exchanges and responding to partners. In general, children with disabilities show fewer initiations to partners than children without disabilities. With more sophisticated partners (i.e., mothers and older siblings) and with friends there are more initiations. Similarly, children with disabilities often have difficulty responding to social partners. Responsiveness is often more problematic for children with more severe disabilities. In addition, disabled children seem to have particular difficulty in matching their responses to those of their partners.

There is particularly limited evidence about the development of more sophisticated social processes for children with disabilities. They are less likely to participate in and be chosen as partners for group play; however, researchers have only speculated about what mechanisms may be responsible. If relationships with partners other than peers (i.e., mothers, fathers, siblings) are seen as precursors to relationships with peers, there is some evidence that more sophisticated play may not be occurring with these other partners for children with disabilities. There is also evidence that mothers of children with disabilities assume the roles of teacher and manager rather than playmate, which would limit time for play activities.

Thus, if social strategies generalize from one partner to another, it is important to realize that children with disabilities may have less early opportunity to practice those strategies with partners other than peers. It may be important to intervene early in some of these social strategies used with parents and other partners in order to facilitate later generalization to peers.

IMPLICATIONS FOR RESEARCH

The literature reviewed in this chapter suggests a number of areas in which future research is needed to understand social competence in young children with disabilities. First, the literature to date has focused on relatively few social strategies that researchers believe to be involved in social interaction. In particular, among those strategies investigated, researchers have focused on some of the very basic strategies used by children, such as the ability to initiate an interaction or the ability to imitate. When researchers have intervened, they have been relatively successful in improving children's ability to use such basic strategies (Kohl & Beckman, 1990; Lefebvre & Strain, 1989). However, despite the success of these strategies, young children with disabilities continue to experience difficulty with social exchanges. In part, this may be because most research efforts have focused on relatively few of the processes identified in this chapter. Those that have been targets of intervention are often the least complex of the strategies used by young children who do not have disabilities. Improving these behaviors, however, may not be sufficient to allow children with disabilities to participate in the sophisticated exchanges that characterize the repertoires of children without disabilities (e.g., coordinating social contact with pretend play). Thus, research is needed that addresses some of the more sophisticated social behaviors.

Second, there is a need for research that focuses on the extent to which social competence in one social system influences social competence in other systems. For example, is the amount of pretend play children engage in with parents related to the amount of pretend play with peers?

Third, there is a need for continued research examining other components of the social context (e.g., environmental influences). The importance of a variety of features of the social context as determinants of the social behavior of young children with disabilities has been emphasized by a number of authors (DeKlyen & Odom, 1989). For example, Kohl and Beckman (1984) demonstrated that patterns of interaction between children with disabilities and their nondisabled peers varied as a function of the type of activity in which the children engaged. In another study, Beckman and Kohl (1987) demonstrated that the interactions of young children with disabilities varied as a function of whether they were in segregated or integrated settings. Other studies have shown that the type of toys available in the setting influenced patterns of social interaction (Beckman & Kohl, 1984; Stoneman, Cantrell, & Hoover-Dempsy, 1983). Strain (1983) found that the social setting to which children returned after peer confeder- ate training was critical to the maintenance of gains. Thus, central to any discussion of the relationship between early social interaction with parents and later social competence with peers is a recognition of the vastly different social contexts provided by each partner. Many variables within each context have the potential for influencing social interaction patterns. Research is needed to identify in various social contexts the features that promote the use of specific social strategies.

IMPLICATIONS FOR PRACTICE

It is clear from this review that knowledge about the use and develop- ment of social strategies by young children with disabilities is in its infancy. Relatively little is known about how processes learned or practiced with social partners in the home generalize to use with peers. Furthermore, there is a dearth of appropriate instruments for teachers to use to assess social competence (Guralnick, 1990; Strain & Kohler, 1988). Given this lack, many teachers have developed goals and designed interventions based on milestones from developmental inventories (e.g., Early Intervention Developmental Profile [Rogers et al., 1981]; Battelle Developmental Inventory [Newborg, Stock, Wnek, Guidubaldi, & Svinicki, 1984]). Using these inventories to develop goals often leads to training in isolated behaviors rather than general strategies. These isolated behaviors consist of one skill from one do- main. It is clear from the review of literature in this chapter that social interaction, as early as at the toddler level, requires coordination of behaviors, behaviors that frequently come from several domains (see Guralnick, Chapter 2, this volume). Thus, one implication for inter- vention is for teachers to receive more information about the complex- ity of the strategies used in social interaction. While evidence is still limited about how social competence develops and what circum- stances affect its development, researchers can provide interven- tionists with a more sophisticated concept of what is involved in social interaction than is provided by the developmental inventories.

Another implication for practice is the importance of using knowledge about the demands of the social context to design environments that encourage social interaction and the development of social competence. First, there is evidence (Guralnick & Groom, 1987b) that children with disabilities are more competent in negotiating social interactions in dyads, rather than larger groups. There are fewer coordinations required and there are fewer complexities when only one other child is involved. Thus, teachers could actively structure opportunities for dyadic exchanges by pairing children for certain activities. Especially for very young children, structured opportunities for dyads might be more beneficial than other traditional practices (e.g., circle time).

Second, teachers should provide a range of toys that promote social coordination and interaction. Although many early intervention programs are equipped with toys that facilitate dramatic play (e.g., housekeeping equipment), not all young children with disabilities are able to use these toys within a social encounter. However, other toys seem to promote social interaction; among these is large motor equipment (e.g., slides, climbing equipment, large cardboard boxes, balls) (DeStefano & Mueller, 1982). What contributes to the effectiveness of these materials is that they play a dual role by promoting social coordination and interaction, and children at more advanced functioning levels can incorporate this equipment into their pretend play.

Third, the competence of the partner needs to be considered. Guralnick (1990) has made an effective case for the importance of integrated settings in supporting the growth of social competence in young children with disabilities. He indicated that when peers who do not have disabilities are integrated with disabled children, the disabled children imitate their behavior, prefer them as play partners, and exhibit play at a higher cognitive level. Evidence from Lieber and Beckman (1990) as well, indicated that when a familiar playmate sibling interacts with a toddler with disabilities, more social interaction occurs.

Fourth, it is important to note that social competence does not develop in one setting at a time. There is increasing evidence that relationships formed with other partners, specifically mothers, fathers, and siblings, have an impact on the development of social competence with peers. Thus, knowledge of the strategies that children use with other significant partners should inform interventions for strategies used with peers.

REFERENCES

Bakeman, R., & Adamson, L.B. (1984). Coordinating attention to people and objects in mother-infant and peer-infant interaction. *Child Development, 55,* 1278–1289.

Beckman, P.J. (1983). The relationship between behavioral characteristics of young children and social interaction in an integrated setting. *Journal of the Division for Early Childhood, 10,* 69–77.

Beckman, P.J., & Kohl, F.L. (1984). The effects of social and isolate toys on the interactions of integrated and nonintegrated groups of preschool children. *Education and Training of the Mentally Retarded, 19,* 169–174.

Beckman, P.J., & Kohl, F.L. (1987). The interactions of handicapped and nonhandicapped preschoolers in integrated and segregated settings: A longitudinal study. *Mental Retardation, 25*(1), 5–12.

Blacher, J., & Meyers, C.E. (1983). A review of attachment formation and disorder of handicapped children. *American Journal of Mental Deficiency, 87,* 359–371.

Brazelton, T.B. (1982). Joint regulation of neonate-parent behavior. In E.Z. Tronick (Ed.), *Social interchange in infancy: Affect, cognition and communication* (pp. 7–22). Baltimore: University Park Press.

Brenner, J., & Mueller, E. (1982). Shared meaning in boy toddlers' peer relations. *Child Development, 53,* 380–391.

Bridges, L.J., Connell, J.P., & Belsky, J. (1988). Similarities and differences in infant-mother and infant-father interaction in the strange situation: A component process analysis. *Developmental Psychology, 24,* 92–100.

Bruner, J.S. (1983). *Child's talk.* New York: Norton.

Campbell, P.H., Leib, S.A., Vollman, J., & Gibson, M. (1989). Interaction pattern and developmental outcome of infants with severe asphyxia: A longitudinal study of the first years of life. *Topics in Early Childhood Special Education, 9*(1), 48–71.

Carlson, L., & Bricker, D. (1982). Dyadic and contingent aspects of early communicative intervention. In D. Bricker (Ed.), *Intervention with at-risk and handicapped infants* (pp. 291–308). Baltimore: University Park Press.

Cohen, L.J., & Campos, J.J. (1974). Father, mother, and stranger as elicitors of attachment behaviors in infancy. *Developmental Psychology, 10,* 146–154.

Cooke, T., Apolloni, T., & Cooke, S. (1977). Normal preschool children as behavioral models for retarded peers. *Exceptional Children, 43,* 531–532.

Corsaro, W. (1979). "We're friends. Right?": Children's use of access rituals in a nursery school. *Language in Society, 8,* 315–336.

DeKlyen, M., & Odom, S.L. (1989). Activity, structure and social interaction with peers in developmentally integrated play groups. *Journal of Early Intervention, 13,* 342–352.

DeStefano, C.T., & Mueller, E. (1982). Environmental determinants of peer social activity in 18-month-old males. *Infant Behavior and Development, 5,* 175–183.

Dunn, J. (1983). Sibling relationships in early childhood. *Child Development, 54,* 787–811.

Dunn, J. (1988). *The beginnings of social understanding.* Cambridge, MA: Harvard University Press.

Dunn, J., & Kendrick, C. (1979). Interaction between young siblings in the context of family relationships. In M. Lewis & L.A. Rosenblum (Eds.). *The child and its family* (pp. 143–168). New York: Plenum.

Dunst, C.J., & Trivette, C.M. (1988). Determinants of parent and child interactive behavior. In K. Marfo (Ed.), *Parent-child interaction and development: Theory, research, and intervention* (pp. 3–31). New York: Praeger.

Easterbrooks, M.A., & Lamb, M.E. (1979). The relationship between quality of infant-mother attachment and infant competence in initial encounters with peers. *Child Development, 50,* 380–387.

Eckerman, C.O., Davis, C.C., & Didow, S.M. (1989). Toddlers' emerging ways of achieving social coordination with a peer. *Child Development, 60,* 440–453.

Fein, G.G., Moorin, E.R., & Enslein, J. (1982). Pretense and peer behavior: An intersectoral analysis. *Human Development, 25,* 392–406.

Field, T. (1979). Differential behavioral and cardiac responses of three month old infants to a mirror and a peer. *Infant Behavior and Development, 2,* 179–184.

Field, T. (1981). Fathers' interactions with their high-risk infants. *Infant Mental Health Journal, 2,* 249–256.

Field, T. (1984). Play behaviors of handicapped children who have friends. In T. Field, J.L. Roopnarine, & M. Segal (Eds.), *Friendships in normal and handicapped children* (pp. 153–162). Norwood, NJ: Ablex.

Fogel, A. (1979). Peer vs. mother directed behavior in 1- to 3-month old infants. *Infant Behavior and Development, 2,* 215–226.

Frye, D. (1981). Developmental changes in strategies of social interaction. In M.E. Lamb & L.R. Sherrod (Eds), *Infant social cognition: Empirical and theoretical considerations* (pp. 315–331). Hillsdale, NJ: Lawrence Erlbaum Associates.

Gallagher, P.A., & Powell, T.H. (1989). Brothers and sisters: Meeting special needs. *Topics in Early Childhood Special Education, 8*(4), 24–37.

Goldberg, S., Lojkasek, M., Gartner, G., & Corter, C. (1989). Maternal responsiveness and social development in preterm infants. In M.H. Borstein (Ed.), *Maternal responsiveness: Characteristics and consequences.* New Directions for Child Development, No. 43. San Francisco: Jossey-Bass.

Goncu, A. (1987). Toward an interactional model of developmental changes in social pretend play. In L.G. Katz (Ed.), *Current Topics in Early Childhood Education* (Vol. 7, pp. 108–125). Norwood, NJ: Ablex.

Guralnick, M.J. (1986). The peer relations of young handicapped and nonhandicapped children. In P.S. Strain, M.J. Guralnick, & H.M. Walker (Eds.), *Children's social behavior* (pp. 93–140). New York: Academic Press.

Guralnick, M.J. (1990). Social competence and early intervention. *Journal of Early Intervention, 14,* 3–14.

Guralnick, M.J., & Groom, J.M. (1987a). Dyadic peer interactions of mildly delayed and nonhandicapped preschool children. *American Journal of Mental Deficiency, 92,* 178–193.

Guralnick, M.J., & Groom, J.M. (1987b). The peer relations of mildly delayed and nonhandicapped preschool children in mainstreamed playgroups. *Child Development, 58,* 1556–1572.

Guralnick, M.J., & Weinhouse, E. (1984). Peer-related social interactions of developmentally delayed young children: Development and characteristics. *Developmental Psychology, 20,* 815–827.

Hanzlik, J.R., & Stevenson, M.B. (1986). Interaction of mothers with their infants who are mentally retarded, retarded with cerebral palsy, or non-retarded. *American Journal of Mental Deficiency, 90,* 513–520.

Hartup, W.W. (1983). Peer relations. In M. Hetherington (Ed.), P.H. Mussen (Series Ed.), *Handbook of child psychology: Vol. 4: Socialization, personality, and social development* (pp. 103–196). New York: John Wiley & Sons.

Hay, D.F. (1985). Learning to form relationships in infancy: Parallel attainments with parents and peers. *Developmental Review, 5,* 122–161.

Hay, D.F., Pederson, J., & Nash, A. (1982). Dyadic interaction in the first year of life. In K. Rubin & H.S. Ross (Eds.), *Peer relationships and social skills in childhood* (pp. 11–39). New York: Springer-Verlag.

Holmberg, M.C. (1980). The development of social interchange patterns from 12 to 42 months. *Child Development, 51,* 448–456.

Howes, C. (1985). Sharing fantasy: Social pretend play in toddlers. *Child Development, 56,* 1253–1258.

Howes, C. (1987). Social competence with peers in young children: Developmental sequences. *Developmental Review, 7,* 252–272.

Howes, C., Unger, O., & Seidner, L.B. (1989). Social pretend play in toddlers: Parallels with social play and with solitary pretend. *Child Development, 60,* 77–84.

Jacobson, J.L. (1981). The role of inanimate objects in early peer interaction. *Child Development, 52,* 618–626.

Jacobson, J.L., Tianen, R.L., Wille, D.E., & Aytch, D.M. (1986). Infant-mother attachment and early peer relations: The assessment of behavior in an interactive context. In E.C. Mueller & C.R. Cooper (Eds.), *Process and outcomes in peer relationships* (pp. 57–78). New York: Academic Press.

Jacobson, J.L., & Wille, D.E. (1986). The influence of attachment pattern on developmental changes in peer interaction from the toddler to the preschool period. *Child Development, 57,* 338–347.

Kohl, F.L., & Beckman, P.J. (1984). A comparison of handicapped and non-handicapped preschooler's interactions across classroom activities. *Journal of the Division for Early Childhood, 8,* 49–56.

Kohl, F.L., & Beckman, P.J. (1990). The effects of directed play on the frequency of reciprocal interactions with moderately handicapped preschoolers. *Education and Training in Mental Retardation, 25,* 258–266.

Lamb, M.E. (1977). Father-infant and mother-infant interaction in the first year. *Child Development, 48,* 167–181.

Lamb, M.E. (1978). Interactions between eighteen month olds and their preschool aged siblings. *Child Development, 49,* 51–59.

Lamb, M.E. (1981). The development of father-infant relationships. In M.E. Lamb (Ed.), *The role of the father in child development* (pp. 459–488). New York: John Wiley & Sons.

Lamb, M.E., & Oppenheim, D. (1989). Fatherhood and father-child relationships. In S.H. Cath, A. Gurwitt, & L. Gunsberg (Eds.), *Fathers and their families* (pp. 11–26). Hillsdale, NJ: The Analytic Press.

Landry, S.H., & Chapieski, M.L. (1989). Joint attention and infant toy exploration: Effects of Down Syndrome and prematurity. *Child Development, 60,* 103–118.

Landry, S.H., & Chapieski, M.L. (1990). Joint attention of six-month-old Down syndrome and preterm infants: I. Attention to toys and mother. *American Journal of Mental Retardation, 94,* 488–498.

Lefebvre, D., & Strain, P.S. (1989). Effects of a group contingency on the frequency of social interactions among autistic and nonhandicapped preschool children: Making LRE efficacious. *Journal of Early Intervention, 13,* 329–341.

Levy-Shiff, R. (1986). Mother-father-child interactions in families with a mentally retarded young child. *American Journal of Mental Deficiency, 91,* 141–149.

Levy-Shiff, R., Sharir, H., & Mogilner, M.B. (1989). Mother- and father-preterm infant relationship in the hospital preterm nursery. *Child Development, 60,* 93–102.

Lieber, J., & Beckman, P.J. (1990, April), *The effect of social context on social interaction in toddlers with handicaps.* Roundtable presentation at the American Educational Research Association, Boston.

Lieber, J., & Beckman, P.J. (1991). The role of toys in individual and dyadic play among young children with handicaps. *Journal of Applied Developmental Psychology, 12,* 189–203.

Lieberman, A.F. (1977). Preschoolers' competence with a peer: relations with attachment and peer experience. *Child Development, 48,* 1277–1287.

McCollum, J.A., & Stayton, V. (1988). Gaze patterns of mothers and infants as indicators of role integration during play and teaching with toys. In K. Marfo (Ed.), *Parent-child interaction and development: Theory, research, and intervention* (pp. 47–63). New York: Praeger.

Mueller, E., & Brenner, J. (1977). The growth of social interaction in a toddler playgroup: The role of peer experience. *Child Development, 48,* 854–861.

Mueller, E., & Lucas, T. (1975). A developmental analysis of peer interaction among toddlers. In M. Lewis & L.A. Rosenblum (Eds.), *Friendship and peer relations* (pp. 223–257). New York: John Wiley & Sons.

Mundy, P., Sigman, M., Kasari, C., & Yirmiya, N. (1988). Nonverbal communication skills in Down Syndrome children. *Child Development, 59,* 235–249.

Newborg, J., Stock, J., Wnek, F., Guidubaldi, J., & Svinicki, A. (1984). *The Battelle Developmental Inventory.* Dallas: DLM Teaching Resources.

Parke, R.D., MacDonald, K.B., Beitel, A., & Bhavnagri, N. (1988). The role of the family in the development of peer relationships. In R.D. Peters & R.J. McMahon (Eds.), *Social learning and systems approaches to marriage and the family* (pp. 17–44). New York: Brunner/Mazel.

Parke, R.D., & Tinsley, B.R. (1981). The father's role in infancy: Determinants of involvement in caregiving and play. In M.E. Lamb (Ed.), *The role of the father in child development* (pp. 429–457). New York: John Wiley & Sons.

Pepler, D., Corter, C., & Abramovitch, R. (1982). Social relations among children: Comparison of sibling and peer interaction. In K.H. Rubin & H.S. Ross (Eds.), *Peer relationships and social skills in childhood* (pp. 209–227). New York: Springer-Verlag.

Quay, L.C., & Jarrett, O.S. (1986). Social reciprocity in handicapped and nonhandicapped children in a dyadic play situation. *Journal of Applied Developmental Psychology, 7,* 383–390.

Richard, N.B. (1986). Interaction between mothers and infants with Down Syndrome: Infant characteristics. *Topics in Early Childhood Special Education, 6*(3), 54–71.

Rogers, S.J., Donovan, C.M., D'Eugenio, D.B., Brown, S., Lynch, E., Moersh, M.S., & Schafer, S. (1981). *Early Intervention Developmental Profile.* Revised edition. Ann Arbor: The University of Michigan Press.

Roopnarine, J.L., & Mounts, N.S. (1985). Mother-child and father-child play. *Early Child Development and Care, 20,* 157–169.

Ross, H. (1982). Establishment of social games among toddlers. *Developmental*

Psychology, 18, 509–518.

Ross, H.S., & Goldman, B.D. (1977). Establishing new social relations in infancy. In T. Alloway, P. Pliner, & L. Drames (Eds.), *Attachment behavior* (pp. 61–79). New York: Plenum.

Slade, A. (1987). A longitudinal study of maternal involvement and symbolic play during the toddler period. *Child Development, 58,* 367–375.

Spieker, S.J. (1986). Patterns of very insecure attachment found in samples of high-risk infants and toddlers. *Topics in Early Childhood Special Education, 6*(3), 37–53.

Stevenson, M.B., Leavitt, L.A., Thompson, R.H., & Roach, M.A. (1988). A social relations model analysis of parent and child play. *Developmental Psychology, 24,* 101–108.

Stone, N.W., & Chesney, B.H. (1978). Attachment behaviors in handicapped infants. *Mental Retardation, 16,* 8–12.

Stoneman, Z., Brody, G.H., & Abbott, D. (1983). In-home observations of young Down syndrome children with their mothers and fathers. *American Journal of Mental Deficiency, 87,* 591–600.

Stoneman, Z., Cantrell, M.L., & Hoover-Dempsey, K. (1983). The association between play materials and social behavior in a mainstreamed preschool: A naturalistic investigation. *Journal of Applied Developmental Psychology, 4,* 163–174.

Strain, P. (1983). Generalization of autistic children's social behavior change: Effects of developmentally integrated and segregated settings. *Analysis and intervention in Developmental Disabilities, 3,* 23–24.

Strain, P.S., & Kohler, F.W. (1988). Social skill intervention with young children with handicaps: Some new conceptualizations and directions. In S.L. Odom & M.B. Karnes (Eds.), *Early intervention for infants and children with handicaps: An empirical base* (pp. 129–143). Baltimore: Paul H. Brookes Publishing Co.

van den Pol, R.A., Crow, R.E., Rider, D.P., & Offner, R.B. (1985). Social interaction in an integrated preschool: Implications and applications. *Topics in Early Childhood Special Education, 4*(4), 59–76.

Vandell, D.L. (1980). Sociability with peer and mother during the first year. *Developmental Psychology, 16,* 355–361.

Vandell, D.L., & Mueller, E.C. (1980). Peer play and friendships during the first two years. In H.C. Foot, A.J. Chapman, & J.R. Smith (Eds.), *Friendship and social relations in children* (pp. 181–208). New York: John Wiley & Sons.

Vandell, D.L., & Wilson, K.S. (1982). Social interaction in the first year: Infants' social skills with peers versus mother. In K.H. Rubin & H.S. Ross (Eds.), *Peer relationships and social skills in childhood* (pp. 187–208). New York: Springer-Verlag.

Vandell, D.L., & Wilson, K.S. (1987). Infants' interactions with mother, sibling, and peer: contrasts and relations between interaction systems. *Child Development, 58,* 176–186.

Vandell, D.L., Wilson, K.S., & Buchanan, N.R. (1980). Peer interaction in the first year of life: An examination of its structure, content, and sensitivity to toys. *Child Development, 51,* 481–488.

Walker, J.A. (1982). Social interactions of handicapped infants. In D. Bricker (Ed.), *Intervention with at-risk and handicapped infants* (pp. 217–232). Baltimore: University Park Press.

4

Classroom Influences on the Development of Social Competence in Young Children with Disabilities

Diane M. Sainato and Judith J. Carta

The preschool classroom is one of the primary places in which young children with disabilities spend their time. This setting is, above all, a social environment in which the physical setting, the materials present, the schedule of activities, the children, and their peers interact to form an environment rich in opportunities for social learning and experiences. The early childhood classroom, and the entire complexity of variables it represents, can set the occasion for frequent and complex interactions with peers or can make social interactions highly unlikely. For young children the development of social competence requires opportunities to interact with peers in a variety of situations. If the classroom setting pre-empts these opportunities, the implications for children's development are clear: children will be less likely to interact with each other and will receive less practice in critical social skills.

The creation of classroom environments rich in social learning opportunities is often solely the responsibility of the classroom teacher. Decisions a teacher makes regarding arrangement of the classroom environment can powerfully affect the likelihood of children's social interactions on a day-to-day basis and the development of their social competence over the long term (Rogers-Warren, 1977). Teachers often make decisions on the arrangement of classroom activities, playgroups, and materials guided by practical considerations, conventional wisdom, and intuition (Fernie, 1985; Kinsman & Berk, 1979; Moore & Cooper, 1982). Fortunately, a long tradition of research focusing on classroom influences on children's social behavior may be tapped to identify optimum social learning environments for children with disabilities.

The purpose of this chapter is to present findings of naturalistic, descriptive, and experimental studies that examine classroom influences on young children's social behavior. A select review of the literature is presented; it focuses on classroom ecological variables including classroom activities, the composition of children's playgroups, spatial variables, toys, materials, and the relationship of these variables to the development of social competence. In addition, this chapter provides a discussion of future directions for research in the design and organization of optimum environments for the social behavior of young children with disabilities.

SETTING EVENTS

Classroom Activities

Most of the research on the effect of classroom activities on social interaction has been descriptive. Researchers have examined the rates of social interaction during various activities of the classroom day, and have reported the activities during which the highest rates of interaction appear for children with and without disabilities. Odom, Peterson, McConnell, and Ostrosky (1990) conducted one such study and found that the highest rates of verbal social interaction occurred during free play and clean-up activities for children with and without disabilities. Both groups of children were relatively less likely to talk with their peers during preacademic activities. Children with disabilities were least likely to talk with peers during language programming, and those without disabilities also showed significantly less verbal social interaction during story, class business, and fine motor activities. Kohl and Beckman (1984) conducted a similar study and found that children without disabilities interacted most during free play, while children with disabilities interacted most during snacktime. Similar to the Odom et al. (1990) study described above, Kohl and Beckman (1984) also determined that children without disabilities were least likely to engage in social interaction during fine motor and circle activities. In summary, in both of these studies, children appear to engage in more interaction with peers during less structured activities and interact less during formally structured activities.

Activity Structure

Literature on the effect of activity structure on social interaction is not very clear, probably because structure can be defined in many ways.

In a review article, Field (1981) noted that activities with less teacher structure should lead to increases in children's social interaction for children both with and without disabilities. A few studies have examined that premise. Burstein (1986) examined the amounts of peer interaction during three activities that varied by the amount of teacher-imposed structure. In this study, amount of structure was defined simply by the type of activity; for example, "rug time" (i.e., story and music periods) was considered highly structured; "center time" (i.e., child chooses from among available pretend, manipulative, or art activities) was considered moderately structured); and outdoor play (i.e., recess) was considered least structured. While no actual measure of teacher involvement in the activities was made, amounts of social interaction for children without disabilities was found to decrease as the amount of structure assumed to be imposed on activity increased. Thus, children without disabilities showed the highest levels of peer interaction during outdoor play and the lowest amounts during rug time. No differences in social interaction levels were found, however, for children with disabilities, who showed the same low rates of peer interaction across all three types of activities. Shores, Hester, and Strain (1976) specifically manipulated the amount of teacher structure within an activity to examine its effect on children's social interaction. In this study, preschoolers with behavior disorders were exposed to three levels of teacher structure: 1) direct teacher involvement in the activity, 2) no teacher involvement, and 3) teacher-structured play. They found that children had the highest levels of social interaction during activities that were teacher-structured. Children were least likely to interact with peers when teachers were directly involved in the activity.

DeKlyen and Odom (1989) also examined the amount of social interaction that occurred during different activities that varied in their levels of teacher-imposed structure. In this study, 25 different play activities were given "amount of structure" scores by the rater. Structure was defined by the degree to which the teacher arranged the activity to facilitate successful peer interactions. Therefore, activities such as water table or Play-Doh received low structure ratings, while bowling was rated as highly structured. Children both with and without disabilities were observed, and their rates of peer interaction and teacher interaction were recorded across various play activities. Rates of peer social interaction covaried with activities' degree of structure, but rates of teacher interaction did not. In other words, children in both groups were most likely to interact with peers in highly teacher-structured activities. They were not more likely to interact with teachers during more highly structured activities. Therefore, highly structured activities that promoted peer interaction may have been structured before children began playing, but once the activity began, teachers were no more involved in these activities than they were in activities rated as less structured.

In summary, some activities appear to lend themselves more naturally to encouraging social interaction among young children. The most notable among these is free play. But the most current literature appears to indicate that "not all free play is created equally;" that is, some play activities promote interaction among peers more than others, especially for children with disabilities. The study by DeKlyen and Odom (1989) indicates that those play activities in which teachers provided a structure through setting rules, establishing the theme, and assigning roles were the ones in which the highest rates of social interaction occurred. While this study examined the role of teacher-provided structure on peer interaction during free play, other research on peer-mediated interventions in elementary grade classrooms (Greenwood, Carta, & Hall, 1988) indicate that similar structures could be provided during other activities during the preschool classroom day.

Group Compositions

A number of studies have investigated the effects of characteristics of the children available as potential playmates and the resulting social interactions that occur in classrooms. Research on group size indicates that peer interaction is most likely to occur in small groups (e.g., two or three children). Two studies have examined the effect of group size on interaction rates of toddlers. Vandell and Mueller (1977) conducted a longitudinal study of toddlers between 16 and 22 months of age in dyadic and polydyadic situations. They determined that toddlers' social interactions increased in number and complexity between the ages of 16 and 22 months only in the dyadic play situation. That is, these children were more likely to vocalize and engage in coordinated actions when in groups of two than when they were in larger groups. Similarly, Howes and Rubenstein (1979), in a descriptive study of the natural rates of conversational interactions in child care settings, found that toddlers were more likely to engage in conversational exchanges in day care homes enrolling three or four children than were toddlers in day care centers enrolling 10 or more children.

Only a few studies have examined effects of group size on preschoolers' social interaction. Asher and Erickson (1979) found greater social activity among children in nursery schools with eight children than in nursery schools with 16 children. Smith and Connolly (1976) found more imaginative play in classes with smaller numbers of children (i.e., 10 children) than in classes with larger numbers of children (i.e., 35 children). But these findings on the effects of group size may be confounded by the composition of the groups being studied. These possible confounding factors include the familiarity of children in the group, their ages, sex, and level of functioning and/or social competence.

Familiarity of Peers   In their review of play behavior, Rubin, Fein, and Vandenberg (1983) reported that children tended to play more and at higher levels of complexity when in the company of a familiar peer than when they were alone or with an unfamiliar child. Doyle, Connolly, and Rivest (1980) conducted a similar study. They found that children were more likely to engage in dramatic play and that this play was more complex when groups contained familiar as opposed to unfamiliar peers. Similarly, Matthews (1977) found that, as groups of 4-year-olds became better acquainted, children engaged in greater amounts and more complex levels of fantasy play. The literature appears to be fairly consistent in such findings.

Age of Peers   The effect of the age of available peers on social interaction rates also is relatively clear. A mix of descriptive and experimental studies show that "sociable acts" (i.e., both conversational and aggressive behaviors) are more likely to occur among children who are similar in age than among groups of children who differ in age by more than 1 year (Hartup, 1983). Whiting and Whiting (1975) conducted a descriptive study and determined that children also were likely to use more help-giving behaviors in the presence of younger peers and more dependent and assistance-seeking behaviors in the presence of older peers.

In an experimental study of preschoolers who were familiar with each other, Lougee, Grueneich, and Hartup (1977) discovered that social interaction was least likely to occur between two 3-year-old children, more likely to occur between 3- and 5-year olds, and most likely between two 5-year-old children. Langlois, Gottfried, Barnes, and Hendricks (1978) obtained a somewhat different finding in an experimental study of familiar peers. They determined that when children were familiar with each other, more social behavior was evident in same-age dyads composed of 3-year-olds and of 5-year-olds than between children in mixed age (i.e., 3- and 5-year-old) dyads. Thus, familiarity may override the effects of age on social interaction among children in a group.

In an experimental study, Furman, Rahe, and Hartup (1979) examined the social interaction rates of socially withdrawn preschool children when they were paired with a same-age peer or with a younger child for a 10-day session. While interaction rates increased over the sessions in both conditions, greater increases in social interaction rates were found when the socially withdrawn children were paired with younger peers. While this finding seems to contradict findings of increased social interaction among same-age peers over mixed-age groupings, the Furman et al. (1979) study may also indicate that socially withdrawn children are best matched for social interaction when they are with younger peers. Thus, it may be that matching groups on the level of social competence skill, rather than age, best facilitates social interaction among peers.

Sex of Peers   The effect of the sex of available peers on social interaction is well-established (Hartup, 1983). Children begin to show a preference for and associate more frequently with same-sex peers beginning in the toddler years. A number of researchers have described greater amounts of associative or cooperative interactions among same-sex peers in preschool (Charlesworth & Hartup, 1967; Clark, Wyon, & Richards, 1969; McCandless & Hoyt, 1961; Serbin, Tronick, & Sternglanz, 1977). Specifically, preschoolers have been found to engage in parallel play twice as often and in cooperative play four times as often with same-sex peers as with opposite sex peers (Serbin et al., 1977). Similarly, preschoolers are more likely to experience reinforcing interactions with same-sex playmates than with opposite-sex peers (Charlesworth & Hartup, 1967).

Some researchers have demonstrated that the facilitative effect of same-sex peers on social behaviors extends to both positive and negative social behaviors. For example, Langlois, Gottfried, and Seay (1973) found that same-sex pairs of familiar five-year-olds were more likely to engage in positive social behaviors such as smiling, talking, and nonword verbalizations than were opposite-sex pairs. They also found the same-sex groups to engage in more aggressive behaviors than the opposite-sex dyads. This finding was replicated by Jacklin and Maccoby (1978). Many reasons are offered for this "sex cleavage" in children's social interaction, including possible "intrinsic gratification" of playing with someone of one's own sex and early socialization by parents. Another hypothesis is that teachers may reinforce same-sex play (Fagot, 1977; Hartup, 1983). Serbin et al. (1977) experimentally manipulated play among opposite-sex peers through teacher attention. After a baseline in which a low rate of opposite-sex interactions was observed, teachers were asked to point out and comment approvingly before the class whenever opposite-sex peers engaged in social interactions. Over a 2-week period, the rate of interaction among opposite-sex peers increased 20%, and no decrease in same-sex interactions was observed. Later, teachers were asked to withhold their approving comments, and children's rates of opposite-sex interactions returned to their baseline levels. Therefore, while more permanent changes in rates of play with opposite-sex peers remain to be demonstrated, children's choice of playmate clearly appears to be sensitive to adult reaction.

Peer Disability Status   One variable that has been suggested as an important correlate to young children's social behavior in classrooms is the presence and level of disability among peers (Strain, Guralnick, & Walker, 1986). Numerous investigations examining patterns of social interaction between preschool children with disabilities and their typical peers suggest that regardless of the ratio of typical children to children with disabilities, typical children tend to interact more frequently with peers who are also typically developing or are mildly disabled, than with peers with moderate or severe disabilities (see Odom & McEvoy, 1988; Strain et al., 1986).

In addition to studies that examined the frequency of social behavior between typical children and their peers with disabilities are those that examine the nature and content of such interactions. For example, Guralnick (1981) reported that preschool children with low developmental level scores engaged in more unoccupied and less onlooker, associative, and cooperative play than children with lesser delays or children without disabilities. In addition, children with disabilities engaged in less constructive play and communicated less effectively with each other than did children with less severe disabilities or children without disabilities. Furthermore, investigations by Guralnick and his colleagues examining the content of social interactions among preschool peers in integrated settings suggested that the social behaviors of typical peers toward children with disabilities may be directive or tutorial in purpose (Guralnick & Paul-Brown, 1984), and that the peer interactions of children with mild delays improved when they were paired with nondisabled older children (rather than with other children with mild delays) (Guralnick & Groom, 1987).

In designing classroom environments to facilitate the social behavior of preschool children with disabilities, teachers should take into account the severity or level of disability of the child, and the number of socially competent peers available for interaction. Although a number of studies have noted that social integration for students with mild disabilities may occur without specific intervention in integrated settings (Guralnick, 1986), children with more severe disabilities may require more specific and direct intervention (Strain & Odom, 1986).

Summary In summary, children may be more or less likely to interact, depending on who is available for interaction. It appears that children interact more frequently with familiar peers or with children who are most like themselves in age, sex, and level of social competence. Ample evidence exists, however, that teachers' intervention can have powerful effects on these natural interaction tendencies. (See Section II of this volume.)

Spatial Variables

Amount of space available is one of the most frequently assessed variables in the study of the effect of classroom influences on social interaction of young children. Most of the studies of this variable have been descriptive analyses that attempt to examine the effects of crowding on peer interaction. For example, Peck and Goldman (1978) reported that children tended to engage in more onlooker behavior and dramatic play when space available for play decreased. Others (e.g., McGrew, 1972; Smith & Connolly, 1976) have reported that decreases in play spaces result in decreases in running and in rough-and-tumble play. However, studies such as these have been difficult to interpret. Many factors affecting spatial density are confounded by variables such as number of resources available, group size, and novelty of crowded and less crowded areas. Smith and Connolly (1976) have argued that at least two factors must be considered in studies of spatial density: 1) effects due to adding to the number of children in a space that is kept constant, and 2) effects due to decreasing the amount of space made available to a constant number of children. In addition, they suggested that the number of materials and their level of novelty be kept constant.

In studies examining spatial density by altering room size while keeping group size and resource density constant, crowding had little effect on social interaction or aggression as long as density was no more than 25 square feet per child (e.g., Aiello, Nicosia, & Thompson, 1979). Reduced frequencies of social interaction have been found with densities greater than 20 square feet per child (Loo, 1972), and increases in rough-and-tumble play have been evident with densities beyond 50 square feet per child. Increases in aggression have been noted in densities that are less than 20 square feet per child (Smith & Connolly, 1976). In studies that independently vary spatial and resource densities, availability of resources appears to account for variance in social interaction and aggression more than does amount of available space (Smith & Connolly, 1976).

One of the few systematic examinations of the effects of spatial density on young children with disabilities was conducted by Brown, Fox, and Brady (1987). These authors used an alternating treatment design to study the effects of two free play conditions: 1) a large area consisting of an entire classroom (58 square feet per child), or 2) a restricted area consisting of one-third of the classroom (19 square feet per child). Other variables (e.g., number of toys) were kept constant. Four of 10 children were observed across 9 observation days, and instances of various types of social interaction were recorded. Group analyses revealed consistently more socially directed behavior in the smaller play area. Increases in aggressive behavior previously associated with crowded conditions (e.g., Hutt & Vaizey, 1966; Smith & Connolly, 1976) were not found in this study. The authors speculated that existing classroom management procedures may have discouraged occurrences of aggressive behavior.

Toys and Materials

Descriptive Studies   Interest in the analysis and description of toys and materials and their impact on play in young children had its beginnings in the growth of the nursery school and child study movements of the 1920s and 1930s (Sponseller, 1982). These early studies focused on typical children's toy preferences and the types of social interactions elicited by certain toys and materials (Phyfe-Perkins, 1979). These naturalistic studies of children's play provided the foundation for later research in social behavior by producing the first large scale reports of young children's earliest social encounters with same-age peers. Illustrative of these early descriptions of children's behavior when playing with specific toys were studies by Hulson (1930) and Van Alstyne (1932). In a 1-year longitudinal study of 10 typical preschool children, Hulson (1930) ranked 18 play materials by their "holding power," or duration of use, and their "social value," or the number of children playing with it together. Both sand and blocks ranked highly as preferred and socially interactive materials. Van Alstyne (1932), in a large-scale study of 112 typical children ranging in age from 2 to 5½ years, assessed the popularity, holding power, use, and social value of 25 play materials. This social value index was indicated by the number of children playing with a particular material and the amount of parallel, passive, and cooperative play that occurred. Among the toys and materials eliciting 30%–48% of the social behavior of children were dishes, hollow blocks, the doll corner, colored cubes, clay, and trucks.

Although few observational studies of children's toys and material preferences were reported in the 1940s and 1950s (due to focus on personality variables and parent influences rather than the impact of setting [Sponseller, 1982]), a renewed interest reflected in the work of researchers in the 1960s and 1970s once again led to studies examining whether specific materials elicit predictable play behaviors. For example, Charlesworth and Hartup (1967) and Rubin (1977) found that solitary and parallel types of play occurred when children were involved with art activities, books, Play-Doh, clay, sand, or water. Rubin (1977) also reported that house play elicited social interaction 55% of the time. In a later observational study of six typically developing children and six children at risk for special education placement, Stoneman, Cantrell, and Hoover-Dempsey (1983) concluded that play materials such as blocks, housekeeping materials, and water play were instrumental in promoting peer interaction.

Interestingly, findings across several studies appear to indicate that certain materials, such as sand, are associated with increased rates of either social *or* nonsocial behavior with children. This indicates a need for careful assessment of children's social behavior prior to use of materials in the context of a social skill intervention program.

The role of toys in facilitating social interactions for infants has been investigated by several researchers (Bronson, 1974; Durfee & Lee, 1973; Mandry & Nekula, 1939). Mueller and his colleagues (Mueller & Brenner, 1977; Mueller & Rich, 1976) suggested that play materials serve as a contextual variable for social interactions between young infant peers, whereby children "find themselves coming together because they share skills for things like opening the Jack-in-the-box or sliding down the slide" (Mueller, 1979, p. 174).

In a study of 44 pairs of typically developing children (i.e., infants 10–12 months and toddlers 22–24 months), Eckerman and Whatley (1977) noted that the presence of toys reduced the frequency of some peer-related behaviors such as duplicating or imitating the actions of peers, but also set the occasion for other types of peer interaction including offering toys to and accepting them from one another. In another investigation, Jacobson (1981) suggested toddlers must be able to focus attention simultaneously on both the toy and the peer before social interactions can take place in an object-centered (e.g., toy) context.

The fact that sustained attention is a precursor to toy play and subsequent object-centered social interactions has implications for infants and toddlers whose disabilities may preclude their opportunities to engage in object-centered play. This link between early toy play and the social-cognitive growth of infants and toddlers with disabilities is an important area for future research.

Hendrickson, Strain, Tremblay, and Shores (1981) employed an observational assessment strategy to determine the relationship between toy- and material-use and the type and occurrence of social interaction displayed by 115 typically developing preschool-age children. Observers recorded four categories of appropriate play behavior including *isolate play* (i.e., playing alone); *parallel play* (i.e., playing within 3 feet of others but not using the same materials); *share/ cooperative play* (i.e., mutual use or exchange of an object); and *physical assistance* (i.e., providing physical aid to another child in a play context).

Interestingly, the authors reported 66% of the materials were used in more than one play context. The authors reported that a majority of the materials were used in an isolate fashion upon occasion. Materials most frequently associated with isolate play included puzzles, shape templates, parquetry blocks, pegboards and pegs, pull toys, and toy animals. Toys and materials that were observed to be used in share/cooperative play for more than 70% of the observed intervals were balls, office toys, wagons, clay, and Play-Doh. The authors suggested that simple data collection should be employed by teachers in order to provide a basic framework for selecting toys and materials to be used in social behavior programs.

Experimental Studies   In one of the first studies attempting to influence the social behavior of children by directly manipulating the type of toys available during free play, Quilitch and Risley (1973) observed groups of boys and girls, averaging about 7 years of age, playing with materials that previously had been determined to be either "social" or "isolate" toys (Quilitch, Christophersen, & Risley, 1977). Social toys included materials such as a deck of playing cards, checkers, and pick-up stix, while the isolate toys were a gyroscope, Tinkertoys, jigsaw puzzles, and Play-Doh. In the first of two experiments, four groups of six children were presented with both social and isolate toys in a counterbalanced order for 15-minute intervals in the 45-minute session. Results of this initial experiment indicated that children engaged in social play 68% of the time in the first social toy condition, while their percentage of time in social play in the first isolate condition dropped to 6%. Upon reinstatement of the social toy condition social play increased to an average of 74%. Comparable results were achieved for the remaining groups of children and during a second experiment in which the composition of the play group was not held constant.

In an experimental investigation of the effects of social and isolate toys on the social behavior of preschool children with and without disabilities, Beckman and Kohl (1984) observed the amount of time children were engaged in toy play, their toy preferences, and the frequency of social interactions. Ten independent raters assigned toys to three categories. These were social toys (i.e., blocks, a ball, cars and trucks, puppets); isolate toys (i.e., books, paper and crayons, Play-Doh, and puzzles); and a mixed set consisting of both social and isolate toys. Observations were conducted randomly across 13 target children, who participated in both integrated and nonintegrated play groups, across the social, isolate, and mixed toy conditions. Results of the study indicated children in both the nonintegrated and integrated groups engaged in more social interaction when only social toys were available.

Summary   The impact of toys and materials on the play of young children has been a pivotal research area since the 1930s. Naturalistic and descriptive studies have documented the positive influence of particular toys and materials on the social and cooperative behavior of typical children. With regard to young children with disabilities, little research has focused upon the impact of the primary use of toys and materials in intervention to improve social behavior. Toys and materials should be viewed as a setting factor that may be used to enhance the effects of direct social behavior interventions. Selection of toys and materials to be included in such interventions should be based upon observations of children who will be participating in the intervention program within the context of their own preschool playtimes.

FUTURE DIRECTIONS

The social ecology of the preschool classroom encompasses a variety of dynamic variables related to the characteristics of the children in the environment, physical setting, and available toys and materials. The study of the impact of classroom influences on children's social behavior may be a guide in creating optimum social environments for children with disabilities. The review of literature in this chapter has focused upon both descriptive and experimental studies detailing the impact of classroom activities, activity structure, the composition of children's playgroups, spatial variables, toys and materials, and the relationship of all these variables to development of social competence. Taken together, this body of research may provide teachers with a framework for creating optimum social environments. However, certain methodological problems suggest caution and future directions for inquiry.

Typically, studies examining ecological variables study one variable at a time. Analysis of the influence of combinations of setting events is lacking, even though information is available concerning the impact of single setting events. In many studies, only the status of the setting event of interest is examined, and its influence, combined with the subsequent impact of other variables is overlooked (e.g., Asher & Erickson, 1979; Brown et al., 1987; Doyle et al., 1980).

In addition, it is difficult to determine in many studies if changes or differences in social behavior resulted from a single setting event of interest (e.g., the type of toys available) or from a combination of variables that were not identified or measured (e.g., Smith & Connolly, 1980). Systematic and detailed examinations of the interplay between combinations of setting events and children's social interactions is needed (Chandler, 1989; Greenwood, Delquadri, Stanley, Terry, & Hall, 1985).

Although it is known that environmental variables may set the occasion for enhanced social behavior in preschool children, the interplay between ecological variables, teacher behavior, and specific interventions to facilitate social interactions of preschool children with disabilities is a potent ecological event and should be considered an important direction for future research.

REFERENCES

Aiello, J.R., Nicosia, G., & Thompson, D.E. (1979). Physiological, social, and behavioral consequences of crowding on children and adolescents. *Child Development, 50,* 195–202.

Asher, K.N., & Erickson, M.T. (1979). Effects of varying child-teacher ratio and group size on day care children's and teacher's behavior. *American Journal of Orthopsychiatry, 49,* 518–521.

Beckman, P., & Kohl, F.L. (1984). The effects of social and isolate toys on the interactions and play of integrated and nonintegrated groups of preschoolers. *Education and Training of the Mentally Retarded, October,* 169–174.

Bronson, W.C. (1974). Competence and the growth of personality. In K. Connolly & J. Bruner (Eds.), *The growth of competence* (pp. 241–264). London: Academic Press.

Brown, W.H., Fox, J.J., & Brady, M.P. (1987). Effects of spatial density on three and four-year-old children's socially directed behavior during free-play: An investigation of a setting factor. *Education and Treatment of Children, 10,* 247–258.

Burstein, N.D. (1986). The effects of classroom organization on mainstreamed preschool children. *Exceptional Children, 52,* 425–434.

Chandler, L. (1989). *Ecobehavioral analysis of the influence of multiple setting events on preschool children's peer social interaction.* Unpublished doctoral dissertation, University of Kansas, Lawrence.

Charlesworth, R., & Hartup, W.W. (1967). Positive social reinforcement in the nursery school peer group. *Child Development, 38,* 993–1002.

Clark, A.H., Wyon, S.M., & Richards, M.P.M. (1969). Free play in nursery school children. *Journal of Child Psychology and Psychiatry, 10,* 205–216.

DeKlyen, M., & Odom, S.L. (1989). Activity structure and social interactions with peers in developmentally integrated play groups. *Journal of Early Intervention, 13,* 342–352.

Doyle, A., Connolly, J., & Rivest, L. (1980). The effects of playmate familiarity on the social interactions of young children. *Child Development, 51,* 217–223.

Durfee, J.T., & Lee, L.C. (1973). Infant-infant interaction in a day care setting. *Proceedings of the 81st Annual Convention of the American Psychological Association, 8,* 63–64.

Eckerman, C.O., & Whatley, J.L. (1977). Toys and social interaction between infant peers. *Child Development, 48,* 1645–1656.

Fagot, B.I. (1977). Consequences of moderate cross-gender behavior in preschool children. *Child Development, 48,* 902–907.

Fernie, D.E. (1985). The promotion of play in the indoor play environment. In J. Frost & S. Sutherland (Eds.), *When children play: Proceedings of the International Conference on Play and Play Environments* (pp. 285–295). Wheately, MD: Association for Childhood International.

Field, T. (1981). Early peer relations. In P.S. Strain (Ed.), *The utilization of classroom peers as behavior change agents* (pp. 1–30). New York: Plenum.

Furman, W., Rahe, D.F., & Hartup, W.W. (1979). Rehabilitation of socially withdrawn preschool children through mixed-age and same-age socialization. *Child Development, 50,* 915–922.

Greenwood, C.R., Carta, J.J., & Hall, R.V. (1988). The use of classwide peer tutoring strategies in classroom management and instruction. *School Psychology Review, 17,* 258–275.

Greenwood, C.R., Delquadri, J., Stanley, S., Terry, B., & Hall, R.V. (1985). Assessment of ecobehavioral interaction in school settings. *Behavior Assessment, 7,* 331–347.

Guralnick, M.J. (1981). The behavior of preschool children at different developmental levels: Effects of group composition. *Journal of Experimental Child Psychology, 31,* 115–130.

Guralnick, M.J. (1986). The peer relations of young handicapped and nonhandicapped children. In P.S. Strain, M.J. Guralnick, & H.M. Walker (Eds.), *Children's social behavior* (pp. 93–140). New York: Academic Press.

Guralnick, M.J., & Paul-Brown, D.P. (1984). Communicative adjustments during behavior request episodes among children at different developmental levels. *Child Development, 55,* 911–919.

Guralnick, M.M., & Groom, J.M. (1987). Peer interactions in mainstream and specialized classrooms: A comparative analysis. *Exceptional Children, 54,* 415–425.

Hartup, W.W. (1983). Peer relations. In P.H. Mussen & E.M. Hetherington (Ed.), *Carmichael's manual of child psychology* (Vol. 4, pp. 103–196) New York: John Wiley & Sons.

Hendrickson, J.M., Strain, P.S., Tremblay, A., & Shores, R.E. (1981). Relationship between toy and material use and the occurrence of social interactive behaviors by normally developing preschool children. *Psychology in the Schools, 18*, 50–55.

Howes, C., & Rubenstein, J.L. (1979). *Influences on toddler peer behavior in two types of daycare.* Unpublished manuscript, Harvard University.

Hulson, E.L. (1930). An analysis of the free play on ten four-year-old children through consecutive observations. *Journal of Juvenile Research, 14*, 188–208.

Hutt, C., & Vaizey, M.J. (1966). Differential effects of group density on social behavior. *Nature, 209*, 1371–1372.

Jacklin, C.N., & Maccoby, E.E. (1978). Social behavior at thirty-three months in same-sex and mixed-sex dyads. *Child Development, 49*, 557–569.

Jacobson, L. (1981). The role of inanimate objects in early peer interaction. *Child Development, 52*, 618–626.

Kinsman, C., & Berk, L. (1979). Joining the block and housekeeping areas: Changes in play and social behavior. *Young Children, 35*(7), 66–75.

Kohl, F.L., & Beckman, P.J. (1984). A comparison of handicapped and non-handicapped preschoolers' interactions across classroom activities. *Journal of the Division for Early Childhood, 8*, 49–56.

Langlois, J.H., Gottfried, N.W., Barnes, B.M., & Hendricks, D.E. (1978). The effect of peer age on the social behavior of preschool children. *Journal of Genetic Psychology, 132*, 11–19.

Langlois, J.H., Gottfried, N.W., & Seay, B. (1973). The influence of sex of peer on the social behavior of preschool children. *Developmental Psychology, 8*, 93–98.

Loo, C.M. (1972). The effects of spatial density on the social behavior of children. *Journal of Applied Social Psychology, 2*, 372–381.

Lougee, M.D., Grueneich, R., & Hartup, W.W. (1977). Social interaction in same- and mixed-age dyads of preschool children. *Child Development, 48*, 1353–1361.

Manry, M., & NeKula, M. (1939). Social relations between children of the same age during the first two years of life. *Journal of Genetic Psychology, 54*, 193–215.

Matthews, W.S. (1977). Modes of transformation in the initiation of fantasy play. *Developmental Psychology, 13*, 212–216.

McCandless, B.R., & Hoyt, J.M. (1961). Sex, ethnicity, and play preferences of preschool children. *Journal of Abnormal and Social Psychology, 62*, 683–685.

McGrew, W.C. (1972). *An ethological study of children's behavior.* London: Academic Press.

Moore, S., & Cooper, C. (1982). "Personal and Scientific Sources of Knowledge about Children." In S. Moore & C. Cooper (Eds.), *The young child: Reviews of research: Vol. 3.* Washington, DC: National Association for the Education of Young Children.

Mueller, E. (1979). (Toys and toddlers) = (An autonomous social system). In M. Lewis & L. Rosenblum (Eds.), *The child and its family.* New York: Plenum.

Mueller, E., & Brenner, J. (1977). The origins of social skills and interaction among playgroup toddlers. *Child Development, 48*, 854–861.

Mueller, E., & Rich, A. (1976). Clustering and socially-directed behavior in a play group of 1-year-olds. *Journal of Child Psychology and Psychiatry, 17*, 315–322.

Odom, S.L., & McEvoy, M.A. (1988). Integration of young children with handicaps and normally developing children. In S.L. Odom & Karnes, M.B. (Eds.), *Early intervention for infants and children with handicaps: An empirical base* (pp. 241–267). Baltimore: Paul H. Brookes Publishing Co.

Odom, S.L., Peterson, C., McConnell, S., & Ostrosky, M. (1990). Ecobehavioral analysis of early education/specialized classroom settings and peer social interaction. *Education and Treatment of Children, 13,* 316–330.

Peck, J., & Goldman, R. (1978). *The behaviors of kindergarten children under selected conditions of the social and physical environment.* Paper presented at the meeting of the American Education Research Association, Toronto, Ontario.

Phyfe-Perkins, E. (1979). *Children's behavior in preschool settings: A review of research concerning the influence of the physical environment.* (ERIC Document Reproduction Service No. ED 168 722)

Quilitch, H.R., Christophersen, E.R., & Risley, T.R. (1977). The evaluation of children's play in materials. *Journal of Applied Behavior Analysis, 10,* 501–502.

Quilitch, H.R., & Risley, T.R. (1973). The effects of play materials on social play. *Journal of Applied Behavior Analysis, 6,* 573–578.

Rogers-Warren, A.K. (1977). Planned change: Ecobehaviorally based interventions. In A.K. Rogers-Warren & S.F. Warren (Eds.), *Ecological perspectives in behavior analysis* (pp. 197–210). Baltimore: University Park Press.

Rubin, K.H. (1977). The social and cognitive value of preschool toys and activities. *Canadian Journal of Behavioral Science/Review of Canadian Science, 9,* 382–385.

Rubin, K.H., Fein, G.G., & Vandenberg, B. (1983). Play. In E.M. Hetherington (Ed.), *Carmichael's manual of child psychology: Socialization, personality, and social development.* New York: John Wiley & Sons.

Serbin, L.A., Tronick, I.J., & Sternglanz, S.H. (1977). Shaping cooperative cross-sex play. *Child Development, 48,* 924–929.

Shores, R.E., Hester, P., & Strain, P.S. (1976). The effects of amount and type of teacher-child interaction on child-child interaction during free-play. *Psychology in the Schools, 13,* 171–175.

Shure, M.E. (1963). Psychological ecology of a nursery school child. *Child Development, 34,* 979–994.

Smith, P.K., & Connolly, K.J. (1976). Social and aggressive behavior as a function of crowding. *Social Science Information, 16,* 601–620.

Smith, P.K., & Connolly, K.J. (1980). *The ecology of preschool behavior.* Cambridge: Cambridge University Press.

Sponseller, D. (1982). Play and early education. In B. Spodek, (Ed.), *Handbook of research in early childhood education* (pp. 215–241). New York: Free Press.

Stoneman, Z., Cantrell, M.L., & Hoover-Dempey, K. (1983). The association between play materials and social behavior in a mainstreamed preschool: A naturalistic investigation. *Journal of Applied Developmental Psychology, 4,* 163–174.

Strain, P.S., Guralnick, M.J., & Walker, H.M. (1986). *Children's social behavior.* New York: Academic Press.

Strain, P.S., & Odom, S.L. (1986). Peer social initiations: Effective interventions for social skills development of exceptional children. *Exceptional Children, 52,* 543–551.

Van Alstyne, D. (1932). *Play behavior and choice of play materials of preschool children.* Chicago: University of Chicago Press.

Vandell, D.L., & Mueller, E.C. (1977, March). *The effects of group-size on tod-dler's social interactions with peers.* Paper presented at the meeting of the Society for Research in Child Development, New Orleans.

Whiting, B.B., & Whiting, J.W.M. (1975). *Children of six cultures.* Cambridge: MA: Harvard University Press.

II

Strategies for Designing Social Competence Interventions

5

Peer Social Competence Intervention for Young Children with Disabilities

Mary A. McEvoy, Samuel L. Odom, and Scott R. McConnell

$\mathbf{P}$articipation in social interactions with peers is a critical developmental milestone for young children. In fact, research has demonstrated that socially competent children develop advanced cognitive, language, and social skills (Damon, 1984; Guralnick, 1981; Hartup & Sancilio, 1986; Murray, 1972; Perrot-Clermont, 1980; Piaget, 1926). Most children begin to interact socially with peers while very young and engage increasingly in more complex interactions throughout their early years. However, some children with special needs do not acquire skills necessary for engaging in successful peer interactions and require specific social interaction training in order to increase their social competence (see Odom, McConnell, & McEvoy, Chapter 1, this volume).

Development and evaluation of procedures for promoting the social competence of young children with disabilities has increased dramatically (Fox, McEvoy, Leech, & Moroney, 1990; Shores, 1987). In a review of the literature, Fox et al. (1990) identified 108 studies conducted from 1965–1990 that sought to teach social skills to, and/or increase the social interaction rates of young children with disabilities. Approximately 75% of the studies were conducted from

Preparation of this chapter was supported, in part, by the Institute on Community Integration, a University of Minnesota Affiliated Program, and by Grant #G008730527 from the U.S. Department of Education.

The authors wish to thank Jolene Schuldt for her research assistance.

1978 to 1990. The social interaction procedures evaluated in these studies can be divided into three major types: 1) procedures that attempted to increase social interaction by manipulating environmental variables, 2) procedures that primarily used teachers to prompt and praise interaction, and 3) procedures that relied on peers as the primary change agent. Research that has evaluated environmental factors and their relationship to the development of social interaction skills is reviewed extensively in Chapter 4 and will not be reviewed here. This chapter reviews research on procedures for increasing social interaction that have employed teacher-mediated and peer-mediated techniques.

The studies reviewed here, for the most part, have been evaluated with children who are socially isolate, have behavior disorders, or who have autism or mental retardation. Other chapters in this book review interventions that have been evaluated primarily with children with visual impairments, hearing impairments, or language impairments.

TEACHER-MEDIATED AND PEER-MEDIATED INTERVENTIONS

McEvoy, Shores, Wehby, Johnson, and Fox (1990) have noted that teachers play a significant and critical role in intervention procedures that address social development. Typically, teacher-directed interventions designed to promote interaction have been divided into two categories: *teacher-mediated* and *peer-mediated* (Odom & Strain, 1986). What follows is an overview of the research that has evaluated these two types of interventions.

Teacher-Mediated Interventions

When using a teacher-mediated intervention, prompts and reinforcers for appropriate social interaction generally are directed by the teacher to the target child (Allen, Hart, Buell, Harris, & Wolf, 1964; Odom & Strain, 1986; Strain, Shores, & Kerr, 1976; Timm, Strain, & Ellers, 1979). Typically, the teacher uses a specific set of verbal statements and physical cues or gestures to prompt a child to use a targeted social initiation, such as sharing or assisting, or to respond to an initiation by a peer. Resultant interaction is then praised by the teacher, either directly in the form of verbal praise, or less obviously in the form of stickers, "happy faces," or other tangible rewards.

Teacher Praise with Reinforcers   A number of researchers have demonstrated the powerful effects that teacher prompts and praise for interaction have on the social behavior of young children with disabilities. For example, Wolfe, Boyd, and Wolfe (1983) investigated the effects of verbal instructions and token reinforcers on the rate of the cooperative play of three preschool children with behavior disorders. Two of the children typically engaged in aggressive interactions with peers; one child was noted to be socially isolate and withdrawn. Prior to a free play activity, target children were given "happy face" charts to wear. After announcing that sharing time had begun, teachers rewarded children verbally for playing cooperatively. In addition, target children (i.e., children who were direct recipients of the intervention) who engaged in cooperative play for an entire minute were given a sticker to place on their "happy face" chart. Children who received a predetermined number of "happy face" stickers were rewarded with 10 minutes of outdoor free play later in the day. In addition, they earned a large "happy face" sticker that they could wear the remainder of the day. Target children who did not earn a happy face sticker were verbally prompted by the teacher to play cooperatively. If this prompt was unsuccessful, the teacher proceeded to use a physical prompt to guide the target child to a play activity. The researchers systematically eliminated the reinforcement procedure by increasing the amount of time that the children had to play cooperatively in order to obtain a reward. The researchers noted that teacher prompting and reinforcement were successful in increasing the levels of cooperative play for all three target children. In addition, generalization of target behavior to another free play setting, while generally unstable, was noted. Implementation of the intervention in the alternate setting produced stable rates of cooperative play.

Teacher Praise Solely   Some researchers have evaluated the effects of teacher reinforcement solely, which generally is praise, on the social interaction rates of children who are withdrawn or isolate or have disabling conditions. In a now classic study, Allen et al. (1964) systematically manipulated adult attention in an attempt to increase the social interaction rates of an isolate child with her peers. Teachers were initially instructed to attend to the target child only when she interacted with a peer. During this intervention, initiations by the target child to an adult caregiver were ignored. Interactions with children rose markedly while interactions with adults decreased. When procedures were reversed (i.e., adult attention was made contingent on target child-adult interaction) rates of interaction with adults increased while rates of interaction with peers decreased. The researchers noted that interaction effects appeared to be durable and the intervention was practical and desirable. Wusterbath and Strain (1980) reported similar results with a child who had been physically abused and neglected.

Generalization   Generalization of learned behavior is an important goal of social interaction training. In an extension of an earlier study (Strain & Timm, 1974), Strain, Cooke, and Apolloni (1976) evaluated the generalized effects of interaction training on peers who had not received direct teacher prompting or reinforcement for social interaction. Three children with behavior disorders participated in a teacher-mediated intervention to increase their rates of interaction with preschool peers. Increases in frequency of positive social behavior were seen for each child when the interventions were applied individually. In addition, for two of the target children, increases in their rates of social interaction were noted when they were given an opportunity merely to observe the teacher prompt and praise another child for interacting. The authors noted that a third child's extreme isolation may have decreased the number of opportunities that he had to observe other children being prompted or praised, thus explaining why no "spillover" effects were noted for him. The authors suggested that opportunities merely to observe the implementation of a social interaction intervention may result in increases in the rates of child-child interaction for some children.

Criticisms of Teacher-Mediated Interventions   While teacher-mediated interventions have proved to be an effective strategy for increasing the social interaction skills of children with disabilities, they are not without their drawbacks (McEvoy & Odom, 1987). One criticism of many teacher-mediated interventions is that children may develop a reliance on either teacher prompts or reinforcements, or both, for interaction (Odom & Strain, 1986). In an attempt to examine the effects of the systematic removal of teacher prompts and praise for interaction, Timm et al. (1979) evaluated the use of response-dependent versus response-independent fading of the procedures. The researchers reported that increases in child-child interaction were noted for three socially withdrawn preschoolers when teacher prompts and reinforcement for interaction were introduced. In addition, response-dependent thinning and fading of the intervention was successful in maintaining child-child interaction at rates similar to those observed during intervention. Despite the successful elimination of teacher prompts and praise, however, the authors noted that the fading procedures required were quite lengthy, thus making it unlikely that they would be used effectively in real life settings. In addition, Strain et al. (1976) have pointed out that, while successful, many teacher-mediated interventions have been evaluated primarily in controlled settings using researchers or well-trained practitioners as "teachers." Finally, Strain and Fox (1981) have noted that teacher praise often disrupts ongoing interaction, regardless of whether it is verbal or in the form of an alternate reinforcer such as "happy faces." Given these limitations, many researchers have turned to developing and evaluating interventions that focus primarily on the peer as both trainer and reinforcer.

Peer-Mediated Interventions

During peer-mediated interventions, peers are taught by teachers to deliver instructional encouragements (Odom & Strain, 1984). The teacher may be present and closely monitoring the procedures; however, she or he does not intervene directly with the target child.

While peer-mediated interventions may include a variety of techniques, discussion here will be limited to those interventions that Odom and Strain (1984) have identified as *peer-initiation* strategies (see Odom & Strain, 1984; Strain & Fox, 1981; and Strain & Odom, 1986 for a broad overview of these and other peer-mediated strategies).

Peer-initiation procedures represent the most frequently used peer-mediated strategy for increasing the interaction between children with disabilities and their peers (Odom & Strain, 1984). When using this procedure, a teacher typically trains a peer to direct social initiations to target children. The peer is also trained to be persistent in order to obtain a response to initiations. As in teacher-mediated interventions, teachers play a critical role in this procedure. They not only train the peers to deliver the social bids and to be persistent, but often are also required to prompt and reinforce the peer for successful social bids (Strain & Odom, 1986). In a series of studies, Day, Powell, and Dy-Lin (1982); Ragland, Kerr, and Strain (1978);Strain (1977); and Strain, Shores, and Timm (1977) trained same-age peers to initiate to preschool children who were isolate or withdrawn. Prior to intervention, peers were trained in separate training sessions by the experimenter, or teacher, to initiate to target children and to persist with their initiations. The experimenter participated in the role-playing activities with the peer trainer and acted out typical patterns of social withdrawal. The peer trainer was reinforced by the experimenter, both verbally and later with a tangible reward, for productive efforts to increase social interaction. In all four studies, child-child interaction increased concomitant with increases in peer initiations, and in the Strain (1977) and Strain et al. (1977) studies, spillover effects for nontarget children were noted.

Several researchers have addressed the issue of generalization of social skills training specifically as it applies to the use of peer-mediated interventions (Furman, Rahe, & Hartup, 1979; Lancioni, 1982; Strain, 1977). Strain (1977), during four 20-minute sessions prior to intervention, trained a confederate peer to initiate to his peers with disabilities. After training, the peer was involved in a 15-minute free play session with three preschool children with behavior disorders. The peer was instructed to have the children play with him. Teachers were instructed not to prompt or praise any interactions. Results indicated that the peer-mediated procedure was effective in increasing the social interaction rates of children with disabilities. More important, however, was the fact that for two of the three target children, increases in interaction were also noted in a separate free play period that took place in their classroom. Strain noted that the differential effects of the intervention (i.e., generalization across settings for trained responses of two of the three target children) may be related to the entry-level behavior of the participants, suggesting that those who showed limited repertoires of social behavior may require more intensive intervention. Other researchers (e.g., Odom, Hoyson, Jamieson, & Strain, 1985; Ragland et al., 1978; Shafer, Egel, & Neef, 1984; Strain, Kerr, & Ragland, 1981) have also noted a lack of generalization across settings for some children with more severely disabling conditions.

In the Strain (1977) study reviewed above, children were observed in a generalization setting that was developmentally segregated. Several researchers have evaluated the effects of developmentally segregated *and* integrated settings on the rate of using generalized social interaction skills (e.g., Hecimovic, Fox, Shores, & Strain, 1985; Strain, 1983, 1984). Hecimovic et al. (1985) evaluated the generalization of social interaction skills to developmentally segregated *and* developmentally integrated settings. Intervention was provided for three preschoolers who were socially withdrawn. Peer confederates were trained prior to intervention using the same training procedure described previously (e.g., Ragland et al., 1978; Strain, 1977; Strain et al., 1977). After training, peers and target children were brought individually to a classroom where they were told they could play. On alternate days, the target children were returned after training to either a developmentally segregated (i.e., the target child and their classmates with developmental delays) or a developmentally integrated setting (i.e., the target child, the peer trainers, and their 20 classmates who did not have disabilities). The authors reported increases in both initiations and responses in the training setting for all target children. In addition, they noted that more peer initiations and subject responses occurred in the developmentally integrated setting. Interestingly, however, the authors noted that most of the interactions that occurred in the generalization setting were between target children and peers who *had not* participated in the training.

Single versus Multiple Peer Trainers   Odom, Strain, Karger, and Smith (1986) evaluated the effectiveness of using single versus multiple peer trainers in a peer-mediated procedure. During one phase, the target child was paired with a single peer trainer who had participated previously in training sessions with the teacher. In the multiple peer trainer condition, the target child participated in a free play session with three previously trained peers. Each peer was instructed to interact with the target child for 2 minutes of the 6-minute session. The results indicated that both single and multiple peer confederates were successful in increasing the social interactions of young children with disabilities. However, the authors suggested that the use of multiple peer trainers may be a more efficient training procedure. In addition, while not addressed specifically in this study, other researchers (e.g., Brady, McEvoy, Gunter, Shores, & Fox 1984; Fox et al., 1984) have noted that the use of multiple peer trainers is an effective way to increase generalized peer interaction.

Reducing the Teacher Intensive Aspect of Teaching Peer Trainers   In the studies reviewed above, peer trainers were taught during separate sessions with a teacher using a series of role-play situations for initiating to children with disabilities. Responding to criticisms that peer-mediated procedures were teacher intensive, several researchers have investigated various other ways of training children to interact with their peers with disabilities. For example, Shafer et al. (1984) included children with autism directly in the training. Thus, peers were given an opportunity to practice the training procedures with the target children prior to intervention. During the training sessions, peers observed teachers interacting with the child with autism and later modeled this behavior. Teachers provided feedback and intermittent verbal prompts. The results indicated that this training procedure was effective in increasing the interactions of preschoolers with autism and their peers during later free play periods. This training procedure appeared to be efficient particularly because it eliminated the peer trainers' need for additional teacher prompts or praises for interaction in free play sessions after training.

Group Training and Reinforcement Procedures   Lefebvre and Strain (1989) evaluated the effects of a group training and reinforcement procedure on the social interactions of young children with and without autism. The purpose of this study was two-fold, that is, to determine if: 1) peers could be taught the previously described peer-mediated procedures during a large group activity in which all children participated, and 2) a group contingency procedure could be used as an effective reinforcer for increased child-child interaction.

During group training, teachers taught both play-initiating and play-responding procedures during a morning circle activity. In addition, children were reinforced for interaction during free play only if (on different days) one, two, or all three triads of children met a pre-established criterion of interaction. While teachers continued to prompt peer initiations during activity in the free play setting throughout the study, the researchers demonstrated that a group training and reinforcement procedure could be used effectively by teachers for training child-child interaction.

While Lefebvre and Strain (1989) evaluated the use of a group reinforcement strategy, McConnell, Sisson, Cort, and Strain (in press) evaluated the use of individual- versus group-oriented contingency management procedures (i.e., prompts and reinforcement), implemented during free play, on the social behavior of young children with and without disabilities. In *individual coaching* teachers provided specific antecedents and consequences for an individual child's social behaviors. During this phase, significant changes in the target children's rates of initiations and peer and target child responses were observed. Little change in reciprocal interaction between the target children and peers was noted. During *group coaching*, prompts and praise for social behavior directed to the whole play group resulted in increases in desired peer behavior, but did not affect the interactive behavior of the target children. The authors also noted that interactions increased for the majority of children during structured training activities. However, increases in these behaviors during activity in a separate free play setting were minimal. The authors discussed the importance of investigating *social reciprocity* as an outcome measure and noted the need to design procedures that produce results that generalize from training to free play settings.

Relative Influence of Various Components of Peer-Initiation Intervention   In an effort to determine the relative influence of the various components of a peer-initiation intervention on child-child interactions, Odom et al. (1985) systematically manipulated teacher prompts and praise and assessed their effects on the initiation rates of young children with and without disabilities. Three preschool children with autistic-like characteristics were targets of intervention. In addition, three typically developing children were the same age peers. Prior to intervention, all three peers participated in a peer-initiation training procedure similar to that described in the Strain (1977) study. In addition, all children participated in three activities: structured free play, an independent table activity, and a variety of learning centers.

Following training, intervention was begun initially in the free play setting and later in multiple-baseline fashion during the table and learning center activities. Teachers reminded the peers prior to the activities that they were to initiate to the target children. If a peer was successful in having a target child respond to an initiation, the teacher drew a "happy face" on a card. If the peers did not initiate to the target children within 15–20 seconds the teacher verbally prompted the peer to do so. At the end of each session, the teacher provided the peer with a reinforcer if he or she had obtained a predetermined number of "happy faces." In each setting, increases in initiations were noted for all children when the intervention was implemented.

Once increases in initiations were observed, the reinforcer (i.e., "happy faces") was withdrawn simultaneously in all three settings. Finally, teacher prompts were reduced, and later restored, across settings. The authors noted that the withdrawal of the token reinforcer system had little effect on the rates of social initiations. However, rates of peer initiations decreased substantially when levels of teacher prompts were reduced. Given the fact that levels of initiations increased when teacher prompts were reinstated, it appears that teacher prompts are a critical part of the peer-initiation strategy. Other researchers (e.g., van den Pol, Crow, Rider, & Offner, 1985) have also noted the critical role that teacher prompts play in maintaining social interactions. Odom et al. (1985) have suggested that interventions are needed that reduce child dependence on teacher prompts for interaction.

In order to address this concern, Odom, Chandler, Ostrosky, Raney, and McConnell (1991) evaluated a procedure to reduce systematically the teacher prompts, while maintaining high rates of peer initiations. Immediately following a peer training activity, teachers provided verbal prompts for social initiations during structured play activities in four different classrooms. Once social initiations increased, teachers introduced a visual feedback system in which "happy faces" were drawn on a card by the teacher each time they "got their friend to play with them," although backup reinforcers were not provided. Across a number of phases, teachers systematically reduced their number of prompts and ultimately discontinued the use of "happy faces." Teachers were able to decrease substantially their use of prompts for interaction in two classrooms and discontinue the use of prompts entirely in two other classrooms. Rates of interactions remained high across all classrooms during the fading procedures. The authors noted that peer social competence played a role in the eventual elimination of teacher prompts, with more socially competent peers requiring less teacher intervention.

Teacher-Mediated versus Peer-Mediated Procedures

Several researchers have attempted to evaluate the relative effectiveness of teacher-mediated versus peer-mediated procedures on the social interaction rates of young children with and without disabilities.

Strain and Timm (1974) measured the rates of social interaction between a preschool child with behavior disorders and her classroom peers using two different interventions: 1) teacher physical contact and praise for interaction directed to the target child (i.e., teacher-mediated); and 2) and teacher physical contact and praise for interaction directed to the classroom peers (i.e., peer-mediated). Teacher prompts for interaction were not included in either intervention condition. The results indicated that both procedures were effective in increasing the initiation and responding rates of *all* children, regardless of the targeted recipient of teacher physical contact and praise.

Odom and Strain (1986) compared the effects of these two intervention strategies on the reciprocity of peer social interactions with children with autism. Using an alternating intervention design, the peer-mediated and teacher-mediated interventions were implemented on different, but adjacent days. The order of intervention was determined randomly. Prior to intervention, peers were trained either to direct social initiations to target children or to respond to and extend target child initiations. Once the children had met a pre-determined training criterion, intervention was implemented in a free play setting. In addition, a token reinforcement system for peers was implemented in both conditions using the previously described "happy face" system with backup reinforcers: "happy faces" were awarded for peer initiations during the peer-mediated phase and for peer responses and extended social interactions in the teacher-mediated phase. The results indicated that the peer-mediated procedure was effective in increasing the social responding of the target children with autism. Similarly, increases in target child initiations and length of interaction were seen when teacher-mediated interventions were in effect. In their conclusion, the authors stated that the intervention strategies may be complementary in increasing various classes of child-child interaction.

Combined Effects of Teacher-Mediated and Peer-Mediated Intervention   Given the differential effects of peer-mediated and teacher-mediated interventions reported by Odom and Strain (1986), Smith, McConnell, Maretsky, Kudray, and Strain (1987) evaluated the *combined* effects of a teacher- and peer- mediated intervention on the social reciprocity of young children with autism and their typically developing peers. Training was conducted during a large group activity and included both children with and without disabilities. Across a series of five sessions, peers were given an opportunity to observe and model teachers role-playing appropriate social interaction; to participate in the role-play situations with the teachers; and, finally, to participate in peer-target child role-play situations. Following training, all children participated in a free play activity. During the peer-mediated phase, peers were prompted by the teachers to initiate to the target children. Similarly, during the teacher-mediated phase, teachers prompted the target children to initiate to their peers. Finally, in the combined intervention phase, teachers prompted both target children and peers to initiate interactions. The results indicated that, as in similar studies, peer-mediated interventions increased the rates of peer initiations and target child responses and the teacher-mediated interventions increased target child initiations and peer responses. During phases when the combined intervention was implemented, more equivalent rates of interaction were obtained. The authors also noted that additional training to teach peers to continue or persist with interactions was successful in increasing the mean length of interactions.

Summary

Teacher-mediated and peer-mediated procedures have been used effectively to increase the social interaction rates of young children with and without disabilities. Taken together, they represent the greatest number of empirically validated procedures available to teachers and parents. In addition, several researchers have incorporated these procedures into curricula that teachers can implement in their programs in order to teach children to interact (e.g., Day et al., 1982; Odom et al., 1988). Finally, these procedures have been evaluated in a number of settings and across a number of disabling conditions.

Regardless of the intervention used, as Odom and Strain (1986) have pointed out, teacher prompts and praise have an important effect on child-child interaction. In addition, the authors noted the importance of choosing peers who are socially skilled. While the criteria for selecting appropriate peers remains an empirical question, several researchers (e.g., Hecimovic et al., 1985; Odom & Strain, 1984; Sasso & Rude, 1987) have suggested certain criteria that teachers may want to consider when selecting peer trainers. These include the social status of the peer, the peer's ability to follow adult instructions, and the peer's willingness to participate. Odom and Strain (1986) point out that the absence of socially skilled peers may affect the outcome of social skills interventions.

Despite the success of intervention procedures, the research evaluating them has several limitations. As discussed previously, there has been a limited demonstration of generalization across settings or children (McEvoy & Odom, 1987; Odom & Strain, 1984). In addition, the criticisms of teacher-mediated procedures discussed previously (i.e., a reliance on teacher prompts and praise for interaction and their evaluation in highly structured settings using well-trained and experienced teachers) apply also to peer-mediated procedures (McEvoy, Niemeyer, & Wehby, 1989; McEvoy, Twardosz, & Bishop, 1990; Strain et al., 1976). Given these concerns, a number of researchers have begun evaluating other types of interventions to promote child-child interaction. These interventions are affection training (Brown, Ragland, & Fox, 1988; McEvoy et al., 1988; Niemeyer & McEvoy, 1990; Twardosz, Nordquist, Simon, & Botkin, 1983); correspondence training (McEvoy, Neimeyer, & Fox, 1989; Odom & Watts, in press; Osnes, Guevremont, & Stokes, 1986; Rogers-Warren & Baer, 1976; Sainato, Goldstein, & Strain, in press) and social script training (Doctoroff, 1990; Goldstein, Wickstrom, Hoyson, Jamieson, & Odom, 1988; Strain, 1975; Strain & Weigerink, 1976). A description of social script training is provided in Goldstein and Gallagher, Chapter 8, this volume. What follows is an overview of research that has looked at the impact of affection activities and correspondence training on the social interaction rates of young children with and without disabilities.

AFFECTION TRAINING PROCEDURES

"Affection activities" were developed by Twardosz et al. (1983) and have been used to increase the interactions of children who are isolate or withdrawn (Twardosz et al., 1983); have autism (McEvoy et al., 1988); have mental retardation (Brown et al., 1988); or have been abused or are at risk for abuse (Niemeyer & McEvoy, 1990). The activities are conducted by the teacher during regularly scheduled large or small group times and include typical preschool songs or activities that have been modified to include prompts for interaction. The procedures are called affection activities because most prompts for interaction are for some type of affectionate response. For example, the children may be told, "If you're happy and you know it hug a friend," or "Give your neighbor a handshake." However, increases in general social interaction (e.g., initiations, responses to initiations, and interactions) and *not* specifically affectionate behaviors (e.g., physical affection, smiling) have been observed in generalization free play settings after the activities were implemented in a separate training setting. (A complete description of the procedures is beyond the scope of this chapter and the reader is referred to McEvoy, Twardosz, and Bishop [1990] for a full overview.) However, the procedures have been used successfully by classroom teachers to increase interactions between children with and without disabilities in both the setting where they are conducted and in generalization free play settings. In addition, McEvoy et al. (1988) and Niemeyer and McEvoy (1990) were able to maintain rates of interaction in the generalization settings even after the affection activities were terminated during the group activities. McEvoy et al. (1988) and Twardosz et al. (1983) have suggested that generalization may have been enhanced by the use of multiple peer exemplars, which would increase the chance that generalization from the training to the nontraining setting would occur (Brady et al., 1984). In addition, the activities incorporate a varied and relatively nonspecific set of teacher prompts. Thus, teachers provide training in a number of responses that may increase the likelihood that generalization will occur (Stokes & Baer, 1977).

The affection activities, while effective, have several drawbacks, First, McEvoy, Twardosz, and Bishop (1990) note that some children may require additional teacher- or peer-mediated procedures in order to interact. Affection activities appear to work best with children who already know how to interact but are not doing so. In addition, these activities may have to be modified for children who are averse to physical affection. Finally, additional research is needed to identify the most critical components of the affection activities for promoting generalization across settings and promoting maintenance.

CORRESPONDENCE TRAINING

A number of researchers have used correspondence training or closely related procedures for training in generalized social responding. Developed initially to increase verbal behavior of young children (Risley & Hart, 1968), these procedures also have been used to increase rates of child-child social interaction (McEvoy, Niemeyer, & Fox, 1989a; Odom & Watts, in press; Osnes et al., 1986; Rogers-Warren & Baer, 1976; Sainato et al., in press). In "say-do" correspondence training, children state initially the behavior that they will use later and are reinforced afterwards for actually engaging in the named behavior. Using this procedure, McEvoy, Niemeyer, and Fox (1989) trained three preschool children to interact with target children with disabilities. Prior to a free play activity, individual peers were asked to name for the teacher a target child that she or he would play with in a subsequent free play activity. Immediately following free play, peers were reinforced with stickers if they had indeed interacted with the named target child. Substantial increases in interaction were noted for all six children (i.e., three with and three without disabilities) involved in the activity. Similar results using this procedure have been reported by Osnes et al. (1986) and Rogers-Warren and Baer (1976).

In a modified version of correspondence training, Odom and Watts (in press) initially taught nondisabled peers to prompt the interactions of young children with autism during a free play activity. After training, peers and target children participated in a free play session during which teachers continued to prompt peers to initiate to the target children. Peer initiations increased in this setting. In a separate setting, the teacher told the peers prior to the free play activity that if they said they would play with a target child and then actually did so, they would receive a reward at the end of the free play activity. In addition to this, Odom and Watts included visual feedback to the peers during the activity by drawing a "happy-face" on an index card in view of the peer each time she or he was observed engaging in social interaction with a target child. Increases in interaction were also noted in this setting. While the individual contribution of the correspondence training procedure toward increases in social behavior was not assessed, the authors noted that the correspondence training/visual feedback procedure was less intrusive than a peer-mediated procedure, and thus may be used more readily by teachers.

Finally, Sainato et al. (in press) used a modified version of correspondence training to increase the use of social interaction strategies by peers with their classmates with autism. Once peers had been trained to use a number of social interaction facilitative strategies (i.e., attracting a friend's attention, getting a friend to play, share, and continue interactions), they were taught to "self evaluate" their performance during a later free play session. Specifically, peers were asked to predict how they would encourage a child with autism to play with them. The peers were then taught to reward themselves with happy faces for interacting successfully with a target child. Later, the peers were given stickers and trinkets by the teacher if they had evaluated their performance accurately. The researchers reported increases in social interaction facilitative strategies with the onset of self-evaluation. In addition, while teacher prompts for interaction never were eliminated during the free play activity, they were reduced substantially. Again, the authors pointed out that the activities were less intrusive than more typical training procedures and required less reliance on teacher prompts.

DIRECTIONS FOR FUTURE RESEARCH

This chapter has attempted to provide a full overview of social interaction training for young children with special needs. The research to date has demonstrated that teachers can effectively promote social interaction between children with and without disabilities. Also, there exists a need to continue to evaluate procedures that are effective, yet can and will be implemented programmatically by teachers. Two issues that future research should address are: 1) a commitment to targeting and training in social skills that are *socially significant*, and 2) an increased emphasis on procedures for providing training in *generalized* social skills.

Parents' and Teachers' Perceptions of Children's Social Behavior

One variable that needs to be considered in targeting skills for intervention is teacher and parent perception of children's social behavior. The essential questions are: 1) do parent's and teacher's perceptions of what is social and what is not social coincide with those of researchers who develop the social interaction training programs; 2) if they differ, in what ways do they differ—do teachers or parents have a more restrictive or inclusive view of social behavior; and 3) if parent's or teacher's perceptions do differ from those of researchers, then how might these differences affect social behavior changes (initial, generalized, and long-term changes) that are attempted through interventions?

That teacher and parent perceptions of child behavior often differ from those of researchers is evident, for example, from research comparing their ratings of children's behavior problems and the problems for which they refer children for psychological services (Achenbach, McConaughy, & Howell, 1987; Simpson & Halpin, 1986; Simpson & Humphrey, 1984; Touliatos & Lindholm, 1981). Unfortunately, the degree to which teachers' and parents' perceptions of specific social behaviors may differ from that of researchers and the implications of this difference on the development and successful implementation of social skills interventions has yet to be addressed adequately (McEvoy, Fox, Cronin, Odom, & McConnell, 1989; Strain & Kohler, 1988). Incorporating teacher and parent judgments in a performance-based approach to assessing children's social competence (see Odom,

McConnell, & McEvoy, Chapter 1, this volume) may be one way of addressing this issue.

Defining Target Social Skills

Generally, in research that has evaluated procedures to increase social interaction, the definitions of target social skills have been somewhat vague (Shores, 1987). Most researchers have described target social behaviors as positive or negative, motor/gestural or vocal/verbal, or simply defined them as initiations or responses and measured them using quantitative analysis (e.g., frequency, duration) (e.g., McEvoy et al., 1988; Strain & Timm 1974; Strain et al., 1976). While noting drawbacks, Greenwood, Todd, Hops, and Walker (1982) suggested that intervening on these consolidated measures of interaction is both cost-effective and pragmatic. However, future research is needed to identify other critical and socially valid targets for intervention for which training can be provided both efficiently and effectively.

Generalization and Maintenance Effects

While the immediate effects of social skills interventions are well documented (e.g., McEvoy & Odom, 1987; Strain & Fox, 1981), researchers have noted the difficulty in demonstrating generalization and maintenance effects of social skills training procedures (Chandler & Lubek, 1990; Fox et al., 1990; McConnell, 1987; Shores, 1987). In their review, Fox et al. (1990) found that in research of the 1980s and 1990s, the number of studies that have specifically programmed for and assessed generalization and maintenance has declined. Moreover, even when it has been assessed, the evaluation of maintenance typically has been conducted over short intervals, for brief lengths of time, and limited to relatively few observations. Although procedures may have been clearly described, most studies failed to employ experimental design tactics to allow verification of the effects of a particular programming tactic on generalization or maintenance. Clearly, researchers must attend more carefully to these critical issues of generalization and maintenance in future research.

Applied social interaction research now has a relatively extended and productive history. Researchers have pursued empirical analyses of the immediate effects of intervention tactics, and, in some instances, albeit limited, have sought to examine the transfer and durability of changes in social interaction skills. However, close inspection of these studies indicates continually unanswered questions. Future research should concentrate on factors and tactics that facilitate (or inhibit) generalized, durable, and socially significant changes in social behavior.

REFERENCES

Achenbach, T.M., McConaughy, S.H., & Howell, C.T. (1987). Child/ adolescent behavioral and emotional problems: Implications of cross-informant correlations for situational specificity. *Psychological Bulletin, 101,* 213–232.

Allen, K.E., Hart, B., Buell, J.S., Harris, F.R., & Wolf, M.M. (1964). Effects of social reinforcement on isolate behavior of a nursery school child. *Child Development, 35,* 511–518.

Brady, M.P., McEvoy, M.A., Gunter, P., Shores, R.E., & Fox, J. J. (1984). Considerations for socially integrated school environments for severely handicapped students. *Education and Training of the Mentally Retarded, 19,* 246–254.

Brown, W.H., Ragland, E.U., & Fox, J.J. (1988). Effects of group socialization procedures on the social interactions of preschool children. *Research in Developmental Disabilities, 9,* 359–376.

Chandler, L.K., & Lubek, R.C. (1990, May). *The generalization and maintenance of young children's social skills: A retrospective review and analysis.* Paper presented at the 16th Annual Conference of the Association for Behavior Analysis: International, Nashville.

Damon, W. (1984). Peer education: The untapped potential. *Journal of Applied Developmental Psychology, 5,* 331–334.

Day, R., Powell, T., & Dy-Lin, T. (1982). An evaluation of the effects of a social interaction training package on mentally handicapped preschool children. *Education and Training of the Mentally Retarded, 17,* 125–130.

Doctoroff, S. (1990). *Effects of sociodramatic script training and peer prompting on the sociodramatic role play and social interaction of socially isolated preschool children.* Unpublished doctoral dissertation, Vanderbilt University, Nashville.

Fox, J.J., Gunter, P., Brady, M.P., Bambara, L., Spiegel-McGill, P., & Shores, R.E. (1984). Using multiple peer exemplars, to develop generalized social responding of an autistic girl. In R. Rutherford & C.M. Nelson (Eds.), *Monograph on Severe Behavioral Disorders of Children and Youth, 7,* 17–26.

Fox, J.J., McEvoy, M.A., Leech, R.L., & Moroney, J.J. (1990, May). *Generalization, maintenance, and social interaction with exceptional children: Ten years after Stones and Baer.* Paper presented at the 16th Annual Convention of the Association for Behavior Analysis: International, Nashville.

Furman, W., Rahe, D., & Hartup, W. (1979). Rehabilitation of socially withdrawn preschool children through mixed-age and same-age socialization. *Child Development, 50*(4), 915–922.

Goldstein, H., Wickstrom, S., Hoyson, M., Jamieson, B., & Odom, S. (1988). Effects of sociodramatic play training on social and communicative interaction. *Education and Treatment of Children, 11,* 97–117.

Greenwood, C.R., Todd, N.M., Hops, H., & Walker, H.M. (1982). Behavior change targets in the assessment and treatment of socially withdrawn preschool children. *Behavioral Assessment, 4,* 273–297.

Guralnick, M.J. (1981). Peer influences on development of communicative competence. In P. Strain (Ed.), *The utilization of peers as behavior change agents* (pp. 31–68). New York: Plenum.

Hartup, W.W., & Sancilio, M.F. (1986). Children's friendships. In E. Schopler & G. Mesibov (Eds.), *Social behavior in autism* (pp. 61–80). New York: Plenum.

Hecimovic, A., Fox, J.J., Shores, R.E., & Strain, P.S. (1985). An analysis of

developmentally integrated and segregated freeplay setting and the generalization of newly-acquired social behaviors of socially withdrawn preschoolers. *Behavior Assessment, 7,* 367–388.

Lancioni, G.E. (1982). Normal children as tutors to teach social responses to
withdrawn mentally retarded school-mates: Training, maintenance, and
generalization. *Journal of Applied Behavior Analysis, 15,* 17–40.

Lefebvre, D., & Strain, P.S. (1989). Effects of a group contingency on the
frequency of social interactions among autistic and nonhandicapped preschool children: Making LRE efficacious. *Journal of Early Intervention, 13,*
392–341.

McConnell, S.R. (1987). Entrapment effects and the generalization and maintenance of social skills training for elementary school students with behavioral disorders. *Behavioral Disorders, 12,* 252–263.

McConnell, S.R., Sisson, L., Cort, C.A., & Strain, P.S. (in press). Effects of
social skills training and contingency management procedures in the interactive social behavior of preschool children. *Journal of Special Education.*

McEvoy, M.A., Fox, J.J., Cronin, P., Odom, S.L., & McConnell, S. (1989,
November). *Teacher perception of social interaction behaviors.* Paper presented
at the 13th Annual Conference on Severe Behavior Disorders of Children
and Youth, Tempe, AZ.

McEvoy, M.A., Niemeyer, J., & Fox, J.J. (1989, October). *The measurement and
development of affection in early childhood settings.* Paper presented at the 5th
International Early Childhood Conference on Children with Special Needs,
Minneapolis, MN.

McEvoy, M.A., Niemeyer, J., & Wehby, J.H. (1989, October). *Measurement of
special education teachers' expression of affection toward preschool children with
handicaps.* Paper presented at the meeting of the American Association of
University Affiliated Programs, Denver.

McEvoy, M.A., Nordquist, V.M., Twardosz, S., Heckaman, K.A., Wehby,
J.H., & Denny, R.K. (1988). Promoting autistic children's peer interaction in
an integrated setting using affection activities. *Journal of Applied Behavior
Analysis, 21,* 193–200.

McEvoy, M.A., & Odom, S.L. (1987). Social interaction training for preschool
children with behavior disorders. *Behavioral Disorders, 12*(4), 242–252.

McEvoy, M.A., & Shores, R.E., Wehby, J.H., Johnson, S.M., & Fox, J.J. (1990).
Special education teachers' implementation procedures to promote social
interaction among children in integrated settings. *Education and Training in
Mental Retardation, 25,* 267–276.

McEvoy, M.A., Twardosz, S., & Bishop, N. (1990). Affection activities: Procedures for encouraging young children with handicaps to interact with
their peers. *Education and Treatment of Children, 13,* 159–167.

Murray, F. (1972). The acquisition of conservation through social interaction.
Developmental Psychology, 6, 1–6.

Niemeyer, J.A., & McEvoy, M.A. (1990, October). *Affection activities: Procedures for teaching young children at-risk for abuse to interact.* Paper presented
at the Annual Conference of the Division for Early Childhood, Albuquer-
que.

Odom, S.L., Bender, M., Stern, M., Doran, L., Honden, P., McInnes, M.,
Gilbert, M., DeKlyen, M., Speltz, M., & Jenkins, J. (1988). *Integrated preschool curriculum.* Seattle: University of Washington Press.

Odom, S.L., Chandler, L.K., Ostrosky, M., Raney, S., & McConnell, S.R.

(1991). *Eliminating teacher prompts in peer mediated interventions.* Manuscript submitted for publication.

Odom, S.L., Hoyson, M., Jamieson, B., & Strain, P.S. (1985). Increasing handicapped preschoolers, peer social interactions: Cross setting and component analysis. *Journal of Applied Behavior Analysis, 18,* 3-16.

Odom, S.L., & Strain, P.S. (1984). Peer mediated approaches to increasing children's social interactions. *American Journal of Orthopsychiatry, 54,* 544–557.

Odom, S.L., & Strain, P.S. (1986). A comparison of peer initiation and teacher-antecedent interventions for promoting reciprocal social interaction of autistic preschoolers. *Journal of Applied Behavioral Analysis, 19,* 59–72.

Odom, S.L., Strain, P.S., Karger, M.A., & Smith, J.D. (1986). Using single and multiple peers to promote social interaction of preschool children with handicaps. *Journal of Division of Early Childhood, 10,* 53–64.

Odom, S. L., & Watts, E. (in press). Reducing teacher verbal prompts in peer-mediated interventions for young children with autism. *Journal of Special Education.*

Osnes, P.G., Guevremont, D.C., & Stokes, T.R. (1986). If I say I'll talk more, then I will: Correspondence training to increase peer-directed talk by socially withdrawn children. *Behavior Modification, 10,* 287–299.

Perrot-Clermont, A.N. (1980). Social interaction and cognitive development in children. *European Monographs in Social Psychology.* London: Academic Press.

Piaget, J. (1926). *The language and thought of the child.* London: Routledge & Kegen Paul.

Ragland, E.U., Kerr, M.M., & Strain, P.S. (1978). Effects of social initiations on the behavior of withdrawn autistic children. *Behavior Modification, 2,* 565–578.

Risley, T., & Hart, B. (1968). Developing correspondence between nonverbal and verbal behavior of pre-school children. *Journal of Applied Behavior Analysis, 1,* 267–281.

Rogers-Warren, A.K., & Baer, D.M. (1976). Correspondence between saying and doing: Teaching children to share and praise. *Journal of Applied Behavior Analysis, 9,* 335–354.

Sainato, D.M., Goldstein, H., & Strain, P.S. (in press). Effects of self-evaluation on preschool children's use of social interaction strategies with their autistic peers. *Journal of Applied Behavior Analysis.*

Sasso, G.M., & Rude, H.A. (1987). Unprogrammed effects of training high-status peers to interact with severely handicapped children. *Journal of Applied Behavior Analysis, 20,* 35–44.

Shafer, M.S., Egel, A.L., & Neef, N.A. (1984). Training mildly handicapped peers to facilitate changes in the social interaction skills of autistic children. *Journal of Applied Behavior Analysis, 17,* 461–476.

Shores, R.E. (1987). Overview of research on social interaction: A historical and personal perspective. *Behavioral Disorders, 12,* 233–241.

Simpson, R.G., & Halpin, G. (1986). Agreement between parents and teachers in using the revised behavior problem checklist to identify deviant behavior in children. *Behavioral Disorders, 12,* 233–241.

Simpson, R.G., & Humphrey, W.R. (1984). Relationship between parent ratings and teacher ratings using the Revised Behavior Problem Checklist. *Diagnostique, 9,* 172–177.

Smith, J.D., McConnell, S.R., Maretsky, S.R., Kudray, R.M., & Strain, P.S. (1987). *Promoting reciprocal social interactions among autistic and normally developing children in an integrated preschool setting.* Unpublished manuscript.

Stokes, T.F., & Baer, D.M. (1977). An implicit technology of generalization. *Journal of Applied Behavior Analysis, 10,* 349–367.

Strain, P.S. (1975). Increasing social play among severely mentally retarded preschool children with socio-dramatic activities. *Mental Retardation, 13,* 7–9.

Strain, P.S. (1977). An experimental analysis of peer social initiations on the behavior of withdrawn preschool children: Some training and generalization effects. *Journal of Abnormal Psychology, 5,* 445–455.

Strain, P.S. (1983). Generalization of autistic children's social behavior change: Effects of developmentally integrated and segregated settings. *Analysis and Intervention in Developmental Disabilities, 3,* 23–24.

Strain, P.S. (1984). Social interactions of handicapped preschoolers in developmentally integrated and segregated settings: A study of generalization effects. In T. Field (Ed.), *Friendships between normally developing and handicapped children* (pp. 187–208). Chicago: Society for Research in Child Development.

Strain, P.S., Cooke, T.P., & Apolloni, T.A. (1976). *Teaching exceptional children: Assessing and modifying social behavior.* New York: Academic Press.

Strain, P.S., & Fox, J.J. (1981). Peer social initiations and the modification of social withdrawal: A review and future perspective. *Journal of Pediatric Psychology, 6,* 417–433.

Strain, P.S., Kerr, M.M., & Ragland, E.U. (1981). The use of peer social initiations in the treatment of social withdrawal. In P.S. Strain (Ed.), *The utilization of classroom peers as behavior change agents* (pp. 101–127). New York: Plenum.

Strain, P.S., & Kohler, F.W. (1988). Social skill intervention with young children with handicaps: Some new conceptualizations and directions. In S. Odom & M. Karnes (Eds.), *Early intervention for infants and children with handicaps: An empirical base* (pp. 129–143). Baltimore: Paul H. Brookes Publishing Co.

Strain, P.S., & Odom, S.L. (1986). Peer social initiatives: Effective intervention for social skill development of exceptional children. *Exceptional Children, 52,* 543–552.

Strain, P.S., Shores, R.E., & Kerr, M.M. (1976). An experimental analysis of "spillover" effects on the social interaction of behaviorally handicapped preschool children. *Journal of Applied Behavioral Analysis, 9,* 31–40.

Strain, P.S., Shores, R.E., & Timm, M. (1977). Effects of peer social initiations on the behavior of withdrawn preschool children. *Journal of Applied Behavior Analysis, 10,* 289–298.

Strain, P.S., & Timm, M.A. (1974). An experimental analysis of social interaction between a behaviorally disordered preschool child and her classroom peers. *Journal of Applied Behavioral Analysis, 7,* 583–590.

Strain, P.S., & Weigerink, R. (1976). The effects of sociometric activities on social interaction among behaviorally disordered preschool children. *Journal of Special Education, 10,* 71–75.

Timm, M.A., Strain, P.S., & Ellers, P. (1979). Effects of systematic response dependent fading and thinning procedures on the maintenance of child-child interaction. *Journal of Applied Behavior Analysis, 12,* 308.

Touliatos, J., & Lindholm, B.W. (1981). Congruence of parents' and teachers' ratings of children's behavior problems. *Journal of Abnormal Child Psychology, 9,* 347–354.

Twardosz, S., Nordquist, V.M., Simon, R., & Botkin, D. (1983). The effect of group affection activities on the interaction of socially isolate children. *Analysis and Intervention in Developmental Disabilities, 13,* 311–338.

van den Pol, R.A., Crow, R.E., Rider, D.P., & Offner, R.B. (1985). Social interaction in an integrated preschool: Implications and applications. *Topics in Early Childhood Special Education, 4*(4), 59–76.

Wolfe, V.V., Boyd, L.A., & Wolfe, D.A. (1983). Teaching cooperative play to behavior problem preschool children. *Education and Treatment of Children, 6,* 1–9.

Wusterbath, N.J., & Strain, P.S. (1980). Effects of adult-mediated attention on the social behavior of physically abused and neglected preschool children. *Education and Treatment of Children, 3,* 91–99.

6

Social Competence Intervention for Young Children with Hearing Impairments

Shirin D. Antia and
Kathryn H. Kreimeyer

Social competence can be broadly thought of as the ability to interact appropriately with others. Children acquire social competence through interaction with parents, other adults, and peers. Social competence includes: 1) the ability to communicate with others using a shared symbol system, and 2) knowledge of the rules governing interaction within various social contexts. Children with hearing impairments may have difficulty acquiring social competence for a variety of reasons. Their inability to express and comprehend language through speech may preclude them from interacting easily with parents and caregivers, thereby restricting opportunities for acquiring social competence. Delays in the development of certain communication skills may reduce opportunities for peer interaction, again precluding the child with a hearing impairment from learning the social rules governing communication. Thus, hearing impairments isolate children from their parents and peers and deprive them of the interactions necessary for the development of social competence. In turn, reduced social competence further decreases opportunities for interaction.

This chapter focuses on two areas of social competence in children with hearing impairments: conversation skills and social interaction skills. The nature of interaction between adults and children with hearing impairments and between children with hearing impairments and their peers with and without hearing impairments is examined. Then various intervention programs designed to increase the conversation and social interaction skills of children with hearing impairments are described.

VARIABLES AFFECTING THE ACQUISITION OF SOCIAL COMPETENCE BY CHILDREN WITH HEARING IMPAIRMENTS

The major variables that may affect social competence in children with hearing impairments are the degree of hearing loss, parental hearing status, age of onset of the loss, amplification, and educational history.

Degree of Hearing Loss and Parental Hearing Status

The degree to which a child's hearing is impaired can range from mild to profound. The term "hearing impairment" generally refers to the entire continuum. Differences in the characteristics of individuals along the continuum make it necessary to classify gradations of loss. The most common classifications are: 1) mild loss: 25–40 dB; 2) moderate loss: 40–55 dB; 3) moderate to severe loss: 55–70 dB; 4) severe loss: 70–95 dB; and 5) profound loss: 95–110 dB (Bess & McConnell, 1981). In general, children with mild and moderate hearing losses are considered to be hard of hearing, while children with severe and profound losses are frequently considered deaf (Moores, 1987). In this chapter, the term hearing impairment refers to all degrees of loss, and the terms mild, moderate, severe, and profound refer to various levels of hearing loss.

The degree of hearing loss may have a considerable influence on the acquisition of communication skills and social competence. In general, children with mild and moderate losses acquire spoken language more easily than children with severe and profound losses. Children with severe and profound losses frequently communicate using sign. The use of sign does not preclude the acquisition of a mature communication system. However, most children with hearing impairments are born to hearing parents who do not begin to learn to sign until after the child's hearing loss is identified. Unfortunately, it is not unusual for severe and profound hearing impairment to be diagnosed as late as at 30–48 months of age (Elssmann, Sabo, & Matkin, 1987). The lack of fluent adult models and interactors, and the late introduction of a systematic symbol system may have a negative impact on the communication skills and social competence of a large number of hearing-impaired children. Hearing-impaired children with hearing-impaired parents may not have similar difficulties because early fluent communication is established between the parents and children. However, these children constitute only about 10%

of the total population of children with severe-profound hearing impairments (Paul & Quigley, 1990). Although children with mild and moderate hearing impairments acquire spoken language more easily than children with severe and profound impairments, those with less severe impairments still are more likely to be diagnosed and their hearing amplified at a later age (Elssmann et al., 1987). Therefore their early interaction with parents and peers may be hampered due to difficulties in the comprehension and expression of spoken language.

Age of Onset of Hearing Loss

The age of onset of the hearing loss is also a factor that influences the acquisition of communication skills. Children who have prelingual hearing losses (i.e., hearing loss that occurred prior to the onset of speech and language) have more difficulty acquiring spoken language than children whose losses occurred postlingually. Most research with hearing-impaired children is conducted on children with prelingual losses.

Amplification and Educational History

Other factors that can influence acquisition of communication skills include the age at which the child receives suitable amplification and the consistency with which amplification is worn. Unfortunately, because of the comparatively low incidence of childhood hearing impairment (Ries, 1986) most researchers are unable to control these variables when selecting subjects. Even more unfortunately, researchers frequently do not describe this information when reporting subject data. Thus, little information is available on the impact of amplification on the development of social competence of children with hearing impairments. A child's educational history, specifically the age at which intervention was initiated and the kind of intervention received, also may affect the acquisition of communication and social competence (Moores, 1987).

It is clear that researchers must consider numerous variables when examining the development of social competence in children with hearing impairments. Despite all these variables, there is a surprising degree of consensus regarding the characteristics of interaction between children with hearing impairments and their parents, teachers, and peers.

CHILDREN'S INTERACTION

Adult-Child Interaction

The child's first opportunity to acquire social competence occurs when interacting with parents or caregivers. Several important conversational skills are acquired during these early interactions, specifically conversational turn-taking and topic initiation and maintenance (Snow, 1981; Terrell, 1985). The following section examines the nature of interaction between children with hearing impairments and their parents and teachers, focusing on those aspects that facilitate or hamper the acquisition of conversational skills.

Parent-Child Interaction

The Research   Several research studies have focused on the differences in dyadic interaction between mothers with hearing-impaired children and mothers with hearing children. Meadow, Greenburg, Erting, and Carmichael (1981) examined the communication patterns between members of four groups of dyads: 1) hearing mothers with their hearing children, 2) hearing mothers with severely/profoundly hearing-impaired children who used oral communication, 3) hearing mothers with severely/profoundly hearing-impaired children who used total (oral and signed English) communication, and 4) hearing-impaired mothers with severely/profoundly hearing-impaired children who used a combination of signed English and American Sign Language. All children were between 3.5 and 5.5 years of age. The hearing-impaired children had prelingual losses that were diagnosed at between 15 and 19 months of age.

The researchers videotaped the dyads in a playroom that contained a variety of toys. Data for each dyad were analyzed from an 8.5-minute transcript. Analysis of the social interaction between members of dyads focused on the duration of interaction, the topic of the interaction, how interactions were elaborated between mother and child, and who initiated the interaction or the elaboration of topic. The results indicated that the hearing mother/hearing-impaired child dyads differed significantly from the other two dyads on several dimensions. These dyads interacted with each other for less time and tended to interact in sequences of one turn each; lengthy sequences of turn-taking were less frequent than with the other dyads. They also tended to have more interactions that were initiated by the mothers. The authors concluded that hearing mother/hearing-impaired child dyads had less mature interactive patterns than hearing-impaired mother/hearing-impaired child dyads and hearing mother/hearing child dyads. The latter two dyads interacted in a very similar manner.

It appears that hearing-impaired children with hearing mothers may have fewer opportunities than hearing children or hearing-impaired children with hearing-impaired mothers to engage in lengthy conversational turn-taking and topic maintenance, two skills important in developing conversational competence. Because no data were available on the children's linguistic competence or the hearing mothers' signing skills, it is not clear how these factors may have contributed to the differences between the dyads.

Wedell-Monig and Lumley (1980) also found that hearing mothers tended to dominate initiations when interacting with their hearing-impaired children. The authors compared six hearing mother/hearing-impaired child dyads with six hearing mother/hearing child dyads. The children were between the ages of 13 and 29 months and were matched for age, gender, and parental educational and occupational status. The hearing-impaired children had severe to profound prelingual losses. Neither the hearing-impaired children nor their mothers had developed sign language skills at the time of the study, although they were enrolled in a total communication intervention program. The dyads were videotaped during six free play sessions conducted 2 months apart. The researchers found that the mothers of the hearing-impaired children averaged 21.8 attempts to interact (i.e., visually, vocally, or physically) during a 5-minute session, compared with 9.6 attempts by the mothers of the hearing children. The hearing-impaired children attempted an average of only 2.3 initiations compared with 12.7 by the hearing children. In contrast to Meadow et al. (1981), Wedell-Monig and Lumley (1980) found that mothers of hearing-impaired children spent more time interacting with their children than mothers of hearing children. However, they also had a greater frequency of interaction than the hearing mother/hearing child dyads, perhaps indicating that, as with the dyads in the Meadow et al. (1981) study, the duration of each interaction was extremely brief.

Henggeler and Cooper (1983) compared the interaction between 15 dyads of hearing mothers and their hearing-impaired children and an equal number of hearing mothers with their hearing children. The children were between the ages of 3.4 and 6 years, and were matched for age, gender, race, social class, and father presence or absence. The hearing-impaired children were being educated in an oral program and had hearing losses ranging from mild to profound. Mothers and children participated in a 15-minute videotaped play period and a 7-minute teaching period. The researchers examined the quantity of interaction between members of the dyads and the control and responsivity of each member of the dyad. They found no significant differences between the two groups of dyads in the amount of interaction. However, there appeared to be more reciprocal communication between mothers and their hearing children than between mothers and their hearing-impaired children. Mothers made significantly more indirect requests of their hearing children, who complied and responded more frequently than did the hearing-impaired children.

Hearing children were more likely to respond to their mother's questions than the hearing-impaired children, even though their mothers asked significantly fewer questions than the mothers of the hearing-impaired children. The hearing children asked significantly more questions of their mothers than did the hearing-impaired children, and their mothers were more likely to respond than the mothers of the hearing-impaired children. These results indicate that, although mothers of hearing-impaired children initiate more interactions with questions than do mothers of hearing children, their children are less likely to maintain the interaction by responding to their questions. Hearing-impaired children appear to initiate fewer interactions and to receive fewer responses to their initiations than hearing children. Thus, a cycle may be established whereby initiations are discouraged. Differences among the hearing-impaired children were not examined despite the wide range in hearing loss. It is possible that children with milder losses would have better oral communication skills and more reciprocal communication with their mothers.

Cheskin (1982, 1983), studied the interaction between three mothers and their hearing-impaired children, who were also enrolled in oral communication programs. The children were between the ages of 1.6 and 2.10 years and were reported to have severe and profound hearing impairments. Each dyad was videotaped for 1 hour in their own home. Cheskin's findings indicated that the most frequent communication of all three mothers was repetitions of their own speech to their children (38%–44% of total utterances). All mothers spent a considerable amount of time describing objects in the child's environment (26%–36% of total utterances). They asked few questions of their children and often did not provide children with opportunities to respond but, instead, answered their own questions after a very brief pause. Cheskin did not examine children's responses to their mothers interactive attempts; thus, it is not possible to draw conclusions on the degree of reciprocity in the interactions. However, it does appear that mothers did not hand over conversational turns to their hearing-impaired children frequently. Because no comparable dyads with hearing children were examined, it is not clear whether the age of the children or their communicative ability was the controlling factor in their interaction.

Conclusions Despite the differences in observation techniques, children's ages, and the wide range of hearing losses among the children studied, the literature on the interaction between mothers and their hearing-impaired children shows some striking similarities in patterns of conversational interaction. Mothers of hearing-impaired children appear to interact frequently with their children; however, they tend to be involved in multiple brief rather than extended sequences of interaction. They seem to take major responsibility for initiating conversation, while the hearing-impaired children tend to be passive interactors, who seldom initiate interaction with their mothers and frequently do not respond to their mothers' conversational attempts. These behaviors on the part of the children seem to establish a cycle. Mothers of nonresponsive children may feel that they have no option but to initiate more interaction with their children. Their dominance of the interaction may discourage their hearing-impaired children from trying to initiate interaction themselves. Thus, the skills of conversation initiation and maintenance may not be learned by the hearing-impaired child.

Teacher-Child Interaction   Children with hearing impairments usually are enrolled in intensive intervention programs shortly after diagnosis. The primary purpose of these programs is to help children develop communication skills. Thus, children with hearing impairments, unlike their hearing peers, often develop conversation skills through interactions with teachers as well as parents.

Classroom discourse generally is dominated by teachers, allowing children few opportunities to initiate or extend conversational topics. Frequently, classroom discourse is characterized by teacher questions that require short answers from children. The teacher retains responsibility for choosing the topic of conversation, keeping the children on topic, and maintaining coherent discourse (Wood, Wood, Griffiths, & Howarth, 1986). At this writing no research on the interaction between teachers and preschool children with hearing impairments is available; therefore, this section reviews the research on teachers' interactions with slightly older (i.e., 6- to 8-year-old) children with hearing impairments. The authors' experience indicates that similar patterns are likely to occur in preschool classrooms.

The Research   An early study by Craig and Collins (1970) used a modification of Flanders Interaction Analysis to obtain data on teacher and child interaction in classes of children with hearing impairments. Data were obtained during several class periods for primary, middle school, and secondary school classrooms, though only the results of primary classrooms (i.e., children 7–8 years of age) are reported here. The authors found that teacher-initiated communication made up 68%–75% of the interactions; student-initiated communication made up 3%–20% of the interactions, and teachers responded less than 1% of the time to these student initiations. It is clear that children with hearing impairments had few opportunities to initiate conversation and even fewer to extend a topic of conversation that they themselves had chosen.

Wood, Wood, Griffiths, Howarth, and Howarth (1982) examined the effects of teacher conversational style on the conversation of children with hearing impairments in four different classrooms. The participating severely/profoundly hearing-impaired children ranged in age from 6 years, 6 months to 10 years, 8 months, and communicated orally. The authors videotaped and transcribed each classroom conversation and categorized each teacher conversational turn (termed a move) by its degree of power. The five categories of teacher moves were: 1) enforced repetitions, in which the teacher requested that the child repeat the teacher's utterance (e.g., "Say, 'I went to the store.'."); 2) two-choice questions (e.g., "Did you go to the park?"); 3) "wh" type questions (e.g., "Who went with you?"); 4) contributions or comments in which the teacher made a statement about the topic of the conversation (e.g., "I like the park too."); and 5) phatics where the teacher took her turn but did not add substantial information to the conversational topic (e.g., "Oh good!"). Enforced repetitions, two-choice questions, and "wh" questions are considered high power teacher moves because they constrain the topic and structure of the child's response. Comments and phatics are considered low power teacher moves because they exercise less control over the child's response. Wood et al. (1982) found that conversations characterized by high levels of teacher power (i.e., when teachers used a high proportion of enforced repetitions and two-choice questions) were associated with low levels of child initiative and a short mean length of turn in words (MLT). Conversely, conversations characterized by low levels of teacher power (i.e., when teachers used high proportions of contributions and phatics) were associated with high levels of child initiative and a long MLT. Questions constituted 48% of all teacher moves but only 1% of all child moves, indicating that hearing-impaired children had few opportunities to initiate conversational topics. Children provided short, unelaborated answers to 47% of teacher questions and contributed to the conversation with statements only 24% of the time. Thus, the children had few opportunities to maintain conversation. Children's moves were highly correlated with teachers' moves: high teacher control moves elicited short unelaborated turns from children, while low teacher control moves elicited longer, more elaborated turns from children. This relationship held true regardless of the mental age or degree of hearing-impairment of the children.

Conclusions   Although the information on teacher-child conversation in the classroom is scanty, it further emphasizes the lack of
opportunity provided to children with hearing impairments to learn
conversational skills. Although dominance of conversation is not
unique to teachers of children with hearing impairments, the effects
of such dominance may be detrimental for these children because
they do not arrive in school with well developed conversational skills.
Also, children with hearing impairments begin formal schooling at a
very early age, and frequently their parents are encouraged by professionals to "teach" language, which often requires following a teacher's model. Because the teacher's model is not one that encourages
child initiation and maintenance of conversation, the parents do not
learn to break the cycle of adult dominance of conversation that already may have been established. Wood et al. (1986), suggested that
some of the difficulties faced by children with hearing impairments in
learning conversational skills are caused by the effect that the impairment has on the adults who significantly influence their development, rather than an inherent inability of the child to learn the necessary skills.

Peer Interaction

As children mature, the context in which social competence is acquired is extended to include interaction with peers as well as adults.
Because of the reciprocal nature of interaction, children who are able
to initiate and maintain interactions with peers are more likely to
receive initiations from peers. As seen in the adult/child literature,
children with hearing impairments may have had limited opportunities to develop the initiation and maintenance skills necessary for
successful interaction; thus, one might anticipate some difficulties
when they interact with their peers, both with and without hearing
impairments.

The literature on the social interaction of preschool children with
hearing impairments is available from two perspectives. A small
group of studies compares the characteristics of social interaction
between dyads of hearing-impaired and dyads of hearing preschoolers. This group of studies identified some of the differences in
peer interaction between hearing-impaired and hearing children and
also provides data on the characteristics of hearing-impaired children's interactions with their hearing-impaired peers. The hearing-
impaired children typically described in these studies are enrolled in
self-contained early education programs. Another group of studies

focuses on the social interaction between hearing-impaired children and their hearing and hearing-impaired peers within integrated early education programs. This group of studies provided data on partner selection and characteristics of interaction between hearing-impaired children and their hearing peers.

Social Interaction Between Hearing-Impaired Children and Their Hearing-Impaired Peers

The Research   The literature that describes the characteristics of interaction between hearing-impaired preschool children and their hearing-impaired peers provides information on the ability of hearing-impaired children to interact with peers who use a common communication system and function with similar communication restrictions. Additionally, this body of literature contrasts the interactive behaviors of hearing-impaired children and similar age, hearing peers.

Higginbotham and Baker (1981) compared the social participation and cognitive play of seven hearing-impaired children who attended a preschool for hearing-impaired students and seven hearing children who attended a nonspecialized preschool. The hearing-impaired children had severe to profound hearing losses and all children were 47–66 months of age. Fifteen 1-minute free play observations over a 6-week period were obtained for each child. Free play behavior was classified for social participation (i.e., solitary, parallel, associative, and cooperative); cognitive play (i.e., functional, constructive, and dramatic); and nonplayful activity (Higginbotham, Baker, & Neill, 1980).

Analysis of the children's social participation indicated that the hearing-impaired children spent significantly more time in solitary play and less time in cooperative play than the hearing children. Analysis of the children's cognitive play indicated that the hearing children spent similar amounts of time in constructive and dramatic play while the hearing-impaired children spent more time in constructive than in dramatic play. Communication used by the hearing-impaired children during their play was primarily nonlinguistic. When the social/cognitive categories were combined, solitary-constructive play was the most preferred mode for the hearing-impaired children. In contrast, the hearing children preferred cooperative-dramatic play. Only three of the seven hearing-impaired children engaged in any cooperative-dramatic play. Hearing-impaired children may have preferred solitary play because their restricted linguistic development limited their ability to engage in the communicative interchanges required for cooperative play. It is also possible that these children had immature social and conversational skills. The results of this study indicate that hearing-impaired children may isolate themselves during play, thus restricting their opportunities to develop social competence through peer interaction.

Vandell and George (1981) observed 16 dyads of preschool hearing-impaired and hearing children between the ages of 41 and 64 months in 15-minute free play sessions to evaluate the frequency and type of interaction initiations and the duration of interactions. The hearing-impaired children in this study received instruction in simultaneous communication; two children had moderate hearing losses, and the others had severe to profound hearing losses. Each hearing-impaired and hearing child was observed once with a hearing-impaired partner and once with a hearing partner. Data were therefore obtained from hearing/hearing dyads, hearing-impaired/hearing-impaired dyads, and hearing-impaired/hearing dyads. Although there were no significant differences in the number of interactions engaged in by the various dyads, significant differences were found in the amount of time spent in interaction, with hearing dyads interacting an average of 62.3% of a session and hearing-impaired dyads interacting only 24.7% of a session. The mean interaction duration was also significantly different, with hearing dyads averaging 33.8 seconds per interaction and hearing-impaired dyads averaging 11.8 seconds per interaction. The pattern of brief interactions between peers may be an extension of the brief early interactions between hearing-impaired children and their parents. Brief and infrequent interactions appear to be characteristic of hearing-impaired children's interaction with both adults and peers.

McKirdy and Blank (1982) compared conversational interaction between 12 dyads of hearing-impaired and of hearing preschool children during 15-minute play sessions. The hearing-impaired children ranged in age from 52–64 months and had hearing losses that ranged from moderately severe to profound. The hearing children were between the ages of 49 and 63 months and were matched for age, gender, and IQ.

The authors recorded all conversational turns between members of the dyads and then coded the cognitive complexity and summoning power of initiations and the appropriateness of responses. The data indicated that the hearing-impaired dyads initiated significantly fewer conversational turns (mean = 27) than the hearing dyads (mean = 57). When the summoning power of the initiations were analyzed, 57% of the hearing-impaired children's initiations were in a form that contained a clear expectation of a response, termed an oblige. In contrast, 57% of the initiations of the hearing children were in the form of comments that did not contain an explicit demand that the partner respond. When children's responses to their partner's initiations were analyzed, the data indicated that hearing-impaired children rarely responded to comments and responded more frequently to obliges than to comments. Hearing children also responded more successfully to obliges than to comments, but differences between response rates to these two types of initiations were not as pronounced as was observed with the hearing-impaired children. As would be expected, the complexity of language used by the hearing dyads surpassed that observed between members of the hearing-impaired dyads. McKirdy and Blank found that the hearing-impaired children displayed extremely limited instances of sustained conversation and limited their discussion to "here and now" topics. They also had greater difficulties as responders than as initiators.

As noted in the earlier discussion of mother/child interaction characteristics, children with hearing impairments have, from an early age, fewer opportunities to engage in sustained reciprocal communication than their hearing peers. They may, therefore, have less experience than their hearing peers in responding to conversational initiations. Mothers of children with hearing impairments initiate interactions with questions more frequently than mothers of hearing children (Henggeler & Cooper, 1983). Hearing-impaired children's use of obligatory initiation forms with their peers may reflect their experience with this form of initiation during interactions with their mothers. Preschool hearing-impaired children's limited ability to engage in conversational exchanges with their peers may be due to their restricted language skills as well as limited opportunities to develop conversational initiation and maintenance skills at home.

Lederberg, Ryan, and Robbins (1986) evaluated the role of language and the effects of hearing status, familiarity, and experience on the dyadic interaction of hearing-impaired children with their hearing and hearing-impaired peers during 14-minute free play observations. Only data obtained from observations of the hearing-impaired dyads are discussed in this section. Fourteen hearing-impaired children between the ages of 54 and 83 months were the focal children and an additional seven hearing-impaired children, identified by teachers as friends of the focal children, were the hearing-impaired peers. All hearing-impaired children had severe to profound hearing losses and were enrolled in an educational program that used simultaneous communication.

The researchers observed that the dyads of hearing-impaired children used minimal linguistic communication during their interactions with one another, results consistent with previous research (Arnold & Tremblay, 1979; Vandell & George, 1981). Language competence scores were positively correlated with total interaction time, total number of turns, and frequency of interactive bouts containing pretend play. These data indicate that the relationship between language competence and peer interaction is independent of linguistic communication. Language competence scales typically measure nonlinguistic as well as linguistic communication and it may be competence with nonlinguistic communication that facilitates interactive play between hearing-impaired children. It should be noted that no comparative data were obtained from dyads of hearing children.

Conclusions   The research indicates that hearing-impaired children do not interact with one another as frequently as do same-age, hearing peers. Interaction between hearing-impaired children is characteristically nonlinguistic and of brief duration even though the children share a common communication system. Hearing-impaired children appear to have greater difficulty responding to peers' initiations than initiating interaction themselves. It is possible that competence in nonlinguistic communication may be positively correlated with peer social interaction.

Social Interaction Between Hearing-Impaired Children and Their Hearing Peers   Peer interaction with hearing children is likely to be affected by the hearing-impaired children's difficulties in initiating and maintaining successful interactions. Additionally, such interaction may be complicated by the lack of a shared communication system. It is not surprising that the literature on the social interaction between hearing-impaired children and their hearing peers indicates that minimal interaction occurs within integrated settings.

The Research   Arnold and Tremblay (1979) examined the social interaction between five hearing and five profoundly hearing-impaired children between 4 and 5 years of age who were enrolled in an integrated preschool program that emphasized both manual and oral communication. All of the children were videotaped during a 30-minute recess period for 3 weeks. The researchers found no significant differences between the hearing-impaired and hearing children in the frequency of occurrence of vocalizations, gestures, approach, physical contact, imitation, social play, taking and giving objects, and aggression. However, hearing children approached, vocalized, played and engaged in physical contact with other hearing children significantly more than with hearing-impaired children. In contrast, the hearing-impaired children did not show a preference for hearing-impaired partners.

Tendencies toward self-segregation were also obtained by Levy-Shiff and Hoffman (1985) who examined the relationship between social competence and hearing loss by observing the interactive behaviors of hearing and hearing-impaired preschool children during free play sessions. Twenty-four hearing-impaired children (12 with profound hearing impairments and 12 with severe hearing impairments), all of whom communicated orally, and 12 hearing preschoolers between the ages of 48 and 67 months participated in this study, which was conducted in Israeli preschools. The hearing-impaired and hearing children were classmates in five integrated kindergarten programs.

Nineteen behaviors which reflected: 1) ability and willingness to interact with a playmate, 2) expressions of positive or negative affect, or 3) absence of social interaction, were time sampled for each target child during four 15-minute free play sessions conducted over a 1 month period. Observers also recorded whether the target child's partner was a hearing or hearing-impaired child. Results indicated that both the hearing-impaired and hearing children preferred to initiate to, converse with, and positively respond to partners whose hearing status matched their own. The hearing-impaired children, in contrast to the hearing children, relied more heavily on gestures than vocalizations to communicate.

The data from this study also suggested that a relationship may exist between degree of hearing loss and successful interaction with peers. Profoundly hearing-impaired children engaged in significantly less peer interaction (49.3% of the total observation time) than either the severely hearing-impaired (65.8%) or hearing children (68.1%). They also engaged in less conversation than the severely impaired children who, in turn, engaged in less conversation than the hearing children. A variety of factors, including intelligible speech, linguistic ability, or the ability to understand spoken communication, may have contributed toward this relationship.

Brackett and Henniges (1976), in a study of the communicative interactions of 13 hearing-impaired children in an integrated preschool class, observed a relationship between linguistic proficiency and choice of interactive partner. Hearing-impaired children between the ages of 42 and 78 months with hearing losses ranging from mild to profound, and an equal number of hearing children between the ages of 3 and 5 years were enrolled in an integrated class. A battery of language tests were administered to the hearing-impaired children, and the results were used to classify the children as linguistically limited or proficient.

Data on the type of communicative interaction (initiation or response); the communicative partner (hearing peer, hearing-impaired peer, or adult); and the mode of communicative interaction (verbal, vocal, or gestural) were obtained for each hearing-impaired child over two 10-minute observations conducted within a structured language group and a free play setting. The authors found that linguistically proficient hearing-impaired children interacted more frequently with hearing peers than did hearing-impaired children with limited linguistic skills. The latter children showed a definite preference for interaction with other hearing-impaired children. The relationship between degree of hearing loss and peer interaction was also examined and approached significance.

Lederberg et al. (1986) also evaluated the role of language use and competence in peer interaction, as well as the effects of hearing status, familiarity, and experience on the dyadic interaction of hearing-impaired children during free play. Data were obtained on the dyadic interaction of hearing-impaired children with: 1) hearing-impaired peers, 2) familiar hearing peers who regularly interacted with hearing-impaired children, 3) unfamiliar hearing peers who regularly interacted with hearing-impaired children, and 4) unfamiliar hearing peers who had no previous experience interacting with hearing-impaired children. Fourteen hearing-impaired children between the ages of 54 and 83 months were the focal children, and seven additional hearing-impaired children were the hearing-impaired peers. All hearing-impaired children had severe to profound hearing losses and used simultaneous communication. Twenty-one hearing children between the ages of 52 and 86 months were the partners for the hearing-impaired children. Fourteen of these children played with one of the hearing-impaired focal children at least once every 2 weeks, and the remaining seven children had minimal experience with hearing-impaired children. Following are the results concerning interaction between hearing-impaired and hearing children.

Interaction and play between the hearing-impaired/hearing dyads was not related to language use, language competence, nonverbal IQ, or chronological age. The researchers suggested that perhaps interaction between hearing-impaired and hearing children was related more to the abilities and motivation of the hearing than the hearing-impaired children.

Analyses of the effect of partner hearing status, familiarity, and experience, on interaction and communication provided information on several variables previously unexplored. One outcome of this analysis was that hearing-impaired focal children tended to communicate with signs when with a hearing-impaired partner, and with object-related behavior and toy play when with a hearing partner. This is not surprising given the difference in communication systems between the two groups. Hearing-impaired children initiated more interactions with the familiar, experienced, hearing peer than with the hearing-impaired peer, but initiations were equally successful for both partners. Hearing-impaired focal children were significantly more likely to experience initiation success with familiar, experienced hearing peers than with unfamiliar, experienced hearing peers (children who played regularly with other hearing-impaired peers). No significant difference in the initiation success rate was observed when hearing-impaired focal children initiated interaction with unfamiliar, experienced hearing peers and unfamiliar, inexperienced hearing peers (children who had minimal exposure to hearing-impaired children). Familiarity also influenced the kind of communication and play in which the dyads engaged. Hearing children used more gestures, exaggerated facial expressions, and vocalizations with a familiar than with an unfamiliar hearing-impaired peer. Hearing-impaired focal children engaged in more pretend play and physical contact with familiar, experienced hearing peers than with unfamiliar, experienced hearing peers.

Results of this study indicate that familiarity played a more significant role than experience in promoting interaction and communication between hearing-impaired and hearing children. Thus, a hearing child's relationship with a specific hearing-impaired child increased communication and interaction between members of the dyad but did not generalize to situations with other unfamiliar, hearing-impaired children. These data suggest that if hearing-impaired children are to develop social competence skills through interaction with hearing peers, they may need extended opportunities to interact regularly with specific hearing children.

As mentioned earlier, Vandell and George (1981) observed the interaction between hearing-impaired, hearing, and mixed (i.e., hearing and hearing-impaired) dyads of children enrolled in separate preschool programs in the same center. Two groups, each composed of 16 children, came together for lunch, recess, gym, and various classroom activities. Two of the hearing-impaired children had moderate hearing losses and fourteen had severe to profound losses. The hearing children were taught sign language as part of their preschool program. Analysis of the interactions between the three kinds of dyads indicated that there were no significant differences in the total number of interactions, although significant differences were found in the amount of time spent in interaction. The mixed dyads interacted 16.6% of the 15-minute play period, compared with 24.7% for hearing-impaired dyads and 62.3% for hearing dyads. The mean interaction duration also was significantly different, with mixed dyads averaging 9.3 seconds per interaction, hearing-impaired dyads 11.8 seconds, and hearing dyads 33.8 seconds. The authors noted that hearing-impaired children were more likely than hearing peers to be the recipients of inappropriate signals, and, although they initiated significantly more interactions than their hearing counterparts, their initiations were more likely to be rejected. Both of these factors could depress subsequent interaction between hearing-impaired and hearing children.

Conclusions   Several conclusions can be drawn from the above studies. When hearing-impaired and hearing children are presented with opportunities to interact with one another, interaction occurs less frequently and is of shorter duration than when hearing children interact with their hearing peers. Limited data suggest that a negative relationship may exist between the degree of hearing loss and the frequency and duration of interaction between hearing-impaired and hearing children. There also appears to be a relationship between the linguistic proficiency of hearing-impaired children and the amount of interaction with hearing peers. Successful interaction between hearing-impaired and hearing children is more likely when the children are familiar with one another because familiar, hearing peers appear to develop a repertoire of nonlinguistic communication skills.

INTERVENTION

Intervention Programs To Increase Conversation Skills in Children with Hearing Impairments

This section describes two intervention programs designed to develop conversation skills in children with hearing impairments. Wood et al. (1986), described techniques for modifying aspects of teacher talk, and Stone (1988) provided a comprehensive language teaching approach within a conversational framework. Neither method was designed exclusively for preschool children, but the procedures appear to be appropriate for this age group. As with many intervention programs used with children who have hearing impairments, little data are available on the long-term outcomes of either technique. Data on the immediate effects of different styles of teacher talk on the language output of children with hearing impairments are available and are reviewed here.

Modifying Aspects of Teacher Talk　The intervention strategies for developing communication competence suggested by Wood et al. (1986) stem directly from their research on the effects of teacher conversational style on the conversational initiative of children with hearing impairments. Because high levels of teacher control of conversation were found to be correlated with low levels of child initiations, these authors suggested that changing the style of teacher conversation will provide opportunities for children to initiate and maintain conversation. Wood and Wood (1984) asked three teachers of oral/ hearing-impaired children between the ages of 5.6 years and 11.3 years to vary their conversational style by deliberately emphasizing one of the five levels of moves (i.e., enforced repetition, two-choice questions, wh-type questions, contributions, and phatics) in five successive conversations. They found that teachers were able to vary their conversational style, and that the children with hearing impairments responded systematically to these changes. Significant negative correlations were found between adult control of conversation and child initiative and mean length of turn (MLT). Teacher use of phatics yielded the longest child MLT followed by contributions, wh-type questions, and two-choice questions. These results were found for all six children participating in the study, regardless of age. Moreover, they found that children were sensitive to the general tenor of the conversation, as well as to teacher moves within the conversation. For instance, children were more likely to give extended responses to teacher contributions when these occurred frequently in the conversation than when contributions were interspersed with frequent wh-type or two-choice questions. Similarly, children were likely to provide extended responses to teacher questions when these occurred infrequently in conversations dominated by teacher contributions or phatics. In a qualitative analysis of the conversations, Wood et al. (1986) reported that frequent requests for repetitions (used by teachers as a corrective tool) resulted in children ceasing to respond or to initiate conversation. When teachers asked frequent questions children responded nonverbally or with the minimal information required; as question asking conversations progressed, children became increasingly passive. In conversations in which teachers used a high percentage of contributions and phatics, children were more likely to ask questions of the teacher and to contribute original ideas. However, they were also more likely not to respond at all, and, because the teacher did not control the topic of conversation, there was often a lack of coherence in the discourse. The authors suggested that conversations marked by frequent use of teacher contributions and phatics, with occasional use of teacher questions to maintain coherence, appear to be the most useful in providing children opportunities to learn conversational skills.

No data are available as yet on the long-term effectiveness of these techniques. Also, it is not clear that reducing adult control of conversation will have a positive impact on all children with hearing impairments, regardless of age or communication ability. However, there is some evidence that hearing-impaired children with a mean length of utterance as low as 1.0 morphemes will respond positively to the teacher's use of low control conversation moves (Antia & Husby, 1989). Wood and Wood (1984) were able to demonstrate that teachers can change their conversational behavior with children, but there are no data to indicate whether these changes will persist over time. Nevertheless, reducing adult conversational control appears to be a simple and effective way for adults, both parents and teachers, to increase the participation of hearing impaired children in conversation and to give them practice in topic initiation and maintenance.

Comprehensive Language Teaching Within a Conversational Framework   Stone (1988) has described a language instruction approach for children with hearing impairments that is in direct contrast to some traditional approaches that have emphasized knowledge of language structure by instructing children through metalinguistic analysis (McAnnally, Rose, & Quigley, 1987). Because this instructional approach does little to develop conversational skills in children, researchers have suggested that teachers rethink language instruction techniques to develop language structures within the framework of conversation (Kretschmer & Kretschmer, 1978). Stone described methods of using role-play scenarios to develop the conversation skills of initiation, turn-taking, and maintenance. After an initial assessment of conversational skills obtained during teacher-child interaction, specific conversational skills and semantic/syntactic language structures are targeted for instruction. The teacher designs a role-play that is presented to the child in a manner that ensures that the ensuing dialogue results in the child using the required skill. For example, when targeting the skill of maintaining a conversation by producing contingent utterances, the teacher might say, "Let's pretend we're going for a ride in the car. I'll drive and you be the passenger." The teacher would initiate a conversation with a comment by saying, "Look at that barn." The child is expected to respond with a contingent comment such as, "I see some cows."

To facilitate learning, four teacher intervention strategies are described for use within the role-plays. These are teacher clarification, role switching, requesting clarification, and teacher prompting. Teacher clarification requires the teacher to restate the child's part in the dialogue using the appropriate language. Role switching requires the teacher and child to switch roles so that the teacher can model the dialogue required of the child. Requesting clarification involves simply letting the child know that the utterance was not understood by asking questions such as, "What did you say?" or "Pardon me." Teacher prompting requires that the teacher request that the child say something "another way." Stone suggests that teachers can teach children to transfer skills learned in the role-play scenarios to new situations by having different individuals act as partners and by using communication situations that occur during the day for generalization opportunities.

The methods described by Stone are promising because they assist teachers in targeting specific conversational skills and allow children to obtain practice in these, while also targeting semantic/syntactic language. This is in marked contrast to instructional approaches that frequently teach semantic/syntactic language targets to young children in drill-like situations. Unfortunately, no published data are available on the effectiveness of conversational role-plays with young children who have hearing impairments. One difficulty with this approach is that Stone provides relatively few examples of scenarios on topics that would be appropriate for preschool children. However, he does provide a useful scope and sequence chart on the related development of conversation and semantic/syntactic skills of young children.

The interventions described for increasing the conversational competence of children with hearing impairments have focused solely on classroom interventions. As noted earlier, the literature indicates that difficulties in acquiring conversational competence may stem from the characteristics of early interactions between children with hearing impairments and their parents. At this time the authors are not aware of any published intervention programs that address this specific concern. Parents, like teachers, could learn to be less controlling in their interactions with their young children with hearing impairments by using the techniques described by Wood et al. (1986). It is not clear, however, whether hearing mothers can break the cycle of interaction with their children, given the problems surrounding the lack of fluent shared communication.

Intervention Programs To Increase Social Interaction Between Children with Hearing Impairments and Their Peers

A number of intervention programs have been reported to increase the interaction between children with hearing impairments and their peers. The authors have identified three kinds of interventions that have had varying degrees of success: 1) the reduction of the dependence of children with hearing impairments on adults to reward interactions, 2) changing the attitudes and behaviors of peers toward children with hearing impairments, and 3) teaching children with hearing impairments the social skills necessary to interact with peers.

Reduction of Dependence on Adults   Several researchers have reported that children with hearing impairments interact more frequently with adults than do their hearing peers and depend more on adults than on peers to reward social interactions (Antia, 1982; Mc-Cauley, Bruininks, & Kennedy, 1976). Soderhan and Whiren (1985), in an intensive study of a 4-year-old child with a moderate hearing impairment in an integrated preschool setting, noted that there appeared to be a direct relationship between high rates of adult/child interaction and low rates of peer interaction. They attempted to reduce the frequency of adult interactions with the hearing-impaired child by sending a written communication about the value of interaction between the hearing-impaired child and his peers to all participating adults in the preschool. In addition, for a period of 2 weeks, the researchers reminded the adults to monitor their own interactions with the hearing-impaired child and to encourage him to interact with his peers during play periods. No details were provided concerning the strategies used to encourage peer interaction, or how the adults monitored their interactions with the child. The researchers obtained observations on the frequency of adult/child and peer interaction during 14 half-hour, free play periods prior to the intervention, immediately following the intervention, and again 8 weeks after the intervention ceased. Their results indicated that the intervention resulted in a significant decrease in adult interactions with the hearing-impaired child and a corresponding increase in the child's communicative initiations towards his peers and peers' initiations towards him. After 8 weeks, adult/child interactions again increased and peer interaction decreased, although levels of interaction did not return to baseline. The authors concluded that frequent adult/child interaction interfered with children depending on one another for companionship and that adults could be persuaded to decrease their interactions with children, resulting in increased peer interaction.

Although few details of the intervention are provided by the authors, their hypothesis should be considered seriously. Children with hearing impairments spend a large proportion of their time in small groups with a high adult-child ratio. As mentioned earlier (Craig & Collins, 1970), teachers tend to dominate the classroom interaction and, because of this, children with hearing impairments may become dependent on adults for interaction. Furthermore, if adults take the major responsibility for initiating and maintaining the interaction, children may find themselves at a disadvantage when interacting with peers because they have not learned conversation skills.

Changing the Attitudes and Behaviors of Peers Who Do Not Have Disabilities Several researchers have attempted to increase the interactions of children who have disabilities with nondisabled peers by changing the attitudes and behaviors of the nondisabled peers (Shafer, Egel, & Neef, 1984; Strain, Kerr, & Ragland, 1979). When children who do not have disabilities act as change agents they can break the cycle of passivity in which children with disabilities frequently find themselves. Moreover, it may be pointless to change the behaviors of the children with disabilities if the nondisabled children remain unresponsive to their initiations. Vandell, Anderson, Ehrhardt, and Wilson (1982) attempted to modify hearing children's approach to hearing-impaired children by engaging the hearing children in a variety of activities designed to provide them with knowledge of hearing impairment and practice in using communication techniques appropriate when interacting with hearing-impaired children. The intervention consisted of fifteen 15- to 30-minute sessions during which hearing children learned about hearing impairment by reading stories, receiving information about hearing loss and hearing aids, and experiencing simulated hearing loss. They learned communication techniques by receiving instruction in sign language, by engaging in play and classroom activities with a hearing-impaired peer, and by practicing nonlinguistic communication among themselves. The hearing-impaired children in the intervention group were the peers for the hearing children but received no intervention.

Eight hearing and eight hearing-impaired children between the ages of 53 and 55 months participated in the intervention, and a similar number of hearing children were a control group. The hearing-impaired children had severe to profound hearing losses and used simultaneous communication. Researchers obtained data on successful and unsuccessful social initiations and the frequency and duration of interactions by observing each child in dyadic play situations with a same sex child of: 1) opposite hearing status but same intervention condition, and 2) opposite hearing status and opposite intervention condition. Data were obtained before the intervention, immediately following the intervention, and again 6 weeks after the intervention ceased. Contrary to expectations, the authors found that after the intervention, the dyads involving the hearing children who received the intervention interacted less frequently and for shorter durations than dyads involving hearing children who did not receive the intervention. Hearing children in the control group initiated more frequent nonlinguistic initiations toward their hearing-impaired partners than did the hearing children in the intervention group. Hearing-impaired children had more successful initiations with their hearing partners in the control group than with their hearing partners in the intervention group.

Several explanations for the lack of success of the intervention program can be offered. The length and duration of the intervention may have been insufficient to change the behavior of the hearing children. Providing hearing children with knowledge of hearing loss may have heightened awareness of the differences between the two groups of children. Without intensive training in techniques to interact with hearing-impaired children such awareness may have reduced rather than increased interaction. Although the hearing children were provided with opportunities to interact with children with hearing impairments, these opportunities were limited to five half-hour sessions, and may have been insufficient for the hearing children to change their communicative behaviors toward the children with hearing impairments. No specific training or instruction was provided to the hearing children during the simulated activities or during the joint activities with the hearing-impaired children. An assumption seems to have been made that the hearing children could generalize from the information provided about hearing impairment to skills needed to interact with hearing-impaired children. During the joint activities, the hearing children were always paired with a different hearing-impaired child; thus, they had no opportunities to become familiar with any one hearing-impaired child. Finally, no intervention was provided to the hearing-impaired children, and their behavior may have affected the interaction in a negative manner.

Teaching Social Skills to Children with Hearing Impairments   Another approach to increasing positive interaction between children with hearing impairments and their peers is to instruct children with hearing impairments in the social skills that are necessary for interaction. Several studies of the effects of social skill intervention on peer interaction have been conducted in segregated environments, but none have been conducted in integrated environments (Antia & Kreimeyer, 1987; Antia & Kreimeyer, 1988; Barton & Osborne, 1978; Kreimeyer & Antia, 1988).

Barton and Osborne (1978) taught verbal sharing through positive practice to a group of five 6-year-old children with moderate to severe hearing impairments in a self-contained classroom during a 30-minute free play period, 5 days per week, for 15 sessions. The positive practice procedure involved instruction, modeling, and practice. The children practiced the role of the initiator (i.e., the child who asked a peer to share a toy), or the acceptor (i.e., the child who agreed to share). Each time a nonsharer was observed, the teacher modeled and prompted this child to ask a peer to share a toy, or to agree to share a toy with a peer. Observational data on verbal and physical sharing were obtained during an initial baseline condition, intervention, second baseline, and a follow-up session 15 weeks after the second baseline. The positive practice procedure resulted in immediate gains in physical sharing, which were maintained during the second baseline and the follow-up sessions. No changes in verbal sharing occurred, even though the intervention targeted this behavior.

Barton and Osborne demonstrated that hearing-impaired children can benefit from instruction and practice in specific social skills. Further evidence of the success of this approach comes from Antia and Kreimeyer (1987), who taught two groups of young children with hearing impairments between 36 and 48 months of age the following social skills: greeting peers, sharing materials, assisting, complimenting and praising, cooperative play, and inviting. The children had severe and profound hearing impairments and were enrolled in a self-contained preschool program. They received the intervention for 30-minute sessions 5 days a week for 8 weeks in two groups of five and four children, respectively. Preschool activities were modified to allow children frequent opportunities to interact with one another. During the activities, the teachers modeled and prompted (i.e., physically and verbally) the social skills and accompanying linguistic behavior. The effectiveness of the intervention was evaluated using a multiple baseline design. Data were collected daily on the frequency of praise, sharing, conversation, and negative interactions between children during baseline, intervention, and a second baseline during teacher-directed activities and free play probes. The results indicated that the intervention increased the frequency of total positive peer interaction in both situations. Sharing accounted for most of the increase in interaction, though a slight upward trend was observed in conversation. However, interaction decreased once the intervention was withdrawn.

The social skills intervention was extended to encompass the concept of a social interaction routine that provided the children with repetitive and predictable situations in which to practice social skills (Antia & Kreimeyer, 1985; Kreimeyer & Antia, 1988). Three kinds of routines were devised: 1) shared product routines, which required children to work together to complete a single product; 2) cooperative game routines, which required children to participate in simple, repetitive, teacher-designed, and traditional noncompetitive games; and

3) role-play routines, which allowed children to practice various skills within familiar role-play situations, such as going to a restaurant. Although materials and themes were varied across activities, procedures and language remained repetitive within a routine to provide sufficient repetition for learning and generalization.

The effectiveness of this revised social skills intervention program, using the routines together with teacher modeling and prompting of social skills, was examined by Kreimeyer and Antia (1988). The researchers also studied the conditions under which social skills, learned during teacher-directed activities, would generalize to free play settings. Some of the toys used in free play settings were designed as "trained" toys and incorporated into the intervention activities. Toys that were not incorporated into the intervention were designated as "untrained" toys. The researchers incorporated each trained toy into multiple social interaction routines.

The intervention was conducted within a preschool program for children who had hearing impairments with three groups of children (12 children in all) between the ages of 39 and 54 months with hearing losses ranging from moderate to profound. Children received the intervention for 26–28 twenty-minute sessions, 4 days per week. The design of the study and the data collection techniques were similar to Antia and Kreimeyer (1987). The intervention resulted in increased total positive peer interaction during teacher-directed activities for all children on whom data were collected. Sharing increased more than conversation, but each child showed increases in both of these behaviors. Increases in peer interaction generalized to free play sessions in which trained toys were available to the children. Generalization of interaction was not observed during free play sessions in which only untrained toys were available.

Antia and Kreimeyer (1988) continued their research by studying the conditions under which gains in social interaction would be maintained. They used a sequential withdrawal design to determine whether intervention gains were maintained as teacher modeling and prompting were withdrawn. Three children with severe hearing impairments and one child with a moderate hearing impairment, all between the ages of 5 years and 5 years, 10 months, participated in the intervention program, which was conducted for 20 minutes per day, 4 days a week. Social skills were taught during shared product routines, which were incorporated into the regular preschool curriculum. Immediate increases in positive peer interaction were observed for each child upon implementation of the intervention; however, peer interaction returned to baseline levels when the entire intervention was withdrawn abruptly. The intervention was reinstated and then withdrawn in two phases: 1) teachers modeled the social skills prior to the activity and prompted these skills during the first 2 minutes of the activity, and 2) teachers modeled the social skills prior to the activity but did not prompt children to use them. A final baseline period indicated that levels of positive peer interaction were maintained as a result of the gradual withdrawal procedure. An interesting finding of this study was that while both nonlinguistic and linguistic interactions increased during the intervention, during the withdrawal phases, nonlinguistic interaction decreased while linguistic interaction continued to increase. It is possible that nonlinguistic interaction is a precursor to linguistic interaction even in children who have linguistic skills.

The studies described in this section indicate that social skill intervention results in increased peer interaction, generalization of interaction to free play situations, and short-term maintenance of interaction gains. Immediate gains are seen most frequently for nonlinguistic interaction, while increases in linguistic interaction occur at a slower pace, if at all. Inadequate data are available to determine whether gains in linguistic interaction are correlated with linguistic competence. Kreimeyer and Antia (1988) noted that hearing-impaired children with linguistic levels below those of similar-age, hearing-impaired peers made gains equal to the other children in sharing but not in conversation. As mentioned earlier, children need to converse with their peers to sustain cooperative play; intervention programs that increase only nonlinguistic peer interaction may provide hearing-impaired children with skills that are necessary, but not sufficient, for long-term maintenance of interaction. Considerable research remains to be conducted in this area.

SUMMARY

A review of the literature indicates that children with hearing impairments do not have the same opportunities as their hearing peers to engage in reciprocal interaction with adults and peers. Consequently, they do not necessarily acquire the social competence skills learned through these interactions. Several intervention strategies have been described to assist these children in acquiring the skills necessary for adequate interaction with adults and peers. Language intervention programs for young children with hearing impairments that emphasize learning semantic/syntactic structures within a conversational framework, rather than a drill-like context, appear to be promising, but no data on effectiveness are available. Teachers can provide children with opportunities to practice conversation skills by reducing the amount of control they exert during conversational interactions. Although no data are available on the use of this strategy to reduce parental control during parent-child interactions, it may be as effective with parents as it is with teachers. To provide children with opportunities to learn skills acquired in the social context of interaction with peers, it may be necessary for teachers to reduce their interaction with children who have hearing impairments during play. Even teacher praise of peer interaction appears to interrupt rather than increase peer interaction (Kreimeyer, Antia, & Eldredge, 1989).

Unfortunately, even when adults are not present, peer interaction may not increase unless the children with hearing impairments have developed the social skills to interact with peers. Intervention programs that teach specific social skills to these children have been effective in increasing positive interaction with hearing-impaired peers who participated in the intervention. No data are available on generalization of social skills to other situations with peers who did not participate in the intervention. Nor are data available on the effects of social skill intervention programs on interaction with hearing peers.

Increasing interaction between children with hearing impairments and their hearing peers appears to be a more complex process than increasing interaction between children with hearing impairments. Factors such as the linguistic proficiency and speech intelligibility of the children with hearing impairments are likely to have an impact on the amount and quality of interaction with hearing peers, and there are as yet no data to indicate whether intervention programs can be designed to increase interaction despite these factors. Successful interventions probably will need to teach social interaction and communication skills to hearing and hearing-impaired children because both groups of children need to learn how to adapt their communication and interaction strategies to one another. Interventions that focus on providing children with information rather than skills are unlikely to succeed. In addition, intervention needs to be conducted with stable groups of hearing and hearing-impaired children over a lengthy period of time because familiarity appears to be a factor that positively influences the quantity and quality of interaction. Finally, intervention strategies need to be designed to ensure that the teacher's role is monitored carefully and that interaction with the teacher does not interfere with positive peer interaction.

REFERENCES

Antia, S.D. (1982). Social interaction of partially mainstreamed hearing-impaired children. *American Annals of the Deaf, 127,* 18–25.

Antia, S.D., & Husby, B. (1989) *Discourse development and strategies for teaching discourse and social communication skills to hearing-impaired children*. Paper presented at the Annual Conference of the Council for Exceptional Children, Toronto, Canada.

Antia, S.D., & Kreimeyer, K.H. (1985). Social interaction routines to facilitate peer interaction in hearing-impaired children. *Australian Teacher of the Deaf, 26*, 13–18.

Antia, S.D., & Kreimeyer, K.H. (1987). The effect of social skill training on the peer interaction of preschool hearing-impaired children. *Journal of the Division for Early Childhood, 11*(3), 206–216.

Antia, S.D., & Kreimeyer, K.H. (1988). Maintenance of positive peer interaction in preschool hearing-impaired children. *The Volta Review, 90*(7), 325–337.

Arnold, D., & Tremblay A. (1979). Interaction of deaf and hearing preschool children. *Journal of Communication Disorders, 12*, 245–251.

Barton, E.J., & Osborne, J.G. (1978). The development of classroom sharing by a teacher using positive practice. *Behaviour Modification, 2*(2), 231–249.

Bess, F.H., & McConnell, F.E. (1981). *Audiology, education and the hearing impaired child*. St. Louis: C.V. Mosby.

Brackett, D., & Henniges, M. (1976). Communicative interaction of preschool hearing-impaired children in an integrated setting. *The Volta Review, 78*, 276–285.

Cheskin, A. (1982). The use of language by hearing mothers of deaf children. *Journal of Communication Disorders, 15*, 145–153.

Cheskin, A. (1983). The verbal environment provided by hearing mothers for their young deaf children. *Journal of Communication Disorders, 14*, 485–496.

Craig, W.N., & Collins, J.L. (1970). Analysis of communicative interaction in classes for deaf children. *American Annals of the Deaf, 115*, 79–85.

Elssmann, S.F., Sabo, M.P., & Matkin, N.D. (April, 1987). Early identification and habilitation of hearing-impaired children: Fact or fiction? *Proceedings of 1987 symposium in audiology* (pp. 1–34). Rochester, MN: Mayo Clinic-Mayo Foundation.

Henggeler, S.W., & Cooper, P.F. (1983). Deaf child-hearing mother interaction: Extensiveness and reciprocity. *Journal of Pediatric Psychology, 8*, 83–98.

Higginbotham, D.J., & Baker, B. (1981). Social participation and cognitive play differences in hearing-impaired and normally hearing preschoolers. *The Volta Review, 83*, 135–149.

Higginbotham, D.J., Baker, B.M., & Neill, R.D. (1980). Assessing the social participation and cognitive play abilities of hearing-impaired preschoolers. *The Volta Review, 82*(5), 261–270.

Kreimeyer, K., & Antia, S. (1988). The development and generalization of social interaction skills in preschool hearing-impaired children. *The Volta Review, 90*(4), 219–231.

Kreimeyer, K.H., Antia, S.D., & Eldredge, N. (1989). *Social skills intervention procedures*. Unpublished manuscript, University of Arizona.

Kretschmer, R., & Kretschmer L. (1978). *Language development and intervention with the hearing-impaired*. Baltimore: University Park Press.

Lederberg, A., Ryan, H.B., & Robbins, B. (1986). Peer interaction in young deaf children: The effect of partner hearing status and familiarity. *Developmental Psychology, 22*(5), 691–700.

Levy-Shiff, R., & Hoffman, M. (1985). Social behaviour of hearing-impaired and normally-hearing preschoolers. *British Journal of Educational Psychology,* *55,* 111–118.

McAnnally, P.L., Rose, S., & Quigley, S.P. (1987). *Language learning practices with deaf children.* Boston: College-Hill.

McCauley, R.W., Bruininks, R.H., & Kennedy, P. (1976). Behavioral interactions of hearing-impaired children in regular classrooms. *The Journal of Special Education, 10,* 277–284.

McKirdy, L., & Blank, M. (1982). Dialogue in deaf and hearing preschoolers. *Journal of Speech and Hearing Research, 25,* 487–499.

Meadow, K.P., Greenberg, M.T., Erting, C., & Carmichael, H. (1981). Interactions of deaf mothers and deaf preschool children: Comparisons with three other groups of deaf and hearing dyads. *American Annals of the Deaf, 126,* 454–467.

Moores, D. (1987). *Educating the deaf: Psychology, principles and practices.* Boston: Houghton Mifflin.

Paul, P.V., & Quigley, S.P. (1990). *Education and deafness.* White Plains, NY: Longman.

Ries, P. (1986). Characteristics of hearing-impaired youth in the general population and of students in special education programs for the hearing impaired. In A.N. Schildroth & M.A. Karchner (Eds.), *Deaf children in America* (pp. 1–32). San Diego: College-Hill.

Shafer, M.S., Egel, A.L., & Neef, N.A. (1984). Training mildly handicapped peers to facilitate changes in the social interaction skills of autistic children. *Journal of Applied Behavior Analysis, 17,* 461–476.

Soderhan, A.K., & Whiren, A.P. (1985). Mainstreaming the young hearing-impaired child: An intensive study. *Journal of Rehabilitation of the Deaf, 18*(3), 7–14.

Snow, C.E. (1981). Social interaction and language acquisition. In P. Dale & D. Ingram (Eds.), *Child language: An international perspective.* Baltimore: University Park Press.

Stone, P. (1988). *Blueprint for developing conversational competence: A planning/instruction model with detailed scenarios.* Washington, DC: A.G. Bell Association.

Strain, P.S., Kerr, M.M., & Ragland, E.V. (1979). Effects of peer-mediated social initiations and prompting/reinforcement procedures on the social behavior of autistic children. *Journal of Autism and Developmental Disabilities, 9*(1), 41–54.

Terrell, B.Y. (1985). Learning the rules of the game: Discourse skills in early childhood. In D.N. Ripich & F.M. Spinelli (Eds.), *School discourse problems* (pp. 13–27). San Diego: College-Hill.

Vandell, D.L., Anderson, L.D., Ehrhardt, G., & Wilson, K.S. (1982). Integrating hearing and deaf preschoolers: An attempt to enhance hearing children's interactions with deaf peers. *Child Development, 53,* 1354–1363.

Vandell, D., & George, L. (1981). Social interaction in hearing and deaf preschoolers: Successes and failures in initiations. *Child Development, 52,* 627–635.

Wedell-Monig, J., & Lumley, J.M. (1980). Child deafness and mother child interaction. *Child Development, 51,* 766–774.

Wood, D.J., Wood, H., Griffiths, A., & Howarth, I. (1986). *Teaching and talking with deaf children.* New York: John Wiley & Sons.

Wood, D.J., Wood, H.A., Griffiths, A., Howarth S.P., & Howarth, I. (1982).

The structure of conversations with 6- to 10-year-old deaf children. *Journal of Child Psychology and Psychiatry, 23,* 295–308.

Wood, H.A., & Wood, D.J. (1984). An experimental evaluation of the effects of five styles of teacher conversation on the language of hearing-impaired children. *Journal of Child Psychology and Psychiatry, 25,* 45–62.

7

The Social Functioning of Children with Visual Impairments

Annette C. Skellenger, Mary-Maureen Hill, and Everett Hill

For the majority of people in the world the process of attaining the multiple and complex skills that support social competence occurs naturally through observation and practice of day-to-day experiences. As with children who have other disabling conditions, however, the natural development of these skills is delayed for many children with visual impairments. Absence or impairment of the visual sensory modality, which has been estimated to be responsible for transmitting up to 85% of the information people receive (Hill & Blasch, 1980; Telford & Sawrey, 1977), increases the difficulty of interpreting an already complex world. The reduction of visually observable information affects substantially an individual's ability to learn incidentally skills that contribute to social competence (see Chapter 1). Also, as with children with other disabling conditions, the development of social competence of children with visual impairments may require the implementation of interventions to promote social skills.

Although the development of strategies for increasing the social skills of children with other disabling conditions has become the focus of many current researchers (see Odom, McConnell, & McEvoy, Chapter 1, this volume), fewer studies have focused on children with visual impairments. In order to suggest strategies that may be useful for children with visual impairments, this chapter examines some of the factors that affect the social functioning of children with visual impairments and reports on research on the social skills of these individuals. Studies that have examined interventions used with children with visual impairments, as well as strategies used with children with other disabling conditions, provide the basis for a discussion regarding the design of future interventions to increase the social competence of children with visual impairments.

THE IMPACT OF VISUAL IMPAIRMENT ON INFORMATION PROCESSING

The first and most basic component of any learning process is the collection of information through sensory channels. The visual sense is the most versatile of the major senses and provides a substantial proportion and variety of input in the information collection process. Impairment of this sensory modality, therefore, affects a child's ability to gain basic information about and through the environment. Disruption at the initial stage of the learning process has a pervasive and crucial impact on all areas of development (Warren, 1984).

Children with disabling conditions other than visual impairment typically demonstrate the ability to intake visual sensory information about their social environment but experience difficulty either in determining the meaning of the information received, acting upon it, or both (see Odom, McConnell, & McEvoy, Chapter 1, this volume). As a result, interventions with these children have fostered the acquisition of social interaction skills by directly teaching specific skills to children with disabilities or by teaching nondisabled children strategies for increasing and highlighting their social initiations during interaction with children who have disabilities (see McEvoy, Odom, & McConnell, Chapter 5, this volume).

For the child with a visual impairment, the process of social functioning is restricted even before the child has need to process or act upon socially relevant information. Predictably, young children with visual impairments typically demonstrate disruptions in social functioning regardless of mental ability or other impairment, unlike children with other disabling conditions whose lowered social functioning may be related to the mental age or severity of the disabling condition (Guralnick, 1981). In addition, the initial restriction in the visual collection of information may result in lowered ability to process and act upon any other information that *is* available to them (e.g., verbalizations of peers, social toys). For example, understanding the context of the social interaction, which is vital information for choosing an appropriate initiation or response, clearly is restricted by visual impairments. Moreover, for children with visual impairments, the spiralling of effects of not being able to be involved actively in a peer social group, as may be experienced by children with other disabilities (see Odom, McConnell, & McEvoy, Chapter 1, this volume), compounds even further the impact of this basic restriction of information.

In addition to the limitations that result from reduced or absent visual input, further restrictions exist in the insufficient information that hearing provides about the social environment. Researchers including Fraiberg (1977) and Burlingham (1961, 1964, 1979) have recognized and emphasized that auditory input alone provides insufficient motivation and direction for most early skills of children with visual impairments. For the most part, the young, preverbal child with a visual impairment is unable to obtain meaning from and, therefore, make use of sound unless it is consistently associated with tactile cues. Since very few sounds occur naturally in this manner (e.g., the mother's voice or sound of a toy may be distant), opportunities for practicing social skills are severely restricted. Other qualities of sound, such as limited information regarding directionality, cause and effect, and intentionality, also restrict the amount of information available to support social functioning throughout life. As a result, young children with visual impairments are likely to have difficulty moving from an egocentric interpretation of their environment (Sacks, 1988) and many fall into patterns of passivity (Burlingham, 1965; Sandler, 1963). Limitations in sensory input experienced by children with visual impairments are then further compounded by the inadequacy of the remaining sensory channels. These limitations also enter the spiralling pattern of barriers that the young child with a visual impairment must overcome to experience social competence.

"Visual impairment" encompasses a very wide range of visual ability. Individuals with visual acuity of 20/200 or less in the better eye after correction, or with a visual field less than 20° are defined as legally blind, and as such are eligible for educational services in most areas. Although children with similar visual acuity display a wide range of visual functioning (i.e., behavior related to vision use) an acuity of 20/200 often enables the individual to read enlarged print and move around familiar areas without contacting objects. Other children may have field restrictions; for example, they can have relatively clear vision but experience what commonly is termed "tunnel vision."

Access to information to support social functioning therefore also varies among children with visual impairments. Whereas one child may be totally limited to auditory or tactile cues, another may have a small amount of visual information clearly available; yet another may have unrestricted access to information as long as it occurs within a few feet.

When discussing visual impairment it is common to think of children who are totally blind. In fact, the majority of research on children with visual impairments has been conducted with individuals who had virtually no residual vision (Skellenger, 1990). This research provides the basis for this chapter. However, the design of programs to remediate delays in children with visual impairments, unfortunately, cannot be based solely on information that is so clearcut. Children with low vision (i.e., those with some degree of remaining vision) make up the majority of the total population of children with visual impairments (Barraga, 1976). They face multiple and complex problems related to their particular degree and type of vision loss. In highly individual ways these problems affect their ability to function socially (Jose, 1983). It is beyond the scope of this chapter to explore the very unique aspects of low vision and its relationship to social competence. However, this area clearly is in need of research in the future.

FACTORS THAT AFFECT SOCIAL COMPETENCE OF CHILDREN WITH VISUAL IMPAIRMENTS

Numerous skills have been identified by researchers as integral for functioning competently in social situations with peers. Many of these skills are social behaviors used directly in social settings, whereas others support or mediate successful social functioning. Restricted information that results from limited visual input can affect the ability of the young child with a visual impairment to achieve success in each of these skill areas, as described in the following sections.

Impact on Skills that Directly Support Social Competence

Facial and body movements play a large part in communicative interactions of sighted individuals. The importance of such skills is particularly obvious during the prelinguistic months of an infant's life, but these skills continue to have an impact on social competence throughout life.

Prior to the beginning of verbal communication, a major portion of the interaction between sighted infants and caregivers occurs through nonverbal, visually-mediated behaviors, such as eye contact, shared gaze, pointing, and facial expressions (Ainsworth, Blehar, Waters, & Wall, 1978; Bates, Benigni, Bretherton, Camaioni, & Volterra, 1977; Field, 1982). In addition to the immediate communicative message carried in such behaviors, these skills are extremely important in establishing children's understanding and control of their social environment (Tait, 1972a). Children learn the "give and take" in communication, as well as learning their role in such exchanges. The child's competence in such skills has also been found to be extremely important to caregivers' emotional and communicative responsiveness (Goldberg, 1977; Lamb & Easterbrooks, 1981), and is necessary for the establishment of patterns of reciprocity embedded in these early processes. Furthermore, children with visual impairments who show gaze direction have been evaluated by their sighted agemates as having higher social competence, as being more intelligent, and as possessing greater ability to compete with sighted individuals as adults (Raver, 1987a).

Studies of the communicative patterns between parents and their infants with visual impairments, however, indicate the overall failure of infants, as well as their caregivers, to use nonverbal behaviors that mediate the initiation and maintenance of interactions (Imamura, 1965; Kekelis & Andersen, 1984; Preisler, 1988). In addition, the results of a comparative study of 30 sighted and visually-impaired children, 5–15 years of age indicated that the children with visual impairments did not use nonverbal behaviors comparable to their sighted peers (Parke, Shallcross, & Anderson, 1980).

In social interactions with peers and other partners, children with severe visual impairments are limited by their inability to both receive *and* produce nonverbal behaviors that support and often supplant verbal communication. They are severely limited in the ability to utilize physical cues and controls such as permission to take a turn in the conversation or facial expressions that negate a spoken message. Additionally, children with visual impairments have limited ability to indicate their interest in the topic (or individual) through facial expressions or to signal through body positioning a desire for the conversation to end. Without kinesthetic cues, both the child and social partner are further restricted in their ability to monitor continuously the effects of their communication or behavior on each other. Many interactions are even influenced by nonverbal cues that occur as one partner moves toward the other or watches from another side of the room. Once again, individuals with visual impairments are severely restricted in their ability to practice social competence both through the initial restricted intake of sensory information and throughout social interaction.

Although nonverbal communication continues to have an impact on social functioning throughout life, another major component of social interactions after the first year of life is the ability to engage in verbal communication. Children with visual impairments typically display age-appropriate verbal ability and have been reported to achieve appropriate language development milestones (Warren, 1984). It would seem that this is one area in which young children with visual impairments are not restricted in social situations and, indeed, many children with visual impairments excel in their ability to converse with other individuals. Evidence suggests, however, that this is also an area that proves difficult for many young children with visual impairments. Persons with visual impairments have been identified as using interaction behaviors that are characteristically different from those of sighted individuals, and mild to severe disruptions in communications have been found to exist between individuals with visual impairments and sighted individuals (Apple, 1972).

Children with visual impairments, like the majority of children with other disabling conditions, apparently have difficulty beginning conversations and have been found to initiate interactions at much lower rates than agemates who do not have disabilities (Hoben & Lindstrom, 1980; Rogers & Puchalski, 1984). In addition, evidence suggests that once conversation is begun, children with visual impairments also tend to engage in communication behaviors that may negatively affect social interchange (Kekelis, 1988a). Through naturalistic observations, young children with visual impairments were observed to make an inordinate number of demands on their partners and would abruptly shift topics rather than respond to the concerns of others (Andersen, Dunlea, & Kekelis, 1984). Young children with visual impairments also have demonstrated an inability to move beyond simple greetings and requests for information and ask numerous and repetitive questions (Erin, 1986; Mulford, 1983). Their focus remains primarily on their own interests and actions (Dunlea, 1982), and they often do not respond to others' communication attempts (Andersen et al., 1984). In addition, when children with visual impairments wish to become engaged in communication, they tend to reject their peers and seek out teachers or assistants for conversation (Kekelis, 1988a; Parsons, 1986a; Tait, 1972a,b). Furthermore, the failure of *both* partners to initiate, interpret, or respond appropriately to communication has been discussed repeatedly (Adelson, 1983; Andersen et al., 1984; Fraiberg, 1977; Kekelis, 1988a; Rowland, 1984; Urwin, 1978). Thus, the impact of visual loss on social functioning can begin at the very early preverbal stages of interaction and continue to grow in complexity.

Impact on Skills that Mediate Social Functioning

One area of learning is believed to be that which occurs through the support and result of parallel learning in other domains (Piaget,

1952). Development of social competence both requires and results in development in related skill areas such as language and cognition (see Guralnick, Chapter 2, this volume). Limitations in social functioning may also be the result of, and may result in, limited competence in other areas. For children with visual impairments, the impact occurs in areas closely related to social functioning, as well as in areas that are less often associated with social skill.

The need to manage or control the environment is one area not typically associated with social functioning; yet, it is closely tied to the acquisition of social competence for children with visual impairments (Sacks, 1988). Even a relatively simple skill, such as maintaining control over play materials, has been reported to affect the social functioning of young children with visual impairments. Children have been observed to spend the majority of their play periods sitting facing the toy shelves with their backs to their peers, or refusing attempts at interaction for fear of their more boisterous peers inadvertently or intentionally removing toys from their possession (Kekelis & Sacks, 1988; Preisler & Palmer, 1988).

Difficulty in management and control of the environment through efficient, independent mobility presents major obstacles to success for individuals with visual impairment. Children with visual impairments often experience delay and difficulty in nearly all areas of independent movement. Many children with visual impairments do not take their first independent steps before the age of 3 or 4 years (Fraiberg, 1977; Norris, Spaulding, & Brodie, 1957), and for many children with visual impairments this is their first independent movement since, typically, they do not crawl before learning to walk. Even after independent movement is established, many children are limited in their independence by fear, overprotection from parents, lack of visual cues to provide motivation, and restricted ability to orient to and monitor their location.

In addition to the negative impact on overall development, problems with mobility can affect social functioning in multiple ways. Young children with visual impairments often have severely limited opportunities to interact with peers, or other social targets, because of their tendency to be inactive, as well as their limited ability to locate and move to places where social interaction is occurring or might occur. For the child who does attempt to locate social partners, the process of locating and safely moving to their location is complex and time-consuming. In typical childhood settings, social targets rarely remain in one location for any measurable length of time, so that the child with visual impairments, *if* successful in locating and moving to social targets, has limited time in which to interact. In addition, since children with visual impairments lack the opportunity visually to locate their friends from a distance and signal their interest, they are also limited in their ability to bring others to their own location. Frustrating free play or recess periods are but one situation in which mobility limitations can have a severe impact on the social functioning of young children with visual impairments.

Another area more often associated with social success, yet of particular importance to children with visual impairments, is the ability to learn and practice social skills through visually-mediated processes, such as social referencing and imitation (Bandura & Walters, 1963; Fenson & Ramsey, 1980; Meltzoff & Moore, 1977; Walden & Ogan, 1988). At virtually any moment when two people can be observed together the potential exists for a child to observe appropriate or inappropriate ways to interact with another. The sighted, typically-developing child has nearly continuous access to information that can be stored for use at a later time. Not only is this information severely limited for the child with visual impairments, but information available through the remaining sensory modalities is ambiguous and difficult to interpret. The child with visual impairment has few examples available to provide motivation, direction, and assurance to support successful social interaction.

Childhood play, one of the most common vehicles for practice and refinement of social skills, also presents restrictions for children with visual impairments. In her research, Tait (1972a,b) found very immature play skills: a 12–18 month level in children with visual impairments as old as 9 years of age. Young children with visual impairments often spend a high proportion of their play periods in perseverative, self-stimulatory behaviors (Fraiberg, 1977; Parsons, 1986a,b; Preisler, 1988; Preisler & Palmer, 1988; Sokolow, 1983) or tend to seek out a teacher or other adult with whom to become engaged (Parsons, 1986a,b; Tait, 1972a,b). Furthermore, children who do desire to become involved in group play activities are limited in their ability visually to monitor play groups and receive visual permission to enter the group, a crucial factor in the play of sighted children (Cosaro, 1979; Puttalez & Gottman, 1981). In addition to severely restricting the amount of peer interaction that can occur, such limitations also have a negative impact on peer acceptance. Failure to become engaged appropriately with play objects and playmates, in addition to affecting current social practice, also severely limits other benefits of play, such as cognitive growth and language development (see Chapter 1). This in turn affects higher level social skill practice, such as trying out social roles through sociodramatic play.

The studies noted in this section present but a few examples of the pervasive, accelerating effects of visual impairment on social competence. Virtually every area of functioning relies heavily on visual input, and each of these areas can have individual and cumulative impact on successful social functioning.

DEVELOPMENT OF SOCIAL SKILLS
IN YOUNG CHILDREN WITH VISUAL IMPAIRMENTS

Knowledge of behaviors that children with visual impairments display in social situations should direct the choice of social skills interventions and strategies. Unfortunately, very little research exists on the development of peer-related social skills in children with visual impairments. Even less has been published on interventions that might be implemented to increase or otherwise affect social functioning in peer interactions. Because much of the research that is available suffers from methodological flaws, such as small, inadequately defined, heterogenous samples and failure to control for confounding variables such as degree of vision and institutional status (Skellenger, 1990), results must be considered with caution. In addition, generalization and correspondence to other populations is severely limited due to an overall reliance on case or naturalistic studies. Furthermore, information specific to peer social functioning in the preschool years has emerged only since the late 1980s. Much of what has been described about the social functioning of preschool children with visual impairments has been the result of comparative analysis of standardized measures of overall social competence, observation of adult-child communicative interactions, and descriptions of elementary-age or older individuals.

In one of the few comprehensive reviews of social development, Warren (1984) reported on multiple studies published prior to the early 1980s. These studies incorporated the use of social scales such as the Maxfield-Fjeld (1942), Maxfield-Buchholz (1957), and Vineland Social Quotient (Doll, 1953) as measures of the overall social competence of children with visual impairments. Use of such scales resulted in findings that described children with visual impairments as scoring lower than either sighted or deaf children (Bradway, 1937). Partially sighted children scored higher than totally blind children (Bauman, 1973; Maxfield & Fjeld, 1942), and children in itinerant or mainstreamed settings scored higher than children in residential or segregated settings (McGuinness, 1970; Schindele, 1974).

Parent-Child Interactions

Further information on the social functioning of children with visual impairments has been obtained from studies of the communicative patterns of interaction between parents and their preschool children with visual impairments. Rogers and Puchalski (1984) found that 4- to 25-month-old infants with visual impairments engaged in more intervals of no response, more negative affect, and fewer positive responses than same-age, sighted infants. Marked differences occurred in the frequency and type of initiation of topic or interaction. Other researchers have documented that initiations by children with visual impairments occur much less frequently than for sighted children (Imamura, 1965; Kekelis & Andersen, 1984; Rogers & Puchalski, 1984), and a much greater proportion of infants with visual impairments do not initiate at all (Rogers & Puchalski, 1984). Many of the initiations made by the preschoolers with visual impairments have been characterized as "monotonous and repetitious" (Imamura, 1965, p. 236). These children often do not vocalize at expected times (Rowland, 1984); are much more likely to submit to the dominant behaviors of their mothers than are sighted children (Imamura, 1965); and engage in high levels of vocal play that is noncommunicative (Kitzinger, 1987).

Preisler (1988), through monthly observations of the interactions of 16 parent-child dyads across a 2-year period, reported that infants with visual impairments who were 8–9 months of age were observed to initiate contact occasionally, but parents took the leading role in most dialogues and contacts. At 10–12 months, although communicative intent of the infants' body movements or repeated actions was occasionally recognized, most often they were misinterpreted by the parents. By 13–14 months the infants began to take a greater role in turn-taking situations; however, they often chose to focus on newly acquired motor abilities rather than participating in interactions with the parents, and parents often reported feelings of rejection during this period. Children at 15–19 months spent many of their interactions with their parents in vocal exploration, both original and in imitation of their parents' sounds. Body movements and vocalizations were supplemented with spoken language at 20–24 months. At all levels, Priesler reported reciprocity to be a major stumbling point in interactions. In effect, the parent maintained control of the interaction, thus limiting the children's participation to response only.

Despite design and methodological limitations in the research, a consistent picture of impaired social functioning emerges from the small number of studies available in the literature. Even long before the young child has the occasion to interact with peers, social and communicative interactions are notably restricted in number and quality.

Peer Interactions

Much of what is known about the social competence of children with visual impairments in peer interactions is based almost entirely on studies of school-age children. These studies generally present a picture similar to that found in studies of parent-child interactions.

Children with visual impairments have been found to score in low ranges on measures of social acceptance. When classmates of 20 mainstreamed children with visual impairments in grades 4–6 completed sociometric ratings, the students with visual impairments tended to fall below the class medians in most areas (Jones, Lavine, & Shell, 1972). In addition, those sighted children who gave higher rankings of their peers with visual impairments also received low rankings by other classmates. Furthermore, children with visual impairments were found to be rejected by their classmates to a significantly greater extent than other groups of elementary-age children with disabling conditions (Jones & Chiba, 1985).

In an observational study of 22 children with visual impairments (acuities of 20/20 to 20/200) mainstreamed into grades 1–12 (Hoben & Lindstrom, 1980), students with visual impairments engaged in fewer interactions with classmates than their peers who did not have disabilities. Results indicated that nearly half, that is, 45%, of the students with visual impairments had fewer than 10 interactions, as compared with 9% of their sighted peers. In addition, eight students with visual impairments, but none of their sighted peers, engaged in no interactions during the total observation period. The relatively low frequency of social interactions apparently was influenced further by the response behavior of the children with visual impairments. Only 14% of the peers who did not have disabilities were observed to make fewer than 10 responses to their peers' initiations, as compared with 54% of the children with visual impairments. In addition, teachers in this study reported perceiving the children with visual impairments as spending more of their noninstructional time alone, waiting to be approached by classmates.

A naturalistic study of four kindergarten-level children with visual impairments ranging from total to legal blindness provides a narrative picture of each child's situation and thematic discussion of their social functioning (Kekelis & Sacks, 1988). Although specific behaviors across the four children varied with differences in classroom conditions and child-specific factors, each child was described as experiencing difficulties in social interactions. Behaviors included misunderstood or incomplete communications, solitary and aimless wandering, and willful rejection by peers or by the children with visual impairments themselves. Both the children with visual impairments and their classmates were observed to have difficulty monitoring the attention of their partners, often talked about topics not of interest to the other, and often were ignored. The sighted and visually impaired kindergartners also were observed to fail to respond at points in conversation, and neither party attempted to repair the frequent breakdowns in communication.

In another study teachers and aides in both residential and mainstreamed classrooms rated three functionally blind kindergartners on approximately 40 social subskills (Read, 1989). The subskill divisions were: 1) participating in actions with others; 2) maintaining relationships; and 3) developing assertiveness, classroom, and cafeteria skills. While the children's scores varied considerably, common weaknesses were found most often in the category of maintaining relationships. Common major problem areas included use of body language, offering help, complimenting others, and recognizing others' behaviors.

In the only report specifically describing peer interactions of preschool children with visual impairments, Kekelis (1988a) provided naturalistic observations of the peer interaction behaviors of a 3½-year-old girl who was totally blind. She attended a regular preschool and a preschool program for children with visual impairments on alternate days of the week. Although the settings, adults, and number and personalities of the other children in each program differed significantly, only small differences were described in the child's peer interactions between the two settings. Descriptions include examples of normal social interactions between the child and her family, as well as examples of some positive peer interactions in each preschool setting. The interactions that occurred in the regular preschool program, however, were limited in frequency and duration. The success of interactions appeared to be affected by a number of factors, including nearly continuous presence of an adult, failure of sighted peers to read and respond to the blind child's intentions, and occasional failure to interact or outright rejection of involvement in interactions by the child herself. Positive interactions in the classroom with children who had visual impairments also were limited, primarily through the child's preference for solitary play over interaction with her classmates. A similar picture has been provided by Preisler and Palmer (1988) through incidental reports of difficulties experienced during attempts to mainstream six preschoolers with visual impairments into a regular nursery-school program in Sweden. Teachers reported the children's behaviors as deviant and inadequate. The children, ages 2 and 3 years, sat motionless in the midst of boisterous activities and often physically rejected interactions with their peers.

Although information specifically describing peer-peer social functioning of preschool-age children with visual impairments is limited, a picture of their social skills is beginning to emerge. These children tend to engage in low levels of interaction and rarely initiate interaction; when they do occur, interactions frequently are thwarted by the children's failure to respond to the social partner.

Recognition of the impact of restricted visual input on development, as well as the ways in which visual restrictions manifest themselves in the social skills of young children with visual impairments, make a compelling argument for the need for intervention in this area. In addition, such information provides an important basis on which to make decisions about the development of strategies and techniques to affect social competence.

DESIGN OF INTERVENTIONS TO INCREASE SOCIAL SKILLS OF YOUNG CHILDREN WITH VISUAL IMPAIRMENTS

Despite compelling rationale, documentation of delay, and repeated arguments for provision of instruction in social skills (Kekelis, 1988b; Parke et al., 1980; Read, 1989), programs designed to intervene in the social functioning of children with visual impairments have begun to appear in the literature only since the late 1980s. For the most part, systematic examinations of social skills interventions have targeted adolescents and adults almost exclusively (Kekelis, 1988b; Skellenger, 1990). Training in discrete physical skills that support social functioning, such as posture, facial expressions, and eye gaze, have been a primary goal of interventions with adolescents and adults (Howze, 1987; Raver, 1987b; Raver & Dwyer, 1986). Another major portion of the intervention literature has focused on reduction of behaviors that interfere with social interactions (e.g., stereotypies). Interventions of this type have had generally positive results, although the success of these interventions for maintaining the targeted skills across time has yet to be tested.

A much smaller body of literature that focused on interactional skills, such as initiation and duration of interaction, has produced more ambiguous results. Although these studies point toward the general success of interventions to increase the social interactions of children with visual impairments and their peers, methodological issues have limited the clarity of the results.

Through one training program that utilized taped instruction and role-playing, children with visual impairments received training in social behaviors such as meeting persons, sharing and helping, and resolving arguments (Jones & Chiba, 1985). No significant differences were found for the targeted children with visual impairments on any of the observational measures of social interactions. In addition, success of the training program was lower for children with visual impairments than it was for targeted children with other disabling conditions.

In another study, Sacks and Gaylord-Ross (1988) attempted to compare the effectiveness of two techniques for increasing both concomitant physical behaviors (i.e., gaze direction and body posture) and interactive behaviors such as positive social initiations and joining and sharing in group activities. Fifteen legally blind children, 7–12 years old, were divided into three groups. Groups were matched by age, gender, grade level, and amount of vision, and all participants were described as possessing average intelligence. Five children each were assigned to control, peer-mediated, and teacher-directed intervention conditions. Similar amounts and schedules of training were conducted in both intervention conditions. A multiple baseline across behaviors was used to evaluate changes in social behavior. Both types of social skills training were superior to the no intervention condition, and the peer-mediated condition produced more powerful effects than teacher-direction. A number of other factors, however, such as differences in teacher styles, may have affected the results. This study, then, can be taken as merely a beginning point for information regarding social skills intervention for children with visual impairments.

Sisson, Van Hasselt, Hersen, and Strain (1985) conducted a study of the peer-mediated approach to increase socially appropriate play behavior of 9- to 11-year-old children with multiple disabilities, including visual impairments. They also reported positive results, with gains being maintained at a 4-month follow-up. However, these authors did not examine generalization of behaviors to untrained peers or social validity.

A case study/A-B-A design implemented to increase playground interactions with sighted schoolmates (Kekelis, 1988c) is the only reported intervention study involving a preschool child with a visual impairment. The frequency of social initiations by the child's classmates increased through the use of an activity table equipped with high interest toys. Observational data indicated that the activity table acted as a "social prosthesis" by enabling the child to maintain control over the toys and prompting other children to remain in the area of the table, thus motivating increase in their initiations to the target child. Although the strength of these indications was limited by numerous scientific flaws, the study presents an intriguing approach to intervention in that it addresses factors specific to children with visual impairments.

Despite their limitations, these studies provide a basis upon which to design intervention strategies for children with visual impairments.

SUGGESTED STRATEGIES FROM INTERVENTIONS DESIGNED FOR CHILDREN WITH OTHER DISABLING CONDITIONS

As discussed previously, one of the major effects of visual impairment on children's social skills comes from the pervasive and cyclical impact on the child of having restricted sensory input on which to base his or her behavior. In addition to severely restricting the incidental, natural development of social skills, sensory processing limitations also reduce the modes through which one can intervene in the social competence of children with visual impairments. Many interventions designed for children with other disabling conditions depend at least in part on visually-mediated strategies. Adaptation or modification of many of the techniques described elsewhere in this book, therefore, may be required to address some of the unique needs of children with visual impairments.

Environmental Arrangements/Incidental Strategies

The use of environmental arrangement strategies (see Sainato & Carta, Chapter 4, this volume) can circumvent some of the restrictions experienced by children with visual impairments. In a play area of restricted size (i.e., to approximately 10 feet × 10 feet), children have less need for extensive orientation and mobility skills, may have more control over the environment, and can more easily gain access to playmates and materials. In addition, a smaller play area places less dependence on a child's need to utilize nonverbal signals to bring others to his or her own location and increases the probability of children remaining in interactions once they are begun.

By selecting play materials carefully, a teacher or other adult may highlight the capabilities of the child with a visual impairment, thus increasing the child's feelings of control and increasing the likelihood that the child will initiate to peers. Selection of high interest materials may produce shared interest and discussion among peers, and attention to the characteristics of the materials may reduce self-stimulatory or other asocial behaviors (Flavell, 1973; Hopper & Wambold, 1978; Wambold & Bailey, 1979). Creative modification of environmental techniques, such as the activity table described by Kekelis (1988c), can address specific needs of children with visual impairments by further reducing the need for related nonsocial skills such as mobility and reducing the social complexities of especially difficult playground environments.

Other manipulations that focus on the play setting may also indirectly affect social skills. Teachers and parents of children with visual impairments often select toys that have audible or tactual qualities. Although the careful selection of toys in this manner is appropriate and necessary for children who continuously fail to engage in toy play, it is important that teachers attend to the age-appropriateness of materials. A majority of toys with audible or tactual enhancements have been designed primarily for typically developing infants. In addition to these toys being highly age-inappropriate for preschoolers and kindergartners, their simplicity allows limited involvement and invites perseverative, repetitive actions. Even audibly or tactually interesting toys that have been designed for use by older children (i.e., audibly enhanced materials such as sizzling frying pans or electronic games) may elicit self-stimulatory behaviors because the children may selectively attend to the sensory qualities of the toys. Although these toys may bring simple enjoyment and relaxation to children with visual impairments, they also reduce the opportunity for interactions with others in the play setting by drawing a child's interest so directly to the play material. In addition, the perseverative, self-stimulatory behaviors, which so often occur in the use of these toys, reduce the child's acceptability to peers.

A variety of toys, then, should be made available to children with visual impairments. As much as possible, infant toys should be phased out and replaced with more developmentally advanced, age-appropriate toys, such as housekeeping toys; cars and trucks; and zoo, farm, and other pretend play sets. However, the literature suggests that children with visual impairments spend high proportions of their play periods unengaged with peers *or* materials (Parsons, 1986a,b; Tait, 1972a,b). Access to higher level play materials alone may not increase higher level play skills or social interaction without additional intervention. Therefore, it is important that teachers have a systematic plan for supporting their students' use of age-appropriate, socially acceptable toys. Despite some indications that adult involvement in play activities may reduce many of the positive benefits of play (Field, 1980; Silver & Ramsey, 1983), teachers of children with visual impairments may need to find ways systematically to involve themselves in the play of their students in order to promote appropriate play (Chance, 1979; Linder, 1990; Musselwhite, 1986), with the purpose of also increasing peer social interaction. Many early educators have made excellent suggestions of ways to support play, both with typically-developing children (Bergen, 1988; Cherry, 1976; Jeffree, McConkey, & Hewson, 1977; Johnson, Christie, & Yawkey, 1987) and children with disabling conditions (Lear, 1977; Musselwhite, 1986). Also, for children with severely delayed play skills and limited independent movement, it may be that alternatives to outdoor recesses should be arranged to allow practice in object and social interaction. Even beyond the preschool years, it may be that activities such as periods of indoor, semi-structured play or activities used in cooperative group learning strategies (Bina, 1986) should be scheduled regularly.

Techniques for use other than in the play setting may also be incorporated. One relatively simple approach is periodically rotating seating arrangements or working groups to facilitate contact between children with visual impairments and a variety of peers (Kekelis & Sacks, 1988). Also, amount and type of adult support can be monitored carefully and altered continuously to fit the child's needs. The importance of adjusting adult direction and support is especially evident in situations in which an aide remains with a child one-on-one throughout the school day. Although intensive support may be necessary at many points, such as for facilitation of initial learning and transitioning, at many other points the constant presence of an adult severely restricts the opportunity for social interaction with peers, as well as other important experiences. In settings where adult involvement is not crucial, adults can withdraw temporarily or request peer facilitation.

Peer-Mediated and Other Systematic Approaches

In most instances, more systematic approaches, such as the peer-mediated interventions that Sacks and Gaylord-Ross (1988) employed, will provide the greatest benefit for children with visual impairments. Children with visual impairments, like their peers with other disabling conditions, can learn many skills from typically developing peers when carefully structured techniques are implemented. While many of the techniques for social competence intervention described by other authors in this book can and should be used with children who have visual impairments, it may be that intervention addressing additional skills should be incorporated in peer-mediated intervention designed for children with visual impairments.

Effectiveness of peer-mediated strategies may be based upon the peers' understanding of and ability to compensate for the effect of restricted sensory input, in addition to having the typical focus on skills to increase social initiations. Peer training might include a discussion of: 1) strategies for unobtrusively providing environmental information that will facilitate the target child's interactions; 2) discussion of the absence of eye contact, nonverbal cues, and other physical behaviors; 3) the necessity of initiating and responding in absence of those behaviors; and 4) the causes of breakdowns in communication and techniques for repairing breakdowns when they occur (Kekelis & Sacks, 1988). Prompting peers to allow, and facilitate, the target child's access and control over materials, and teaching peers methods for assisting children with visual impairments to decrease the tendency to rely on verbalizations rather than actions could also be important features of an intervention.

In addition to changes in peer involvement, more extensive adult involvement may be necessary, particularly at the initial stages of an intervention. Adult involvement may include longer, more extensive training periods for peers; more extensive prompting systems; or physical involvement of the adult as a model in the social setting. It is crucial, however, that the adult not become the target of the children's interactions and that he or she act only to facilitate interaction between the peers. In addition, for intervention to be effective, plans must be incorporated for the systematic and complete withdrawal of adult involvement.

An additional strategy may include the initial use of older playmates as peers to facilitate the withdrawal of initial teacher direction and involvement, and to increase the effectiveness of peer-mediated approaches to intervention. The level of understanding and accommodation necessary to facilitate interactions with children who have visual impairments may be difficult for preschool-age children, who themselves need to focus on learning and practicing new social and play skills. Initial phases of intervention, then, may include high levels of teacher involvement in training, and interactions with older peers. Teacher involvement can be faded and, as children with visual impairments acquire initial social skills under the support of the more capable, older peers, same-age peers may be trained and incorporated into the intervention.

Child-Specific Approaches

As noted earlier, many of the interventions designed for children with visual impairments involve attempting to teach skills that support social functioning directly to the children (i.e., in contrast with peer-mediated interventions). The majority of researchers have used behavior modification techniques to increase skills such as eye gaze and head position (Miller & Miller, 1976; Rapoff, Aultman, & Christopherson, 1980; Raver, 1984, 1987a,b; Raver & Dwyer, 1986; Van Hasselt, Hersen, Kazdin, Simon, & Mastantuono, 1983; Van Hasselt, Simon, & Mastantuono, 1982). However, use of other strategies that focus on direct instruction and practice of social skills by children with social delays are being examined (see McConnell, McEvoy, & Odom, Chapter 11, this volume) and show promise for use with children who have visual impairments. Even young children with visual impairments can understand ways in which limited vision affects their social interactions with peers. Curricula can be designed to include practice in skills such as soliciting joint attention to an activity. In addition, modifications of existing curricula, such as DUSO (Dinkemeyer, 1970), could be used to supplement children's knowledge of correct ways to act in social situations, which they are unable to obtain through observational learning.

CONCLUSION

The strategies presented in this chapter are only a few of the possible strategies that can be designed to increase the social skills of young children with visual impairments. A combination of strategies probably will be required for a successful impact on peer-related social competence, particularly with children who have severe impairments. It may be that effective strategies for increasing nonverbal, physical behaviors that support social interaction should be combined with strategies designed for increasing initiation, social interaction, and appropriate communications. For some children, additional intervention may be required to reduce asocial behaviors such as self-stimulatory or perseverative play. In addition, social skills interventions should be interfaced carefully with interventions in related domains such as daily living skills and orientation and mobility. Interventions that focus on the increase of any one type of social skill in isolation will have limited impact on the overall social competence of children with visual impairments.

The development of social competence that will support successful involvement in the increasingly complex global village of the 1990s and the next century presents a challenge for young children with visual impairments and their peers with other disabling conditions. Obviously, it is unwise to leave the development of social competence of children with disabling conditions to chance. Regardless of the intervention strategies implemented, the most important component for successful improvement of social skills in children with visual impairments is the commitment of teachers and other adults to the absolute necessity of these skills for future success, social and otherwise. Social competence should be valued as a goal for *all* children. Particularly for children with visual impairments, it is important that this goal be addressed by the development and implementation of programs of *systematic* intervention in social skills development.

REFERENCES

Adelson, E. (1983). Precursors of early language development in children blind from birth. In A. Mills (Ed.), *Language acquisition in the blind child* (pp. 1–12). San Diego: College-Hill.

Ainsworth, M.D., Blehar, M.C., Waters, E., & Wall, S. (1978). *Patterns of attachment, a psychological study of the strange situation.* Hillside, NJ: Lawrence Erlbaum Associates.

Andersen, E.S., Dunlea, A., & Kekelis, L.S. (1984). Blind children's language: Resolving some differences. *Journal of Child Language, 11,* 645–664.

Apple, M.M. (1972). Kinesic training for blind persons: A vital means of communication. *New Outlook for the Blind, 66,* 201–208.

Bandura, A., & Walters, R.H. (1963). *Social learning and personality development.* New York: Holt, Rinehart & Winston.

Barraga, N.C. (1976). *Visual handicaps and learning: A developmental approach.* Belmont, CA: Wadsworth Publishing.

Bates, E., Benigni, L., Bretherton, I., Camaioni, L., & Volterra, V. (1977). From gesture to the first work: On cognitive and social prerequisites. In M. Lewis & L. Rosenblum (Eds.), *Interaction, conversation, and the development of language* (pp. 247–307). New York: John Wiley & Sons.

Bauman, M.K. (1973). *The social competency of visually handicapped children.* Paper presented at the conference on The Blind Child in Social Interaction: Developing Relationships with Peers and Adults, New York.

Bergen, D. (Ed.). (1988). *Play as a medium for learning and development: A handbook of theory and practice.* Portsmouth, NH: Heinemann.

Bina, M.J. (1986). Social skills development through cooperative group learning strategies. *Education of the Visually Handicapped, 18,* 27–40.

Bradway, K.P. (1937). Social competence of exceptional children: III, The deaf, the blind, and the crippled. *Exceptional Children, 4,* 64–69.

Burlingham, D. (1961). Some notes on the development of the blind child. *Psychoanalytic Study of the Child, 26,* 121–145.

Burlingham, D. (1964). Hearing and its role in the development of the blind. *Psychoanalytic Study of the Child, 19,* 95–112.

Burlingham, D. (1965). Some problems of ego development in blind children. *Psychoanalytic Study of the Child, 20,* 194–208.

Burlingham, D. (1979). To be blind in a sighted world. *Psychoanalytic Study of the Child, 34,* 5–31.

Chance, P. (1979). *Learning through play.* New York: Johnson & Johnson.

Cherry, C. (1976). *Creative play for the developing child: Early lifehood education through play.* Belmont, CA: Fearon Pittman Publishers.

Corsaro, W.A. (1979). "We're friends, right": Children's use of access rituals in nursery school. *Language in Society, 8,* 315–336.

Dinkmeyer, D. (1970). *Developing understanding of self and others.* Circle Pines, MN: American Guidance Service.

Doll, E.A. (1953). *A measurement of social competence: A manual for the Vineland Social Maturity Scale.* Educational Test Bureau.

Dunlea, A. (1982). The role of visual information in the emergence of meaning: A comparison of blind and sighted children. (Doctoral dissertation, University of Southern California, 1982). *Dissertation Abstracts International, 43,* 1130-A.

Erin, J.N. (1986). Frequencies and types of questions in the language of visually impaired children. *Journal of Visual Impairment and Blindness, 80,* 667–674.

Fenson, L., & Ramsey, D.S. (1980). Decentration and integration of the child's play in the second year. *Child Development, 51,* 171–178.

Field, T. (1980). Preschool play: Effects of teacher/child ratios and organization of classroom space. *Child Study Journal, 10,* 191–205.

Field, T. (1982). Interaction coaching for high-risk infants and their parents. In H.A. Moss, R. Hess, & C. Swift (Eds.), *Early intervention programs for infants: Prevention in human services* (Vol. 1, No. 4, pp. 5–23). New York: Hawthorn Press.

Flavell, J. (1973). Reduction of stereotypies by reinforcement of toy play. *Mental Retardation, 11,* 21–23.

Fraiberg, S. (1977). *Insights from the blind.* New York: Meridian.

Goldberg, S. (1977). Social competence in infancy: A model of parent-infant interaction. *Merrill-Palmer Quarterly, 23,* 163–177.

Guralnick, M.J. (1981). The social behavior of preschool children at different developmental levels: Effects of group composition. *Journal of Experimental Child Psychology, 31,* 115–130.

Hill, E., & Blasch, B.B. (1980). Concept development. In R.L. Welsh & B.B. Blasch (Eds.), *Foundations of orientation and mobility* (pp. 265–290). New York: American Foundation for the Blind.

Hoben, M., & Lindstrom, V. (1980). Evidence of isolation in the mainstream. *Journal of Visual Impairment and Blindness, 74*(8), 289–292.

Hopper, C., & Wambold, C. (1978). Improving the independent play of severely mentally retarded children. *Education and Training of the Mentally Retarded, 13,* 42–46.

Howze, Y.S. (1987). The use of social skills training to improve interview skills of visually impaired young adults: A pilot study. *Journal of Visual Impairment and Blindness, 81*(6), 251–255.

Imamura, S. (1965). *Mother and blind child.* New York: American Foundation for the Blind (Research Series, No. 14).

Jeffree, D., McConkey, R., & Hewson, S. (1977). *Let me play.* London: Souvenir Press.

Johnson, J.E., Christie, J.F., & Yawkey, T.D. (1987). *Play and early childhood development*. Glenview, IL: Scott, Foresman.

Jones, R., & Chiba, C. (1985). *Social skills assessment and intervention*. Final report prepared for the National Institutes of Health. Washington, DC: National Institutes of Health.

Jones, R.L., Lavine, K., & Shell, J. (1972). Blind children integrated in classrooms with sighted children: A sociometric study. *New Outlook for the Blind, 66*(3), 75–80.

Jose, R. (1983). *Understanding low vision*. New York: American Foundation for the Blind.

Kekelis, L.A., & Andersen, E.S. (1984). Family communication styles and language development. *Journal of Visual Impairment and Blindness, 78*(2), 54–65.

Kekelis, L.S. (1988a). A case study of a blind child in two school settings. In S. Sacks, L. Kekelis, & R. Gaylord-Ross (Eds.), *The social development of visually impaired students*. San Francisco: San Francisco State University.

Kekelis, L.S. (1988b). Increasing positive social interactions between a blind child and sighted kindergartners. In S. Sacks, L. Kekelis, & R. Gaylord-Ross (Eds.), *The social development of visually impaired students*. San Francisco: San Francisco State University.

Kekelis, L.S. (1988c). Peer interactions in childhood: The impact of visual impairment. In S. Sacks, L. Kekelis, & R. Gaylord-Ross (Eds.), *The social development of visually impaired students*. San Francisco: San Francisco State University.

Kekelis, L.S., & Sacks, S.Z. (1988). Mainstreaming visually impaired children into regular education programs: The effects of visual impairment on children's interactions with peers. In S. Sacks, L. Kekelis, & R. Gaylord-Ross (Eds.), *The social development of visually impaired students*. San Francisco: San Francisco State University.

Kitzinger, M. (1987). The role of repeated and echoed utterances in communication with a blind child. *British Journal of Discourse of Communication, 19*, 135–146.

Lamb, M.E., & Easterbrooks, M.A. (1981). Individual differences in parental sensitivity: Origins, components, and consequences. In M.E. Lamb & L.R. Sherrod (Eds.), *Infant social cognition: Empirical and theoretical considerations* (pp. 127–153). Hillsdale, NJ: Lawrence Erlbaum Associates.

Lear, R. (1977). *Play helps: Toys and activities for handicapped children*. London: Heinemann Health Books.

Linder, T.W. (1990). *Transdisciplinary play-based assessment: A functional approach to working with young children*. Baltimore: Paul H. Brookes Publishing Co.

Maxfield, K.E., & Buchholz, S. (1957). *A social maturity scale for blind preschool children: A guide to its use*. New York: American Foundation for the Blind.

Maxfield, K.E., & Fjeld, H.A. (1942). The social maturity of the visually handicapped preschool child. *Child Development, 13*, 1–27.

McGuinness, R.M. (1970). A descriptive study of blind children educated in the itinerant teacher, resource room, and special school setting. *American Foundation for the Blind Research Bulletin, 20*, 1–56.

Meltzoff, A.N., & Moore, M.K. (1977). Imitation of facial and manual gestures by human neonates. *Science, 198*, 75–78.

Miller, B., & Miller, W. (1976). Extinguishing "blindisms:" A paradigm for intervention. *Education of the Visually Handicapped, 8*, 6–15.

Mulford, R. (1983). Referential development in blind children. In A.E. Mills (Ed.), *Language acquisition in the blind child* (pp. 89–107). San Diego: College-Hill.

Musselwhite, C.R. (1986). *Adaptive play for special needs children.* San Diego: College-Hill.

Norris, M., Spaulding, P.J., & Brodie, F.H. (1957). *Blindness in children.* Chicago: Chicago University Press.

Parke, D.L., Shallcross, R., & Anderson, R.J. (1980). Differences in coverbal behavior between blind and sighted persons during dyadic communication. *Journal of Visual Impairment and Blindness, 74*, 142–149.

Parsons, S. (1986a). Function of play in low vision children (Part 2): Emerging patterns of behavior. *Journal of Visual Impairment and Blindness, 8*(6), 777–784.

Parsons, S. (1986b). Function of play in low vision children (Part 1): A review of the research and literature. *Journal of Visual Impairment and Blindness, 80*, 627–631.

Piaget, J. (1952). *The origins of intelligence in children.* New York: International Universities Press.

Preisler, G. (August, 1988). *The development of communication in blind infants.* Paper presented at the International Symposium on Visually Impaired Infants and Young Children: Birth to Seven, Edinburgh, Scotland.

Preisler, G., & Palmer, C. (1988). The blind child goes to nursery school with sighted children. *Child Care, Health and Development, 476*, 45–52.

Putallatz, M., & Gottman, J.M. (1981). Social skills and group acceptance. In S.R. Asher & J.M. Gottman (Eds.), *The development of children's friendships* (pp. 116–149). New York: Cambridge University Press.

Rapoff, M.A., Aultman, K., & Christopherson, E.R. (1980). Suppression of self-injurious behavior: Determining the least restrictive alternative. *Journal of Mental Deficiency Research, 4*, 37–46.

Raver, S.A. (1984). Modification of head droop during conversation in a 3-year-old visually impaired child: A case study. *Journal of Visual Impairment and Blindness, 78*(7), 307–310.

Raver, S.A. (1987b). Training blind children to employ appropriate gaze direction and sitting behavior during conversation. *Education and Treatment of Children, 10*, 237–246.

Raver, S.A. (1987a). Training gaze direction in blind children: Attitude effects in the sighted. *Remedial and Special Education (RASE), 8*, 40–45.

Raver, S., & Dwyer, R. (1986). Using a substitute activity to eliminate eye poking in a 3-year-old visually impaired child in the classroom. *The Exceptional Child, 33*, 65–72.

Read, L.F. (1989). An examination of the social skills of blind kindergarten children. *Education of the Visually Handicapped, 20*(4), 142–155.

Rogers, S.J., & Puchalski, C.B. (1984). Social characteristics of visually impaired infants' play. *Topics in Early Childhood Special Education, 3*(4), 52–56.

Rowland, C. (1984). Preverbal communication of blind infants and their mothers. *Journal of Visual Impairment and Blindness, 78*(7), 297–302.

Sacks, S. (1988). The social development of visually handicapped children: A theoretical perspective. In S. Sacks, L. Kekelis, & R. Gaylord-Ross (Eds.), *The social development of visually impaired students.* San Francisco: San Francisco State University.

Sacks, S., & Gaylord-Ross, R. (1988). Peer-mediated and teacher-directed social skills training for visually impaired students. In S. Sacks, L. Kekelis, & R. Gaylord-Ross (Eds.), *The social development of visually impaired students.* San Francisco: San Francisco State University.

Sandler, A.M. (1963). Aspects of passivity and ego development in the blind infant. *Psychoanalytic Study of the Child, 18,* 343–361.

Schindele, R. (1974). The social adjustment of visually handicapped children in different educational settings. *American Foundation for the Blind Research Bulletin, 28,* 125–144.

Silver, P.G., & Ramsey, P.G. (1983). Participant observation: Broadening points of view. *Early Child Development and Care, 10,* 147–156.

Sisson, L.A., Van Hasselt, V.B., Hersen, M., & Strain, P.S. (1985). Peer intervention: Increasing social behaviors in multihandicapped children. *Behavior Modification, 9,* 292–321.

Skellenger, A.C. (1990). *Play and social skills of children with visual impairments: A review of the literature.* Unpublished manuscript, Peabody College of Vanderbilt University, Nashville.

Sokolow, A. (1983). Differences in play and language development in a pair of blind and sighted twin infants. In M.E. Mulholland & M.V. Wurster (Eds.), *Help me become everything I can be* (pp. 117–122). New York: American Foundation for the Blind.

Tait, P.E. (1972a). The effect of circumstantial rejection on infant behavior. *New Outlook for the Blind, 66,* 139–151.

Tait, P.E. (1972b). Play and the intellectual development of blind children. *New Outlook for the Blind, 66,* 361–369.

Telford, C.W., & Sawrey, J.M. (1977). *The exceptional individual* (2nd ed.). Englewood Cliffs, NJ: Prentice-Hall.

Urwin, C. (1978). The development of communication between blind infants and their parents. In A. Lock (Ed.), *Action, gesture and symbol* (pp. 74–108). London: Academic Press.

Van Hasselt, V.B., Hersen, M., Kazdin, A.E., Simon, J., & Mastantuono, A. (1983). Training blind adolescents in social skills. *Journal of Visual Impairment and Blindness, 77,*(5), 199–203.

Van Hasselt, V.B., Simon, J., & Mastantuono, A.K. (1982). Social skills training for blind children and adolescents. *Education of the Visually Handicapped, 14*(1), 34–40.

Walden, T.A., & Ogan, T.A. (1988). The development of social referencing. *Child Development, 59*(5), 1230–1240.

Wambold, E., & Bailey, R. (1979). Improving leisure-time behaviors of severely/profoundly mentally retarded children through toy play. *American Association for the Education of the Severely and Profoundly Handicapped Review, 4,* 237–250.

Warren, D.H. (1984). *Blindness and early childhood development.* New York: American Foundation for the Blind.

8

Strategies for Promoting the Social-Communicative Competence of Young Children with Specific Language Impairment

Howard Goldstein
and Tanya M. Gallagher

$\mathbf{T}$his chapter provides a description of the characteristics of children with specific language impairment (SLI). An examination of developments in peer relationships and social competence is offered to stimulate a consideration of a general change in the focus of assessment and intervention strategies for serving children with SLI. This change in perspective is required because relatively little attention has been placed on the identification and remediation of the social-communicative difficulties that children with SLI are likely to encounter during their interactions with their peers. A number of interventions that have the potential for improving the ability of children with SLI to communicate effectively with peers have been developed, but most often with other clinical populations. Four promising intervention approaches are described and suggestions for using these interventions with children with SLI are presented.

Specific language impairment is a developmental language disability that is not attributable to any of the major disabling conditions

Preparation of this chapter was supported by Grant No. HD23705 from the National Institute of Child Health and Human Development, awarded to the University of Pittsburgh, and by the McGill-IBM Cooperative Project of McGill University, Montreal.

189

that account for other types of language disability. Children with SLI do not have clinically significant sensory, intellectual, neurological, emotional, or oral-motor impairments. They have normal visual and hearing acuity; test within normal limits on nonverbal measures of intellectual functioning; and demonstrate functioning within normal limits on neurological, emotional, and oral-motor assessments. Although other terms have been used to refer to this type of language problem, including "developmental aphasia," "childhood aphasia," "congenital aphasia," "language delay," and "specific developmental language disorder," the term "specific language impairment" currently is the most widely used (NIH, 1990).

Attempts to identify the etiology of the disorder have focused on three major parameters: 1) characteristics of the language learning environment; 2) auditory processing abilities; and 3) nonlinguistic representational abilities, such as symbolic play (see Lahey, 1988; Leonard, 1987; Stark & Tallal, 1988 for reviews). Each of these parameters has been studied extensively. Results across investigations have been inconsistent, however, suggesting that none of these parameters sufficiently accounts for the language difficulties children with SLI experience. The observation that SLI runs in families with higher-than-expected frequencies (Tallal, Ross, & Curtiss, 1989; Tomblin, 1989) has led to the current hypothesis that the cause of the disability is a genetic deficiency (Gopnik, 1990). Further research along this line is necessary, however, before conclusions regarding this hypothesis can be reached.

In the absence of a clearly identifiable etiology, specific language impairment continues to be defined by exclusion criteria. These criteria, framed broadly in the DSM–III–R classification of the disorder (American Psychiatric Association, 1987), were specified most precisely by Stark and Tallal (1981). Their definition has been accepted widely in the clinical literature. According to Stark and Tallal (1981), in order to be considered to have a specific language impairment, children must demonstrate overall language performance that is at least 12 months below their chronological and mental age as determined by a performance intelligence test; receptive language performance that is at least 6 months below their mental age; expressive language performance that is at least 12 months below their mental age; hearing levels of at least 25 dB from 250 Hz to 6000 Hz; IQ scores of at least 85 on the Performance Scale of the WISC-R or WPPSI; no frank neurological signs or history of head trauma or epilepsy; no severe behavioral or emotional problems; no oral-motor anomalies; and reading performance (if 7 years of age or older) within 6 months of their overall language age.

Prevalence estimates of SLI among children vary but are all below 1% (see Lahey, 1988 for a review). Follow up studies of children identified as having specific language impairment in early childhood suggest that for a substantial number of the children the problem is not resolved with age (Aram & Nation, 1980; Hall & Tomblin, 1978). Children who are identified in their preschool years as having specific language impairment tend to experience academic difficulties when they enter school and at that time may be labelled as "learning disabled" (National Joint Committee on Learning Disabilities, 1987).

CHARACTERISTICS OF CHILDREN WITH SLI

Language Structural Characteristics of Children with SLI

Just as it has been difficult to determine the cause(s) of specific language impairment, despite over 20 years of intensive research, it also has been difficult to determine the language structural commonalities that characterize children with the disorder. Three major conclusions can be drawn from the literature. One is that the nature of the syntactic, semantic, lexical, and phonological problems of children with SLI and the severity of those problems vary considerably from child to child. In language structural terms it has even been difficult to identify reliable subgroups of children. The second conclusion is that, although the language structural performance of children with SLI cannot adequately be described as "delayed," it is more similar to that of younger children who produce utterances of the same approximate length than it is to chronological-age–matched peers. The third conclusion is that, within the overall variability that characterizes the children's language structural performance, they tend to have relatively greater difficulty learning grammatical morphology and complex syntax than learning other grammatical features of language.

Conversational Characteristics of Children with SLI

Although the conversational characteristics of children with SLI have not been studied as extensively as their language structural characteristics, major features of their communicative interactions have been investigated. One major line of research has identified the functions of the language the children use. The commenting and requesting functions have received particular attention (Gallagher & Craig, 1984; Prinz, 1982; Prinz & Ferrier, 1983; Snyder, 1978). Another major line of research has examined the discourse regulation abilities of children with SLI. These studies have included studies of turn-taking (Craig & Evans, 1989); cohesion (VanKleeck & Frankel, 1981); conversational repair (Brinton, Fujiki, Winkler, & Loeb, 1986; Gallagher & Darnton, 1978); responses to requests (Brinton & Fujiki, 1982); and acknowledgements of comments (Craig & Gallagher, 1986). The results of these studies are similar to those reported in the language structural literature. Children with SLI can have problems with any of these communicative functions or discourse regulation devices, although the extent of the difficulties and their relationships to language structural problems that the children may also have are not predictable. In general, children with SLI are not communicating as effectively as their chronological age peers, in part, due to language structural difficulties and, in part, due to difficulties they experiences in the integration of discourse and language structural knowledge. Taken together, the language structural difficulties and conversational characteristics of children with SLI may put them at risk for social difficulties.

PEER RELATIONSHIPS AND SOCIAL CONSEQUENCES FOR CHILDREN WITH SLI

The impact of a diminished ability to participate effectively in conversational interactions is best understood within the context of the social demands inherent in peer relationship development. Based upon an extensive review of the literature, much of which included their own work, Gottman and colleagues (Gottman, 1983; Gottman & Mettetal, 1986; Gottman & Parkhurst, 1980; Parker & Gottman, 1989) proposed that peer relationships among children from 3 to 17 years of age could be broadly characterized in terms of three developmental periods.

Periods of Development

The first period, early childhood, extends approximately from 3 to 7 years of age. Gottman and colleagues proposed that during this developmental period the goal of children's peer interactions is the coordination of interactive temporal play sequences. They further suggest that, in terms of meeting children's friendship needs of solidarity and amity, types of coordinated play can be arranged into a hierarchy. The lowest level of coordinated play is parallel play and the highest level is nonstereotyped fantasy play. Parallel play is the least demanding in terms of children's needs to accommodate each other. It has the lowest potential for disagreement and conflict, which disrupt coordinated play. But it is also the least satisfying socially. The highest and most satisfying level of coordinated play is nonstereotyped fantasy play. This level of play places the greatest demands upon children in terms of continual negotiation of play roles and has the greatest potential for disagreement and conflict. It is verbally demanding and requires behavioral inhibition and perspective-taking in order to be sustained. For these reasons fantasy play is fragile and easily susceptible to breakdown. Children must be comfortable with one another, be able to anticipate one another, and be willing to accommodate each other in order to attain and sustain this valued level of play. Gottman and colleagues hypothesize that it is probably for these reasons that researchers have observed that the frequency of fantasy play among young children increases with familiarity (Matthews, 1978). It also has been noted that children's regard for each other relates to their potential as play partners (Berndt & Perry, 1986; Furman & Buhrmester, 1985).

Gottman (1986) speculated that fantasy play is highly valued in early childhood because it provides a means for practicing social roles and for resolving major fears. He observed that young children seemed to "work through" their fears with their friends by means of fantasy play. Children took turns acting out fantasies dealing with some fear; setting up a drama pertaining to the fear; ensuring that there was a satisfactory resolution, however improbable the solutions were; and then repeating the fantasy over and over again with some variations. Gottman (1986) noted several recurrent themes in this play: parental abandonment, growing up, power and powerlessness, life and death, and transformations of the self. Corsaro (1985) noted similar themes in the fantasy play of preschool children. He identified three recurrent themes: "lost-found," "danger-rescue," and "death-rebirth." Fantasy play seemed to provide a means by which children, who were largely unable to reflect upon their fears and openly discuss them, could address them within the supportive context of peers.

Parker and Gottman (1989) summarized the theme of the early childhood period of peer relationship development as the maximization of excitement, entertainment, and affect during play. This characterization of young children's friendships suggests that children who have limited receptive and/or expressive language skills would have limited coordinated play partner potential and, therefore, not be highly valued interaction partners. This perspective on the social cost of specific language impairment is an important one for designing effective intervention strategies.

The second period of peer relationship development, middle childhood, extends from 8 to 12 years of age. The theme of this period is inclusion by peers. A concern about self-presentation and the desire to avoid rejection are predictable consequences of this theme.

Gottman and colleagues noted that school increases the complexity of children's social worlds. The number and variability among the children with whom interaction occurs is typically much greater than they experienced in the preschool years. Children begin to form peer groups that differ in status and power (Crockett, Losoff, & Petersen, 1984; Hartup, 1984). This contributes to their insecurities about peer acceptance. They highly value group inclusion, and yet, they also view membership within groups as volatile and to some extent capricious. Negative-evaluation gossip is the primary means by which children establish solidarity, reaffirm group membership, and determine peer attitudes about behaviors for which probable group reactions are not known. Humor in the form of teasing also is used to serve these functions. Parker and Gottman (1989) suggested that negative-evaluation gossip and teasing may be used to sample unknown peer group attitudes because they are low risk strategies. Children can use them to determine group attitudes without risking personal exposure by actually becoming engaged themselves in the behaviors yet to be judged.

During this period of development children with SLI again are at social risk, not only because many of the group norms deal with the acceptability of content and styles of talking, but also because negative gossip and teasing are themselves sophisticated verbal behaviors. Children who have weak language skills, therefore, are at a tremendous social disadvantage.

The third period of peer relationship development is adolescence. This period extends from approximately 13 to 18 years of age. Gottman and colleagues propose that the theme of this period is self-exploration and self-definition. As with the themes of the other periods, the means for addressing this theme is highly verbal. In the context of discussions with friends, adolescents explore who they are, what they believe, what they want to become, and so forth, what Goffman (1959) called the territories of the self. Additionally, they use talking with their friends as a problem-solving strategy. Adolescents with SLI also have limited access to participation in this highly verbally intensive period of peer relationship development.

Consequences of Limited Peer Access

The communicative difficulties children with SLI experience put them at risk for access to peers throughout these important periods of peer relationship development. Children not only obtain a sense of social support and self-esteem from peer relationships, but peers also serve as an important means by which children learn critical communicative skills. These skills relate to the importance of clear communication; effective interpersonal perspective-taking; code-switching; communicative appropriateness and politeness; and, in the broadest sense, the role of communication in the social commerce of daily life. A careful examination of this list highlights the fact that peers not only may be the most effective teachers of appropriate child communicative skills, but also actually may be the only ones who can impart some of this knowledge. In this sense, peer interactions may be the communicative analogue of the mother-child interaction routines that characterize a child's early development (Bruner, 1977). Peers, who become more important to the child from preschool age, may play a role in the next phase of the child's conversational development that is parallel to the role played originally by the mother (caregiver).

Adults do not have easy or reliable access to the kinds of information that make up child communicative competence across developmental age ranges, particularly at the younger ages. Even if such information were available to adults, they might be unable to sustain child roles long enough to be effective models of these behaviors because of their pervasive adult perspectives. Furthermore, adults adopting child communicative styles when interacting with communicatively limited language users such as children with SLI, could actually exacerbate the child's interactional problems by blurring social role information that is essential for achieving the full range of communicative competence.

Limited access to the development of positive peer relationships, therefore, should be a concern for the management of intervention programs for children with SLI. Attention to peer relationships may be central to accomplishing the goals of communication intervention.

DESIGNING AND IMPLEMENTING INTERVENTIONS

Although there is not an abundance of research on the conversational characteristics of children with SLI or on their interaction and development of peer relationships, it is clear that SLI places children at significant risk for social difficulties. Relatively little attention has been placed on remediating the social-communicative difficulties children with SLI are likely to encounter during their interactions with peers. Indeed, many of the intervention approaches recommended in the following sections represent extensions of research conducted with children who have other disabilities. A number of intervention approaches have the potential for improving the ability of children with SLI to communicate effectively with peers. These interventions employ a variety of strategies including teaching specific alternatives to socially penalizing behaviors; teaching general scripts for routine social activities; setting the occasion for social interaction through peer intervention; and teaching social interaction skills directly.

Identifying Alternatives to Socially Penalizing Behaviors

Observers of the peer interactions of children with SLI should be particularly attentive to communicative behaviors that elicit negative peer reactions. These behaviors should be noted because they result in high social-interaction penalties (Tomblin & Liljigreen, 1985). Socially negative peer reactions can aid the observers' identification of these behaviors by directing observers' attention to them.

Negative descriptive statements about children with SLI by peers, teachers, or other significant individuals in their lives also can be used to direct observers' attention toward those communicative behaviors that might have contributed to the negative impressions underlying the descriptions obtained. Open-ended questions about the children's communicative behaviors can elicit these descriptive comments. Once these are obtained, care should be taken to try to determine whether there are specific behaviors that may have contributed substantially to the development of these impressions of the children. These behaviors may be highly aversive and/or particularly noticeable to communicative partners so that they respond in overtly negative ways to them or subsequent to them; partners appear to be uncomfortable and/or try to disengage from the communicative interaction. Such partner reactions are helpful in identifying and targeting socially penalizing communicative behaviors within the interactions of children with SLI.

Gallagher and Craig (1984) used this type of identification procedure to study the use of a socially penalizing communicative behavior, the phrase, "It's gone," by Clark, a 4-year-old boy with SLI. He used this phrase frequently in his dyadic interactions with two chronological-age–matched peers and two 2-year-old, MLU (mean length of utterance) matched peers. His chronological peers responded to the phrase by saying things like, "What does, 'It's gone,' mean?", "Why do you always say, 'It's gone?' ", and "Don't say, 'It's gone,' any more." His 2-year-old partners tended to look confused or upset and would walk away, turn their backs to Clark, or use some other means to disengage from interaction. Clark, however, continued to use the phrase throughout his peer interactions. The negative reactions he received from three of the four children with whom he interacted did not seem to discourage him from continuing to use the phrase. Gallagher and Craig (1984) studied Clark's use of the phrase and concluded that he was using it as a play access strategy. This strategy probably was a remnant of the "appearance-disappearance" game that he had played with his mother, a highly frequent mother-child interactional routine among mothers and very young children (Bruner, 1974, 1975, 1977; Ratner & Bruner, 197?; Snow, 1978). This game was associated in Clark's social repertoire with affectively positive social interaction, and he seemed to be using it to invite his peers to play with him. The difficulty with the strategy was not only that it was typically unsuccessful in achieving its purpose, but also that it was socially aversive or at least uncomfortable for most of his peers.

Subsequent to the completion of the study Clark was enrolled in a language intervention program. One of the goals of the program was to replace the socially penalizing communicative play access phrase, "It's gone," with a phrase that was functionally equivalent in purpose, but more successful and interactionally acceptable to peers. Because Clark's expressive language skills were limited, it was determined that this new phrase would be taught as a compensatory routine to replace his earlier phrase, while language structural intervention continued to focus on enhancing his expressive language skills. The compensatory routine, "Let's play," was taught as a means of facilitating more positive peer interactions while language structural intervention proceeded. Clark learned the phrase and it was received more positively by peers. Interestingly, his use of the phrase, "It's gone," decreased proportionally, although there were no explicit efforts to discourage its use.

This is an example of establishing functional equivalence. If it is determined that a socially penalizing behavior of a child with SLI is serving a major communicative function, discouraging its use essentially would be trying to discourage the child from having that communicative need. Even if this were possible, which probably is unlikely except in very restricted contexts, it would be counterproductive because children with SLI should be encouraged to participate fully in peer interactions. In the above example, Clark was not discouraged from using the phrase "It's gone." Once its function within his communicative repertoire was determined, a more socially acceptable alternative behavior was taught. Its use in peer interactions was reinforced naturally by the more positive reactions the alternative phrase, "Let's play," received. The new phrase, therefore, more successfully met the original communicative purpose of "It's gone," which was play access, and quickly replaced it in his communicative system.

This approach to identifying functionally equivalent behavior was illustrated in dramatic fashion by Carr and Durand (1985) in their work with children with autism. First, they conducted controlled observations to generate hypotheses about the conditions responsible for maintenance of maladaptive behavior in a number of autistic children to identify the communicative function of these behaviors. They posited that the behavior problems were demonstrated by some children when they encountered difficult tasks rather than easy tasks and by some children when they encountered infrequent access to teacher attention rather than consistent access to teacher attention. These assessments distinguished between children whose misbehavior was escape-motivated and children whose misbehavior was attention-motivated. Following this functional analysis it became possible to select alternative behaviors more astutely. Children were taught to say, "I don't understand," as a more appropriate way to escape from difficult demands, and children were taught to ask, "Am I doing good work?" as a more appropriate way to gain attention. Subsequent experimental analyses confirmed that only when the functionally equivalent utterances for escape-motivated and attention-motivated behaviors were taught did misbehavior virtually disappear in those contexts.

Tomblin and Liljigreen (1985) discussed similar issues relative to designing an intervention program for a 12-year-old child with a language impairment. They concluded, "The product of this approach should lead to the identification of those aspects of the child's communication that bring the greatest social penalties. As a result, changes brought about by clinical intervention should yield the greatest positive gain to the child's quality of life" (p. 229).

Script Training

A number of investigators contend that a key to peer social interaction is sharing common knowledge and expectations (e.g., Bower, Black, & Turner, 1979; Nelson, 1981; Nelson & Gruendel, 1979; Nelson & Seidman, 1984). Children are much more likely to engage in interactive communication when they share social scripts for the routine events to be expected in a particular situation. Goldstein and his colleagues (Goldstein, Wickstrom, Hoyson, Jamieson, & Odom, 1988) applied this notion of social scripts in teaching sociodramatic play skills to preschoolers with and without developmental disabilities.

Sociodramatic play is incorporated into curricula for most preschool programs. The quality of interactions during sociodramatic play may be depressed, however, when children's common knowledge does not extend to all the characters and to how the scenario progresses for a particular theme. The usual approach to teaching sociodramatic play skills involves making specific materials available and providing informal teacher intervention in the form of participation in and/or direction of activity. Script training offers a means of formalizing these intervention efforts with the intention of minimizing the active participation of adults during play activities.

An intervention based on script training might involve triads of preschoolers who are taught scripts comprising three roles and behaviors associated with common play scenarios, such as going to dinner or going shopping (Goldstein et al., 1988). Scripts provide a general framework in which groups of children can contribute verbally or nonverbally (depending on individual capabilities) to a theme, such as going to a hamburger stand. An example of a script for a visit to a pet store is provided in Figure 8.1. Notice that, unlike a script for a dramatic production, a variety of nonverbal and verbal forms are suggested as the activity progresses, with an equal number of contributions planned for each child. After the children are taught the script through a process of prompting and fading, they are allowed to play that activity with minimal intrusion by the trainer. The trainer may need to prompt children to stay in their roles and help them exchange roles to help maintain improved communicative interaction during free play. In an experimental evaluation of the effects of script training, Goldstein and his colleagues (1988) found improved social interaction subsequent to script training, with minimal teacher prompting during play time. The benefits of script training were replicated with a variety of children, including children with SLI as well as children with developmental disabilities and typical children.

The specific steps to implementing this script training intervention include: 1) teaching scripts to children, and then 2) encouraging role-related behavior during free play. A teacher might use 15 minutes per day for at least 1 week to teach a script that includes three roles (e.g., a cook, salesperson, and customer at a hamburger stand). Each child is provided opportunities to perform each role, with variations adapted to individuals' communicative abilities. When the script is first introduced the teacher models responses and tells children whose turn it is, what to do, and what to say. Thereafter, the teacher attempts to employ fewer and less explicit prompts. After a couple of days it is not difficult to complete the script three times in 15 minutes. Deviations from the script are permissible and should be encouraged to reinforce elaborations and to maintain novelty in play activities. A current investigation demonstrated that training time tended to be reduced with the introduction of successive scripts (Goldstein & Cisar, in press).

After children have learned the scripts they are monitored during play periods. During a play period, it is helpful to reassign roles so that each child has an opportunity to be each character. A minimal amount of prompting may be necessary. Prompting should be limited

Setting: PET SHOP

Characters: Salesperson (S), Animal Caretaker (A), Customer (C)

Stuffed animals representing familiar cartoon characters were used, such as Snoopy, Garfield, Spuds, Kermit, and Benji. Smaller versions of these stuffed animals were used to represent the "puppies." Crates served as cages for the pets. Cards with the animals' names and pictures were placed on each cage.

		Minimal Verbal	Nonverbal	Elaborated
1. S:	Tells A to let the people in.	Open.		It's time to open the store and let the people in.
2. A:	Welcomes customers. (Flips sign and opens door.)	Hi, come in.	Waving/ motioning in gesture.	Hi, come in and look at all the pets.
3. S:	Offers assistance to C.	Need help?		What type of animal are you looking for?
4. C:	Expresses interest in an animal.	Dog.	Points to animal type.	I'd like a small, playful house dog.
5. S:	Assists C to pet cages.	Follow me.	Guides C to a cage.	Just follow me, we have about five dogs in our store today.
6. A:	Offers 1st animal to C. (Gets animal out of cage.)	Here.	Gives animal to C.	Here's a small beagle that we just received.
7. C:	Receives animal from A.	Nice doggie.	Extends arms to obtain dog.	He sure is a friendly dog.
8. A:	Tells C the animal's name.	Snoopy.	Gives C a picture card with the animal's name.	The dog's name is Snoopy.
9. S:	Assists C to 2nd animal cage.	Follow me.	Guides C to the second pet cage.	There's another dog over here.
10. A:	Tells C the animal's name.	Spuds.	Gives C a picture card with the animal's name.	His name is Spuds.
11. A:	Offers 2nd animal to C.	Here.	Gives animal to C.	Wow, he's a heavy little dog.
12. C:	Receives animal from A.	Thank you.	Extends arms to obtain dog.	You're right, he sure is heavy.
13. S:	Asks C about interest in a particular animal.	You like?		Is this the type of pet you are looking for?
14. C:	Responds.	Yes/no.	Nods yes/no.	This is exactly what I had in mind.
15. S:	Draws C's attention to the new animals.	Puppies.	Points to puppy cage.	Look at all the new puppies over here.
16. A:	Asks C about desire to see an animal.	Which one?	Offers choice of animal cards to C.	Which one of the puppies would you like to see?
17. C:	Responds.	Baby Spuds.	Chooses animal card from A or points to puppy.	I'd like to see the small, white puppy in the corner.
18. A:	Restates C's request. (Gets the desired animal.)	Spuds.	Points to puppy or to the animal card.	Okay, I'll get that one.
19. A:	Offers 3rd animal to C.	Here.	Gives animal to C.	He's really a little puppy.
20. C:	Receives 3rd animal from A.	Cute puppy.	Extends arms to obtain animal.	Thanks, this is the cutest puppy.
21. S:	Asks C about decision to buy an animal.	Buy one?		Have you made up your mind which one you want to buy yet?
22. C:	Responds.	Snoopy.	Points to dog or chooses animal card.	I've decided I'd like to buy Snoopy.
23. S:	States the cost of the animal.	Ten dollars.	Gives the bill to C.	That dog costs 10 dollars.
24. C:	Offers money to S.	Here.	Hands money to S.	Here's **10 dollars.**

(continued)

Figure 8.1. An example of a sociodramatic play script.

Figure 8.1. (continued)

25. S:	Receives money from C.	Thank you.	Receives money from C.	Thank you very much.
26. S:	Tells A to get a leash.	Leash.	Points to leash.	Please get a leash for Snoopy.
27. A:	Offers a leash to C.	Here.	Gives leash to C.	Here's a black leash that matches Snoopy's ears.
28. C:	Receives leash.	Thank you.	Receives leash from A.	This will look good on him.
29. A:	Offers C the requested animal.	Here.	Gives animal to C.	Snoopy is all ready to go home with you.
30. C:	Receives animal.	Thank you.	Extends arms to obtain animal.	Thanks, have a good day.

primarily to reminders about the activity and the role that a child is portraying (e.g., "Remember, you are the salesperson at the hamburger stand"). Once the children have learned the roles during script training, it is rarely necessary to specify desired responses. However, it is sometimes helpful to ask a child, "What do you do now?"

It is worth noting that Goldstein et al. (1988) found improvements in theme-related behavior not specifically targeted in the script. Goldstein and Cisar (in press) found that the effects of training were magnified with the introduction of each of three successive scripts. Script training seems to impose an expectation for interaction and communication among children. This is especially important in mainstream classrooms, where structure often must be imposed to ensure that children with disabilities interact (see Odom & Strain, 1984). In addition, there may be long-term benefits to the heterogeneous grouping of children. For example, the more linguistically sophisticated children may model more advanced language skills for less sophisticated peers.

Peer-Mediated Approaches

To compensate for impairment in social-communicative competence of children with SLI, interventionists can engineer situations to set the occasion for use of interaction skills. Teaching typical classmates to serve as intervention agents should be particularly effective when children with SLI are socially withdrawn and consequently neglected by peers (see McEvoy, Odom, & McConnell, Chapter 5, this volume for a complete review of peer mediated approaches). Briefly, targeted behaviors in peer intervention studies refer to social behaviors or strategies that typical peers (sometimes called peer confederates) are asked to direct to their classmates with disabilities. Most interventions teach peers to initiate interactions with peers with disabilities at high rates (e.g., Day, Powell, Dy-Lin, & Stowitschek, 1982; Odom, Hoyson, Jamieson, & Strain, 1985; Ragland, Kerr, & Strain, 1978; Strain, 1977; Strain, Kerr, & Ragland, 1979; Strain, Shores, & Timm, 1977; Tremblay, Strain, Hendrickson, & Shores, 1981). Such social initiation strategies include asking a child to play; suggesting play ideas (i.e., "play organizers"); asking peers to share toys or offering to share toys; and offering assistance. Other peer interventions have focused more on peers as reinforcement agents who hand out requested materials, praise social behavior, provide social attention, and offer hugs (e.g., Guralnick, 1976; McEvoy et al., 1988; Wahler, 1967; Young & Kerr, 1979). It should be noted that these interventions were developed for children who were socially withdrawn, including children with behavior disorders, autism, and other developmental disabilities. These interventions may prove generally useful with a broad range of children with and without disabilities who have difficulty forming and maintaining relationships with peers.

Goldstein and his colleagues have sought to adapt these peer-mediated approaches to focus on communicative interaction among preschoolers (Goldstein & Ferrell, 1987; Goldstein, Kaczmarek, Pennington, & Shafer, 1991; Goldstein & Wickstrom, 1986). The strategies taught to typical peers have included: 1) establishing eye contact, 2) establishing joint focus of attention, 3) initiating joint play, 4) prompting requests, 5) describing one's own or other children's play, and 6) responding by repeating or expanding children's utterances or by requesting clarification. The use of these strategies by peers generally resulted in increased interaction rates, especially responses, on the part of their classmates with moderate to severe developmental disabilities.

Goldstein et al. (1991) taught a set of strategies as a chain of behaviors to typical preschoolers. Peers learned to: 1) establish mutual gaze, 2) comment on ongoing activities, and 3) acknowledge and respond to their partner's communicative behaviors. An important characteristic of this intervention was the lack of reliance on initiation strategies that demanded responses. The development of the intervention was based on ecobehavioral analyses of communicative interaction in dyads of typical children (Ferrell, 1990). This descriptive research revealed that obligatory demands (e.g., commands, questions) were embedded in a context characterized by more frequent nonobligatory communication (e.g., comments). This approach to intervention was more consistent with behavior typical of preschoolers; it also turned out to be responsive to the criticism that prior interventions have emphasized compliance to peers' initiations. The intervention was surprisingly effective in improving the social interaction of five children with autism. Even with strategies that did not require compliance, target children demonstrated more social behavior in their interactions with peers. Children with SLI, because of their more sophisticated linguistic abilities, might be expected to experience far greater gains in verbal interaction skills from similar interventions.

Although these developments in peer interventions should prove useful in applications to children with SLI, they may not be sufficient. Many children with SLI would not be considered socially withdrawn; rather they may initiate interaction, but do so inappropriately. Peers may need to be sensitized to different topographies that indicate an initiation and perhaps acknowledge the initiation with an appropriate model. For example, the peer may learn to say, "Oh, you meant to ask me if I would hide," after a child with SLI says, "It's gone."

Teaching peers to use strategies in a role-play situation may not guarantee their use during play with their classmates with SLI. Rarely is this accomplished without encouragement from the adult monitoring the play activity (Odom et al., 1985; Sainato, Goldstein, & Strain, in press). Most often the peers are prompted by an adult monitor who suggests strategies for the peers to try. These verbal prompts can be provided quickly and easily. However, they can interrupt the children's play, and, furthermore, the effects of strategy use are confounded because the child with disabilities also is likely to hear the prompt. Goldstein and his colleagues (1986, 1987) were able to reduce these problems by teaching peers to recognize posters illustrating the strategies. An adult prompted the peers during the play sessions by directing their attention to a poster depicting the suggested strategy. It is possible that gestural cues (e.g., pointing to one's eyes, ears, or mouth) could be instituted in a similar manner to reduce the intrusiveness of prompting still further.

Prior to the implementation of peer intervention, it is not uncommon to find a tendency for adult monitors to direct a majority of their prompts to children with disabilities (Goldstein & Ferrell, 1987; Sainato et al., in press). Prompting children with disabilities can be reduced considerably once peer intervention is instituted. Peer intervention usually has been successful in increasing the rate of social responses with few prompts directed to the children with disabilities, even for children with autism and severe behavior problems (e.g., Odom et al., 1985; Odom, Strain, Karger, & Smith, 1986). In some peer intervention studies, consistent albeit unprogrammed declines in adult prompts were seen (Goldstein & Ferrell, 1987; Goldstein &

Wickstrom, 1986). This natural reduction in adult prompts provides a positive outlook for the maintenance of strategy use as prompts are deliberately faded.

Maintenance and generalization of intervention effects are likely to depend on the behavior of the peers when they are no longer being prompted to use facilitative strategies and reinforced for doing so. One should expect that if peers continue to use these strategies, then their classmates with SLI will continue to display higher rates of communicative interaction. The more pervasive these reciprocal relationships are, the more likely that natural contingencies will take hold and widespread generalization as well as maintenance will accrue. Reciprocity may range from interactions involving the obvious give-and-take of play, such as catching and throwing a ball or chasing and being chased in a game of tag, to more sophisticated conversational interactions involving role enactment, such as taking turns, talking on a telephone, or playing salesperson and customer. However, peers are not likely to continue using strategies if the effort to do so outweighs the rewards inherent in the interactions. If children with SLI experience a reduction in initiations from classmates, they may in turn take more responsibility for initiating and maintaining peer interactions. That is, they may compensate for the reduced effort of the peers in order to sustain the level of reciprocal interaction experienced previously. It is possible that increased initiations by the children with SLI will result in more balanced interaction patterns. Clearly, the greatest testimony to the success of intervention programs would be the maintenance of friendships among children with SLI and typical children after active intervention has been withdrawn.

It is unlikely that peer intervention approaches would be implemented with children who have SLI without other language skills being addressed in early intervention settings. Peer intervention does provide a context for learning new social and communication skills. Peers model behaviors that children with SLI can learn observationally. They may provide verbal instructions and prompts, and may differentially reinforce desired social behavior contributing to a shaping of new behavior. But peer intervention is not as well-suited to the learning of new skills as it is to setting the occasion for the generalization of present skills (Strain, 1983). Therefore, peer intervention should be included in a more comprehensive program of communication training that contains adult-administered teaching components.

Typically, other language skills, such as receptive and expressive vocabulary, semantic relations, morphology, and syntax are taught. One can argue that peer intervention is likely to enhance the effects of such programming. Providing a receptive context for interaction with peers allows children with SLI the opportunity to practice previously acquired or trained language skills. It also provides an opportunity for peers to be exposed to improvements in social and communicative skills in children with SLI that might otherwise go unnoticed and therefore, not be reinforced. This opportunity for peers to perceive their classmates with SLI in new ways may enhance social acceptance.

Teaching Social Interaction Skills Directly

Perhaps the most obvious strategy for enhancing the social-communicative competence of children with SLI is teaching communicative interaction skills directly. The paucity of research in attempting to teach children with SLI critical skills for interacting with peers may be attributable to the difficulty in pinpointing which skills should be taught (Gallagher & Craig, 1984). Research is needed to identify interaction skills that can be taught effectively and that yield improved conversations with peers. The application of an ecobehavioral approach like the one used to identify facilitative strategies for peers may prove valuable in identifying strategies to teach the children with SLI (e.g., see Sainato & Carta, Chapter 4, this volume). Indeed, it might be profitable to augment the peer intervention approach by teaching facilitative strategies to children with SLI along with their typical classmates. As is similar in the script training approach, a common set of expectations and shared knowledge can be generated.

Ongoing assessments of peer interactions may provide a useful context for identifying strategies that should be encouraged or that could be taught directly to other children with SLI. That is, the advent of improved interactions may provide a good context for conducting ecobehavioral analyses to help interventionists select facilitative behaviors that can be prompted and reinforced in other children with SLI during peer interactions.

Teachers or speech-language pathologists may teach interaction skills using a social skills curriculum or episodically within the classroom setting. Teaching skills such as, saying "please" and "thank you," learning how to share and how to resolve conflicts, respecting the rights or acknowledging the feelings of others, and acknowledging other's verbalizations often require children with SLI to generalize those skills to other contexts. Hence, the approach of teaching social interaction skills directly may not be sufficient to produce significant improvements in interactive behavior and peer acceptance during play times. A peer intervention component is likely to produce better results than those attained through this type of adult-mediated teaching alone. The coupling of social skills training with peer intervention has proved profitable with older children (e.g., Ladd, 1981; Oden & Asher, 1977), but researchers rarely have employed this tactic with preschoolers (Factor & Schilmoeller, 1983).

The design of a curriculum for teaching interactive skills may need to individualize content for children with different characteristics. For example, children who lack assertive skills may need to learn a repertoire of entry behaviors. What may amount to brief scripts might be introduced. For instance, a child with SLI might be taught to observe children who are playing with a set of toys, select a toy that fits into the activity, and then offer a descriptive statement about the ongoing play.

Children with SLI who tend to be nonresponsive or slow to respond might be taught a different set of adaptive behaviors. For instance, a child might be encouraged to repeat peers' utterances as a way to hold the floor while formulating a response. In addition, a child might be taught that it is important to answer when asked questions or at least to acknowledge a question.

Both initiation and responsive behaviors may be more difficult to regulate when the child with SLI is grouped with more than one peer. Instruction might encourage the child to observe peers who hold the floor and detect subtle cues based on eye contact that indicate a designation of the expected next speaker.

Once target behaviors have been identified, direct instruction in social-communicative skills tends to include four components. The first component is teaching the behavior. Various means are used including verbal instruction, modeling, and role-playing. As Fey (1986) has indicated, heavy reliance on the first of these, verbal instruction, may not be possible with young children who have very limited language skills. The second component is practicing the new behavior until it is under the child's control. This "behavioral rehearsal" is usually adult guided until the behavior is under the child's volitional control. The third component is developing evaluative skills to enable the child to recognize the social utility of the new behavior. This is sometimes referred to as the feedback phase of the program. The fourth component is developing self-monitoring skills. This phase involves being able to monitor one's own behavior and substitute alternative social behaviors on the basis of interactive feedback. Asher's (1985) review of social skills training research provides an excellent discussion of this type of intervention program.

Direct instruction programs have been used most often with elementary school-age children who are neglected by peers. These programs have focused on increasing children's social knowledge and social proficiency. Social knowledge includes awareness of what constitutes social behavior and the role these behaviors play in interpersonal contexts. Social proficiency includes the use of interpersonal self-awareness or the ability to evaluate social performance accurately and adjust it on the basis of interpersonal feedback (Ladd & Mize, 1983). Positive behavioral changes have been noted as a result of direct instruction programs; however, results indicating sociometric improvements have been mixed (see Bierman, 1986). Variability seems to be related to differences in subject selection criteria, assessment of individual needs in terms of program content, and types of outcome measures used. Despite these problems, direct instruction programs hold considerable promise.

SUMMARY

This chapter represents a divergence from much of the literature on children with SLI, which has focused on their language structural characteristics. Currently, attention paid to conversational characteristics has revealed that children with SLI do not communicate as effectively as their typical peers. An examination of the development of peer relationships provides an illuminating perspective on the complexity of the social and communication demands inherent in peer interaction and friendship development.

This chapter has pointed out that from a young age, peers play an important role in the socialization of children. From the early stages of peer relationship development, children who have limited receptive and/or expressive language skills are at a distinct disadvantage given the demands of coordinated play routines. Gottman and others (Gottman & Mettetal, 1986; Parker & Gottman, 1989) have noted the potential role of these early play routines as a means of practicing social roles and resolving major fears. Children's ability to address these needs depends heavily on opportunities to interact communicatively with their peers. Of course, as children grow older the social and communicative requirements become more complicated. Elaborations on the basic social system require more sophisticated receptive and expressive communicative skills to conform to the expectations of the peer group and to maintain group inclusion. By adolescence access to friends may be limited if adolescents with SLI cannot keep up with the heavy demands involved in talking to friends as part of a process of self-exploration and self-definition. Clearly, the increasing sophistication of communicative skills needed to function effectively in more demanding social situations underscores the need to ameliorate communicative impairments as early as possible.

A serious consideration of peer relationships and social competence changes the focus of assessment and intervention strategies for serving children with SLI. Both assessment and intervention must be conducted in appropriate social contexts. Analyses of natural social contexts rarely have been stressed by interventionists, who have focused largely on the language structural characteristics of children with SLI. Researchers must acknowledge the importance of language structural characteristics because of their critical role in diagnosing a disability defined mainly by exclusion criteria. Nevertheless, a recognition of the importance of analyzing communication in social contexts implies a more challenging approach to assessment and intervention. To meet this challenge, researchers must incorporate examination of interactional contexts that include children, as well as contexts that include adults, as they evaluate the extent of communicative impairments as well as intervention options.

The intervention options presented in this chapter share a number of underlying principles. First, the identification of intervention goals should be based on individualized assessment. Specific goals are selected to conform to the communicative intentions being expressed. The actual form of these goals can vary greatly depending on the linguistic sophistication of the individual children. Even if these communicative intentions are being expressed in a socially penalizing manner, the interventionist should seek an alternative form of expression rather than an elimination of the intention. If less penalizing alternative forms of expression are well chosen, they should quickly come under control of positive social consequences.

Second, teaching specific communicative skills should be coupled with strategies for ensuring that a receptive social environment will occasion and reinforce the use of those skills. Peers are involved either directly or indirectly in these intervention efforts. Strategies are presented for taking advantage of play routines and for improving upon them to generate greater sharing of common knowledge and expectations among children with and without disabilities. In particular, a reliance on adult direction of the communicative contributions of children with SLI during interactions with peers is discouraged. The natural reinforcement stemming from reciprocal interaction and self-monitoring of communicative skills and their effects should be relied upon to encourage maintenance and generalization of improved social-communicative functioning among children with SLI.

The authors hope that this chapter inspires greater interest in the study of social competence in children with SLI. The extent of impairments in social competence in children with SLI is not well-delineated. Nonetheless, children with SLI are clearly at risk for serious impairments in the development of social relationships. Both descriptive and experimental research are warranted. Clearly, investigations of all intervention efforts with children who have SLI should examine effects in a variety of social contexts. In particular, this chapter provides an impetus for examining the effects of intervention on children with SLI within the context of peer interactions and peer relationship development.

REFERENCES

American Psychiatric Association. (1987). *Diagnostic and statistical manual of mental disorders* (3rd ed., revised). Washington, DC: Author.

Aram, D.M., & Nation, J.E. (1980). Preschool language disorders and subsequent language and academic difficulties. *Journal of Communication Disorders, 13,* 159–170.

Asher, S. (1985). An evolving paradigm in social skill training research with children. In B. Schneider, K. Rubin, & J. Ledingham (Eds.), *Children's peer relations: Issues in assessment and intervention* (pp. 157–171). New York: Springer-Verlag.

Berndt, T.J., & Perry, T.B. (1986). Children's perceptions of friendships as supportive relationships. *Developmental Psychology, 22,* 640–648.

Bierman, K.L. (1986). Process of change during social skills training with preadolescents and its relation to treatment outcome. *Child Development, 57,* 230–240.

Bower, G.H., Black, J.B., & Turner, T.J. (1979). Scripts in memory for text. *Cognitive Psychology, 11,* 177–250.

Brinton, B., & Fujiki, M. (1982). A comparison of request-response sequences in the discourse of normal and language-disordered children. *Journal of Speech and Hearing Disorders, 47,* 57–62.

Brinton, B., Fujiki, M., Winkler, E., & Loeb, D. (1986). Responses to requests for clarification in linguistically normal and language-impaired children. *Journal of Speech and Hearing Disorders, 51,* 370–378.

Bruner, J. (1974). Organisation of early skilled action. In M. Richards (Eds.), *The integration of a child into a social world* (pp. 167–184). London: Cambridge University Press.

Bruner, J. (1975). The ontogenesis of speech acts. *Journal of Child Language, 2,* 1–20.

Bruner, J. (1977). Early social interaction and language acquisition. In H. Schaffer (Ed.), *Studies in mother-infant interaction* (pp. 271–289). London: Academic Press.

Carr, E.G., & Durand, V.M. (1985). Reducing behavior problems through functional communication training. *Journal of Applied Behavior Analysis, 18,* 111–126.

Corsaro, W.A. (1985). *Friendship and peer culture in the early years.* Norwood, NJ: Ablex.

Craig, H., & Evans, J. (1989). Turn exchange characteristics of SLI children's simultaneous and non-simultaneous speech. *Journal of Speech and Hearing Disorders, 54,* 334–347.

Craig, H., & Gallagher, T. (1986). Interactive play: The frequency of related verbal responses. *Journal of Speech and Hearing Research, 62,* 474–482.

Crockett, L., Losoff, M., & Petersen, A.C. (1984). Perceptions of the peer group and friendship in early adolescence. *Journal of Early Adolescence, 4*, 155–181.

Day, R., Powell, T., Dy-Lin, E., & Stowitschek, J. (1982). An evaluation of the effects of a social interaction training package on mentally handicapped preschool children. *Education and Training of the Mentally Retarded, 17*, 125–130.

Factor, D.C., & Schilmoeller, G.L. (1983). Social skill training of preschool children. *Child Study Journal, 13*, 41–56.

Ferrell, D.R. (1990). *Communicative interaction between handicapped and nonhandicapped preschool children: Identifying facilitative strategies.* Unpublished doctoral dissertation, University of Pittsburgh.

Fey, M. (1986). *Language intervention with young children.* San Diego: College-Hill.

Furman, W., & Buhrmester, D. (1985). Children's perceptions of the personal relationships in their social networks. *Developmental Psychology, 21*, 1016–1024.

Gallagher, T., & Craig, H. (1984). Pragmatic assessment: Analysis of a highly frequent repeated utterance. *Journal of Speech and Hearing Disorders, 49*, 368–377.

Gallagher, T., & Darnton, B. (1978). Conversational aspects of the speech of language-disordered children: Revision behaviors. *Journal of Speech and Hearing Research, 21*, 118–135.

Goffman, E. (1959). *Presentation of self in everyday life.* New York: Doubleday.

Goldstein, H., & Cisar, C.L. (in press). Promoting interaction during sociodramatic play: Teaching scripts to typical preschoolers and classmates with handicaps. *Journal of Applied Behavior Analysis.*

Goldstein, H., & Ferrell, D.R. (1987). Augmenting communicative interaction between handicapped and nonhandicapped preschoolers. *Journal of Speech and Hearing Disorders, 19*, 200–211.

Goldstein, H., Kaczmarek, L., Pennington, R., & Shafer, K. (1991). *Improving interaction skills of preschoolers with developmental disabilities: Effects of low-demand peer intervention.* Unpublished manuscript.

Goldstein, H., & Wickstrom, S. (1986). Peer intervention effects on communicative interaction among handicapped and nonhandicapped preschoolers. *Journal of Applied Behavior Analysis, 19*, 209–214.

Goldstein, H., Wickstrom, S., Hoyson, M., Jamieson, B., & Odom, S. (1988). Effects of sociodramatic play training on social and communicative interaction. *Education and Treatment of Children, 11*, 97–117.

Gopnik, M. (1990). Feature-blind grammar and dysphasia. *Nature, 344*, 715.

Gottman, J.M. (1983). How children become friends. *Monographs of the Society for Research in Child Development, 48*(3, Serial No. 201).

Gottman, J.M. (1986). The observation of social process. In J.M. Gottman & J.G. Parker (Eds.), *Conversations of friends: Speculation on affective development* (pp. 51–102). New York: Cambridge University Press.

Gottman, J., & Mettetal, G. (1986). Speculations about social and affective development: Friendships and acquaintanceship through adolescence. In J.M. Gottman & J.G. Parker (Eds.), *Conversations of friends: Speculation on affective development* (pp. 192–237). New York: Cambridge University Press.

Gottman, J.M., & Parkhurst, J.T. (1980). A developmental theory of friendship and acquaintanceship processes. In W.A. Collins (Ed.), *Minnesota sym-*

posia on child development: Vol. 13: Development of cognition, affect, and social relations (pp. 197–253). Hillsdale, NJ: Lawrence Erlbaum Associates.

Guralnick, M.J. (1976). The value of integrating handicapped and nonhandicapped preschool children. *American Journal of Orthopsychiatry, 42*, 236–245.

Hall, P.K., & Tomblin, J.B. (1978). A follow-up study of children with articulation and language disorders. *Journal of Speech and Hearing Disorders, 43*, 227–241.

Hartup, W.W. (1984). The peer context in middle childhood. In W.A. Collins (Ed.), *Development during middle childhood: The years from six to twelve* (pp. 240–282). Washington, DC: National Academy Press.

Ladd, G.W. (1981). Effectiveness of a social learning method for enhancing children's social interaction and peer acceptance. *Child Development, 52*, 171–178.

Ladd, G.W., & Mize, J. (1983). Social skills training and assessment with children: A cognitive-social learning approach. In G.W. Ladd (Ed.), *Social skills training for children and youth* (pp. 61–74). Binghamton, NY: Hayworth Press.

Lahey, M. (1988). *Language disorders and language development*. New York: Macmillan.

Leonard, L. (1987). Is specific language impairment a useful construct? In S. Rosenberg (Ed.), *Advances in applied psycholinguistics: Disorders of first-language development* (pp. 1–39). Cambridge: Cambridge University Press.

Matthews, W.S. (1978). Sex and familiarity effects upon the proportion of time young children spend in spontaneous fantasy play. *Journal of Genetic Psychology, 133*, 9–12.

McEvoy, M.A., Nordquist, M.M., Twardosz, S., Heckaman, K.A., Wehby, J.H., & Denny, R.K. (1988). Promoting autistic children's peer interaction in an integrated early childhood setting using affection activities. *Journal of Applied Behavior Analysis, 21*, 193–200.

National Institutes of Health. (1990). *Epidemiology of specific language impairment*. RFP NIH-DC-90-19. Washington, DC: Author.

National Joint Committee on Learning Disabilities. (May, 1987). Learning disabilities and the preschool child. *Asha, 29*, 35–38.

Nelson, K. (1981). Social cognition in a script framework. In J.H. Flavell & L. Ross (Eds.), *Social cognitive development: Frontiers and possible futures* (pp. 97–118). Cambridge: Cambridge University Press.

Nelson, K., & Gruendel, J.M. (1979). At morning it's lunchtime: A scriptal view of children's dialogues. *Discourse Processes, 2*, 73–94.

Nelson, K., & Seidman, S. (1984). Playing with scripts. In I. Bretherton (Ed.), *Symbolic play: The development of social understanding* (pp. 45–71). Orlando: Academic Press.

Oden, S., & Asher, S.R. (1977). Coaching children in social skills for friendship making. *Child Development, 48*, 495–506.

Odom, S.L., Hoyson, M., Jamieson, B., & Strain, P.S. (1985). Increasing handicapped preschoolers' peer social interactions: Cross-setting and component analysis. *Journal of Applied Behavior Analysis, 18*, 3–16.

Odom, S.L., & Strain, P.S. (1984). Peer-mediated approaches for promoting children's social interaction: A review. *American Journal of Orthopsychiatry, 54*, 544–557.

Odom, S.L., Strain, P.S., Karger, M.A., & Smith, J. (1986). Using single and multiple peers to promote social interaction of preschool children with handicaps. *Journal of the Division for Early Childhood, 10,* 53–64.

Parker, J., & Gottman, J. (1989). Social and emotional development in a relational context. In T. Berndt & G. Ladd (Eds.), *Peer relationships in child development* (pp. 95–131). New York: John Wiley & Sons.

Prinz, P. (1982). An investigation of the comprehension and production of requests in normal and language-disordered children. *Journal of Communication Disorders, 15,* 75–93.

Prinz, P., & Ferrier, L. (1983). "Can you give me that one?": The comprehension, production and judgement of directives in language-impaired children. *Journal of Speech and Hearing Disorders, 48,* 44–54.

Ragland, E.U., Kerr, M.M., & Strain, P.S. (1978). Behavior of withdrawn autistic children: Effects of peer social initiations. *Behavior Modification, 2,* 565–578.

Ratner, N., & Bruner, J. (1978). Games, social exchange and the acquisition of language. *Journal of Child Language, 5,* 391–401.

Sainato, D.M., Goldstein, H., & Strain, P.S. (in press). Effects of self-monitoring on preschool children's use of social interaction strategies with their autistic peers. *Journal of Applied Behavior Analysis.*

Snow, C.L. (1978). The conversational context of language acquisition. In R.N. Campbell & P.T. Smith (Eds.), *Recent advantages in the psychology of language: Language development and mother-child interaction* (pp. 253–269). New York: Plenum.

Snyder, L. (1978). Communicative and cognitive abilities and disabilities in the sensori-motor period. *Merrill-Palmer Quarterly, 24,* 161–180.

Stark, R., & Tallal, P. (1981). Selection of children with specific language deficits. *Journal of Speech and Hearing Disorders, 46,* 114–122.

Stark, R., & Tallal, P. (1988). *Language, speech, and reading disorders in children.* Boston: College-Hill.

Strain, P.S. (1977). Effects of peer social initiations on withdrawn preschool children: Some training and generalization effects. *Journal of Abnormal Child Psychology, 5,* 445–455.

Strain, P.S. (1983). Generalization of autistic children's social behavior change: Effects of developmentally integrated and segregated settings. *Analysis and Intervention in Developmental Disabilities, 3,* 23–34.

Strain, P.S., Kerr, M.M., & Ragland, E.U. (1979). Effects of peer-mediated social initiations and prompting/reinforcement procedures on the social behavior of autistic children. *Journal of Autism and Developmental Disorders, 9,* 41–54.

Strain, P.S., Shores, R.E., & Timm, M.A. (1977). Effects of peer social initiations on the behavior of withdrawn preschool children. *Journal of Applied Behavior Analysis, 10,* 289–298.

Tallal, P., Ross, R., & Curtiss, S. (1989). Familial aggregation in specific language impairment. *Journal of Speech and Hearing Disorders, 54,* 167–173.

Tomblin, J.B. (1989). Familial concentration of developmental language impairment. *Journal of Speech and Hearing Disorders, 54,* 287–295.

Tomblin, J., & Liljigreen, S. (1985). The identification of socially significant communication needs in older language impaired children: A case example. In D. Ripich & F. Spinelli (Eds.), *School discourse problems* (pp. 219–230). San Diego: College-Hill.

Tremblay, A., Strain, P., Hendrickson, J.M., & Shores, R.E. (1981). Social interactions of normal preschool children: Using normative data for subject and target behavior selection. *Behavior Modification, 5,* 237–253.

VanKleeck, A., & Frankel, T. (1981). Discourse devices used by language disordered children: A preliminary investigation. *Journal of Speech and Hearing Disorders, 46,* 250–257.

Wahler, R.G. (1967). Child-child interactions in free field settings: Some experimental analyses. *Journal of Experimental Child Psychology, 5,* 278–293.

Young, C.C., & Kerr, M.M. (1979). The effects of a retarded child's social initiations on the behavior of severely retarded school-aged peers. *Education and Training of the Mentally Retarded, 14,* 185–190.

9

Contributions of Siblings to the Development of Social Competence Interventions for Young Children with Disabilities

James J. Fox, Judith Niemeyer, and Sarah Savelle

Paula is a 4-year-old-girl diagnosed as having Down syndrome. Observing her at the developmentally-integrated preschool she attends, it is quickly apparent that she has a quick smile, takes an active interest in the materials and activities around her, and generally cooperates with her teachers' instructions. However, it is equally apparent that, although she frequently observes the interactions of other children, she rarely interacts with them herself. On the few occasions when she does initiate to her classmates or they to her, Paula does not respond either in quite the right way or quickly enough to maintain the interaction.

Ross is a 10-year-old boy who has been identified as having autism. Like Paula, Ross rarely interacts with other students with or without disabilities. Unlike Paula, however, he actively avoids interactions and seems to prefer solitary activities, some of which are repetitive stereotypic behaviors. When approached, Ross does not make direct eye contact but may watch the other person out of the corner of his eye. He may step back from the

Preparation of this chapter was supported by the Center for Early Childhood Learning and Development of East Tennessee State University. The author wishes to acknowledge Karon Smiley for her assistance in the preparation of the manuscript.

approaching persons or even push them away if they press their initiations.

Tommy is an 8-year-old boy in a regular education classroom. He has yet to be identified as having any disabling condition; however, he is beginning to fall behind grade level in several subject areas. More to the point, Tommy also has difficulties in peer interaction. Unlike Paula and Ross, Tommy interacts with other students, sometimes in a positive manner, but more often negatively. Even his positive interactions often become negative, degenerating into teasing, arguing, and, periodically, fighting. Some children have begun to avoid him, and many of the children can be heard to speak negatively about him to other students.

These descriptions are composites from the author's experience with similar students. Of course, they are not precise characterizations of all children with Down syndrome, autism, or conduct disorder. Yet, such problems of social withdrawal, social avoidance, and negative peer interactions do occur. They have a number of serious short-term and long-term implications for the child, especially a child with other cognitive and behavioral disabilities, and they *can be* some of the most persistent problems with which teachers must cope. Fortunately, applied researchers have produced a number of social skills interventions (McEvoy & Odom, 1987) and intervention packages (Fox, McEvoy, & Day, 1991) that can be used successfully by teachers in classroom settings to improve the social competence of these children with their classmates.

Suppose, however, the situations are slightly altered. Instead of problems in peer interaction, difficulties in interactions with siblings exist. These interactions are at least as important as those with peers, since the family, and particularly siblings, typically offer the earliest and, potentially, the most enduring social relationships (Fox & Savelle, 1987). Researchers have begun to elucidate the negative implications of problems in sibling relationships for later development (Richman, Stevenson, & Graham, 1982). What can be offered to those children and their families for whom the more typical sibling interactions do not develop, or for whom sibling interactions are excessively negative? Can the social skills training technology developed for peer relations be applied to the difficulties in sibling relations that may be presented by children with disabilities? What role can and should siblings play in assisting their sisters and brothers with disabilities in the development of social competence? What additional questions do social interaction researchers need to address to improve, expand, and guide the existing technology as it is applied to interactions between siblings with and without disabilities?

PEER SOCIAL COMPETENCE
AND SCHOOL-BASED INTERVENTIONS

Other chapters in this volume address peer social competence interventions more specifically and at greater length, and there are numerous additional articles on this topic (e.g., the special issue of *Behavioral Disorders*, 1987, *12*). Consequently, their treatment here will be brief and in terms of their relevance to sibling interaction interventions.

Social interaction research, which began in the mid 1960s, has produced well over 100 published studies detailing various interventions for teaching social skills to children with disabilities and increasing their positive interaction with other children (Fox, McEvoy, Leech, & Moroney, 1989). For the most part, these interventions and intervention packages have a learning theory or direct teaching orientation, so they have several common characteristics. They rely on specification of directly observable classes of social behavior as intervention targets. Some investigators have gone so far as to identify and teach more precisely the specific social skill components of peer interaction (e.g., Strain, 1983; Tremblay, Strain, Hendrickson, & Shores, 1981; Walker, Greenwood, Hops, & Todd, 1979). The goal of these interventions is to produce positive, reciprocal interaction between the child and his or her peers (Fox, Shores, Lindeman, & Strain, 1986; Strain & Shores, 1977), and various direct measures of peer interaction have been used to evaluate these interventions. In some cases other measures of social validation (e.g., Antia & Kreimeyer, 1987; Bradlyn, Himadi, Crimmins, Graves, & Kelly, 1983; Haring, Rogers, Lee, Breen, & Gaylord-Ross, 1986; James & Egel, 1986; Lerger et al., 1979; Powell, Salzberg, Rule, Levy, & Itzkowitz, 1983; Shafer, Egel, & Neef, 1984) and sociometric acceptance (e.g., Maheady & Sainato, 1985; Paine et al., 1982; Rynders, Johnson, Johnson, & Schmidt, 1980; Strain, 1981) have also been obtained.

The specific procedures and tactics employed to teach positive peer interaction have been quite varied, but they can be divided into three basic groups (McEvoy & Odom, 1987). The first approach, *environmental arrangement or re-arrangement*, includes such things as alterations of the nonsocial, physical environment; the activities in the classroom; and/or the social composition of the classroom. By altering the physical space in which children are to interact (Brown, Fox, & Brady, 1987; Spiegel-McGill, Bambara, Shores, & Fox, 1984); the materials they are to use (Beckman & Kohl, 1984; Quilitch & Risley, 1973); or providing socially competent peers for them to interact with (Hecimovic, Fox, Shores, & Strain, 1985; Strain, 1983), one can create setting conditions that will enable, though not ensure, positive interactions with peers.

The other two approaches are *teacher-mediated* and *peer-mediated* applications of direct instruction and intervention tactics. Essentially, they involve application of behavioral procedures such as modeling, prompting, and differential reinforcement of social skills and interactions (McEvoy & Odom, 1987; Strain & Fox, 1981). The basic difference between these two applications is that teacher-mediated procedures rely primarily upon the teacher (or other adult) to model, prompt, and/or differentially reinforce changes in the social skills of the child with disabilities; peer-mediated approaches involve altering the social behaviors and responses of the peer group, which in turn produces and supports changes in the child's social repertoire. Thus, in teacher-mediated intervention adult trainers have used modeling, behavior rehearsal, role-playing, and feedback to teach appropriate peer social skills directly to aggressive students and those with mental retardation (e.g., Elder, Edelstein, & Narick, 1979; Geller, Wildman, Kelly, & Laughlin, 1980) as well as physical and verbal prompts and contingent praise to increase play interactions between children with mental retardation, behavior disorders, or autism, and other children with and without disabilities (Fox et al., 1986; Odom & Strain, 1985; Romanczyk, Diament, Goren, Trunell, & Harris, 1975; Timm, Strain, & Eller, 1979). Peer-mediated interventions include prompting and differentially reinforcing other students to increase their initiations to the child with disabilities (e.g., Hendrickson, Strain, Tremblay, & Shores, 1982; Strain, 1977); having peers model appropriate social behaviors (e.g., Apolloni, Cooke, & Cooke, 1977; Fleming & Fleming, 1982); and directing peers to prompt social responses from students with disabilities (e.g., Haring et al., 1986).

Beyond the individual tactics and approaches, combinations of these procedures and intervention packages have also been developed and applied. Group affection (McEvoy et al., 1988; Twardosz, Nordquist, Simon, & Botkin, 1983) and group socialization (Brown, Ragland, & Fox, 1988) training incorporate teacher-mediated procedures (modeling, prompting, and differential reinforcement); peer-mediated procedures (peer initiations); and environmental organization (grouping children with and without disabilities; use of interactive songs and games) to teach social skills and increase interaction. In addition there are other, more formal, field-tested social skills training curricula that address both young children and adolescents with mild to severe disabilities (e.g., Day, Fox, Shores, & Lindeman, 1982; Day et al., 1984; Day, Powell, & Stowitschek, 1980; Goldstein, Sprafkin, Gershaw, & Klein, 1980; McEvoy, Shores,

Wehby, Johnson, & Fox, 1990; McGinnis & Goldstein, 1984; Shores et al., 1986; Walker et al., 1985).

Clearly, there is an increasingly well-defined and empirically validated technology of school-based social skills training for children with disabilities. Moreover, researchers are beginning to concentrate more effort on identifying ways in which the initial effects of social skills training can be extended across different situations and maintained over time (Fox, 1990; Stokes & Osnes, 1987).

SIBLING INTERACTIONS AND INTERVENTIONS

Given the substantial and successful research dealing with peer social competence interventions, one might expect that the same or similar procedures should be applicable to improving the interactions between children with disabilities and their siblings. After all, one is dealing with child-child interactions (or the lack thereof) in both cases. Furthermore, if peer social competence researchers have been thorough, then the interventions they have developed should be effective across particular situations.

There is, however, at least one flaw with such reasoning. The available descriptive data suggest that the interactions between siblings differ in important ways from those between unrelated children. Brody, Stoneman, and MacKinnon (1982) and Stoneman, Brody, and MacKinnon (1984) have examined the various interaction roles children take when playing with friends and when playing with younger siblings. Friend interactions were characterized by more equality in the roles assumed. The interactants were most likely to act as playmates with one another. In contrast, sibling interactions were characterized by more unequal roles, with the older child acting more as a teacher or manager of the younger sibling. Consequently, there is some reason to question the generalizability of peer social skills interventions to sibling interaction.

Of course the best test of the appropriateness and effectiveness of social competence interventions is actually applying them to children with disabilities and their siblings and empirically evaluating their effects. Unfortunately, there have been very few family-based studies of social competence training (Fox & Savelle, 1987). This is surprising given the importance attached to sibling interaction (Dyson & Fewell, 1989; Gallagher & Powell, 1989) in childhood socialization and researchers' active pursuit of descriptive analyses of sibling interaction, especially of young children (Abramovitch, Corter, & Lando, 1979; Abramovitch, Corter, & Pepler, 1980; Abramovitch, Corter, Pepler, & Stanhope, 1986; Arnold, Levine, & Patterson, 1975; Brody & Stone-

man, 1986; Brody et al., 1982; Brody, Stoneman, MacKinnon, & Mac-
Kinnon, 1985; Corter, Abramovitch, & Pepler, 1983; Donnellan, An-
derson, & Mesaros, 1984; Dunn & Kendrick, 1980; Dunn & Kendrick,
1979, 1981a,b; Lamb, 1978; Lichstein & Wahler, 1976; Loeber, Weissman, & Reid, 1983; Martin & Graunke, 1979; Mash & Johnston, 1983;
Mash & Mercer, 1979; Minnett, Vandell, & Santrock, 1983; Pepler,
Abramovitch, & Corter, 1981; Stoneman & Brody, 1983; Stoneman &
Brody, 1984; Stoneman, Brody, Davis, & Crapps, 1987; Stoneman,
Brody, & MacKinnon, 1984). In a review of investigations published
between 1965 and 1987, Fox, Neimeyer, and Savelle (1988) identified 23
studies that reported observational data *describing* the topographies
and frequencies of interactions between siblings, nine (39%) of which
included descriptions of interactions between children with disabilities
and their siblings. In contrast, a separate analysis of social interaction
intervention studies published between 1965 and 1989 revealed that
out of 106 studies published in that period only six (5%) targeted
problems in sibling interaction (Fox et al., 1989). What follows is a brief,
illustrative review of this social interaction intervention literature. It is
divided into those studies dealing with lack of interaction between
siblings and those dealing with negative sibling interaction patterns.

Interventions To Encourage Positive Interaction Between Siblings

One of the first studies in which school-based, peer social competence training procedures were applied to sibling interaction was reported by Powell et al. (1983). These investigators adapted the
materials, procedures, and behavioral targets of the *Social Competence
Intervention Package for Preschool Youngsters* (SCIPPY) (Day et al., 1980),
a social interaction training package previously developed and field-
tested with teachers of young children with diverse disabilities (i.e.,
mental retardation, behavioral disorders, social withdrawal). Through
assigned readings of a manual, a workshop, and periodic contingent
feedback, parents were taught how to target specific, effective social
initiations (e.g., sharing, verbally organizing play, assisting) and to
apply modeling, prompting, and reinforcement procedures to increase their children's reciprocal social initiations and interactions.
The participants in this study were four children with moderate mental retardation, their nondisabled siblings (three older and one younger than their brother or sister with a disability), and their mothers.
Results indicated that during initial baseline observation, there was
little or no interaction between the children with disabilities and their
siblings, and this did not improve during the next phase when parents were simply told to do their best to encourage their children to
interact. However, once parent training in the SCIPPY materials and
procedures was accomplished and parents used the program with

their children during brief (i.e., 10-minute) sessions at home, the frequency and duration of siblings' play interactions increased. Also, three of the four sibling dyads were observed to increase their positive interactions at times other than when training was being conducted.

Fox and his colleagues (Blackman, 1986; Savelle & Fox, 1987) conducted several studies in an attempt to replicate and extend the initial findings of Powell et al. (1983). Because they reported only a single, broadly defined category of reciprocal interaction as the dependent measure, Powell et al. (1983) were unable to determine if changes in interaction resulted from increases in the initiations of the child with a disability, the sibling, or both children. Also, the transfer of increases in sibling interactions across situations in the Powell et al. (1983) study occurred only with those dyads for whom assessments were conducted the next day (i.e., 24 hours after the intervention sessions); no transfer was found for that dyad in which assessment was conducted soon (i.e., 20 minutes) after the training sessions that same day. Finally, there has as yet been no assessment of the persistence of increased sibling interactions over longer time.

The first replication was directed at determining the relative effects of the adapted SCIPPY procedures on the interactive skills of a 7-year-old girl with moderate mental retardation and her nondisabled 5-year-old sister (Fox, Shores, Spiegel-McGill, & Bambara, 1984). This analysis was important in terms of the reciprocal model of social competence. Truly reciprocal child-child interaction would be characterized by changes in both children's initiations and responses to one another, which would be sustained once the parent-mediated intervention procedure was reduced or eliminated. By using a continuous, sequential observation system that recorded the identity of initiator and responder in these interactions, and by gradually reducing or fading the intervention procedure (Fox et al., 1986), the researchers could address these issues. As the parents implemented the social interaction training procedures, the initiations, responses, and interactions of both children increased, with the initiations of the child with mental retardation increasing somewhat more than those of her sister. As the parent-mediated intervention gradually was reduced, there was some reduction in each child's initiations; however, their extended interactions actually increased. At a final follow-up observation 6 months after intervention had ended, the children's initiations remained within intervention frequencies, but extended interactions had decreased.

In an effort to understand how the timing of assessments might affect the amount of sibling interaction, another study was undertaken (Blackman, 1986). The sibling interactions of two girls (4 and 6 years of age) with moderate disabilities and their older sisters (both 7 years old) were the focus of this analysis. The same parent-implemented intervention package was used, and its effects were assessed during the training sessions and again during two different free play times in the home, one immediately after each training session and the other immediately before the next day's training session. Although the siblings' interactions increased during training sessions, there was little evidence of systematic change in their interactions during either of the two types of free play assessment sessions.

The procedures used in sibling studies described so far were applied in a parent-mediated fashion; that is, the parent directly modeled, prompted, and reinforced interactions between the siblings. Other studies have evaluated sibling-mediated applications of these procedures, that is, those in which the nondisabled sibling is trained to arrange and support interactions directly with the child with disabilities.

Perhaps the earliest report of a sibling-mediated social interaction intervention is one by Miller and Cantwell (1976). They described the case study of an 11-year-old boy identified as "moderately retarded with autistic features." At first, the boy's four older siblings were taught to use mild reprimand and brief time out procedures contingent upon the boy's food stealing. In addition, each sibling was briefly (i.e., 15 minutes) to engage the boy in a one-on-one activity (e.g., playing cars, going for a walk) each day. At these times, they were to "encourage eye contact, coherent speech, and appropriate social behaviors." Although no quantitative measures of interaction were provided, anecdotal reports were that positive interactions were increased.

A data-based evaluation of sibling-mediated social behavior training was reported by James and Egel (1986). Three socially withdrawn young (each 4 years old) children with mental retardation; their older (ages 6–8 years), nondisabled siblings; their mothers; and a nondisabled friend of a sibling were the focus of an intervention package consisting of three components.

The first component involved training sessions in which the experimenters used modeling, rehearsal, verbal prompts, and feedback to train the nondisabled siblings to initiate interactions, prompt responses, and reinforce both initiations and responses of the child with a disability. In the second component nondisabled siblings were taught through modeling, role playing, and feedback to use incidental teaching procedures to increase the disabled child's verbal or gestural requests for desired toys. This second component was added when the first component failed to increase initiations by the children with disabilities sufficiently. The third component was implemented to increase sibling interaction during generalization probes and involved mothers giving the children a general prompt (e.g., "Go play") once during each probe session. Initiations and reciprocal interactions were observed in the home during: 1) free play probes consisting of the sibling dyads and experimenter, 2) generalization probes involving the sibling dyads and/or nondisabled friend, 3) parent (but excluding the experimenter) involvement, and 4) 6-month follow-up probes similar to the generalization probes.

Results showed that: 1) the sibling-mediated intervention increased initiations and interactions between the siblings during free play probes, and these gains persisted at the 6-month follow-up; 2) similar increases in sibling initiations and interactions occurred during the generalization probes without intervention; 3) response prompting by the mother further magnified the interaction increases during these probes; 4) nondisabled friends' initiations to children with disabilities increased slightly during generalization probes but disabled children's initiations to friends did not; and 5) generalization of sibling interaction across settings also was noted.

A later study by Clark, Cunningham, and Cunningham (1989) described a sibling-mediated, problem-solving strategy to increase positive social behaviors between children with autism and their siblings who did not have disabilities. This package consisted of several components designed to increase the nondisabled siblings' use of two behaviors—positive attending to the sibling with autism and use of standard sign language—and to reduce a third class of behavior—controlling commands and questions.

First, nondisabled siblings observed adult trainers as they role-played the parts of disabled and nondisabled children in problem interaction situations, for example, having difficulty engaging the child with autism in positive play interactions. Next, nondisabled siblings were asked for solutions to these problem situations, after which they observed again as the adults role-played these solutions to "master" the problem. Following this the nondisabled siblings were given practice and feedback in enacting these solutions themselves, first as they rehearsed them with the adult trainers and then with their autistic siblings.

Free play observations conducted in a clinic playroom revealed that nondisabled siblings' attending and signing to their autistic siblings increased, and controlling behaviors decreased as the problem-solving sessions were used sequentially across three behaviors. Some, but not all, of these social behavior changes were reported to persist at the 6-month follow-up assessment. In addition, siblings' and parents' ratings suggested improvement in interactive behavior at home, which persisted at the 6-month follow-up assessment. Unfortunately, neither direct observation of the autistic children's social behavior at the clinic play sessions nor either sibling's behavior at home was obtained.

Interventions To Reduce Negative Sibling Interactions and Increase Positive Sibling Interactions

Use of family-based interventions that seek to reduce child behavior problems is not unusual; indeed, it is quite common. However, those that seek to reduce negative *and* increase positive interactions between siblings are used considerably less frequently, especially those that report direct observational measures of both classes of interaction.

O'Leary, O'Leary, and Becker (1967) sought directly to increase positive interaction between a 6-year-old boy with behavior disorders and his younger brother in their home. Prior to intervention, the boys' play interactions were characterized by a variety of negative behaviors, including fighting, breaking toys and furniture, tantrums, and noncompliance to parents' instructions. The experimenters and, later, the parents used differential reinforcement of cooperative play and time out for negative behaviors. Reliable increases in cooperative play between the siblings occurred.

Two variations of this differential attention procedure were examined by Leitenberg, Burchard, Burchard, Fuller, and Lysaught (1977). Six children with behavior problems and their siblings were the focus of this study. Parents and a trained observer conducted in-home observations of: 1) verbal and physical aggression (labeled "sibling conflict"); 2) appropriate interaction (e.g., playing games together, sharing, helping, conversation); and 3) no interaction. Following baseline, parents implemented one of two different interventions in alternating weeks. Differential reinforcement of other behavior (DRO) involved parents delivering contingent praise and pennies to both children for each minute in which sibling conflict did not occur. The second procedure, reinforcement of appropriate interaction (RAI), consisted of the same rewards but they were delivered only after an interval in which the siblings had interacted appropriately. DRO and RAI reduced sibling conflict equally, and both were associated with increase in appropriate interaction. However, RAI resulted in substantially more appropriate sibling interaction.

In the authors' research the effects of the SCIPPY social interaction training package on positive and negative interactions were investigated with a young boy with moderate mental retardation and his older sister (Savelle & Fox, 1987). These children had a history of predominantly negative interaction, rather than simply a lack of interaction. The observation and social interaction training procedures were implemented as described in the Savelle and Fox (1987) study. A reversal design was used to contrast successive phases of no intervention with parent use of social interaction training. Results showed that: 1) both initiations and interactions for the child with a disability increased following the parent-implemented social interaction training; 2) negative initiations and interactions between the siblings were eliminated; 3) when the intervention was terminated, positive initiations and interactions decreased but did not return to baseline levels.

In contrast to the adult-mediated procedures of the preceding studies, Lavigueur (1976) evaluated both sibling- and parent-mediated procedures in a slightly different approach to increasing siblings' positive interactions and reducing negative interactions. Two disruptive children from two different families and their siblings were involved. Interval recording sampled the occurrence of positive and negative verbalizations, offering and giving help, aggression, noncompliance, playing, and positive affect. After baseline two procedures were contrasted in sequential phases: 1) parent use of differential attention and time out contingent upon the occurrence of target behaviors, and 2) use of differential attention by both parents and siblings. Initial targets were positive and negative verbalizations; offering help and giving help were added later. In one family, positive interactions increased when the parent-only intervention was used. Although introduction of the combined parent- and sibling-intervention produced no further increases in positive interactions, negative verbalizations did not decrease until the sibling-mediated component was added. In the second family all target behaviors were changed by the parent intervention alone. During the last two phases of parent and parent-sibling intervention, play between the siblings (never a direct intervention target) also increased. Thus, although increases were obtained in several categories of positive interaction, the sibling-intervention effects were minimal.

Summary

Considered together these few studies indicate that siblings as well as parents can be taught to use specific, behavioral procedures similar to those employed in school-based, peer competence interventions, that is, modeling, prompting, and differential reinforcement procedures. Some have been parent-mediated (Leitenburg et al., 1977; O'Leary et al., 1967; Powell et al., 1983), while others (Clark et al., 1989; James & Egel, 1986; Lavigueur, 1976) have included siblings as direct trainers or intervention agents for their brother or sister with a disability.

These interventions typically have increased positive initiations and interactions between children with disabilities and their nondisabled siblings. The data further show that often these increased sibling interactions have also tended to occur in other situations, with other children, and persisted over time (Fox, Shores et al., 1984; James & Egel, 1986; Powell et al., 1983) although this has not been true in every case (Fox, Shores et al., 1984; Powell et al., 1983).

SIBLING SOCIAL COMPETENCE INTERVENTIONS RECONSIDERED

Given the very positive outcomes of these sibling intervention studies and the related results from the more extensive peer social competence data base, there would appear to be a readily available technology for addressing problems of both positive and negative interaction between siblings. Despite these encouraging outcomes, there remain a number of important and unresolved issues facing researchers and practitioners alike. These include the adequacy of the current descriptive data base in guiding clinical applications of these procedures; the adequacy of experimental and intervention studies in addressing the generalization and maintenance of changes in child-sibling interaction; the range of variables that must or would be advantageous to consider in evaluating changes in these interactions; and social validation of sibling-based interventions.

Adequacy of the Current Descriptive Data Base

Those who do intervention research often are asked such questions as, "How little interaction is enough to warrant intervention?", and "How much change in interaction can and should be produced?" Descriptive studies of naturally occurring interaction in families with children who do not have disabilities or families with children who have disabilities in which interaction is considered appropriate *might* be used to answer these and other related questions.

However, use of this data base for normative comparisons is made difficult by several factors. First, there is an unequal distribution of studies across different populations. Most analyses have centered upon siblings without disabilities, followed by those centered on children with conduct disorders (Fox et al., 1988). In addition, the vast majority of these studies have been conducted with young children and their brothers or sisters. How the frequency, topography, and function of sibling interactions may differ for older children and adolescents largely has been ignored.

A second problem concerns the setting conditions of these investigations. Parameters that have been or could be used to describe setting conditions include the physical location of the study (e.g., laboratory versus clinic versus home); the specific area of the home in which observations were conducted; the particular family members present; instructions to and other requirements of the participants (e.g., free play versus structured tasks or activities); restrictions (or lack of restrictions) on family members' activities during the observation (e.g., television or radio on or off, limitations on telephone calls or visitors); and the area of the home to which family members have or have not been restricted. Those studies conducted by the same or by related research groups usually describe the same setting parameters and tend to employ the same particular setting conditions. However, when one looks across different research groups, the setting parameters reported and the particular setting conditions used often have varied considerably.

That at least certain of these setting variables affect children's interactions with parents or siblings is apparent from experimental studies. For example, Gene Brody, Zolinda Stoneman, and their colleagues have documented the reductive effects of television viewing on children's interactions with their fathers as well as the differences in interactions when both or only one parent is present (e.g., Brody & Stoneman, 1983; Brody, Stoneman, & Sanders, 1980). Thus, descriptions of prevailing interaction rates are not likely to be informative without description of and comparison with the prevailing setting conditions for a study or group of studies.

Depending upon the specific independent variables under study, it may be appropriate, for example, to follow the lead of Gerald Patterson and his colleagues at the Oregon Social Learning Center who, across their specific investigations, employ a standard set of observation setting conditions that include the following:

1. Everyone in the family must be present.
2. No guests.
3. The family is limited to two rooms.
4. The observers will wait only 10 minutes for all to be present in the two rooms.
5. Telephone: No calls out; briefly answer incoming calls.
6. No TV.
7. No talking to observers while they are coding.
8. Do not discuss anything with observers that relates to your problems or the procedures you are using to deal with them. (Patterson, 1982, p. 49)

Of course, not all studies can or should use identical setting conditions. Also, it will be important to examine *systematically* how variations in setting conditions by themselves and in concert with other direct interventions may alter child-sibling interactions.

A third, and possibly more limiting factor of existing descriptive (and experimental) studies, concerns the measurement procedures used and the units of analysis. The most frequently reported observation tactic in the studies to date has been some form of time sampling/interval recording. Although efficient and often highly reliable, such recording procedures present problems in social interaction research. Methodological studies have shown that interval recording does not accurately represent either frequency or duration of the behavior measured (Harrop & Daniels, 1984; Powell, Martindale, Kulp, Martindale, & Baumann, 1977; Repp, Roberts, Slack, Repp, & Berkler, 1976). Also, because interval recording procedures artificially divide an observation into discontinuous segments, they do not permit a precise analysis of interaction sequences and exchanges.

In viewing interaction with siblings and parents from a reciprocal perspective, the best measurement tactic is continuous, sequential recording (Patterson, 1982). Continuous, sequential recording permits an analysis of social behaviors in terms of their actual social antecedents and consequences. This approach has proved fruitful in identifying effective social interaction skills in children's interactions with classroom peers (Savelle & Fox, 1988; Strain, 1983; Tremblay et al., 1981) and in evaluating the effects and social validity of social interaction interventions for children with disabilities (Day, Powell et al., 1982; Fox et al., 1986; Hendrickson et al., 1982). However, this measurement tactic rarely has been used in descriptive studies of children's interactions with siblings (Fox et al., 1988).

For these reasons the author and his colleagues initiated their own descriptive analysis of the sibling interactions of children with and without disabilities (Savelle, Fox, & Phillips, 1987). Standard home setting conditions similar to those of Patterson (1982) and a continuous sequential observation system that assessed disabled child, sibling, and parent initiations and responses to one another were used in this study. Children with mental retardation and their siblings initiated more to one another than did sibling pairs in which neither child had a disability. However, nondisabled sibling pairs were more responsive to one another's initiations. In effect, interactions between children with mental retardation and their siblings appeared less reciprocal.

A somewhat different inequality was noted between parents and children. Children with mental retardation and nondisabled children initiated to their parents at roughly similar rates. However, parents of children with mental retardation initiated to their children more and responded to a higher proportion of their children's initiations than did parents of nondisabled children.

There is a need not only for more descriptive studies, but also for studies that: 1) describe a common set of setting condition parameters; 2) systematically examine the effect of changes in particular setting conditions, such as the area of the home, presence/absence of certain family members, use of specific instructions or tasks during the observation; 3) repeatedly assess children's interactions with family members over time to evaluate the stability of these interactions; and 4) use continuous, sequential observation procedures to identify specific social behaviors and the social responses of family members to them. It is through such refinements that the descriptive data base will become most useful in understanding naturally occurring family interactions and in guiding intervention research and applications.

Adequacy of Research in Addressing Generalization and Maintenance of Improved Interaction

To date there have been few intervention studies targeting sibling interaction and even in these few studies parents typically have been the primary intervention agents. In terms of adult involvement, research on social interaction training with siblings of children with disabilities has evidenced a history similar to that of school-based studies of social interaction training (McEvoy & Odom, 1987; Strain & Fox, 1981).

Again, progress in this area will not be simply a matter of increasing the number of intervention studies dealing with sibling or parent interactions of children with disabilities. Of course, replications are needed, but it seems clear from the existing data that both parents and siblings *can* intervene effectively to teach social skills to children with disabilities and increase their positive interactions with family members. In addition, researchers must also begin to address more complex questions including: 1) whether parent- or sibling-mediated intervention is the more efficient approach with regard to training time, effort, and the magnitude and generalization of the social gains for children with disabilities; 2) what, if any, side effects, positive or negative, result from using parents or siblings as social interaction trainers; 3) how children with disabilities may be taught a set of skills to recruit and shape positive interactions with family members as has been done in classroom settings (Graubard, Rosenberg, & Miller, 1971; Morgan, Young, & Goldstein, 1983; Polirstok & Greer, 1977); and 4) what long-term outcomes for the child, sibling, and parents do these social interaction interventions have?

Perhaps one of the most critical of these questions has to do with the "generalization" and "maintenance" of the effects of sibling interaction training. Several studies have reported that once increases in sibling interaction were obtained under training conditions, similar increases also were obtained between siblings under nontraining conditions (Clark et al., 1989; James & Egel, 1986; Powell et al., 1983) and between the child with disabilities and other children (James & Egel, 1986). To some extent, increases persisted over time (James & Egel, 1986).

However, it is not entirely clear that these are instances of generalization. In the traditional use of the term, generalization involves the spread of control by the stimulus. Control of the response extends from that stimulus directly associated with the intervention conditions to other stimuli that are similar to the original training stimulus in some respect. This occurs without the generalization test stimuli having been associated with the intervention or other environmental changes.

Changes in social behavior that are observed to occur across stimuli (i.e., situations, people) may indicate stimulus generalization; they also may be the result of other environmental changes that directly or indirectly result from the original social interaction intervention. For example, in both the Powell et al. (1983) and the James and Egel (1986) studies, some of the target behaviors taught to the disabled and nondisabled siblings, that is, sharing, verbally organizing play, assistance, and affection, were behaviors that previous research (Fox et al., 1986; Savelle & Fox, 1987; Tremblay et al., 1981) had shown to have a high probability of receiving a positive response from other children. In effect, these behaviors appear to have a "natural community of reinforcement." Teaching these behaviors as part of a social competence intervention program would, therefore, constitute the application of a particular programming tactic (Kohler & Greenwood, 1986; Marholin & Siegel, 1978; Stokes & Baer, 1977; Stokes & Osnes, 1987, 1989). If this were, indeed, the case, then the changes across situations in social behavior in the Powell et al. (1983) and James and Egel (1986) studies might represent the effects of generalization programming, an important outcome that appears topographically similar to generalization but actually results from the intervention itself, that is, teaching behaviors that other children are likely to reinforce (Fox et al., 1989; McConnell, 1987; Stokes & Osnes, 1987). Much the same argument can be made concerning reports of maintenance of changes in social interaction between siblings.

This is an issue of practical as well as conceptual importance. In the development of an applied technology of social competence intervention, researchers must not only evaluate their ability to produce initial changes in social behavior, but also understand how to arrange for these changes to occur reliably across relevant situations (Baer, Wolf, & Risley, 1968). For this reason, it is necessary to assess whether or not changes in sibling interaction occur across different situations, people, and time, as well as to analyze systematically specific tactics for promoting generalization of social behavior change.

How this type of analysis can be accomplished has been discussed at length elsewhere (Fox et al., 1989). However, it can be illustrated briefly here with the Powell et al. (1983) and James and Egel (1986) studies. Given that some of the behavioral targets of sibling interaction training were more socially effective (i.e., more likely to receive a positive response) than others, one could compare the degree to which these two different response classes were found to occur across situations or time. If, indeed, these more socially effective behaviors generalized and the less effective behaviors did not, then this would *suggest* that it was the immediate response of siblings to these behaviors that was responsible, rather than the empirical phenomenon of generalization.

It would be necessary to test this hypothesis further, perhaps by deliberately reducing the siblings' responsiveness to the socially effective behavior targets during the generalization sessions. If the socially effective behaviors then decreased during these sessions, this would strengthen the case for contingency control rather than generalization of these behaviors.

Of course, the analysis cannot and should not be left simply after a demonstration of contingency control in sibling interaction. Certainly changes in sibling responsiveness will be necessary to support and extend the social repertoires of children with disabilities. At the same time efforts might begin to focus on how deliberately to produce more generalized durable change (Stokes & Baer, 1977; Stokes & Osnes, 1987, 1989) through the use of deliberate generalization programming tactics, such as multiple exemplar training (Brady et al., 1984; Brady, Shores, McEvoy, Ellis, & Fox, 1987; Fox et al., 1984; Gaylord-Ross, Haring, Breen, & Pitts-Conway, 1984; Gunter, Fox, Brady, Shores, & Cavanaugh, 1988) and/or reinforcement thinning and fading tactics (Fox et al., 1986; Romanczyk et al., 1975; Timm et al., 1979).

Sibling and Peer Social Interaction

Another unresolved issue has to do with the relationship between children's interactions with siblings and their interactions with peers. This general issue can be addressed at two levels. On one level researchers might ask what effect, if any, increasing the interactions between children with disabilities and their siblings would have on their interactions with peers (or vice versa). To some degree this is a variation of the generalization questions just discussed.

Several studies have directly contrasted the sibling and peer interactions of nondisabled children in the home. Siblings' play interactions are characterized by role inequalities, the older sibling more often acting in a teacher/manager role, that is, more directive, and the younger sibling more often assuming a learner/managee role (Brody et al., 1982; Stoneman et al., 1984). In contrast, child-friend interactions typically have been described as more egalitarian, that is, with more sharing of social roles and cooperative play, in these same studies. When all three children (i.e., friend, older and younger siblings) were observed together, the older child and friend still assumed a more managerial role relative to the younger sibling but did so less frequently than in the dyadic play sessions. Furthermore, in this triadic arrangement the younger child engaged in more solitary behavior than in dyadic play sessions.

Berndt and Bulleit (1985) not only assessed the interactions between nondisabled preschoolers and their older or younger siblings but compared them with these same preschoolers' interactions with classmates at school. They replicated the more cooperative, egalitarian nature of child-peer interactions but otherwise found only a very few moderate correlations between children's behavior at home and at school (i.e., initiating aggression, onlooker, and unoccupied behaviors).

There have been fewer such analyses of children with disabilities. In an intensive observational case study of a young boy with autism, Lichstein and Wahler (1976) found comparatively little interaction between this boy and his older, nondisabled sister or the sister's friend, nor was the boy observed to engage peers in much interaction at school. Unfortunately, neither the specific topographies of social behavior nor the relative amounts of sibling and friend interaction were recorded. In the James and Egel (1986) study intervention-related increases in the initiations and interactions between disabled and nondisabled siblings were accompanied by what appeared to be "spontaneous" increases in interactions between children with disabilities and an untrained peer.

The existing data on the relationship between sibling and peer interaction are too few and the measurement procedures used to collect them too varied to allow any firm conclusions. However, it does not appear that there is an exact, point-by-point relationship between child-sibling and child-peer interactions (Berndt & Bulleit, 1985), at least under naturally occurring conditions. When a child's social skills and interactions with his or her sibling are deliberately increased, this *may* improve interactions with other children (e.g., James & Egel, 1986).

Perhaps researchers should not expect very close correspondence between sibling and peer interactions, since the topographies and functions of these interactions seem rather different (Brody et al., 1982; Stoneman et al., 1984). It may also be that the setting conditions for these interactions as well as the status of the interactants may modulate the relationship between sibling and peer interactions. For example, if peer interactions are observed between a child at home or in his or her neighborhood (rather than at school), they may bear a closer relationship to or be more affected by interactions with his or her sibling at home.

The other level of the issue of the relationship between sibling and peer interactions concerns the role that can and should be anticipated for siblings in social interaction training. To what degree should siblings be expected to fulfill the same role that classroom peers have, that is, the role of social skills trainer or intervention agent for their brother or sister with a disability? What effects might this role as trainer have on their social interactions? Should siblings become the primary interaction partners for their brothers or sisters outside of school?

These questions go beyond the earlier issue of whether or not siblings *can* fulfill these roles. Research has shown that in their naturally occurring interactions, older siblings often act as teachers and managers for their younger brothers or sisters (Brody et al., 1982; Stoneman et al., 1984). With a certain amount of training and supervision by adults, siblings certainly are capable of participating in the teaching of social (Clark et al., 1989; James & Egel, 1986; Lavigueur, 1976) as well as other skills (e.g., Schriebman, O'Neill, & Koegel, 1983).

Variables To Consider in Evaluating Changes in Interaction

However, it is unclear what factors may mitigate the effectiveness or appropriateness of siblings as active trainers or even partners in social skills training programs for children with disabilities. Some studies have reported increased social isolation, depression, and stress in families of children with disabilities (e.g., Breiner & Young, 1985; DeMeyer & Goldberg, 1983; Galbreath, Daurelle, & Fox, 1987; Gallagher, Beckman, & Cross, 1983; McAllister, Butler, & Lei, 1973). In studying the families of children with conduct disorders, Wahler and his colleagues (Dumas & Wahler, 1983; Wahler, 1980; Wahler, Leske, & Rogers, 1979) reported that parents' "social insularity" (low rates of interactions with friends, high amounts of negative interactions with relatives and helping agencies) was associated with the occurrence of problem interactions between parents and children and a reduced likelihood that these families would sustain the gains of a standard behavioral parent training program.

The particular implications for sibling interaction or for the effectiveness of sibling-mediated intervention are largely unknown. However, it is not improbable that these personal and family system variables have some mediating role (Gallagher & Powell, 1989). A study by Dyson and Fewell (1989) found that, as a group, siblings of children with disabilities did not differ significantly in self-concept from siblings of children who did not have disabilities, although a few had very low self-concept scores. Mash and Johnston (1983) reported that measures of maternal self-confidence and stress were negatively related to the amount of interaction between hyperactive boys and their siblings.

It is important from both a research and a clinical standpoint to determine more precisely the extent to which such variables as poor self-concept, pre-existing negative relations, the amount of caretaking responsibilities, and other family system variables may affect or be affected by nondisabled children's participation in and use of social competence interventions with their siblings who have disabilities. Deliberate alterations in other areas of a family's ecology may positively or negatively affect the in-home interactions between children with disabilities, siblings, and parents. It is not inconceivable that such ecological interventions may augment or facilitate more direct social competence interventions for children with disabilities (see Krantz & Risley, 1977 for an example of effective ecological interventions in preschools). Some currently popular "interventions" that take place outside of the home (parent and sibling support groups and respite care) may indeed have beneficial effects on actual family interactions within the home. However, the authors know of no published or ongoing studies that relate family members' participation in these out-of-the-home activities to in-home interactional changes.

Social Validity of Sibling-Based Social Competence Interventions

Several of the specific questions addressed in the section immediately preceding touch upon topics that also may be treated as issues of social validity, for example, should siblings be social skills trainers; what kinds of interactive behaviors between siblings with and without disabilities should intervention attempt to increase? One might even include those questions relating to the effects of social skills training on sibling interaction, peer interaction, and family functioning. From this perspective, sibling social competence training might be considered socially valid: 1) if there are concurrent changes in a child's acceptance by a sibling, peers, or other family members; 2) if the procedures used to effect these changes are in some way acceptable to siblings or parents; and/or 3) if there are positive effects on family interaction beyond the sibling dyad.

The traditional approach to social validity (Wolf, 1978) has been to inquire of significant others as to their opinions about such social validity outcomes, usually by administering some form of checklist, rating scale, or other questionnaire. Several sibling intervention studies cited earlier have used just such an approach and usually have reported positive reactions to the interventions and outcomes. Thus, James and Egel (1986) and Powell et al. (1983) found that observationally measured changes in siblings' social interactions were supported by parents' positive ratings of those interactions at the end of the studies. Powell et al. (1983) also noted that parents positively rated the utility and effectiveness of the interaction training package that they were trained to use.

Such information *can* be valuable to researchers and practitioners alike. For it to be useful, however, social validation must be pursued beyond the summative and indirect manner in which it has been pursued so far. There are at least two related problems with such an approach, that is, the "validity" of social validation and the limited manner in which such validation has been conducted.

First, regarding the "validity" of social validation, when significant others such as parents, siblings, teachers, and so forth are asked to render summary judgments of children's behavior, their ratings may comport with direct observational data as in the James and Egel (1986) and Powell et al. (1983) studies; however, their judgements may also indicate behavior change where no such change has occurred (e.g., Wahler & Fox, 1980) or fail to identify behavior change when it has in fact occurred (e.g., Wahler & Leske, 1973).

This is not to say that social validation judgments are unimportant. In fact, they are probably quite important in that most parents, teachers, and so forth make these judgments anyway, and social validation is simply the researcher's way of formalizing and attempting to measure them objectively. What is, perhaps, even more important is discovering what variables control these judgments, and, when these judgments diverge from directly measured behavior change in the child, what can be done to improve the accuracy of parents' judgments or perceptions of their child's behavior.

For example, Wahler and Leske (1973) asked two groups of teachers to make summary judgments of a boy's distractible behavior. The only procedural difference between the two groups was that one group simply rated the child's behavior at the end of each videotaped segment. The other group of teachers was asked to make direct frequency counts of distractible behavior while watching the tape and then to rate the boy's behavior using the rating scale at the end of each segment. The latter group's ratings were much more sensitive to actual changes in the boy's distractibility than the former group.

Replication of this study with siblings and parents in regard to their interactions with a family member with disabilities would yield information of both scientific and practical importance. It would allow researchers (or the families) to take practical action, particularly if it were combined with an analysis of how these perceptions in turn might affect moment-to-moment sibling interactions or the accurate implementation of social competence training procedures.

The second and related point regarding social validation has to do with the absolute as opposed to the relative way in which it has been assessed. To be truly informative, social validation assessments must ask more than whether parents or siblings find a particular intervention procedure acceptable, that is, whether they find a particular level of change in sibling interaction of sufficient magnitude or desirable. Instead, researchers must begin to ask to what extent family members find a particular procedure more acceptable, effective, efficient, and so forth, relative to some other procedure (e.g., parent-mediated versus sibling-mediated) or to no intervention at all. These relative judgements might be even more informative once researchers can and do supply parents with information regarding the relative durability and generalization of intervention effects, and their potential "side-effects." Some parents may consider sibling-mediated social skills interventions time-consuming and/or an unwarranted intrusion upon the child who does not have a disability. However, they may find certain family scheduling or home environmental rearrangements more acceptable. Alternatively, if the longer-term consequences of not intervening in some way in siblings' interactions involve a worsening of the relationship between the disabled and nondisabled child (e.g., increased negative interaction), a relatively intensive intervention that is faded out over time may be regarded as more acceptable by parents and siblings.

SUMMARY

For the most part research on siblings' contribution to social interaction with and social competence interventions for their brothers or sisters with disabilities has paralleled and benefited from peer social competence studies. There have been ample demonstrations that peers can contribute effectively and directly to the development of social skills in children with disabilities. From the few existing studies with siblings, it is apparent that siblings can fulfill a similar function.

However, research on sibling interaction and intervention must now move beyond this "demonstration" phase. Researchers must address more complex and, ultimately, more interesting and socially significant issues. These include understanding the conditions under which it is practical and effective for siblings to act as trainers for their brothers or sisters with disabilities, and how to analyze and describe more systematically the situational influences on sibling interaction, and the long-term individual and family consequences of these interventions.

REFERENCES

Abramovitch, R., Corter, C., & Lando, B. (1979). Sibling interaction in the home. *Child Development, 50,* 997–1003.

Abramovitch, R., Corter, C., & Pepler, R.D. (1980). Observations of mixed-sex sibling dyads. *Child Development, 51,* 1268–1271.

Abramovitch, R., Corter, C., Pepler, D., & Stanhope, L. (1986). Sibling and peer interaction: A final follow-up and comparison. *Child Development, 57,* 217–229.

Antia, S.D., & Kreimeyer, K.H. (1987). The effect of social skill training on the peer interaction of preschool hearing-impaired children. *Journal of the Division of Early Childhood, 11,* 206–216.

Apolloni, T., Cooke, S.A., & Cooke, T.P. (1977). Establishing a non-retarded peer as a behavioral model for retarded toddlers. *Perceptual and Motor Skills, 44,* 231–241.

Arnold, J., Levine, A., & Patterson, G. (1975). Changes in sibling behavior following family intervention. *Journal of Consulting and Clinical Psychology, 43,* 683–688.

Baer, D.M., Wolf, M.M., & Risley, T.R. (1968). Some current dimensions of applied behavior analysis. *Journal of Applied Behavior Analysis, 1,* 91–97.

Beckman, P.J., & Kohl, F.L. (1984). The effects of social and isolate toys on the interactions and play of integrated and nonintegrated groups of preschoolers. *Education and Training of the Mentally Retarded, 19,* 169–174.

Berndt, T.J., & Bulleit, T.N. (1985). Effects of sibling relationships on preschoolers' behavior at home and at school. *Developmental Psychology, 21,* 761–767.

Blackman, J. (1986). *Parent-mediated treatment of exceptional children's social withdrawal.* Unpublished doctoral dissertation. George Peabody College for Teachers, Vanderbilt University, Nashville.

Bradlyn, A.S., Himadi, W.G., Crimmins, D.B., Graves, K.G., & Kelly, J.A. (1983). Conversational skills training for retarded adolescents. *Behavior Therapy, 14,* 314–325.

Brady, M.P., McEvoy, M.A., Wehby, J., & Ellis, D. (1987). Using peers as trainers to increase an autistic child's social interactions. *Exceptional Child, 34,* 213–219.

Brady, M.P., Shores, R.E., Gunter, P., McEvoy, M.A., Fox, J.J., & White, C. (1984). Generalization of an adolescent's social interaction behavior via multiple peers in a classroom setting. *Journal of The Association for Persons with Severe Handicaps, 9*, 278–286.

Brady, M.P., Shores, R.E., McEvoy, M.A., Ellis, D., & Fox, J.J. (1987). Increasing the social interactions of severely handicapped autistic children. *Journal of Autism and Developmental Disorders, 17*, 375–390.

Breiner, J., & Young, D.L. (1985). Social interaction: A comparison of mothers with noncompliant, nondelayed and developmentally delayed children. *Child and Family Behavior Therapy, 7*, 1–7.

Brody, G.H., & Stoneman, Z. (1983). The influence of television viewing on family interactions. *Journal of Family Issues, 4*, 329–348.

Brody, G.H., & Stoneman, Z. (1986). Contextual issues in the study of sibling socialization. In J.J. Gallagher & P.M. Vietze (Eds.), *Families of handicapped persons: Research, programs, and policy issues* (pp. 197–217). Baltimore: Paul H. Brookes Publishing Co.

Brody, G.H., Stoneman, Z., & MacKinnon, C. (1982). Role asymmetries in interactions among school-aged children, their younger siblings, and their friends. *Child Development, 53*, 1364–1370.

Brody, G.H., Stoneman, Z., MacKinnon, C., & MacKinnon, R. (1985). Role relationships and behavior between preschool-aged and school-aged sibling pairs. *Developmental Psychology, 21*, 124–129.

Brody, G.H., Stoneman, Z., & Sanders, A. (1980). Effects of television viewing on family interactions: An observational study. *Family Relations, 29*, 216–220.

Brown, W.H., Bryson-Brockman, W., & Fox, J.J. (1986). The usefulness of J. R. Kantor's setting event concept for research on children's social behavior. *Child and Family Behavior Therapy, 8*, 15–25.

Brown, W.H., Fox, J.J., & Brady, M.P. (1987). The effects of spatial density on the socially directed behavior of 3 and 4 year old children during freeplay: An investigation of a setting factor. *Education and Treatment of Children, 10*, 247–258.

Brown, W.H., Ragland, E.U., & Fox, J.J. (1988). Effects of group socialization procedures on the social interactions of preschool children. *Research in Developmental Disabilities, 9*, 359–376.

Clark, M.L., Cunningham, L.J., & Cunningham, C.E. (1989). Improving the social behavior of siblings of autistic children using a group problem solving approach. *Child and Family Behavior Therapy, 11*, 19–33.

Corter, C., Abramovitch, R., & Pepler, D. (1983). The role of the mother in sibling interaction. *Child Development, 54*, 1599–1605.

Day, R., Fox, J.J., Shores, R.E., & Lindeman, D. (1982). The social competence intervention project: Developing educational procedures for teaching social interaction skills to handicapped children. *Behavior Disorders, 8*(2), 120–127.

Day, R.M., Lindeman, D.P., Powell, T.H., Fox, J.J., Stowitschek, J.J., & Shores, R.E. (1984). Empirically-derived teaching package for socially withdrawn handicapped and non-handicapped children. *Teacher Education and Special Education, 7*, 46–55.

Day, R.M., Powell, T.H., Dy-Lin, E.B., & Stowitschek, J.J. (1982). An evaluation of the effects of a social interaction training package on mentally retarded handicapped preschool children. *Education and Training of the Mentally Retarded, 17*, 125–130.

Day, R.M., Powell, T.H., & Stowitschek, J.J. (1980). *The Social Compe-*

tence Intervention Package for Preschool Youngsters. (Available from Dr. Sarah Rule, Department of Special Education, Utah State University, Logan, Utah.)

DeMyer, M.K., & Goldberg, P. (1983). Family needs of the autistic adolescent. In E. Schopler & G. Mesibov (Eds.), *Autism in adolescents and adults* (pp. 225–250). New York: Plenum.

Donnellan, A.M., Anderson, J.L., & Mesaros, R.A. (1984). An observational study of stereotypic behavior and proximity related to the occurrence of autistic child-family member interactions. *Journal of Autism and Developmental Disorders, 14,* 205–210.

Dumas, J.E., & Wahler, R.G. (1983). Indiscriminate mothering as a contextual factor in aggressive-oppositional child behavior: "Damned if you do and damned if you don't." *Journal of Abnormal Child Psychology, 13,* 1–17.

Dunn, J., & Kendrick, C. (1979). Interactions between young siblings in the context of family relationships. In M. Lewis & L. Rosenblum (Eds.), *The child and its family* (pp. 143–168). New York: Plenum.

Dunn, J., & Kendrick, C. (1980). The arrival of a sibling: Changes in patterns of interaction between mother and first-born child. *Journal of Child Psychology and Psychiatry, 21,* 119–132.

Dunn, J., & Kendrick, C. (1981a). Interactions between young siblings: Association with the interaction between mother and first-born child. *Developmental Psychology, 17,* 336–343.

Dunn, J., & Kendrick, C. (1981b). Social behaviors of young siblings in the family context: Differences between same-sex and different-sex dyads. *Child Development, 52,* 1265–1273.

Dyson, L., & Fewell, R.R. (1989). The self-concept of siblings of handicapped children: A comparison. *Journal of Early Intervention, 13,* 230–238.

Elder, J.P., Edelstein, B.A., & Narick, M.M. (1979). Adolescent psychiatric patients: Modifying aggressive behavior with social skills training. *Behavior Modification, 3,* 161–178.

Fleming, E.R., & Fleming, D.C. (1982). Social skills training for educable mentally retarded children. *Education and Training of the Mentally Retarded, 17,* 44–50.

Fox, J.J. (Ed.). (1987). Social interactions of behaviorally disordered children and youth [Special issue]. *Behavioral Disorders, 12.*

Fox, J.J. (1990). Ecology, setting events and environmental organization: An interbehavioral perspective on arranging classrooms for behavioral development. *Education and Treatment of Children, 13,* 364–373.

Fox, J.J., Gunter, P., Brady, M.P., Bambara, L., Speigel-McGill, P., & Shores, R.E. (1984). Using multiple peer exemplars to develop generalized social responding of an autistic girl. In R.B. Rutherford (Ed.), *Severe behavior disorders of children and youth* (Vol. 7, pp. 17–26). Reston, VA: Council for Children with Behavioral Disorders.

Fox, J.J., McEvoy, M.A., & Day, R.M. (1991). An empirically-based, educational approach to developing social competence in young children: Outcomes and issues. J.S. Benninga (Ed.), *Moral, character, and civic education in the elementary school* (pp. 227–242). New York: Teachers College.

Fox, J.J., McEvoy, M., Leech, R., & Moroney, M. (1989, November). *Generalization, maintenance and behavioral interventions with handicapped students: Illustrations from social interaction research.* Paper presented at the 13th Annual TECBD National Conference on Severe Behavior Disorders of Children and Youth, Tempe, AZ.

Fox, J.J., Niemeyer, J., & Savelle, S. (1988, March). *Interactions in families of mentally retarded and behaviorally disordered children and youth.* Paper presented at The Gatlinburg Conference on Research in Mental Retardation and Developmental Disabilities, Gatlinburg, TN.

Fox, J., & Savelle, S. (1987). Social interaction research and families of behaviorally disordered children: A critical review and forward look. *Behavioral Disorders, 12,* 276–291.

Fox, J., Shores, R., Lindeman, D., & Strain, P. (1986). Maintaining social initiations of withdrawn handicapped and nonhandicapped preschoolers through a response-dependent fading tactic. *Journal of Abnormal Child Psychology, 14,* 387–396.

Fox , J.J., Shores, R.E., Spiegel-McGill, P., & Bambara, L. (1984, March). *Generalization and maintenance in social interaction training with mentally retarded young children: Past is prologue.* Paper presented at the Gatlinburg Conference on Research and Theory in Mental Retardation and Developmental Disabilities, Gatlinburg, TN.

Galbreath, H., Daurelle, L., & Fox, J.J. (1987, March). *Community interactions and leisure time activities in families of handicapped and nonhandicapped children.* Paper presented at The Gatlinburg Conference on Research in Mental Retardation and Developmental Disabilities, Gatlinburg, TN.

Gallagher, J.J., Beckman, P., & Cross, A.H. (1983). Families of handicapped children: Sources of stress and its amelioration. *Exceptional Children, 50,* 10–19.

Gallagher, P.A., & Powell, T.H. (1989). Brothers and sisters: Meeting special needs. *Topics in Early Childhood Special Education, 8*(4), 24–37.

Gaylord-Ross, R., Haring, T., Breen, C., & Pitts-Conway, V. (1984). The training and generalization of social interaction skills with autistic youth. *Journal of Applied Behavior Analysis, 17,* 229–247.

Geller, M.I., Wildman, H.E., Kelly, J.A., & Laughlin, C.S. (1980). Teaching assertive and commendatory social skills to an interpersonally-deficient retarded adolescent. *Journal of Clinical Child Psychology, 9,* 17–21.

Goldstein, A.P., Sprafkin, R., Gershaw, N., & Klein, P. (1980). *Skillstreaming the adolescent.* Champaign: Research Press.

Graubard, P., Rosenberg, H., & Miller, M. (1971). Student application of behavior modification to teachers and environments or ecological approaches to social deviancy. In S. Ramp & B. Hopkins (Eds.), *A new direction for education: Behavior analysis* (pp. 80–101). Lawrence: University of Kansas.

Gunter, P., Fox, J.J., Brady, M.P., Shores, R.E., & Cavanaugh, K. (1988). Nonhandicapped peers as multiple exemplars: A generalization tactic for promoting autistic students' social skills. *Behavioral Disorders, 13,* 116–126.

Haring, T., Roger, B., Lee, M., Breen, C., & Gaylord-Ross, R. (1986). Teaching social language to moderately handicapped students. *Journal of Applied Behavior Analysis, 19,* 159–171.

Harrop, A., & Daniels, M. (1984). Methods of time sampling: A reappraisal of momentary time-sampling and partial interval recording. *Journal of Applied Behavior Analysis, 17,* 73–77.

Hecimovic, A., Fox, J., Shores, R., & Strain, P. (1985). An analysis of developmentally integrated and segregated freeplay settings and the generalization of newly-acquired social behaviors of socially withdrawn preschoolers. *Behavioral Assessment, 7*, 367–388.

Hendrickson, J.M., Strain, P.S., Tremblay, A., & Shores, R.E. (1982). Interactions of behaviorally handicapped preschoolers: Functional effects of peer social initiations. *Behavior Modification, 6*, 323–353.

James, S., & Egel, A. (1986). A direct prompting strategy for increasing reciprocal interactions between handicapped and nonhandicapped siblings. *Journal of Applied Behavior Analysis, 19*, 173–186.

Kohler, F.W., & Greenwood, C.R. (1986). Toward a technology of generalization: The identification of natural contingencies of reinforcement. *The Behavior Analyst, 9*, 19–26.

Krantz, P., & Risley, T.R. (1977). Behavior ecology in the classroom. In K.D. O'Leary & S.G. O'Leary (Eds.), *Classroom management: The successful use of behavior modification* (2nd ed., pp. 349–366). New York: Pergammon.

Lamb, M. (1978). The development of sibling relationships in infancy: A short-term longitudinal study. *Child Development, 49*, 1189–1196.

Lavigueur, H. (1976). The use of siblings as an adjunct to the behavioral treatment of children in the home with parents as therapists. *Behavior Therapy, 7*, 607–613.

Leitenberg, H., Burchard, J., Burchard, S., Fuller, E., & Lysaught, T. (1977). Using positive reinforcement to suppress behavior: Some experimental comparisons with sibling conflict. *Behavior Therapy, 8*, 168–172.

Lerger, H.J., Groff, D., Harris, V.W., Finfrock, L.R., Weaver, F.H., & Kratochwill, T.R. (1979). An instructional package to teach communication behaviors in a classroom setting. *Journal of School Psychology, 17*, 339–346.

Lichstein, K., & Wahler, R.G. (1976). The ecological assessment of an autistic child. *Journal of Abnormal Child Psychology, 4*, 31–54.

Loeber, R., Weissman, W., & Reid, J.B. (1983). Family interactions of assaultive adolescents, stealers, and nondelinquents. *Journal of Abnormal Child Psychology, 11*, 1–14.

McAllister, R.J., Butler, E.W., & Lei, T. (1973). Patterns of social interaction among families of behaviorally retarded children. *Journal of Marriage and Family*, 93–100.

McConnell, S.R. (1987). Entrapment effects and the generalization and maintenance of social skills training for elementary school students with behavioral disorders. *Behavioral Disorders, 12*, 252–263.

McEvoy, M.A., Nordquist, V.M., Twardosz, S., Heckaman, K.A., Wehby, J.H., & Denny, R.K. (1988). Promoting autistic children's peer interactions in an integrated early childhood setting using affection activities. *Journal of Applied Behavior Analysis, 21*, 193–200.

McEvoy, M.A., & Odom, S.L. (1987). Social interaction training for preschool children with behavioral disorders. *Behavioral Disorders, 12*, 242–251.

McEvoy, M.A., Shores, R.E., Wehby, J.H., Johnson, S., & Fox, J.J. (1990). Special education teachers' implementation of procedures to promote social interaction among children in integrated settings. *Education and Training of the Mentally Retarded, 25*(3), 267–276.

McGinnis, E., & Goldstein, A. (1984). *Skillstreaming the elementary school child.* Champaign, IL: Research Press.

Maheady, L., & Sainato, D. (1985). The effects of peer tutoring upon the social status and social interaction patterns of high and low status elementary school students. *Education and Treatment of Children, 8*, 51–66.

Marholin, D., & Siegel, L.J. (1978). Beyond the law of effect: Programming for the maintenance of behavioral change. In D. Marholin (Ed.), *Child behavior therapy* (pp. 107–149). New York: Gardener Press.

Martin, S., & Graunke, B. (1979). A behavioral analysis of the home environment of autistic children. In L. Hammerlynck (Ed.), *Behavioral systems for the developmentally delayed: Volume 1. School and family environments* (pp. 172–192). New York: Brunner-Mazel.

Mash, E.J., & Johnston, C. (1983). Sibling interactions of hyperactive and normal children and their relationship to reports of maternal stress and self-esteem. *Journal of Clinical Child Psychology, 12,* 91–99.

Mash, E.J., & Mercer, B. (1979). A comparison of deviant and nondeviant boys while playing alone and interacting with a sibling. *Journal of Child Psychology and Psychiatry and Applied Disciplines, 20,* 197–207.

Miller, N., & Cantwell, D. (1976). Sibling as therapist: A behavioral approach. *American Journal of Psychiatry, 133,* 447–450.

Minnett, A., Vandell, D., & Santrock, J. (1983). The effects of sibling status on sibling interaction: Influence of birth order, age-spacing, sex of child, and sex of sibling. *Child Development, 54,* 1064–1072.

Morgan, D., Young, R., & Goldstein, S. (1983). Teaching behaviorally disordered students to increase teacher attention and praise in mainstream classrooms. *Behavioral Disorders, 8,* 265–273.

Odom, S., & Strain, P. (1985). A comparison of peer-initiation and teacher-antecedent interventions for promoting reciprocal social interaction of autistic preschoolers. *Journal of Applied Behavior Analysis, 19,* 59–71.

O'Leary, K.D., O'Leary, S.G., & Becker, W.C. (1967). Modification of a deviant sibling interaction pattern in the home. *Behaviour Research and Therapy, 5,* 113–120.

Paine, S.C., Hops, H., Walker, H.M., Greenwood, C.R., Fleischman, D.H., & Guild, J. (1982). Repeated treatment effects: A study of maintaining behavior change in socially withdrawn children. *Behavior Modification, 6,* 171–199.

Patterson, G.R. (1982). *Coercive family processes: A social learning approach* (Vol. 3). Eugene: Castalia Publishing.

Pepler, D.J., Abramovitch, R., & Corter, C. (1981). Sibling interaction in the home: A longitudinal study. *Child Development, 51,* 1344–1347.

Polirstok, S., & Greer, D. (1977). Remediation of mutually aversive interactions between a problem student and four teachers by training the student in reinforcement techniques. *Journal of Applied Behavior Analysis, 10,* 707–716.

Powell, J., Martindale, B., Kulp, S., Martindale, A., & Baumann, R. (1977). Taking a closer look: Time sampling and measurement error. *Journal of Applied Behavior Analysis, 10,* 325–332.

Powell, T.H., Salzberg, C.L., Rule, S., Levy, S.M., & Itzkowitz, J. (1983). Teaching mentally retarded children to play with their siblings using parents as trainers. *Education and Treatment of Children, 6,* 343–362.

Quilitch, H.R., & Risley, T.R. (1973). The effects of play materials on social play. *Journal of Applied Behavior Analysis, 6,* 573–578.

Repp, A., Roberts, D., Slack, D., Repp, C., & Berkler, M. (1976). A comparison of frequency, interval, and time-sampling methods of data collection. *Journal of Applied Behavior Analysis, 9,* 501–508.

Richman, N., Stevenson, J., & Graham, P. (1982). *Preschool to school: A behavioural study.* London: Academic Press.

Romanczyk, R.G., Diament, C., Goren, E.R., Trunell, G., & Harris, S.L. (1975). Increasing isolate and social play in severely disturbed children: Intervention and postintervention effectiveness. *Journal of Autism and Childhood Schizophrenia, 5,* 57–70.

Rynders, J., Johnson, R.T., Johnson, D.W., & Schmidt, B. (1980). Producing positive interaction among Down's Syndrome and non-handicapped teenagers through cooperative goal setting. *American Journal of Mental Deficiency, 85,* 268–273.

Savelle, S., & Fox, J.J. (1987a, March). *The role of parents and siblings in handicapped children's social development: Initial findings and future perspective.* Paper presented at the Gatlinburg Conference on Research and Theory in Mental Retardation and Developmental Disabilities, Gatlinburg, TN.

Savelle, S., & Fox, J.J. (1988). Differential effects of training in two classes of social initiation on the positive responses and extended interactions of preschool-aged autistic children and their non-handicapped peers. *Monograph in Severe Behavior Disorders of Children and Youth, 11,* 75–86.

Savelle, S., Fox, J., & Phillips, M. (1987b, March). *Handicapped and nonhandicapped children's social interactions with their siblings: A preliminary descriptive analysis.* Paper presented at the Gatlinburg Conference on Research and Theory in Mental Retardation and Developmental Disabilities, Gatlinburg, TN.

Schriebman, L., O'Neill, R.E., & Koegel, R.L. (1983). Behavioral training for siblings of autistic children. *Journal of Applied Behavior Analysis, 16,* 129–138.

Shafer, M., Egel, A., & Neef, N. (1984). Training mildly handicapped peers to facilitate changes in the social interaction skills of autistic children. *Journal of Applied Behavior Analysis, 17,* 461–476.

Shores, R.E., McEvoy, M.A., Fox, J.J., Denny, R.K., Heckaman, K., & Wehby, J.H. (1986). *The social integration of severely handicapped children.* Nashville: John F. Kennedy Center for Research on Education and Human Development, George Peabody College, Vanderbilt University, Nashville.

Spiegel-McGill, P., Bambara, L., Shores, R.E., & Fox, J.J. (1984). The effects of proximity on socially-oriented behaviors of severely multiply handicapped children. *Education and Training of the Mentally Retarded, 7*(4), 365–378.

Stokes, T.F., & Baer, D.M. (1977). An implicit technology of generalization. *Journal of Applied Behavior Analysis, 10,* 349–367.

Stokes, T., & Osnes, P.G. (1987). Programming generalization of children's social behavior. In P. Strain, M. Guralnick, & H. Walker (Eds.), *Children's social behavior: Development, assessment and intervention* (pp. 408–443). New York: Academic Press.

Stokes, T.F., & Osnes, P.G. (1989). An operant pursuit of generalization. *Behavior Therapy, 20,* 337–355.

Stoneman, Z., & Brody, G. (1983). Family interactions during three programs. *Journal of Family Issues, 4,* 349–365.

Stoneman, Z., & Brody, G.H. (1984). Research with families of severely handicapped children: Theoretical and methodological considerations. In J.A. Blacher (Ed.). *Severely handicapped young children and their families* (pp. 179–214). New York: Academic Press.

Stoneman, Z., Brody, G.H., Davis, C.H., & Crapps, J.M. (1987). Mentally retarded children and their older same-sex siblings: naturalistic in-home observations. *American Journal of Mental Retardation, 92,* 290–298.

Stoneman, Z., Brody, G., & MacKinnon, C. (1984). Naturalistic observations of children's activities and roles while playing with their siblings and friends. *Child Development, 5,* 617–627.

Strain, P.S. (1977). An experimental analysis of peer social initiations on the behavior of withdrawn preschool children: Some training and generalization effects. *Journal of Abnormal Child Psychology, 5,* 445–455.

Strain, P.S. (1981). Modification of sociometric status and social interaction with mainstreamed mildly developmentally disabled children. *Analysis and Intervention in Developmental Disabilities, 1,* 157–169.

Strain, P.S. (1983). Generalization of autistic children's social behavior change: Effects of developmentally integrated and segregated settings. *Analysis and Intervention in Developmental Disabilities, 3,* 23–34.

Strain, P.S., & Fox, J.J. (1981). Peers as behavior change agents for socially withdrawn classmates. In B. Lahey & A. Kazdin (Eds.), *Advances in child clinical psychology* (pp. 167–198). New York: Plenum.

Strain, P.S., & Shores, R.E. (1977). Social interaction development among behaviorally handicapped preschool children: Research and educational implications. *Psychology in the Schools, 14,* 493–502.

Timm, M., Strain, P., & Eller, P. (1979). Effects of systematic response-dependent fading and thinning on the maintenance of child-child interaction. *Journal of Applied Behavior Analysis, 12,* 308.

Tremblay, A., Strain, P.S., Hendrickson, J.M., & Shores, R.E. (1981). Social interactions of normally developing preschool children: Using normative data for subject and target behavior selection. *Behavior Modification, 5,* 237–253.

Twardosz S., Nordquist, V.M., Simon, R., & Botkin, D. (1983). The effect of group affection activities on the interaction of socially isolate children. *Analysis and Intervention in Developmental Disabilities, 3,* 311–338.

Wahler, R.G. (1980). The insular mother: Her problems in parent-child treatment. *Journal of Applied Behavior Analysis, 13,* 207–219.

Wahler, R.G., & Fox, J.J. (1980). Solitary toy play: A desirable family treatment component for children with aggressive and oppositional behavior. *Journal of Applied Behavior Analysis, 13,* 23–29.

Wahler, R.G., & Leske, G. (1973). Accurate and inaccurate observer summary reports. *Journal of Nervous and Mental Disease, 165,* 386–394.

Wahler, R.G., Leske, G., & Rogers, E.S. (1979). The insular family: A deviance support system for oppositional children. In L.A. Hamerlynck (Ed.), *Behavioral systems for the developmentally disabled: I. School and family environments* (pp. 102–127). New York: Brunner/Mazel.

Walker, H.M., Greenwood, C.R., Hops, H., & Todd, N.M. (1979). Differential effects of reinforcing topographic components of social interaction. *Behavior Modification, 3,* 291–321.

Walker, H.M., McConnell, S., Holmes, D., Todis, B., Walker, J., & Golden, N. (1985). *The Walker social skills curriculum: The ACCEPTS program.* Austin: Pro-Ed.

Wolf, M.M. (1978). Social validity: The case for subjective measurement or how applied behavior analysis is finding its heart. *Journal of Applied Behavior Analysis, 11,* 203–214.

10

Promoting Children's Social/Survival Skills as a Strategy for Transition to Mainstreamed Kindergarten Programs

Lynette K. Chandler

Nancy graduated from a special education preschool program last year and entered a mainstreamed kindergarten program this fall, at age 5. The adjustment to the change in programs has been slow and difficult for Nancy. She has difficulty following group directions and working without constant teacher attention. She does not play with the other children in class and usually does not answer children who talk to her. The other children in class have stopped trying to invite Nancy to play and seldom direct initiations to her. Her teacher is concerned because many of the skills that Nancy used in preschool have not generalized to the kindergarten setting. For example, Nancy's preschool summary report indicated that she worked independently on academic tasks for a period of 10 minutes. However, in kindergarten, Nancy often daydreams or leaves her seat during academic periods. Nancy's teacher spends considerable time with Nancy trying to teach her skills that the other children in class already use, such as following rules, asking for help appropriately, using the girl's (not boy's) restroom, cleaning her desk, and following group routines after completing tasks. Nancy's teacher says that she wishes Nancy had learned these skills in preschool. Nancy's parents are concerned because Nancy has not adjusted well to kindergarten and cries each morning as she goes to school. They wish Nancy could have stayed in preschool for 1 more year.

Marianne also graduated from a special education preschool program last year and, at age five, entered a mainstreamed kindergarten program this fall. Marianne's adjustment to the change in programs has been fairly easy. She learned in preschool to follow group directions and work without teacher attention on most tasks. Like the other children in class, Marianne is able to raise her hand to ask for help and to follow group routines upon completing tasks. Although Marianne seldom initiates to children in the class, she does respond when children talk to her and will play with many of the children when asked. At the beginning of the year Marianne did not follow classroom rules, but she has learned to do so by imitating other children. Marianne's teacher is concerned that Marianne's academic abilities are lower than those of the other children in class but feels she can work on these because Marianne uses many important social and academic support skills such as staying in her seat, following group directions, and engaging in cooperative play. Marianne's parents are pleased with her progress in kindergarten and her obvious enjoyment of the program, and are relieved that she is adjusting well to the change in programs.

Both of these children have made a transition from a specialized preschool program to a mainstreamed kindergarten program. For one child the transition process has been easy; for the other, it has been difficult. Success in transition is largely dependent on the type of transition preparation a child has experienced. Preparation within Marianne's preschool helped her acquire many of the skills that her kindergarten teacher considered critical to her successful transition (e.g., following group directions). Nancy's preschool did not provide transition preparation activities; consequently, Nancy may not have been prepared for a mainstreamed kindergarten program. The purpose of this chapter is to provide information to help practitioners develop preparation programs that will increase the probability that children with disabilities will be placed in mainstreamed kindergarten programs and that will facilitate smooth and successful transitions.

Transition is an indispensable component of a child's educational experience. Within the field of education, transition can be defined as the process of moving from one program to another or from one service delivery mode to another. Transition usually begins in the sending program (i.e., the program from which the child is moving) as program staff and the child's family prepare for transition. The end of transition usually is indicated by teacher and family agreement that the child has adjusted successfully to the new classroom environment (i.e., the receiving program). The specific beginning and end point of the transition process may differ for each child and family (Odom & Chandler, 1990).

Children move from one program to another for a variety of reasons, including chronological age, academic and social progress, health status, parent decision, and change in diagnostic or categorical label. Chronological age is the most common reason cited for transition from early intervention services to public school programs (Fowler, Hains, & Rosenkoetter, 1990; Thurlow, Ysseldyke, & Weiss, 1988). Unfortunately, as illustrated by Nancy's experience, chronological age alone does not determine a child's readiness for kindergarten and success in transition (Spillman & Lutz, 1985; Wolery, 1989). For many children, planning in the sending and receiving programs is critical to ensure a smooth and systematic transition and to maximize the probability of success in a new program. When transition is well planned and children are prepared for the new program, transition can be a very exciting time for children, families, and teachers. When transition is not well planned and children are not prepared for the new program, transition can be a time of uncertainty and vulnerability (Rice & O'Brien, 1990). The transition from a specialized preschool to a mainstreamed kindergarten program presents children with the opportunity to learn new skills, make new friends, generalize skills from one setting to another, and use existing skills in new ways. For some children, such as Marianne, transition is an easy and rewarding process and the time needed to adjust to the change in programs is short. For other children however, such as Nancy, transition can be a time of stress, and the adjustment period may be difficult and quite long.

IMPORTANCE OF TRANSITION

The importance of transition to children, families, and program staff has been underscored in professional literature (e.g., Fowler, 1988; Ianacone & Stodden, 1987; Neisworth, 1990); federal funding priorities from the Office of Special Education and Rehabilitative Services (OSERS); state plans for special education services; and federal legislation such as Public Law 99-457, the Education of the Handicapped Act Amendments, 1986 (Fowler et al., 1990). Many investigators consider successful transition as a primary goal of early childhood special education, equal in status to the traditional goal of remediation of the disabling condition (e.g., Fowler, 1982; Noonan & Kilgo, 1987; Salisbury & Vincent, 1990). For example, McCormick and Kawate (1982) stress the need for early intervention programs to shift from a solely developmental perspective to one that encompasses preparation for transition into the next environment.

Preparation for transition will influence a child's success in kindergarten and the success of future transitions (Diamond, Spiegel-McGill, & Hanrahan, 1988). It will affect a child's ability to meet the demands imposed in the mainstreamed setting and to be an accepted member of the social network of the classroom. Children often experience difficulty in the new program when they have not acquired skills that are expected in the new setting or they do not generalize critical skills from the preschool to the kindergarten classroom (Hains, Fowler, Schwartz, Kottwitz, & Rosenkoetter, 1989). A child's experience may be problematic also when he or she requires inordinate amounts of teacher time or assistance; does not follow classroom rules and routines; does not participate in group activities; is withdrawn or aggressive in peer interactions; and has behavior problems (Sainato & Lyon 1989; Walter & Vincent, 1982). Children who encounter problems during transition may show signs of stress, such as crying, withdrawal, noncompliance, illness, tantrums, and school phobia (Fowler, 1982; Johnson, Chandler, Kerns, & Fowler, 1986).

Many of the behaviors used (or not used) by children who have difficulty during transition prohibit them from realizing the potential benefits of mainstreaming, such as social interaction and/or friendship with classroom peers, improved self-concept, imitation of appropriate academic and social behavior, and acquisition of academic skills (Bricker, 1978; Peterson & Haralick, 1977; Walter & Vincent, 1982). These behaviors also may result in placement in more restrictive settings (Carden-Smith & Fowler, 1983).

The ease or difficulty of transition from preschool to kindergarten also may have a significant and long-range impact on the course of subsequent transitions (Polloway, 1987). A rewarding experience with early transitions can have a positive impact on future transitions in terms of child behavior and expectations and family and teacher planning, support, and communication (Hains, Fowler, & Chandler, 1988).

Transition, as a goal of early childhood special education, includes two components: 1) preparing children (and other family members) for the move to the next, often less-restrictive environment (Vincent et al., 1980), and 2) ensuring that children adjust to the new environment (Hains et al., 1988). In order to achieve these goals teachers first need to identify the skills necessary to function in and adjust to the new program. Teachers then need to teach these critical skills before the child enters the new program. In addition, teachers must support and continue the training that occurred in preschool as the child moves into the new program (Hains et al., 1988; Ianacone & Stodden, 1987).

ACADEMIC/PREACADEMIC AND SOCIAL/SURVIVAL SKILLS

Two types of skills are important to consider in transition planning. These are academic/preacademic skills and social/survival skills. Academic and preacademic skills make up much of a traditional kindergarten curriculum and typically are assessed on developmental screening and kindergarten readiness assessments (see Goodwin & Driscoll [1982] for a discussion of school readiness tests). Table 10.1 presents a list of academic and preacademic skills that might be assessed on kindergarten screening or readiness tests.

Survival skills are skills and behaviors that a child will need to cope with the demands of the mainstreamed kindergarten program and to function well across a variety of social activities and situations, including academic tasks, free play activities, small and large group activities, and activity transitions (Chandler, 1991; Hutinger, 1981; Vincent et al., 1980). Examples of survival skills include playing cooperatively with peers, attending to and following group instructions, seeking assistance appropriately, taking care of personal belongings, working without disrupting peers, and following common classroom rules and routines.

Many of the skills and behaviors that are identified as survival skills also are encompassed in the concept of social competence. For example, social competence has been defined as a complex set of skills that include effective peer interaction, adaptive and independent behaviors, communication skills, problem-solving and conflict resolution skills, group entry skills, acceptance of authority, self-esteem, and task-related behaviors (Dodge, 1985; Gresham, 1982; McConnell & Odom, 1986; Vaughn & Ridley, 1983). A child is judged as socially competent when he or she interacts with others in ways that are socially acceptable and at the same time personally and/or mutually beneficial (Combs & Slaby, 1977; McConnell & Odom, 1986).

Social/Survival Skills

Given the similarity of skills and behaviors that are encompassed in the concepts of survival skills and social competence, it may be helpful to combine the concepts in a discussion of transition and to refer to these as social/survival skills.

Information about the social/survival skills needed in mainstreamed kindergarten is not readily available from commercial resources. Social/survival skills usually are not part of a traditional kindergarten curriculum and may not be assessed on readiness or kindergarten screening tests or traditional developmental assessments (Hains et al., 1988; Vincent et al., 1980). For example, McCormick and Kawate (1982) compared teacher-identified social/survival skills with nine developmental assessments and screening tests such as Learning Accomplishments Profile (Sanford, 1973); the Denver Developmental Screening Test (Frankenburg & Dodds, 1975); and the

Table 10.1. Sample academic and preacademic kindergarten readiness skills

Telling full name, address	Understanding left-right
Telling telephone number	Understanding prepositions
Understanding simple ideas (e.g., big-small, above-below)	Printing letters and numbers
Understanding simple number ideas (e.g., 1 hat, 2 crayons)	Writing first name
Identifying objects by use	Recognizing letters and words
Discussing stories	Matching letters and numbers
Telling stories	Matching pictures and shapes
Describing own experience	Grouping by two characteristics
Identifying familiar objects	Sorting by category
Identifying colors	Reasoning about future events
Identifying environmental sounds	Completing a 12–20 piece puzzle
Drawing simple figures	Defining 5–10 words
Drawing a person, with a head and parts	Knowing name of penny, nickel, dime
Copying circles, squares	Making opposites analogies
Copying letters, numbers	Cutting out a picture following a general shape
Describing how common objects are used	Acting out stories
Identifying and labeling body parts	Telling simple rhymes
Identifying and labeling numbers	Visually matching
Identifying and labeling shapes	Responding to questions about time
Understanding concepts of size	Copying horizontal block pattern
Understanding concepts of same-different	

These skills were compiled from the following references: Hains et al. (1989); Johnson-Martin, Attermeier, and Hacker (1990); National Education Association (1983); Sanford (1973); Virginia Department of Education (1986) (cited in Polloway, 1987).

Developmental Profile (Alpern & Boll, 1972). They reported that few social/survival skills were included in these assessments. All assessments failed to identify skills in the areas of independent task work, appropriate classroom behavior, and functional communication. These investigators indicated that programs that use developmental assessments and readiness tests to design curricular goals and methods probably will not address sufficiently a child's transition needs in the area of social competence. In support of this statement, Hains et al. (1988) noted that many of the problems encountered in transition occur even though children have passed kindergarten screening or readiness tests.

Although information about social/survival skills is not readily available from commercial resources, it can be obtained from professional literature. Several investigators have identified, through teacher nomination and classroom observation, social/survival skills that are critical to the success of transition from specialized preschool programs to mainstreamed kindergarten classrooms. These skills and corresponding references are listed in Table 10.2.

Academic/preacademic and social/survival skills are important to transition; both will influence a child's adjustment to and success in the future program. Academic/preacademic skills that approximate those of typical children allow a child with disabilities to be integrated during academic periods. Academic integration may provide the child who has disabilities with the opportunity to participate in group instruction, work on cooperative academic tasks, observe the behavior of typical peer models, and receive assistance from peers (Chandler, 1991; Donder & York, 1984).

Social/survival skills have received more attention in the literature concerning transition than academic/preacademic skills because impairments in social competence are considered more of a deterrent to success in mainstreamed classrooms than are academic problems (Fowler, 1982; Hutinger, 1981; Johnson & Mandell, 1988; Sainato & Lyon, 1989). For example, Vincent and her colleagues (1980) reported that teachers identified social/survival skills impairments, rather than preacademic, academic, language, or motor skill difficulties as contributors to unsuccessful transitions. Hains and her associates (1989) reported that teachers rated social interaction, self-help, following instructions, conduct, and communication as priority skill areas for transition into mainstreamed kindergarten programs. Noonan and Kilgo (1987) reported that social/survival skills were more significant predictors of success in transition than preacademic skills.

Social/survival skills are considered critical to transition because they: 1) facilitate referral to mainstreamed or least-restrictive kinder-

Table 10.2.   Social/survival skills critical for successful transitions

Social behaviors and classroom conduct
    Separating from parents and accepting school personnel
    Expressing emotions, affection, and feelings appropriately
    Understanding role as part of a group
    Respecting others and their property
    Playing cooperatively
    Sharing toys and materials
    Interacting without aggression
    Defending self appropriately
    Playing independently
    Imitating peer actions
    Lining up and waiting appropriately
    Sitting appropriately
    Focusing visual attention on a speaker
    Taking turns and participating appropriately in games
    Willingness to try something new
    Following classroom rules and routines
    Responding to warning words (e.g., stop, no)
    Reacting appropriately to changes in routine
    Using time between activities appropriately
    Spontaneously beginning play activities
    Playing for an appropriate length of time
    Interacting verbally with peers
    Playing with peers for an appropriate length of time

Communication behaviors
    Following two- to three-part direction
    Following group instructions
    Recalling and following directions for tasks previously described
    Asking peers for information or assistance
    Asking teachers for information or assistance
    Initiating and maintaining peer interactions
    Modifying behavior when given verbal feedback
    Answering questions
    Relating ideas and experience to others
    Communicating own needs and wants
    Raising a hand for teacher attention when necessary

(*continued*)

garten programs, 2) influence how well a child adjusts to the social and academic expectations of the environment, and 3) influence how well a child functions in a new setting. Social/survival skills often are necessary for the initiation and completion of academic tasks as well

Table 10.2. *(continued)*

Task-related behaviors

Finding materials needed for a task

Not disrupting peers during activities

Staying in own space for an activity

Beginning a task at an appropriate time without extra teacher attention

Working on an activity for an appropriate time with minimal supervision

Seeking teacher attention appropriately

Following task directions in a small or large group

Completing a task on time

Replacing materials and cleaning up work space

Following a routine in transition

Completing a task of ability level near criteria

Making the transition from one activity to the next with a general group verbal or contextual cue

Complying quickly with teacher instructions

Generalizing skills across tasks and situations

Attending to the teacher in a large group activity

Making choices

Using a variety of curriculum materials

Monitoring own behavior, knowing when a task is done

Self-help behaviors

Locating and caring for personal belongings

Attending to toileting needs without supervision

Feeding self independently

Getting on and off school bus with minimal supervision

Avoiding obvious dangers

Taking outer clothing on and off in a reasonable length of time

Recognizing a problem exists and trying strategies to solve the problem

This list was compiled from the following references: Carden-Smith and Fowler (1983); Hains et al. (1989); McCormick and Kawate (1982); Thompson (1979); Vincent et al. (1980); Walker and Rankin (1982); Walter (1979); Walter and Vincent (1982).

as social activities and are useful across a variety of situations (Hops & Cobb, 1973). For example, asking for materials or for assistance, following instructions, and waiting for a turn are behaviors that may be necessary across academic, art, and play tasks, and transition periods.

Social/survival skills not only affect the child's ability to fit in and adjust to the new program, but also influence the teacher's perception of achievement and the child's maintenance in the program (McCormick & Kawate, 1982; Rice & O'Brien, 1990). For example, many referrals for psychological services and segregated placement identify social/survival skills impairments, such as poor peer interaction or inappropriate behaviors, as factors in referral (Carden-Smith & Fowler; 1983; Strain, Cooke, & Apolloni, 1976). Children with social/survival skill impairments may be judged as less verbal and academically skilled, immature, and as presenting more behavior problems than children who have similar academic abilities, but who do have adequate social/survival skills (Greenwood, Walker, Todd, & Hops, 1979; Michelson & Mannarino, 1986; Strain et al., 1976).

Children with disabilities who have been judged, by their teachers, as successful in transition have used appropriate social/survival skills such as compliance, attending, appropriate on-task behavior, peer initiation, self-discipline, following directions, and group participation (Walter & Vincent, 1982). They also required less instructional assistance and attention for behavior problems than children who were considered unsuccessful in transition.

Children's need for social/survival skills training may affect teachers for two reasons. First, teachers typically do not have curricula to assist in the development of lesson plans to teach social/survival skills. Odom, McConnell, and Chandler (1990) reported that 90% of a sample of preschool special education teachers from five states indicated that they did not have sufficient curriculum materials or information to assist in designing social/survival skills instructional programs for their students. Teachers might be more willing and able to help children develop social competence if they had in-service training and curricula that addressed social/survival skills.

Second, children who do not have requisite social/survival skills tend to require inordinate amounts of attention and assistance in the classroom and in planning efforts. It may be difficult for teachers to give extra assistance or attention to individual children in a mainstreamed kindergarten program in which the child-teacher ratio is high and teacher attention must be divided among all children. In such programs, teachers often do not have the luxury of dealing with children on an individual basis. As a result teachers may not be able adequately to assist children who require extensive and highly individualized help (Jalongo, 1986).

The Prevalence of Social and Survival Skill Impairments

Little information is available concerning the number of children who experience difficulties during transition as a result of poor social/survival skills. However, it is agreed generally that a large proportion of children who exit preschool special education programs and enter mainstreamed kindergarten programs do display poor social/survival skills and that these skill impairments can affect the ease, length, and overall success of transition (Fowler, 1982; Hutinger, 1981; Salisbury & Vincent, 1990; Vincent et al., 1980).

According to Jalongo (1986), most children today enter kindergarten programs with previous school experience and good social/survival skills. Unfortunately, children with developmental disabilities, while they may have previous school experience, often do not have the type of experience or training that promotes critically needed social competence. Guralnick (1986) and Odom and McEvoy (1988) pointed out that care settings and early childhood special education programs for children with disabilities usually are not mainstreamed. Rather, they are homogeneous, usually containing children who also display social and developmental delays. As a result children with disabilities do not have appropriate peer models of social/survival skills and may have fewer opportunities for peer interaction. The lack of experience with skilled peers can lead to difficulties for the child in his or her transition into a less-restrictive, mainstreamed kindergarten program. The differences between the experiences and expectations of preschool and mainstreamed kindergarten programs may be quite large for children with disabilities who have attended special education preschool programs and minimal for children from regular education preschool or day care programs. Reducing the differences for children with disabilities who have been enrolled in preschool special education programs should be the primary focus of child preparation.

PREPARING A CHILD FOR TRANSITION

The responsibility for preparing a child for transition and helping a child adjust to the change in programs must be shared by the sending and receiving programs. Teachers and staff in the sending program are responsible for planning and initiating the transition process and providing the type of experiences and instruction that prepare the child for the next educational environment. Teachers and staff in the receiving program are responsible for preparing the classroom environment, classroom peers, and educational curricula to accommodate the child's adjustment during transition.

Although the importance of social/survival skills is widely recognized and critical social/survival skills have been identified, transition planning and child preparation often are the weakest components in special education preschool programs (Hutinger, 1981). Transition planning services may be fragmented, isolated, or nonexistent (Hutinger & Swartz, cited in Noonan & Kilgo, 1987). This may be because there are few commercially available social/survival skills curricula (Odom et al., 1990). As a result, teachers in sending and receiving programs must decide which skills are necessary for successful transition to mainstreamed programs. Teachers then must decide which skills are most important and feasible to teach in the preschool program. Additionally, it is necessary for teachers to maintain a balance of the goals needed in the current program and those needed in the future program (Vincent et al., 1980).

Preparation in the Sending Program

Teachers and staff in the sending program should begin child preparation activities during the child's last year in preschool. There are several strategies that teachers in the sending program may use to identify and prioritize skills to include in transition preparation activities. Teachers may select as priority those skills identified by kindergarten teachers in their district as crucial social/survival skills for peer interaction in mainstreamed kindergarten settings. Or, they may teach children social/survival skills that are required to complete academic tasks such as attending, compliance, and responding (Cartledge & Milburn, 1980; Dettre, 1983). Carden-Smith and Fowler (1983) recommended that preparation activities focus on reducing inappropriate or disruptive behaviors such as aggression, noncompliance, and rule infraction, all of which cause a need for excessive teacher attention. Salisbury and Vincent (1990) recommended that teachers train children for mastery of social/survival skills at a level displayed by kindergarten children mid-year. This would increase the probability of children functioning well during the transition period. However, they also recommended increasing the receiving teacher's acceptance and ability to tolerate and work with children with diverse behaviors and developmental abilities.

A common approach, termed criterion of the next environment, can assist teachers in identifying skills to address in preparation activities (Salisbury & Vincent, 1990; Vincent, Brown, & Getz-Sheftel, 1981; Vincent et al., 1980; Walter & Vincent, 1982). The criterion of the next environment approach involves attending to the demands of the receiving program and addressing those demands in the curriculum of the sending program. In this approach, teachers first analyze the differences between the sending and receiving programs in terms of environmental supports, teaching strategies, teacher requirements and expectations, and classroom activities and routines. Table 10.3 presents a list of variables that may differ across specialized preschool programs and mainstreamed kindergarten programs. The Appendix presents an example of a transition checklist, which is an observation sheet that will guide the identification of differences between pro-

Table 10.3. Potential differences between special education preschool programs and mainstreamed kindergarten programs

Teacher-child ratio
Skill level of children in the classroom
Social and play skill expectations
Length of class periods
Length of activity periods (e.g., academic work periods)
Expected level of independent performance
Size of instructional groups
Amount and availability of teacher attention
Amount and availability of teacher assistance
Type of teacher instruction
Expectations for personal property
Expectations during activity transitions
Locations of areas (e.g., restrooms, playground)
Expected tool and material skills
Classroom rules
Behavior management procedures
Seating arrangements
Number and type of children in the classroom
Transportation
Parent involvement

grams. After the differences are identified with this approach they are then incorporated into the curriculum design and programming of the specialized preschool program. Four steps should be followed in the criterion of the next environment approach:

1. Analyze the teaching approaches, academic and social/survival skill expectations, rules and routines, physical environment, curricular materials, and so forth, in the new environment.
2. Compare information from this analysis to the environment in the child's existing program. Include in this comparison information on the current status of the classroom environment and the status of the environment at the end of the preschool year. Identify potential differences between programs.
3. Assess the academic and social/survival skills currently used by the child in the preschool program.
4. Assist the child in learning identified skills. Teachers may implement child preparation by arranging the classroom environment, routines, and activities, or through direct and indirect (e.g., incidental, milieu) instruction.

It is important to point out that the competencies or skills identified from the criterion of the next environment approach are *not* readiness criteria that may be used to exclude a child from placement in a mainstreamed setting. Rather, they are preparatory goals to increase the likelihood of a child being placed in a mainstreamed program and being successful in the new setting (Salisbury & Vincent, 1990).

Teachers can use a variety of methods to analyze the skills and expectations of the next environment. These include: 1) classroom observation; 2) information exchange through teacher interview; 3) exchange of teacher expectation surveys (e.g., Hains et al., 1989; McCormick & Kawate, 1982); 4) examination of readiness tests; 5) examination of social/survival skills lists such as Table 10.2; 6) exchange of core curricula and daily lesson plans; and 7) information sharing through interagency meetings.

Preparation in the Receiving Program

The receiving teacher is responsible for promoting smooth and successful transition when a child enters the kindergarten program. Fulfulling this responsibility entails learning about the strengths and needs of the child entering the program and adapting the program to build on the child's strengths and address his or her other needs. The receiving teacher also can follow the criterion of the next environment approach in order to help the child learn requisite skills and behaviors as he or she enters the kindergarten program. After the receiving teacher has identified differences between programs, he or she may:

1. Adjust his or her expectations concerning required skills and behaviors in the classroom to reflect the skills and behavior requirements of the preschool program.
2. Initially use the type and number of cues, directions, rules, assistance, behavior management techniques, and so forth, that approximate those to which the child is able to respond.
3. Gradually increase the number or type of classroom skills that the child is expected to use (Fowler & Chandler, 1986).
4. Use familiar preschool tasks, materials, and teaching practices as a supplement to the kindergarten curriculum.
5. Alter the physical layout of the classroom to build on child strengths and meet child needs (e.g., reduce distractions and alter seating arrangements and placement of task materials).

Receiving teachers also are responsible for preparing typically-developing children to interact with a child who has disabilities. Activities to prepare typical children in mainstreamed programs generally have produced benefits for children in terms of social acceptance (Binkard, 1985; Odom & McEvoy, 1988). Preparation activities might provide information about different disabling conditions or about specific children with disabilities who will enter the class. For example, a receiving teacher might arrange for "the Kids on the Block" program to be presented during the first few days of school to increase the typical childrens' acceptance and understanding of disability (this program uses life-size puppets with disabilities who discuss their disabling conditions and the similarities between typically-developing children and children with disabilities). Or, teachers might use simulation activities to increase the childrens' understanding of disability (Johnson & Johnson, 1986).

Preparation for the Generalization of Social/Survival Skills

Many children with disabilities experience difficulty in transition because they do not use the skills they had in preschool when they come to the kindergarten program (Fowler, 1982). In addition to teaching skill acquisition, a goal of transition preparation in sending and receiving programs should be to promote the generalization of social/survival skills. Generalization occurs when a behavior that is learned in one situation is used in a new situation or is maintained across time after training ends. Generalization may occur across settings (e.g., preschool and kindergarten classrooms); persons (e.g., different teachers); and situations (e.g., different materials, cues, or reinforcers).

Generalization is important to transition because it promotes stability and consistency of behavior across changing situations. Children who are able to generalize behaviors will not need to relearn those skills in the new program, and so can spend time on skill acquisition. In addition, they need not experience the potentially negative consequences that may occur from not generalizing expected skills. If generalization to the kindergarten program does not occur, there is little practical, educational, or clinical utility to the gains made in preschool (Chandler, Lubeck, & Fowler, 1991).

Generalization and maintenance of social/survival skills has been difficult to find in research concerning social competence and preschool-age children with disabilities (Chandler et al., 1991; Haring, 1987; Strain, 1981). This may be because many studies have not included generalization as a goal of training and have not addressed generalization as a component of social/survival skills interventions (Haring, 1987). Strategies to promote generalization and maintenance have been outlined by several investigators (e.g., Baer, 1981; Haring,

1987; Koegel & Rincover, 1977; Stokes & Baer, 1977; Stokes & Osnes, 1986; Strain, 1981). The following eight of these strategies are directly applicable to transition preparation.

1. Teach Functional Target Behaviors　Teachers should select and teach social/survival skills or behaviors that will be useful to a variety of individuals, including the child, and that will be useful across a variety of settings (including preschool and kindergarten) and tasks. For example, teachers might select seeking assistance appropriately as a social/survival skill because it is a skill that is useful in preschool and kindergarten classes and across preacademic, academic, and large group activities. This strategy promotes generalization because a behavior that is useful to the child and others and that may be used in several settings is more likely to be used and then reinforced in the new setting.

2. Program Common Stimuli and Consequences　Teachers should use stimuli and consequences during training that are likely to be present across multiple situations (e.g., preschool and kindergarten settings). For example, teachers may use materials (e.g., worksheets); teaching methods (e.g., verbal praise and a hug); or behavior management techniques (e.g., time out) that approximate those used in other settings. The greater the similarity between the special education preschool environment and the environment of the mainstreamed kindergarten program, the greater the probability that a child's skills and behaviors will generalize across settings (Noonan & Kilgo, 1987).

Teachers should incorporate stimuli and consequences during training that are a natural part of the existing program, such as verbal praise. Natural stimuli and consequences are more likely to exist across programs than stimuli and consequences that are developed solely for the purpose of skill acquisition (e.g., a sticker program). Using stimuli and consequences that are part of the child's natural environment increases the probability that the child will respond to those stimuli in other settings and that the child's behavior will be maintained by consequences that are common across programs.

3. Specify a Fluency or Training Criterion　Teachers should specify a level of consistency and proficiency of the social/survival skill that must occur before training is terminated. For example, such a fluency criterion may reflect the behavior of other children (a normed criterion) or it may be set to exceed the behavior of other children so that it is well-learned (i.e., overlearning). Several researchers have speculated that generalization and maintenance may not occur because the behavior was not sufficiently learned during training (Baer, 1981; Kazdin, 1975). A social/survival skill that is performed consistently or proficiently may be more likely to be used in other settings and then to receive positive consequences in those settings.

4. Train Loosely and Use Sufficient Exemplars Social/survival skills training should include a variety of materials, cues, consequences, people, settings, and examples of the behavior. For example, in the course of teaching a child to answer questions: 1) teachers may address questions individually to the child or to a group of children; 2) they may ask questions about a variety of topics such as color identification, snack preference, and favorite toy; 3) they may ask questions at various times of the day or during different activities; or 4) a variety of teachers may ask the child questions and provide consequences for the child's answer. The greater the number of variations a child learns, the more probable skill generalization will be (Dowrick, 1986).

5. Use Indiscriminable Contingencies Although continuous consequences may be required while the child is learning a social/survival skill, it is important to change from continuous to indiscriminable or unpredictable contingencies after the behavior is learned. For example, a teacher may immediately attend to a child each time he or she asks for assistance during the acquisition phase of this skill. However, once the skill has been learned, the teacher may ask the child to wait for a period of time before providing assistance, prompt the child to ask a peer for assistance, or attend to the child every second or third time the child seeks assistance. This strategy should promote generalization because it gives the child experience with the types of contingencies that are likely to exist in the classroom after training is terminated, such as delayed consequences or consequences that are delivered with varying frequency.

6. Reinforce Generalization Teachers should reinforce unprompted use of the social/survival skill in the preschool, home, and kindergarten setting. Behavior that is not reinforced is not likely to generalize across settings or to be maintained when training ends (Baer, 1981). Therefore, it is important to ensure that reinforcement is provided for desired behavior. Positive consequences may be contingent on the target child's behavior (i.e., the child who is expected to learn the social/survival skill) or they may be contingent on the behavior of other children, so that the target child is able to observe other children receiving reinforcement.

7. Recruit Natural Communities of Reinforcement This strategy involves training individuals in the preschool or kindergarten setting to administer intervention contingencies. For example, typical children in the kindergarten classroom may be trained to prompt and reinforce appropriate peer interaction skills. Or children in the preschool or kindergarten classroom may be asked to ignore aggressive or disruptive behavior in order to reduce support for behavior that is incompatible with positive social/survival skills.

8.   Use Sequential Modification   If generalization does not occur when one or more of the above strategies has been used, it may be necessary to provide training in the social/survival skill in the new kindergarten setting. Training in the new program also may be necessary if a social/survival skill is not reinforced in the new program because it is performed poorly or inconsistently. Often, additional training improves the consistency or proficiency of a behavior to a point where it is followed by reinforcement, resulting in maintenance of the skill in the new program.

INTEGRATING TRANSITION PREPARATION AND CORE CURRICULUM GOALS

Although the goal of planning in the preschool program is to prepare a child for the next environment, this should not be accomplished through sacrifice of the skills and behaviors needed in the current program. In the receiving program, child adjustment and the acquisition or generalization of social/survival skills should not be accomplished at the expense of core curriculum skills. The goal of transition planning and child preparation should not be to make the preschool program an early kindergarten, nor to make the kindergarten program a temporary preschool (Fowler & Chandler, 1986). Rather, transition preparation should provide children with training and experiences that facilitate and augment existing child goals, teaching activities, and classroom routines. One way to do this is to combine transition goals with other curriculum goals and activities. Transition preparation may be more likely to succeed if preparation activities become an integral part of the core curriculum and are accomplished in the context of typical school activities and routines (Chandler, 1991; Fowler, 1982; Hutinger, 1981).

Teachers can include child preparation activities as part of classroom practices by following the steps for class-wide and child-specific activities outlined in Table 10.4. Preparation can occur at a class-wide level in which all children participate in preparation activities, or at a child-specific level, in which preparation activities are designed to meet the needs of individual children. To implement class-wide activities teachers should develop a list of social/survival skills that can be incorporated into existing goals and classroom activities and routines. For example, teachers can gradually increase the amount of

Table 10.4.   Steps to implementing class-wide and child-specific transition preparation strategies

1. Identify a general set of kindergarten readiness skills that might be useful to any child making a transition. Include academic/preacademic and social/survival skills.

2. Develop methods for teaching these skills to all children, and integrating these methods into ongoing classroom activities and routines (class-wide focus). For example, all children learn to imitate in Simon Says games.

3. Identify children who need extra help learning general readiness skills.

4. Develop and implement child-specific methods to teach skills to individual children (e.g., use physical prompting to help a child share; work with one child on color identification).

5. When a new program is selected, identify skills that are specific to that program. Assess whether the child uses these skills.

6. Teach these skills on a class-wide basis, if possible (e.g., introduce worksheets for all children).

7. Identify children who need extra help with these skills. Use child-specific methods to teach skills (e.g., use worksheets with one child). Child-specific methods also may be used to teach skills that are not appropriate for all children to learn (e.g., teaching a child to ride the bus).

time children are expected to work on existing academic or play tasks. Or, teachers might teach all children choice-making behavior during daily snack activities by offering more than one type of food (e.g., children may select cookies, crackers, or cereal).

Preparation may be introduced at a child-specific level for two reasons. It may be the first choice after a child's new program has been selected and the skills required or recommended in that program are identified (Chandler, 1991). For instance, one kindergarten program may teach math skills by asking a child to complete simple worksheets, while another program requires a child to answer math questions verbally. Teachers may use a child-specific approach to teach individual children academic and survivals skills that vary across future programs. Teachers should consider, however, whether the skills needed in individual programs might be beneficial for all children in the class to learn. If most children in the class would benefit from learning a skill, it may be more cost-efficient in terms of teacher time to use a class-wide approach. For instance, all children may be taught to use worksheets and to answer questions verbally.

Child-specific preparation techniques also may be used for children who have not acquired skills from participation in class-wide activities (Chandler, 1991). Teachers may design intensive, individualized methods to teach these children. For instance, teachers may use a home-school sticker notebook to manage and teach appropriate rule-following or self-management behavior for the child who does not follow rules consistently.

In designing methods for teaching social/survival skills at a classwide or child-specific level it is helpful to consider the number and type of settings or activities in which the skills will be used or required, the level of proficiency required for the skill to be useful, and normative examples of the quantity and quality of behavior across settings or activities (Chandler et al., 1991). These considerations will help the teacher select goal attainment criteria that reflect characteristics of the next environment.

PARENT INVOLVEMENT IN CHILD PREPARATION

Parents also may be involved in preparing a child for transition. Parents and other family members tend to be a valuable, but underutilized resource during the transition period (Chandler, 1991). They can provide a multi-environmental view of their child's strengths and needs and a historical perspective of their child's previous transition experiences (e.g., from early intervention to preschool or daycare services). Parents also may provide information that facilitates the selection of transition goals and activities. For example, parents may inform receiving teachers about their child's reinforcer preferences, need for predictability, or difficulties in specific skill areas.

Family members can assume responsibility for some child preparation. For example, they can teach survival skills that are not easily taught in a school setting, such as walking to the new school. Parents also might provide opportunities for their child to engage in peer interaction with typical children by taking their child to neighborhood play groups or church day-care settings. They can show the child the new school, visit the new classroom, and talk to the child about the change in programs. Additionally, parents can assist the transition process by identifying potential and current problems and working with teachers to address them.

Parents may be essential to the generalization and maintenance of social/survival skills and behaviors. They can increase the probability of skill generalization by using similar materials, rules, contingencies, and activities across a variety of settings, such as the child's home or neighborhood play groups. They also can promote generalization by teaching skills at home that the child is learning at preschool or kindergarten. They can promote the maintenance of critical skills if there is a break between leaving preschool and kindergarten enrollment. Additionally, parents can provide the receiving teacher with information concerning materials, rules, and behavior management techniques, as well as reinforcers that the teacher may incorporate as common stimuli across programs.

Methods for involving family members in transition planning, benefits to family members from participation in the transition process, and the need for individualized family involvement have been well documented and are beyond the scope of this chapter. Readers are referred to the following sources for further information concerning family involvement in transition from preschool to kindergarten programs: Chandler, Fowler, and Lubeck (1986); Conn-Powers, Ross-Allen, and Holburn (1990); Fowler, Chandler, Johnson, and Stella (1988); Haines et al. (1988); Hanline (1988); Hanline and Knowlton (1988); Johnson et al. (1986).

SUMMARY

The success of a child's early placements is a good predictor of the success of subsequent placements (Edgar, McNulty, & Gaetz, 1984; Vincent et al., 1980). Therefore it is imperative that efforts in the preschool be aimed at providing children who have disabilities with the experiences and skills that will facilitate transition to mainstreamed kindergarten programs.

Activities to prepare a child for transition should increase the likelihood that a child will adjust well to the social and academic requirements of the kindergarten classroom and will remain in the mainstreamed program. Social/survival skills are the most important contributors to a child's adjustment to the new program and the willingness of teachers to support a child in the mainstreamed program. Acquisition and generalization of social/survival skills are a critical goal of preparation activities in sending programs as well as receiving programs.

The success of a child's transition is a function of multiple factors that include a child's academic/preacademic and social/survival skills; preparation efforts in the sending and the receiving programs; family involvement in transition planning; and child preparation. Teachers from the sending and receiving programs must assess and consider a child's needs and abilities, the physical environment, the social community, and the expectations of each program as they develop methods to prepare a child for the new program and to accommodate the child after he or she enters the new program. Teachers then must identify which skills and behaviors are important to teach in each program and develop methods that can be integrated with existing curricular goals, teaching methods, and classroom activities to teach these skills and promote generalization.

Transition preparation to meet the goal of smooth and successful transitions presents many challenges for teachers in sending and receiving programs. The goal of smooth and successful transitions can be met, in part, through the development and implementation of curricula that focus on social/survival skills that are essential to successful transitions.

REFERENCES

Alpern, G.D., & Boll, T.J. (1972). *The developmental profile*. Aspen: Psychological Development Publications.

Baer, D.M. (1981). *How to plan for generalization*. Lawrence, KS: H & H Enterprises.

Binkard, B. (1985). A successful handicapped awareness program run by parents. *Teaching Exceptional Children, 18*(1), 12–16.

Bricker, D.D. (1978). A rationale for the integration of handicapped and nonhandicapped preschool children. In M.J. Guralnick (Ed.), *Early intervention and the integration of handicapped and nonhandicapped children* (pp. 3–26). Baltimore University Park Press.

Carden-Smith, L., & Fowler, S.A. (1983). An assessment of student and teacher behavior in treatment and mainstreamed classes for preschool and kindergarten. *Analysis and Intervention in Developmental Disabilities, 3*, 35–57.

Cartledge, G., & Milburn, J.F. (1980). *Teaching social skills to children: Innovative approaches*. New York: Pergamon.

Chandler, L.K. (1991). Strategies to promote physical, social and academic integration in mainstreamed programs. In G. Stoner, M.R. Shinn, & H.M. Walker, (Eds.), *Intervention for achievement and behavior problems* (pp. 305–331). Washington DC: National Association for School Psychologists.

Chandler, L.K., Fowler, S.A., & Lubeck, R.C. (1986). Assessing family needs: The first step in providing family-focused intervention. *Diagnostique, 11*, 233–245.

Chandler, L.K., Lubeck, R.C., & Fowler, S.A. (1991). *The generalization and maintenance of preschool children's social skills: A critical review and analysis*. Manuscript submitted for publication.

Combs, M.L., & Slaby, D.A. (1977). Social-skills training with children. In B.B. Lahey & A.E. Kazdin (Eds.), *Advances in clinical child psychology* (Vol. 1, pp. 161–201). New York: Plenum.

Conn-Powers, M.C., Ross-Allen, J., & Holburn, S. (1990). Transition of young children into the elementary education mainstream. *Topics in Early Childhood Special Education, 9*(4), 91–105.

Dettre, J. (1983). Bridges to academic success for young at-risk children. *Topics in Early Childhood Special Education, 3*(3), 57–64.

Diamond, K., Spiegel-McGill, P., & Hanrahan, P. (1988). Planning for school transition: An ecological-developmental approach. *Journal of the Division for Early Childhood, 12*, 245–252.

Dodge, K.A. (1985). Facets of social interaction and the assessment of social competence in children. In B. Schneider, K. Rubin, & J. Ledingham (Eds.), *Children's peer relations: Issues in assessment and intervention* (pp. 3–22). New York: Springer-Verlag.

Donder, D.D., & York, R. (1984). Integration of students with severe handicaps. In N. Certo, N. Haring, & R. York, (Eds.), *Public school integration of severely handicapped students: Rational issues and progressive alternatives* (pp. 1–14). Baltimore: Paul H. Brookes Publishing Co.

Dowrick, P.W. (1986). *Social survival for children: A trainer's resource book.* New York: Brunner/Mazel.

Edgar, E., McNulty, B., & Gaetz, J. (1984). Educational placement of graduates of preschool programs for handicapped children. *Topics in Early Childhood Special Education, 4,* 19–29.

Fowler, S.A. (1982). Transition from preschool to kindergarten for children with special needs. In K.E. Allen & E.M. Goetz (Eds.), *Early childhood education: Special problems, special solutions* (pp. 309–334). Rockville, MD: Aspen Systems.

Fowler, S.A. (1988). Transition planning. *Teaching Exceptional Children, 20,* 62–63.

Fowler, S.A., & Chandler, L.K. (1986). *Transitions in early childhood services for handicapped children.* Workshop presented to the North Dakota Department of Public Instruction, Bismark, ND.

Fowler, S.A., Chandler, L., Johnson, T.J., & Stella, M. (1988). Individualizing family involvement in school transitions: Gathering information and choosing the next program. *Journal of the Division for Early Childhood, 12,* 208–216.

Fowler, S.A., Hains, A.H., & Rosenkoetter, S. (1990). The transition between early intervention services and preschool services: Administrative and policy issues. *Topics in Early Childhood Special Education, 9*(4), 55–65.

Frankenburg, W.K., & Dodds, J.B. (1975). *Denver Developmental Screening Test.* Boulder: University of Colorado Medical Center.

Goodwin, W.L., & Driscoll, L.A., (1982). *Handbook for measurement and evaluation in early childhood education.* San Francisco: Jossey–Bass.

Greenwood, C.R., Walker, H.M., Todd, N.H., & Hops, H. (1979). Selecting a cost-effective screening measure for the assessment of preschool social withdrawal. *Journal of Applied Behavior Analysis, 12*(4), 639–652.

Gresham, F.M. (1982). Misguided mainstreaming: The case for social skills training with handicapped children. *Exceptional Children, 48*(5), 422–433.

Guralnick, M.J. (1986). The peer relations of young handicapped and nonhandicapped children. In P.S. Strain, M.J. Guralnick, & H.M. Walker, (Eds.), *Children's social behavior: Development, assessment, and modification* (pp. 93–140). New York: Academic Press.

Hains, A.H., Fowler, S.A., & Chandler, L.K. (1988). Planning school transitions: Family and professional collaboration. *Journal of the Division for Early Childhood, 12,* 108–115.

Hains, A., Fowler, S., Schwartz, I., Kottwitz, E., & Rosenkoetter, S. (1989). A comparison of preschool and kindergarten teacher expectations for school readiness. *Early Childhood Research Quarterly, 4,* 75–88.

Hanline, M.F. (1988). Making the transition to preschool: Identification of parent needs. *Journal of the Division for Early Childhood, 12,* 98–107.

Hanline, M.F., & Knowlton, A. (1988). A collaborative model for providing support to parents during their child's transition from infant intervention to preschool special education public school programs. *Journal of the Division for Early Childhood, 12,* 116–125.

Haring, N. (1987). *Investigating the problem of skill generalization: Literature review III.* Seattle: Washington Research Organization.

Hops, H.H., & Cobb, J. (1973). Survival behaviors in the educational setting: Their implications for research and intervention. In L. Hamerlynck, L. Haney, & E. Mash (Eds.), *Behavior change: Methodology, concepts, and practice.* Champaign, IL: Research Press.

Hutinger, P.L. (1981). Transition practices for handicapped young children: What the experts say. *Journal of the Division for Early Childhood, 2,* 8–14.

Ianacone, R.N., & Stodden, R.A. (1987). Transition issues and directions for individuals who are mentally retarded. In R.N. Ianacone & R.A. Stodden (Eds.), *Transition issues and directions* (pp. 1–7). Washington, DC: Council for Exceptional Children.

Jalongo, M.R. (1986). What is happening to kindergarten? *Childhood Education, 62*(3), 155–160.

Johnson, D.W., & Johnson, R.T. (1986). Integrating handicapped students into the mainstream. *Exceptional Children, 47,* 90–99.

Johnson, R., & Mandell, C. (1988). A social observation checklist for preschoolers. *Teaching Exceptional Children, 20*(2), 18–21.

Johnson, T.J., Chandler, L.K., Kerns, G., & Fowler, S.A. (1986). What are parents saying about family involvement in school transitions? A retrospective transition interview. *Journal of the Division for Early Childhood, 11,* 10–17.

Johnson-Martin, N.M., Attermeier, S.M., & Hacker, B.J. (1991). *The Carolina curriculum for preschoolers with special needs.* Baltimore: Paul H. Brookes Publishing Co.

Kazdin. A.E. (1975). *Behavior modification in applied settings.* Homewood, IL: The Dorsey Press.

Koegel, R.L., & Rincover, A. (1977). Research on the differences between generalization and maintenance in extra-therapy responding. *Journal of Applied Behavior Analysis, 10*(1), 1–12.

McConnell, S., & Odom, S.L. (1986). Sociometrics: Peer-referenced measures and the assessment of social competence. In P.S. Strain, M.J. Guralnick, & H.M. Walker (Eds.), *Children's social behavior: Development, assessment, and modification* (pp. 215–284). Orlando, FL: Academic Press.

McCormick, L., & Kawate, J. (1982). Kindergarten survival skills: New direction for preschool special education. *Education and Training of the Mentally Retarded, 17*(3), 247–252.

Michelson, L., & Mannarino, A. (1986). Social skills training with children: Research and clinical application. In P.S. Strain, M.J. Guralnick, & H.M. Walker, (Eds.), *Children's social behavior: Development, assessment, and modification* (pp. 373–406). New York: Academic Press.

National Education Association. (1983). *How to prepare your child for school.* New York: Avon Books.

Neisworth, J.T. (Ed.). (1990). Transition. *Topics in Early Childhood Special Education, 9*(4).

Noonan, M.J., & Kilgo, J.L. (1987). Transition services for early age individuals with severe mental retardation. In R.N. Ianacone & R.A. Stodden (Eds.), *Transition issues and directions* (pp. 25–37). Washington, DC: Council for Exceptional Children.

Odom, S.L., & Chandler, L.K. (1990). Transition to parenthood for parents of infants with chronic health care needs. *Topics in Early Childhood Special Education, 9*(4), 43–54.

Odom, S.L., McConnell, S., & Chandler, L.K. (1990). *Acceptability and feasibility of classroom-based social interaction interventions for young children with disabilities.* Manuscript submitted for publication.

Odom, S.L., & McEvoy, M.A. (1988). Integration of young children with handicaps and normally developing children. In S.L. Odom & M.B. Karnes (Eds.), *Early intervention for infants and children with handicaps: An empirical base* (pp. 241–267). Baltimore: Paul H. Brookes Publishing Co.

Peterson, N.L., & Haralick, J.G. (1977). Integration of handicapped and non-handicapped preschoolers: An analysis of play behavior and social interaction. *Education and Training of the Mentally Retarded, 12,* 235–245.

Polloway, E.A. (1987). Transition services for early age individuals with mild mental retardation. In R.N. Ianacone & R.A. Stodden (Eds.), *Transition issues and directions* (pp. 11–24). Washington, DC: Council for Exceptional Children.

Rice, M.L., & O'Brien, M. (1990). Transitions: Times of change and accommodation. *Topics in Early Childhood Special Education, 9*(4), 1–14.

Sainato, D.M., & Lyon, S.R. (1989). Promoting successful mainstreaming transitions for handicapped preschool children. *Journal of Early Intervention, 13*(4), 305–314.

Salisbury, C.L., & Vincent, L.J. (1990). Criterion of the next environment and best practices: Mainstreaming and integration 10 years later. *Topics in Early Childhood Special Education, 10*(2), 78–90.

Sanford, A. (1973). *Learning accomplishments profile.* Chapel Hill: University of North Carolina.

Spillman, C.V., & Lutz, J.P. (1985). Focus on research: Criteria for successful experiences in kindergarten. *Contemporary Education, 56*(2), 109–113.

Stokes, T.F., & Baer, D.M. (1977). An implicit technology of generalization. *Journal of Applied Behavior Analysis, 10*(2), 349–367.

Stokes, T.F., & Osnes, P. (1986). Generalizing children's social behavior. In P.S. Strain, M.J. Guralnick, & H.M. Walker (Eds.), *Children's social behavior: Development, assessment, and modification* (pp. 407–443). Orlando: Academic Press.

Strain, P.S. (1981). Peer-mediated treatment of exceptional children's social withdrawal. *Topics in Early Childhood Special Education, 1,* 94–105.

Strain, P.S., Cooke, T.P., & Apolloni, T. (1976). *Teaching exceptional children: Assessing and modifying social behavior.* New York: Academic Press.

Thompson, B. (1979). *Out of the nest: Instructional strategies to prepare young exceptional children for the mainstream.* Madison: The Wisconsin EC:EEN Project, Department of Public Instruction.

Thurlow, M.L., Ysseldyke, J.E., & Weiss, J.A. (1988). Early childhood special education exit decisions: How are they made? How are they evaluated? *Journal of the Division for Early Childhood, 12*(3), 253–262.

Vaughn, S.R., & Ridley, C.A. (1983). A preschool interpersonal problem solving program: Does it affect behavior in the classroom? *Child Study Journal, 13*(1), 1–11.

Vincent, L., Brown, L., & Getz-Sheftel, M. (1981). Integrating handicapped and typical children during the preschool years: The definition of best educational practice. *Topics in Early Childhood Special Education, 1*(1), 17–24.

Vincent, L., Salisbury, C., Walter, G., Brown, L., Gruenwald, L., & Powers, M. (1980). Program evaluation and curriculum development in early childhood/special education: Criterion of the next environment. In W. Sailor, B. Wilcox, & L. Brown (Eds.), *Methods of instruction for severely handicapped students* (pp. 303–328). Baltimore: Paul H. Brookes Publishing Co.

Walker, H.M., & Rankin, R. (1983). Assessing the behavioral expectations and demands of less restrictive settings. *School Psychology Review, 12*, 274–284.

Walter, G. (1979). *The survival skills displayed by kindergarteners and the structure of the regular classroom environment.* Unpublished master's thesis, University of Wisconsin, Madison.

Walter, G., & Vincent, L. (1982). The handicapped child in the regular kindergarten program. *Journal of the Division for Early Childhood, 6*, 82–95.

Wolery, M. (1989). Transitions in early childhood special education: Issues and procedures. *Focus on Exceptional Children, 22*, 2–16.

Appendix

TRANSITION CHECKLIST

The following questions provide information that may be used to identify transition-related goals. Space is provided for indicating whether the items on this form differ between the sending and receiving programs. These differences may be potential problems during transition and may be addressed through child and family preparation procedures.

This checklist may be completed during one classroom visit or completed by and shared with individual teachers.

Program name _____ Date _____

Teacher name _____

Does this differ from your program?

| | Yes | No |

Classroom Composition

1. How many teacher, aides, and other adults are in the classroom? _____   _____   _____
2. How many children are in the classroom? _____   _____   _____
3. Do children with special needs attend the classroom? ____ How many? _____   _____   _____

Physical Arrangement

1. List places where children sit for group instruction (e.g., desks, tables, mats).

   A. _____   _____   _____
   B. _____   _____   _____
   C. _____   _____   _____

Does this differ from your program?

	Yes	No

2. List places where children sit for individual instruction.

A. _____   _____   _____
B. _____   _____   _____
C. _____   _____   _____

3. Are work and play areas separated? ____   _____   _____
4. Where are the restrooms located? _____   _____   _____
5. Are boy and girl restrooms separate? __   _____   _____
6. How are restrooms marked? _____   _____   _____
7. Where do children eat lunch? _____   _____   _____
8. Where do children attend PE? _____   _____   _____

Daily Schedule

1. What hours do children attend daily sessions? _____   _____   _____

2. How many minutes a day do children spend:

A. In large group _____   _____   _____
B. In small group _____   _____   _____
C. In academic/fine motor activities

_____   _____   _____

D. In free play _____   _____   _____
E. In recess and large motor activities _____   _____   _____
F. In transition between activities ___   _____   _____

3. List new activities or routines in this classroom or program that are not in the child's current program (e.g., library, gym, lunch).

A. _____   _____   _____
B. _____   _____   _____
C. _____   _____   _____

Classroom Rules and Routines

1. Are children required to raise hands? ___   _____   _____
   When is this required? _____   _____   _____

2. How should children seek assistance?

_____   _____   _____

3. Do children manage all or some of their own materials? _____   _____   _____

4. Do children line up? _____   _____   _____
   When is this required? _____   _____   _____

**Does this differ from
your program?**

Yes   **No**

5. What do children do when they finish
   an activity? _____   _____   _____
6. How are classroom rules taught (e.g.,
   verbal instruction, pictures)? _____   _____   _____

Academics

1. Are there minimum competency levels for this program or a
   readiness checklist? Compare the skills on this list to those currently
   taught in your program.
2. List the five most important academic skills that most children
   entering the program should have.

   A. _____   _____   _____
   B. _____   _____   _____
   C. _____   _____   _____
   D. _____   _____   _____
   E. _____   _____   _____

3. List the academic subjects that are taught.

   A. _____   _____   _____
   B. _____   _____   _____
   C. _____   _____   _____
   D. _____   _____   _____
   E. _____   _____   _____

4. List the types of curricular materials used (e.g., worksheets, pencils,
   blackboard, manipulatives).

   A. _____   _____   _____
   B. _____   _____   _____
   C. _____   _____   _____

5. List how academic lessons generally are taught (e.g., large group,
   small group, individual instruction).

   A. _____   _____   _____
   B. _____   _____   _____

6. Are academic centers used? _____   _____   _____
7. Do curricular materials require:

   A. Written responses? _____   _____   _____
   B. Verbal responses? _____   _____   _____
   C. Matching skills? _____   _____   _____
   D. Child to follow written or pictorial
      directions? _____   _____   _____

	Does this differ from your program?	
	Yes	**No**

8. How long are children expected to work or play independently? _____   _____   _____

Teacher Attention

1. How often do teachers attend to children? _____   _____   _____

2. Do teachers use special rewards for good behavior (e.g., stickers, notes to home)? _____   _____   _____
   List these.

   A. _____   _____   _____
   B. _____   _____   _____
   C. _____   _____   _____

3. List methods teachers use to consequate inappropriate and disruptive behavior.

   A. _____   _____   _____
   B. _____   _____   _____

4. Do children play or work in groups where no adult is immediately present?

   _____   _____   _____

5. List the types of teacher assistance provided during activities (e.g., verbal, physical guidance, multi-step directions).

   A. _____   _____   _____
   B. _____   _____   _____

Self-Help Skills

1. List the five most important self-help skills that most children entering the program should have.

   A. _____   _____   _____
   B. _____   _____   _____
   C. _____   _____   _____
   D. _____   _____   _____
   E. _____   _____   _____

2. Do children use the toilet independently? _____   _____   _____

3. Are children allowed to choose the location and type of their activities during free play? _____   _____   _____

Does this differ from your program?

Yes   No

4. Are children expected to put on and
    take off outer clothing independently? __   _____   _____

Parent Involvement

1. Do parents serve as program
    volunteers? _____   _____   _____
2. Do parents observe in the classroom? __   _____   _____
3. Are parents asked to work at home with
    their child? _____   _____   _____
4. Are parent and family needs assessed?

    _____   _____   _____
5. List the types of contact parents usually have with program staff
    (e.g., IEP meetings, telephone calls, notes, newsletter).
    A. _____   _____   _____
    B. _____   _____   _____
6. How often do parents usually have contact with program staff? List
    by type of contact.
    A. _____   _____   _____
    B. _____   _____   _____

Support Systems

1. What support systems are available?
    A. Resource room _____   _____   _____
    B. Speech therapy _____   _____   _____
    C. Physical or occupational therapy

        _____   _____   _____
    D. Paraprofessional aides _____   _____   _____
    E. Student tutors _____   _____   _____
    F. Others, please list _____   _____   _____

        _____   _____   _____

Social Skills

1. List the five most important social skills for most children entering
    the program to have.
    A. _____   _____   _____
    B. _____   _____   _____
    C. _____   _____   _____
    D. _____   _____   _____
    E. _____   _____   _____

**Does this differ from
your program?**

                    Yes   **No**

2. When are children expected to share materials?

    A. Academic activities _____   _____   _____
    B. Play activities _____   _____   _____
    C. Art and fine motor activities _____   _____   _____

3. How long are children expected to play
   independently? _____   _____   _____

4. What type of behavior management system is used to reward
   positive behavior and to reduce undesirable behavior?

    A. _____   _____   _____
    B. _____   _____   _____

5. List the types of toys, games, and social materials that most
   children use during play periods.

    A. _____   _____   _____
    B. _____   _____   _____
    C. _____   _____   _____
    D. _____   _____   _____
    E. _____   _____   _____

11

Implementation of Social Competence Interventions in Early Childhood Special Education Classes

Current Practices and Future Directions

Scott R. McConnell, Mary A. McEvoy, and Samuel L. Odom

Since the 1930s, substantial progress has been made in both our knowledge regarding social development of children with and without disabilities, and the practical base of applications to promote this aspect of development. Beginning in the 1930s and continuing through present day, developmental psychologists have articulated many normative processes for the development of play skills (Fewell & Kaminski, 1988; Parten, 1932); peer affiliation and interaction (Greenwood, Walker, Todd, & Hops, 1979); social initiations (Tremblay, Strain, Hendrickson, & Shores, 1981); friendships (Hartup, 1983); and other correlates of social development (Dodge, 1983; Gottman, 1983).

Support for the research described here, and for preparation of this chapter, was provided by Grant G008730527, "Social Interaction Skills Training for Young Children with Handicaps: Analysis of Program Features," from the United States Department of Education to Vanderbilt University and the University of Minnesota. However, the opinions described here are those of the authors only, and no official endorsement should be inferred.

The authors are indebted to Rick Spicuzza for assistance in data management and analyses, and to Carla Peterson, Micki Ostrosky, and the staff of the Vanderbilt-Minnesota Social Interaction Project that assisted in data collection and analysis.

Since the early 1960s, investigators have developed an array of intervention techniques for application in the absence of normative levels of social development (a complete review of these interventions appears in McEvoy, Odom, & McConnell, Chapter 5, this volume). This rapid development of intervention procedures to promote social interaction competence of preschool children with disabilities parallels concerns and instructional objectives among teachers of these children, but does not appear to be influencing intervention in early childhood special education classrooms in any direct way. In a national survey, a vast majority of teachers reported moderate to great need for social interaction competence interventions for their students, but over 90% indicated a relative dearth of curriculum and intervention materials for use in classroom programs (Odom, McConnell, & Chandler, 1990). In short, teachers report a need for social interaction competence interventions but see little formal support for providing them.

In spite of the relative dearth of formal curricula or intervention programs, teachers suggest that social skills and social competence are formal goals of their classroom programs. As seen in detail later, over half of the children in early childhood special education (ECSE) classes have one or more goals or objectives for increased social competence on their individualized education programs (IEP). This suggests that, even in the absence of curricula that formally translate research on social development and intervention into practice, teachers are engaged in planning, teaching, and organizing classroom activities in this area. While it is essential to understand the level and extent of current practice as one part of intervention research and development (McConnell & Odom, 1989), to date there is little, if any, empirical evidence regarding the extent to which social interaction interventions are actually applied in community-based early childhood special education classes.

The purpose of this chapter is to present some direct and indirect evidence regarding the extent of intervention to promote social development and social competence in contemporary ECSE classes. Following an overview of the potential significance of assessing current practice as a necessary step in translative research, a brief review of earlier efforts to assess intervention practices in ECSE is presented. Next, findings are presented from a series of studies that specifically assessed the importance and implementation of social competence interventions in ECSE classrooms. Finally, several possible areas for future research to increase the impact and integrity of social competence interventions in ECSE are outlined.

TRANSLATING RESEARCH INTO
PRACTICE: THE ROLE OF CURRENT PRACTICE

Odom and McConnell's model of translative research (McConnell & Odom, 1989; Odom, 1988) is an effort to articulate the variables that promote or inhibit the translation of research findings into practical applications. One potential outcome measure of translative research is the *impact* of an intervention, or the extent to which that intervention promotes desired change in a wide variety of children across a wide variety of intervention settings.

McConnell and Odom (1989) suggest that the *impact* of a given intervention, or the degree to which it improves outcomes for a group of children served in a variety of community-based settings, can be conceptualized as the product of two related but distinct factors: *impact = effectiveness × likelihood of implementation. Effectiveness* is the extent to which an intervention produces reliable effects in the behavior of children as demonstrated in internally valid experimental investigations, and *likelihood of implementation* is the extent to which an intervention is implemented as designed in typical intervention settings (e.g., community-based ECSE classrooms).

This relationship between effectiveness and likelihood of implementation suggests that the overall impact of an intervention may fluctuate due to variations in *either* factor. Thus, interventions that have been demonstrated to be extremely powerful in well-controlled laboratory settings but that employ atypical or socially unacceptable procedures and/or demand a wide variety of expensive resources for implementation and thus are implemented rarely, may have less overall impact than interventions that have been demonstrated to be less effective in well-controlled laboratory settings but employ well-accepted procedures and/or readily available resources and are implemented more often.

Researchers work to develop intervention procedures that are maximally effective; this is a traditional approach to intervention research and development in psychology and education. To maximize impact in applied settings, however, investigators also must build these interventions into procedures that are acceptable to teachers and that can be implemented with the resources available in typical classroom settings. While the relationship between acceptability, implementation, and effectiveness remains largely unknown (Peterson, 1990), logical analysis suggests that increased attention must be paid to factors that affect the likelihood of implementation for interventions in applied settings.

One way to judge the acceptability and likelihood of implementation of various intervention procedures is to assess the current practices of intervention agents (i.e., teachers, aides) in criterion settings (i.e., community-based classrooms). This assessment of current practice can provide evidence of the extent to which highly effective intervention procedures are already in place. Additionally, this assessment can provide evidence of classroom activities or settings in which more powerful intervention procedures could be added more easily.

With respect to the development of social competence interventions, this assessment of current practice is designed to address six questions:

1.   Are social competence interventions important to teachers?
2.   Are social competence interventions a significant part of children's individualized education programs?
3.   In which classroom activities are young children with disabilities most likely to interact with peers?
4.   How do teachers allocate time for social competence interventions, and how is this time spent?
5.   To what extent do teachers implement social competence interventions that are empirically valid?
6.   What are the social competence outcomes for young children in early childhood special education classrooms?

EARLIER EFFORTS TO ASSESS PRACTICE IN ECSE

While research and practice in ECSE often seem to exist in separate and unconnected domains (Odom, 1988), there have been several notable and productive earlier efforts to assess different aspects of current practice in early childhood special education classrooms. While these earlier efforts have not addressed interventions to promote social competence *per se,* the methods and procedures employed and results obtained do bear on the current discussion.

Sainato and Lyon (as described in Carta, Sainato, & Greenwood, 1989) compared the types and intensities of intervention provided to children in ECSE, regular preschool, and kindergarten classrooms. In each setting, Sainato and Lyon asked the teacher to identify the "most independent" and "least independent" child prior to observation. In this way, these investigators could compare and contrast different standards of performance in a single classroom, as well as compare typical levels of performance across types of classrooms.

Comparisons of most and least independent students within ECSE classrooms suggested markedly different educational programs for these two groups of children. In particular, Sainato and Lyon found that children in both groups spent a large proportion (over 40%) of available classroom time engaged in solitary activities. When engaged in other, more interactive activities, however, children identified as more independent by the teacher were more likely to participate in teacher-guided or teacher-directed activities. Overall, this comparison of students suggested that those children identified as least independent received intervention that was less intensive than that received by more competent classmates.

Carta and Greenwood (described in Carta et al., 1989) also compared performance of children with disabilities and those without disabilities in typical classroom environments. Using a well-established instrument for observational assessment of ecobehavioral interactions, the Ecobehavioral System for Complex Assessments of Preschool Environments (ESCAPE) (Carta, Greenwood, & Atwater, 1985), Carta and her colleagues found evidence that children in ECSE classrooms spend little time engaged in preacademic activities or using instructional materials, and spend a large portion of the day passively attending to the teacher, peers, or classroom activities. Again, these data suggest in a general way that the intensity of intervention in some ECSE classes is not very high.

Carta, Atwater, Schwartz, and Miller (1990) described a series of studies that represent the most complete ecobehavioral assessments of ECSE classrooms completed to date. In one investigation, researchers observed randomly selected boys and girls from ECSE and regular education kindergarten classes twice, for a total of 4 hours, using ESCAPE. Molar analyses of category base rates indicated that the two types of classrooms differed significantly with respect to time spent in designated activities, time spent in various instructional arrangements, and types and amounts of behavior displayed by individual children. For instance, ECSE classrooms in this study allocated more time each day for play and fine motor activities, while regular kindergarten classes devoted more time to transitions and class business. Additionally, children in ECSE classes spent the vast majority of their time in solitary, one-on-one, and small group activities, whereas regular kindergarten students spent a very large percentage (75%) of their time in large group activities. More molecular analyses suggested that ECSE students received about as many prompts as children in kindergarten classes, but these prompts were delivered under remarkably different conditions. In the ECSE classes, teachers prompted primarily during preacademic, fine motor, and transition activities; Carta and colleagues suggested that these prompts functioned more as "precorrections" or instructions for competent child performance. By contrast, teachers in kindergarten classes prompted more during play activities and story time; these findings may suggest that prompts function as consequences for undesired child behavior. Carta and her colleagues demonstrated that levels of intervention vary across classrooms within groups (e.g., ECSE) but that variations also occur between classrooms in different groups. Along with others, Carta et al. (1990) suggested that only the assessment of intervention intensity in ECSE classrooms will enable researchers to identify intervention designs and practices that actually produce reliable changes in the performance of young children with disabilities.

ASSESSING CURRENT SOCIAL COMPETENCE INTERVENTIONS IN ECSE

To describe current practices in the provision of social competence interventions in ECSE classrooms, a series of studies was conducted under the auspices of the Vanderbilt-Minnesota Social Interaction Project during the 1987/1988 academic year. The purpose of these investigations was to describe the relative importance of social competence interventions in community-based ECSE classrooms and to assess directly the extent to which effective procedures to promote social competence were implemented in these classrooms.

Most of these studies were conducted in 28 preschool classrooms in Tennessee and Minnesota and included 222 child participants. Twenty-two of the participating classrooms were part of ECSE programs operated by local school districts or other public agencies; a total of 167 children with disabilities enrolled in these classrooms participated in these investigations. Six additional day care or preschool classrooms were included in these studies to provide a normative base; 55 children without identified disabilities were the child participants from these classes.

A wide variety of measures were gathered to describe both intended and actual intervention programs in each classroom. These measures included direct observations of children and classroom activities during the entire school day, observational assessment of social behavior during free play activities, performance-based assessment of social competence for all child participants, assessment of teachers' schedules and plans for allocation of classroom time, and analysis of students' individualized education programs (for students with disabilities only). In addition, a survey of intervention acceptability and feasibility was conducted with a national sample of 131 ECSE teachers that included the teachers from the 22 participating classrooms.

Taken together, data produced by these measures yielded a detailed picture of the relative importance of social competence interventions in community-based ECSE classrooms, and the ways in which these interventions currently are being conducted. These data can help researchers assess the extent to which previous research on social competence interventions is making an impact on current practice in ECSE, and also can guide researchers in the development of a new generation of interventions that may increase the overall effect on social competence development for students in typical ECSE classrooms. In the following sections the results of these studies are reviewed; then suggestions for future research are presented.

Are Social Competence Interventions Important to Teachers?

Odom, McConnell, and Chandler (1990) presented the results of a national survey of ECSE teachers designed to assess: 1) the relative importance of social competence interventions, 2) the need for additional intervention programs in this area, and 3) the relative acceptability, feasibility, and current use of individual intervention components developed in earlier research. One hundred thirty-one ECSE teachers from throughout the United States participated. They were largely female (99.3%) and averaged 6 years of experience (range = 1–20) as preschool teachers. The vast majority of teachers (98%) held appropriate certification for ECSE in their home state, and 79% of these participants had completed at least some graduate courses beyond their entry-level degree.

Teachers were asked two sets of questions. First, they were asked to judge the relative importance of social competence intervention, and the number of children enrolled in their classroom who were likely to need such intervention. Second, teachers were asked to rate 37 brief descriptions of social competence intervention procedures drawn from a review of the empirical literature. Each procedure was to be rated on three different dimensions: 1) *acceptability* (i.e., the extent to which a particular procedure "fits your philosophy of teaching social interactions skills to young children with disabilities"); 2) *feasibility* (i.e., the extent to which a teacher could implement a particular procedure "given your current resources—personnel, materials, space, training, etc."); and 3) *current use* (i.e., the extent to which a particular procedure was already implemented in the respondent's classroom).

Teachers responding to this questionnaire indicated a great need for social competence interventions. Teachers reported that an average of 74% of their students (range = 2%–100%) needed and/or were receiving social competence interventions. Additionally, 43% of the respondents reported a great need and 47% reported a moderate need for additional intervention procedures.

Teachers' ratings of acceptability of individual procedures varied somewhat, suggesting some differential preference for various components. Most widely accepted intervention procedures included teaching social skills to children, teaching them to label emotions, praising individuals and groups for the use of social skills (especially cooperation), providing appropriate toys and materials, and arranging developmentally heterogeneous play groups. Less acceptable interventions included mastery tests of social skills, using self-management procedures, using tangible reinforcers for social interaction, using videotaped examples of social interaction, and providing activities with high structure for social interaction. In general, however, mean ratings of acceptability across all intervention procedures were high (4.14–4.41 on a five-point scale), perhaps suggesting general teacher acceptance for any of the presented intervention procedures.

Similar results were obtained for feasibility of individual items, although teacher ratings on this dimension were somewhat lower overall (mean ratings of 3.82–4.24 on a five-point scale). Teachers reported that it was most feasible to teach, model, and praise social skills and cooperative play; to create developmentally heterogeneous play groups; to provide appropriate materials; and to conduct play activities in small, well-defined spaces. Less feasible procedures included testing the mastery of social skills instruction, teaching children self-monitoring, providing tangible reinforcement and direct instruction to peers, providing videotaped examples of social interaction, running highly structured play activities, and arranging for play groups that include children with and without disabilities.

Teachers reported lower overall ratings of current use for individual intervention procedures (mean ratings 3.35–3.88 on a five-point scale). However, there was remarkable similarity between relative rankings of current use and feasibility; in general, the results suggested that teachers were likely to report highest levels of use for those items previously identified as most feasible.

Results from the Odom, McConnell, and Chandler (1990) study suggested that social competence interventions are a strong concern of ECSE teachers; that a wide variety of intervention procedures are judged both acceptable and feasible by teachers; and that teachers report already using, to some extent, many of these intervention procedures in their classrooms. While these findings differ somewhat from direct assessment of intervention in ECSE classrooms, they also indicate a need for additional work in the design, evaluation, and dissemination of effective yet acceptable interventions.

Are Social Competence Interventions a Significant Part of Children's Individualized Education Programs?

Teacher judgments of the importance of social competence interventions, as reported by Odom, McConnell, and Chandler (1990), offer initial evidence of the potential impact and significance of research and development activities in this area. However, a different and, perhaps, more direct assessment of the importance of social competence interventions for individual children can be conducted through examination of the IEP. These documents are developed by an ECSE teacher in conjunction with a child's parents and are intended to describe the appropriate education program for that child. As part of an assessment of current practices in social competence intervention, a review of students' IEPs can provide assessment of: 1) the extent to which social competence goals and objectives are included in education programs for students enrolled in ECSE, and 2) the relative importance of these social competence goals and objectives, or their proportion of the total goals and objectives across all developmental areas.

Teachers in classrooms participating in the Vanderbilt-Minnesota Social Interaction Project provided access to current IEPs for all 167 children with disabilities. Trained members of the research team reviewed each IEP and evaluated individual goals and objectives using standard, project-developed definitions. Using these standard definitions, each long-term goal and short-term objective was counted under one of seven mutually exclusive, exhaustive categories: 1) social, 2) cognitive, 3) preacademic, 4) language/communication, 5) gross motor, 6) fine motor, and 7) self-help. These frequencies then served as the basis for calculating the proportion of long-term goals and short-term objectives in each developmental domain.

Table 11.1 presents the actual and relative distributions for long-term goals and short-term objectives by developmental domain. These data suggest that, on the average, preschool children with disabilities have between zero and six long-term social goals, and between 0 and 10 short-term social objectives. Additionally, teachers and parents of young children with disabilities appear to identify one long-term social goal for every two children (i.e., mean frequency of .58 social goals for sample) and 1.66 short-term social objectives for students.

Interestingly, approximately 10% of the long-term goals and short-term objectives identified for young children with disabilities pertain to social interaction and social competence. In a relative sense, young children appear to have slightly more social than self-

Table 11.1. Mean frequency, range, and percentage of total IEP long-term goals and short-term objectives by developmental domain

	Long-term goals			Short-term objectives		
Domain	Mean	Range	% of total	Mean	Range	% of total
Social	.57	0–6	10.7	1.66	0– 10	10.2
Cognitive	.83	0–8	12.7	3.86	0– 27	12.4
Preacademic	.96	0–9	14.7	8.31	0–123	15.8
Language/ Communication	1.40	0–6	29.0	5.51	0– 32	28.6
Gross motor	.62	0–5	11.0	2.21	0– 11	8.6
Fine motor	.82	0–5	13.4	3.72	0– 29	14.3
Self-help	.56	0–7	8.5	5.78	0–138	10.1
Totals	5.76		—	31.05		—

help goals and objectives, approximately the same proportion of social and gross or fine motor goals and objectives, and significantly more cognitive, preacademic, and language/communication than social goals and objectives. These relative rankings are consistent with D. Baumgart's work (personal communication, October, 1990), which demonstrated that teachers assign relatively less value to social interaction goals and objectives than they do to other developmental goals for both typical preschool-age children and those with significant disabilities.

These data suggest that intervention in the area of social competence is an important need, but not the most frequently identified one, for young children with disabilities and their families. These findings largely replicated Odom, McConnell, and Chandler's (1990) survey results, indicating that a large proportion of children in ECSE require some type of social competence intervention. However, it is also clear from these data that social competence interventions should not supplant other intervention services, especially in the areas of cognitive development, language and communication performance, and preacademic skills development.

In Which Classroom Activities Are Young Children with Disabilities Most Likely To Interact with Peers?

To investigate further the extent to which early childhood special education teachers implement social interaction interventions, it is essential to know in what activities or situations children are most likely to interact. One can logically assume that activities or situations in which social interaction *already* occurs are both good opportunities for observing teacher intervention, and the best activities for any additional interventions.

Odom, Peterson, McConnell, and Ostrosky (1990) conducted an observational study to identify those settings and situations in which social interaction was most likely to occur for both children with disabilities in special education classrooms and typically-developing children in regular education classrooms. A total of 127 children, 94 of whom had disabling conditions, were observed using ESCAPE (Carta et al., 1985). Observations were conducted for 2.5–3.5 hours per child, covering all activities scheduled for either the entire portion of a half-day program, or the morning portion of a full-day program.

Because ESCAPE does not include a specific measure of social interaction, a stand-in measure was used instead. Talk to Peers, one of four child verbal behaviors included in ESCAPE, includes topographies that typically are included in observational categories for social interaction, but also excludes some other (i.e., nonverbal) behaviors that might be defined as social interaction. As a result, Talk to Peers was considered by Odom and colleagues to be a conservative estimate of child-child social interaction and was used as the stand-in measure for subsequent analyses.

Table 11.2 (adapted from Odom et al., 1990) summarizes the base rates of Talk to Peers for young children with disabilities in each of 12 designated activities. Historically, curriculum developers have assumed *a priori* that social interaction occurs in a variety of classroom activities, including play, snack, gross motor, fine motor, and transi-

Table 11.2. Mean proportion (and standard deviation) of intervals of Talk to Peers, by designated activity, for young children with disabilities ($N = 127$)

Designated activity	Mean (standard deviation), Talk to Peers
Play	7.0
Clean up	3.7
Fine motor	3.4
Transition	3.2
Snack	2.7
Gross motor	2.4
Class business	2.3
Story	1.9
Music and recitation	1.5
Self-care	1.3
Pre-academics	1.2
Language programming	0.7

tion periods. Observations conducted by Odom, Peterson and colleagues (1990) partly confirm these assumptions, indicating relatively high rates of Talk to Peers during Play and Transition activities. However, these results also indicated that relatively little Talk to Peers occurred during most other classroom activities, including Snack, Gross Motor, and Fine Motor periods.

For the current discussion, these data suggest that play activities are the most likely activities for social interaction generally, and for interventions to increase competence in this area specifically. While both direct (e.g., social skills training) and indirect (e.g., language intervention, fine motor skills instruction) interventions may take place during other periods, researchers interested in social competence might target interventions provided during play activities to assess teachers' current practices in this area.

How Do Teachers Allocate Classroom Time for Social Competence Interventions, and How Is This Time Actually Spent?

Another, more indirect, measure of the importance of social competence interventions is the time that is allocated to and actually spent in classroom activities that promote the development of social competence. Time is perhaps one of the scarcest and most important resources available to ECSE teachers, and its allocation and use is of major concern (Bailey & Wolery, 1984). Thus, it can be expected that there is some relationship between the amount of time allocated or devoted to a particular topic and the relative importance of that topic for children in ECSE classrooms.

Ostrosky, Skellenger, Odom, McConnell, and Peterson (1990) examined teachers' schedules of classroom activities and the time actually devoted to these activities in the 22 ECSE classrooms participating in the Odom, Peterson et al. (1990) descriptive study. Immediately prior to observational assessment, teachers completed a detailed schedule of the allocation of time in their classroom programs. These activities were then coded, using ESCAPE activity definitions, into one of 12 mutually exclusive and exhaustive categories: 1) transition, 2) preacademic, 3) language programming, 4) storytime, 5) fine motor, 6) gross motor, 7) music and recitation, 8) play, 9) class business, 10) self-care, 11) snack, and 12) clean-up. ESCAPE observations were then conducted in each of these classrooms, with a total of 94 children with disabilities observed for all or a significant portion of their classroom day. One part of this observation included ongoing assessment of the activity currently underway for each child observed, with assignment to one of the 12 categories mentioned earlier. Across these two sources of data, Ostrosky, Skellenger, and colleagues were able to estimate the amount of time *allocated* to different types of classroom activities (i.e., proportion of classroom day indicated on the teacher schedule), and the amount of time actually *engaged* in these activities (i.e., proportion of classroom day the activity was observed to take place).

Table 11.3 presents an adaptation of Ostrosky, Skellenger, and colleagues' (1990) findings, with classroom activities ranked by the time allocated to each. Ostrosky and colleagues reported a high degree of correspondence between the time teachers allocated for activities and the time actually devoted to them; in nine of the 12 categories, percentage of time allocated did not differ significantly (less than 3% of the classroom day) from the percentage of time activities were actually observed to occur. In three categories, however, scheduled allocations differed significantly from actual time engaged, with magnitudes of difference that either exceeded by 5% (i.e., Play and Transition) or doubled (i.e., Storytime) the scheduled rate.

Table 11.3. Mean proportion (and standard deviation) of allocated and actual time by type of classroom activity

Activity	Allocated time	Observed time
Play	19.87 (10.47)	14.21 (8.2)
Pre-academic	18.83 (14.58)	15.08 (9.76)
Snack	12.52 (8.11)	11.32 (6.85)
Fine motor	9.78 (10.3)	13.65 (8.08)
Gross motor	8.99 (8.62)	8.10 (5.63)
Transition	7.16 (5.79)	15.06 (4.21)
Class business	6.32 (5.2)	3.93 (2.94)
Self-care	5.82 (5.4)	3.28 (2.29)
Music/recitation	4.92 (6.59)	3.93 (3.45)
Story time	3.20 (3.49)	6.88 (4.29)
Clean up	.94 (1.88)	1.92 (1.04)
Language programming	.93 (3.30)	2.27 (3.06)

Play received the highest proportion of *allocated* time (i.e., 19.87% of the classroom day) and the second highest proportion of *engaged* time (i.e., 14.21% of the classroom day), suggesting that teachers in ECSE classrooms devote substantial proportions of time in their programs to activities in which social interaction is most likely to occur. However, it is important to note significant differences between allocated and engaged time for Play. Ostrosky and colleagues' (1990) results indicated that children spent only 71% of the time scheduled for Play actually engaged in this activity (i.e., 19.87% scheduled time, 14.21% engaged time); these results suggested that a substantial portion of possible Play time may be used instead in Transition activities. Thus, improvements in overall classroom management, using available procedures to speed classroom transitions (Carta, Schwartz, Atwater, & Connell, 1989; Sainato, Strain, Lefebvre, & Rapp, 1987), may produce more opportunities for play and social interaction.

This evidence suggests possible opportunities for social interaction by young children with disabilities; however, it is not yet clear whether teachers actually provide intervention services to promote social competence during these naturally occurring play activities. Evaluations of teacher intervention efforts are described next.

To What Extent Do Teachers Implement Social Competence Interventions that Are Empirically Validated?

Thus far, this chapter has reviewed somewhat indirect measures of the extent to which teachers implement social competence interventions. These indirect measures have included social validity assessments of the importance of social interaction goals and objectives, file reviews of the extent to which these types of goals and objectives are represented on IEPs, estimates of the extent to which social interaction occurs in different activities, and measures of the extent to which teachers allocate and actually engage their students in activities associated with higher base rates of social interaction. Taken together, these data suggest that social interaction skills, and activities to facilitate the acquisition of these skills, are a significant part of the educational program for young children with disabilities. However, these data offer little evidence of the extent to which teachers *explicitly intervene* to increase social interaction of young children with disabilities.

As part of the Vanderbilt-Minnesota Social Interaction Project descriptive study, observational ratings were collected to assess more directly the degree of implementation for a large number of intervention procedures. Prior to initiation of the descriptive study, a review of the empirical literature on social interaction skill interventions for young children with and without disabilities was completed. Empirical evaluations of social interaction skill interventions were identified using a combination of computer searches; reviews of journals typically publishing this research (e.g., *Journal of Applied Behavior Analysis, Behavior Modification, Journal of Special Education, Journal of Early Intervention, Analysis and Intervention in Developmental Disabilities*); conference presentations; and requests for recently completed but unpublished work. Based on this review, a total of 49 intervention tactics (i.e., discrete procedures that had been manipulated either as independent variables [e.g., teacher prompts for social initiations] or as components of multielement intervention packages) were identified. These intervention tactics were then grouped logically into three categories: 1) *environmental arrangements,* or procedures in which the teacher arranges features of the physical (e.g., toys or space available) or social (e.g., peers present, structured activities) environment to promote social interaction; 2) *child-specific interventions,* in which the teacher provides instruction, prompts, praise, or other intervention directly to children for whom increased social interaction is a goal; and 3) *peer-mediated interventions,* in which the teacher directs instruction, prompts, praise, or other intervention to peers who interact with the target child (see Sainato & Carta, Chapter 4, and McEvoy, Odom, & McConnell, Chapter 5, this volume for detailed reviews of intervention procedures in each of these three categories).

As described earlier, trained observers conducted day-long ESCAPE observations for 94 children enrolled in 22 participating ECSE classrooms (Odom, Peterson et al., 1990). At the end of each day observers completed ratings of the extent to which each of the previously identified intervention tactics was implemented during the observation session. Five-point Likert-type ratings were completed for each of the 49 intervention tactics identified in the literature review, with a rating of 1 signifying that an individual intervention component was "not observed or not descriptive of the classroom program," a rating of 3 indicating that an intervention was "implemented for small period of time or somewhat descriptive of classroom program," and a rating of 5 indicating that an intervention "was implemented throughout the period or item is very descriptive of classroom program." Ratings were completed from one to 16 times per classroom (X = 8.63), depending on the number of ESCAPE observations completed in each class, and mean ratings were computed across all observations for each classroom.

Table 11.4 presents the results of these observation-based ratings. Generally, these results suggested that few of the previously identified, empirically evaluated intervention components were widely

Table 11.4. Individual social interaction skill interventions and mean (standard deviation) ratings of implementation in early childhood special education classrooms

Intervention component	Observer rating M (SD)
Environmental Arrangements	
1. Children play in relatively small, well-defined areas that are associated with specific play themes, activities, or materials (in contrast to playing in a large, undifferentiated play area).	3.23 (.77)
2. Toys that promote social interaction are present in play areas (e.g., sociodramatic play materials, blocks that could promote pretend play).	3.65 (.91)
3. Teacher introduces play activities, specifies children's roles, suggests play ideas, before the children begin to play.	1.82 (.66)
4. Teacher selects activities that have a high structure (i.e., limited number of roles, roles clearly defined, materials related to a single play theme) versus low structure (i.e., roles not clearly defined, materials related to multiple play themes, unlimited roles possible).	1.95 (.81)
5. Child's play group is developmentally heterogeneous.	2.44 (1.02)
6. Child's play group includes disabled and nondisabled children.	1.50 (.87)
7. Teacher provides filmed or videotaped models of social interaction.	1.03 (.08)
8. Teacher reads or tells stories that model social interaction.	1.02 (.06)
Child-Specific Interventions	
9. Teacher directly teaches words that label emotions and feelings.	1.17 (.23)
10. Child is taught to recognize or label peers' emotional states (e.g., anger, happiness).	1.14 (.23)
11. Child is taught to identify and solve interpersonal social problems (e.g., aggression related to materials, transgressions related to turn-taking, others calling the child names).	1.35 (.36)
12. Child is taught specific social skills (e.g., sharing, turn-taking, starting interactions) in an instructional setting	1.28 (.41)
13. Teacher uses effective instructional techniques to teach social skills and concepts (e.g., rapid pacing, frequent responding by students, procedures that keep student on-task).	1.15 (.32)

(continued)

Table 11.4. (*continued*)

Intervention component	Observer rating M (SD)
14. Teacher develops individualized programs to teach social interaction skills to child (accounting for differences in environment, language/cognitive skill, and current level of social interaction skill).	1.10 (.25)
15. Teacher models or demonstrates social skills and concepts *during* instructional periods.	1.18 (.31)
16. Teacher describes possible applications for social skills or concepts *during* instructional periods.	1.06 (.14)
17. Teacher directly tests child's mastery of skill or concept *during* instructional periods.	1.08 (.19)
18. Teacher praises child for demonstration of social skills or concepts *during* instructional periods.	1.20 (.36)
19. Teacher corrects child regarding application of social skills or concepts *during* instructional periods.	1.19 (.39)
20. Student receives multiple opportunities to rehearse social skills *during* instructional period.	1.14 (.30)
21. Teacher models or demonstrates social skills and concepts *outside* of instructional setting.	1.28 (.35)
22. Teacher describes possible applications for social skills or concepts *outside* of instructional setting.	1.14 (.32)
23. Teacher directly tests child's mastery of skill or concept *outside* of instructional setting.	1.10 (.21)
24. Teacher praises child for demonstration of social skills or concepts *outside* of instructional setting.	1.40 (.47)
25. Teacher prompts child to demonstrate social skills or concepts *outside* of instructional setting.	1.54 (.51)
26. Teacher corrects child regarding application of social skills or concepts *outside* of instructional setting.	1.43 (.45)
27. Student receives multiple opportunities to rehearse social skills *outside* of instructional setting.	1.44 (.53)
28. Teacher praises application of social interaction skills or concepts in *multiple* settings.	1.20 (.31)
29. Teacher provides opportunities for child to monitor (i.e., record and evaluate) own social interaction skill performance in various environments.	1.04 (.14)
Peer-Mediated Interventions	
30. Children work in cooperative groups that have a joint purpose, explicit theme of cooperation, and shared group (versus individual) objective.	1.22 (.55)
31. Teacher prompts groups to work or play cooperatively.	1.47 (.61)

(*continued*)

Table 11.4. *(continued)*

Intervention component	Observer rating M (SD)
32. Teacher models cooperative behavior (sharing, offering assistance) for the group.	1.36 (.52)
33. Teacher praises cooperative behavior.	1.43 (.57)
34. Teacher instructs peers (i.e., at least one or two peers) in specific strategies for communicating with disabled target children (i.e., children who are targets of the training programs).	1.10 (.34)
35. Teacher instructs peers to persist in their social interactions with disabled target children *in an instructional setting.*	1.06 (.31)
36. Teacher instructs peers to share materials with disabled target children *in an instructional setting.*	1.07 (.33)
37. Teacher instructs peers to request materials (i.e., share request) from disabled target children *in an instructional setting.*	1.08 (.37)
38. Teacher instructs peers to compliment disabled target children *in an instructional setting.*	1.05 (.29)
39. Teacher instructs peers to be affectionate with disabled target peers in an instructional setting.	1.05 (.26)
40. Teacher instructs peers to suggest specific play activities to disabled target children in an instructional setting.	1.05 (.26)
41. Teacher prompts peers to persist in their social interactions with disabled target children *outside* instructional settings.	1.06 (.20)
42. Teacher prompts peers to share materials with disabled target children *outside* instructional settings.	1.14 (.26)
43. Teacher prompts peers to request materials (i.e., share request) from disabled target children *outside* instructional settings.	1.12 (.27)
44. Teacher prompts peers to compliment disabled target children *outside* instructional settings.	1.04 (.22)
45. Teacher prompts peers to be affectionate with disabled target children *outside* instructional settings.	1.03 (.12)
46. Teacher prompts peers to suggest specific play activities to disabled target children *outside* instructional settings.	1.03 (.10)
47. Teacher praises peers for interacting with disabled target children *outside* instructional settings.	1.06 (.13)
48. Teacher praises groups of children for social interaction with individual child (including child and one peer).	1.05 (.19)
49. Teacher provides activity or tangible reinforcement for group based on social interaction of individual child.	1.04 (.15)

used in early childhood special education classrooms. Mean ratings for all items fell below 4.0 ("tactic implemented for large portion of time or item is fairly descriptive of classroom program"), and only items 1, 2, and 5 had mean ratings higher than 2.0 (tactic "implemented for short period of time, or item barely descriptive of classroom program"). However, ratings for 26 of the items indicated very low levels of implementation across all classrooms, with mean ratings below 1.15; in fact, four additional items (i.e., items 45, 46, and 47) occurred at extremely low levels, with ratings above 1.0 for only one classroom.

Content analyses of items with low versus high means offer tentative information regarding the types of social competence interventions already provided in ECSE classrooms. The three items that had highest mean ratings all were described as "environmental arrangements" interventions. These intervention tactics focused on molar organizational and environmental variables related to ways that teachers structured play activities. In particular, these ratings suggested that teachers were relatively more likely to provide toys that promoted social interaction; organize play activities in small, well-defined spaces; and create developmentally heterogeneous play groups. While each of these intervention tactics has been associated, either alone or in combination with others, with increases in social interaction (e.g., Brown, Fox, & Brady, 1987; McEvoy & Skellenger, 1990; Quilitch & Risley, 1973; Strain, 1984), all three of these intervention tactics are molar, structural interventions that require little ongoing or direct teacher intervention.

By contrast, items with lower mean ratings are associated with more direct, response-intensive teacher intervention. The three items that were observed only in a single classroom described specific instructional features of peer-mediated interventions (cf. Odom & Strain, 1984). In fact, 70% of the peer-mediated items had mean ratings less than 1.1; although peer-mediated interventions often are assumed to be the most powerful available procedures for increasing social interaction rates for young children with disabilities, specific features of these interventions were observed rarely in typical ECSE classrooms.

Child-specific intervention tactics were observed only slightly more often. Only 35% of the mean ratings for child-specific intervention tactics exceeded 1.25 (i.e., items 11, 12, 21, 24, 25, 26, and 27). Interestingly, these items assessed the extent to which teachers provided training in specific social interaction skills, as well as providing prompts, praise, and corrective feedback during social interaction activities. It has been demonstrated empirically that these tactics produce the largest gains in social interaction rates during child-specific intervention (McConnell, Peterson, Fox, & Odom, 1990).

This assessment of implementation of intervention procedures has several significant shortcomings. First, ratings were conducted on a nominal scale, offering only general information regarding the degree of implementation for individual tactics. Second, assessments in participating classrooms were conducted over relatively short periods of time; it is possible that more active intervention was in place during portions of the school year other than those observed here. Third, data presented here do not allow for evaluation of possible levels of intervention, nor for evaluation of relationships among different intervention procedures. As noted earlier, it is essential to assess the extent to which intervention *can* be implemented, given available resources and staff training, as well as the extent to which intervention *is* implemented. Fourth, data presented here do not allow for evaluation of variables other than those included in the assessment that also may increase social interaction and competence for young children with disabilities.

However, these data do strongly suggest that ECSE classrooms, as represented in the current descriptive sample, are currently implementing, at moderate to extremely low levels, intervention procedures that have been identified in the empirical literature as effective. Additionally, these results suggest that teachers are more likely to implement structural, somewhat indirect intervention tactics that affect large groups of children and are relatively less likely to implement more active and intensive intervention procedures for individual children. Further research, including more direct assessment of interventions and outcomes for individual children, may be necessary to assess both the variables controlling teacher implementation of intervention tactics, and the extent to which these interventions are effective. However, the results of the present assessment suggest that further work is needed to translate existing intervention tactics into classroom procedures that are, indeed, implemented.

What Are Social Competence Outcomes for Young Children in ECSE Classrooms?

Given low levels of implementation for social interaction skill interventions, one must question the current levels of social competence of children enrolled in ECSE classrooms. On the one hand, intervention procedures may not be implemented frequently because children enrolled already display adequate levels of social interaction and competence. On the other hand, the low level of implementation observed for these interventions may be problematic if children enrolled in ECSE classrooms are demonstrating low levels of social competence. In this latter situation, it would be essential to identify ways to increase the absolute level of intervention to increase social competence among these children.

To address the question of social competence outcomes for young children in ECSE classrooms, performance-based assessments of social competence were collected for students with disabilities in ECSE classrooms and children without disabilities participating in the Vanderbilt-Minnesota Social Interaction Project descriptive study. This assessment, based on Odom and McConnell's (1985) conceptual model for an empirical, multiple-measure definition of social competence, combined 11 different variables from four different measurement sources: 1) teacher ratings of social competence, as collected with the California Preschool Scale of Social Competency; 2) peer ratings of sociometric status; 3) eight variables drawn from observational assessment of child-child interaction in free play settings, including percentage of time in social interaction, mean length of interactions, total number of interactions, rate of target child initiations to peers, rate of peer responses to target child initiations, rate of peer initiations to target child, rate of target child responses to peer initiations, and a "sociability ratio" of target child initiations to peer initiations; and 4) the total score from a 16-item Observer Impressions Rating Scale (McConnell & Odom, 1988), in which trained observers provided qualitative ratings of social behavior following 5-minute direct observation sessions. Individual scores on the 11 variables were submitted to a principal components analysis, and factor scores were computed for each child on the first principal component (McConnell & Odom, 1991).

Eight of the eleven individual variables loaded (.3 or greater) on the first principal component; mean length of interaction loaded at a more moderate level (.24) and peer sociometrics and the sociability ratio calculated from observational data loaded at lower levels, but were retained for subsequent analyses. Comparison of the resulting factor score for children with disabilities ($X = -.194$, $SD = .954$, $n = 140$) and for children without disabilities ($X = .633$, $SD = .886$, $n = 43$) indicated significant differences between groups ($F(1,181) = 25.58$, $p < .0001$). Thus, children with disabilities in this sample both received little direct intervention to increase social interaction skills and competence, and were observed to have significantly lower rates of social competence than same-age children without disabilities.

INCREASING THE IMPACT AND INTEGRITY OF
SOCIAL INTERACTION RESEARCH WITH RESPECT TO
CURRENT USE OF INTERVENTIONS IN ECSE CLASSROOMS

Taken together, results of descriptive studies presented in this chapter and earlier research lead to some tentative conclusions regarding current applications of social interaction skills interventions in preschool programs for young children with disabilities. First, it appears that teachers and parents judge social competence outcomes to be important for children with disabilities, although these outcomes are not judged to be as important as goals and objectives in other developmental areas.

Second, teachers of young children with disabilities report a need for more intensive social interaction skill interventions. It does not appear that these types of interventions are addressed routinely in preservice training programs for early childhood special education teachers, and no methods texts exist in this area. Instead, teacher reports and experience to date suggest that in-service training, including assistance in classroom implementation, may be an appropriate format for increasing teachers' access to these types of interventions.

Third, teachers allocate significant portions (almost one-fifth) of the classroom day to activities that are designed to promote social interaction and that can serve as settings for social competence interventions. However, in most classrooms less time is spent actually engaged in these activities than is allocated in the classroom schedule. Additionally, during these activities, teachers are observed to use some, but not many, empirically valid intervention tactics to increase social competence. While some intervention tactics are implemented at moderate levels (especially those that are more global and less intensive), tactics that are assumed to be most powerful but that require relatively higher levels of teacher involvement with individual children appear less likely to be implemented. To increase the overall impact of social competence interventions in ECSE classrooms, researchers and program administrators may have to find ways to increase the implementation of more powerful, and more demanding, interventions in these settings.

Fourth, in spite of direct and indirect reports from parents and teachers regarding the importance of social competence for young children, and the amount of intervention allocated and actually in place to promote development in this domain, children with disabilities in ECSE classrooms demonstrate lower levels of social competence than do same-age children without disabilities. This suggests that either more intervention, or different types of intervention, must be implemented to achieve social competence goals established by these children's parents and teachers.

Evaluating Impact of Interventions

McConnell and Odom (1989) and others (Kazdin, Kratochwill, & Vanden Bos, 1986; Odom, 1988) have discussed the importance of systematic efforts to translate research findings into practical applications. Other chapters of this volume describe some extremely promising social competence interventions to emerge from research and development activities. However, results presented here would suggest that without some change in research, dissemination, or service delivery systems, this empirical work will have little practical effect on intervention programs or developmental outcomes for young children enrolled in community-based ECSE classrooms.

As noted earlier, the overall impact of an intervention is assumed to vary as a function of both the effectiveness of that intervention and the likelihood that it will be implemented (McConnell & Odom, 1989). Evaluating intervention effectiveness is well-understood by researchers in psychology and special education, and serves as the major focus for many well-accepted research and development models (cf. Walker, Hops, & Greenwood, 1984). For interventions to produce broad, socially valid impact, it is essential that careful attention be paid to the development and empirical evaluation of intervention procedures. Yet, while development of effective interventions is a necessary condition for establishing high degrees of impact, this alone may not be sufficient.

Factors controlling the likelihood of implementation, or "intervention integrity" (Peterson, 1990; Yeaton & Sechrest, 1981), are less well understood. These factors may include the acceptability or social validity of intervention procedures (e.g., Elliott, 1988; Kazdin, 1980, 1981; Witt & Elliott, 1985); the feasibility or resource demands for intervention implementation (e.g., Odom, McConnell, & Chandler, 1990; Witt, Martens, & Elliott, 1984); and the degree of training, consultation, and other supports available to agents initiating intervention (Peterson, 1990). Relatively little is known about covariation among these and other intervention integrity factors or their direct relationship to intervention impact, and to date most of the research on these relationships has been correlational and based on analogue situations (Peterson, 1990).

It is possible that an analysis of factors affecting likelihood of intervention—as with intervention effectiveness—may be necessary for achieving broad impact on child behavior, but is not sufficient for this outcome. Rather, it may be that *both* intervention effectiveness and likelihood of implementation must be optimized to achieve broad scale positive impact. If this is true, then existing research and development models will have to be extended beyond their current focus on intervention effectiveness, to include systematic analysis of factors that promote intervention implementation in typical intervention settings.

Extending Research and Development Models To Increase Intervention Impact

Research and development (R&D) models guide the overall design and evaluation of systematic efforts to develop standardized interventions (Paine, Bellamy, & Wilcox, 1984). These models establish some general parameters for series of empirical investigations and, to some extent, dissemination activities. As a result, existing R&D models may provide a strong foundation for extending current practices to produce intervention programs that have broader impact.

Walker et al. (1984) describe the research and development model employed at the Center at Oregon for Behavioral Research with the Handicapped (CORBEH). This model, which served as the basis for development and evaluation of four standardized intervention packages at CORBEH and has guided numerous other intervention development projects, includes three phases. Phase I, Component Evaluation and Package Development, is devoted to carefully controlled experimentation (typically in experimental classrooms or settings operated by the investigators) leading to the identification of a maximally effective, yet efficient, array of procedures for remediating a specific behavior disorder. This phase is characterized by small-sample experimental research, in which investigators carefully manipulate independent variables to identify a small number of extremely powerful tactics that serve as the foundation for intervention.

Phase II, Adaptation and Standardization of Package Components, provides opportunities to replicate Phase I procedures in a broader variety of classrooms and situations and to identify a final, standardized pattern for implementing interventions in applied settings. As in Phase I studies, most of the intervention procedures in this phase are implemented by members of the research team; unlike in Phase I studies, however, work in this latter phase is conducted in more typical intervention settings (e.g., community-based classrooms).

Phase III, Field Testing under Normal Conditions of Use, assesses the generalizability and external validity of intervention packages when implemented in typical intervention settings by the profession-als who work in those settings. Walker and colleagues (1984) acknowl-edge the logistical complexity of this phase of research and identify a number of procedures to reduce this effect, including carefully select-ing field test sites, identifying an individual on-site to serve as liaison with researchers, having members of the original research team pro-vide preintervention training, and paying participating intervention agents "for additional time and effort expended in the inservice train-ing/implementation effort" (Walker et al., 1984, p. 69).

The CORBEH R&D model has proved to be an effective strategy for developing intervention packages that produce reliable changes in child behavior in typical intervention settings (e.g., Greenwood et al., 1979; Walker & Hops, 1979); that is, the resulting packages are *effec-tive*. Relatively less systematic information is available, however, re-garding the likelihood of implementation for packages developed ac-cording to this model.

Table 11.5 presents a slight extension to the CORBEH R&D model that is designed specifically to assess, and maximize, both intervention effectiveness and likelihood of implementation. Four specific phases are suggested for this extended R&D model. First, intervention development should begin with assessment of the ac-ceptability, feasibility, and current use of potential intervention com-ponents. As noted earlier, these three variables are assumed to influ-ence likelihood of intervention implementation; as research identifies other variables controlling implementation, they should be included in this phase of model development.

The second phase of this proposed model follows closely the initial phase of the original CORBEH model. However, initial experi-mental activities focus on intervention procedures that were identi-fied in the first phase of the extended model as most likely to be implemented in applied settings.

The third phase again follows the original CORBEH model close-ly, adding only explicit analyses of variables to maximize intervention implementation. These variables might include different models of in-service training, different formats for presenting intervention compo-nents, or different degrees of ongoing intervention support. Specific variables would be determined both by the specific intervention un-der development and prior research on variables that increase the implementation or integrity of interventions.

Fourth, this extended model proposes follow-up assessment of the impact of an intervention package in various intervention set-tings. This analysis might be conducted through replication of pro-

Table 11.5. Research and development model to maximize intervention effectiveness and likelihood of implementation

Translative research and development model	CORBEH research and development model
Assess acceptability, feasibility, and current use of potential intervention components.	
Identify necessary intervention components in controlled study, lab school setting, starting with tactics judged most acceptable and most frequently implemented, and assemble intervention package.	Identify necessary intervention components in controlled study, conducted in lab-school setting.
Evaluate effects of intervention package implemented by R&D staff in naturalistic setting.	Evaluate effects of intervention package implemented by R&D staff in naturalistic setting.
Evaluate effects of intervention package implemented by district staff in naturalistic setting, including analysis of procedures for increasing likelihood of implementation.	Evaluate effects of intervention package implemented by district staff in naturalistic setting.
Assess impact of intervention in community-based intervention settings.	

cedures implemented in the initial phase of research, including direct assessment of intervention practices in a sample of classrooms or other intervention settings. In this phase of research, investigators would evaluate the extent to which intervention procedures are adopted and implemented, and assess the outcomes they produce, in settings and situations not included in earlier phases of research.

This translative model of research and development attempts to incorporate experimental methods for developing maximally effective interventions with systematic efforts to identify and affect variables associated with likelihood of implementation to produce intervention procedures that are most likely to produce significant change in the developmental course of a large group of children in community-based programs. The ultimate test for validity of this model, however, is the extent to which it guides the development of intervention procedures with greater impact than do those procedures currently available.

CONCLUSION

This chapter has reviewed the emerging literature on both assessment of current practices in early childhood special education generally, and assessment of current practices for promoting social competence particularly. Results from both prior research and the descriptive analyses presented here are consistent with Odom's (1988) assertion that research and practice in early intervention exist in largely separate domains. In short, reciprocal influences between research and practice are difficult to discern, and, perhaps, ought to be strengthened.

The extended research and development model reviewed in this chapter suggests one approach to increasing the degree to which research activities influence practical applications. While less apparent in the model proposed here, it may be equally important that activities and needs in applied settings influence the direction and content of research activities. Parents, teachers, administrators, and students should have some ways directly to influence ongoing systematic efforts to improve early intervention services in applied settings.

Focus on the reciprocal influences of researchers and practical settings may produce some friction between programmatic and problem-oriented approaches to research. Yet some blend of basic programmatic research and applied problem-oriented research may be the most productive approach to strengthening the knowledge base and improving the quality and quantity of services in early intervention.

REFERENCES

Bailey, D.G., & Wolery, M.R. (1984). *Teaching infants and preschoolers with handicaps.* Columbus: Merrill.

Brown, W.A., Fox, J.J., & Brady, M.P. (1987). Effects of spatial density on 3- and 4-year old children's socially directed behavior during freeplay: An investigation of a seating factor. *Education and Treatment of Children, 10,* 247–258.

Carta, J.J., Atwater, J.B., Schwartz, I.S., & Miller, P.A. (1990). Applications of ecobehavioral analysis to the study of transitions across early childhood settings. *Education and Treatment of Children 12,* 298–315.

Carta, J.J., Greenwood, C.R., & Atwater, J.B. (1985). *ESCAPE: Ecobehavioral system for complex assessments of preschool environments.* Unpublished coding manual for observational system, Juniper Gardens Children's Project, Kansas City.

Carta, J.J., Sainato, D.M., & Greenwood, C.R. (1989). Advances in the ecological assessment of classroom instruction for young children with handicaps. In S.L. Odom & M.B. Karnes (Eds.), *Early intervention for infants and children with handicaps: An empirical base* (pp. 217–239). Baltimore: Paul H. Brookes Publishing Co.

Carta, J.J., Schwartz, I., Atwater, J., & Connell, M. (1989, October). *Teaching classroom survival skills to students with learning problems.* Paper presented at the annual meeting of the Division of Early Childhood, Council for Exceptional Children, Minneapolis.

Dodge, K. (1983). Behavioral antecedents of peer social status. *Child Development, 54,* 1386–1399.

Elliot, S.N. (1988). Acceptability of behavioral treatments: Review of variables that influence treatment selection. *Professional Psychology: Research and Practice, 19,* 68–80.

Fewell, R.R., & Kaminski, R. (1988). Play skills development and instruction for young children with handicaps. In S.L. Odom & M.B. Karnes (Eds.), *Early intervention for infants and children with handicaps: An empirical base* (pp. 145–158). Baltimore: Paul H. Brookes Publishing Co.

Gottman, J.M. (1983). How children become friends. *Monographs of the Society for Research in Child Development, 48*(Serial No. 201).

Greenwood, C.R., Walker, H.M., Todd, N.M., & Hops, H. (1979). Selecting a cost-effective screening device for the assessment of preschool social withdrawal. *Journal of Applied Behavior Analysis, 12,* 639–652.

Hartup, W.W. (1983). Peer relations. In M. Heatherington (Ed.), *Handbook of child psychology* (Vol. iv., pp. 103–196). New York: John Wiley & Sons.

Kazdin, A.E. (1980). Acceptability of alternative treatments for deviant child behavior. *Journal of Applied Behavior Analysis, 13,* 259–273.

Kazdin, A.E. (1981). Acceptability of child treatment techniques: The influence of treatment efficacy and adverse side effects. *Behavior Therapy, 12,* 493–506.

Kazdin, A.E., Kratochwill, T.R., & Vanden Bos, G.R. (1986). Beyond clinical trials: Generalizing from research to practice. *Professional Psychology: Research and Practice, 17,* 391–398.

Jenkins, J.R., Speltz, M.L., & Odom, S.L. (1985). Integrating normal and handicapped preschoolers: Effects on child development and social interaction. *Exceptional Children, 52,* 7–18.

McConnell, S.R., & Odom, S.L. (1988, October). *Peer-related social competence of preschoolers with handicaps: Instructional emphasis, acceptability of treatment, and performance-based assessment of social competence.* Symposium conducted at the annual meeting of the Division of Early childhood, Council for Exceptional Children, Nashville.

McConnell, S.R., & Odom, S.L. (1989, May). *Translative research in applied behavior analysis: Developing effective and efficient social interaction skill interventions.* Symposium conducted at the Fifteenth annual meeting of the Association for Behavior Analysis, Milwaukee.

McConnell, S.R., & Odom, S.L. (1991, April). *Assessment of peer social competence for young children with disabilities.* Paper presented at the biennial meeting of the Society for Research on Child Development, Seattle.

McConnell, S.R., Peterson, C., Fox, J., & Odom, S.L. (1990, May). *Effects of child-specific intervention on social interaction rates for young children with handicaps: Selection of treatment components.* Unpublished manuscript, Vanderbilt-Minnesota Social Interaction Project, University of Minnesota, Minneapolis.

McEvoy, M., & Skellenger, A. (1990, May). *Manipulating environmental vari-*

ables in preschool classrooms to promote interaction: Is it sufficient? Paper presented at the Sixteenth Annual Convention of the Association for Behavior Analysis, Nashville.

Odom, S.L. (1988). Research in early childhood special education. In S.L. Odom & M.B. Karnes (Eds.), *Early intervention for infants and children with handicaps: An empirical base* (pp. 1–21). Baltimore: Paul H. Brookes Publishing Co.

Odom, S.L., & McConnell, S.R. (1985). A performance-based conceptualization of social competence of handicapped preschool children: Implications for assessment. *Topics in Early Childhood Special Education, 4,* 1–9.

Odom, S.L., McConnell, S.R., & Chandler, L. (1990). *Acceptability and feasibility of classroom-based social interaction interventions for young children with disabilities.* Unpublished manuscript, Vanderbilt-Minnesota Social Interaction Project, Vanderbilt University, Nashville.

Odom, S.L., Peterson, C., McConnell, S.R., & Ostrosky, M. (1990). Ecobehavioral analysis of classroom settings that support peer social interaction of young children with and without disabilities. *Education and Treatment of Children, 13,* 274–287.

Odom, S.L., & Strain, P.S. (1984). Peer-mediated approaches to increasing children's social interaction: A review. *American Journal of Orthopsychiatry, 54,* 544–557.

Ostrosky, M., Chandler, L., Odom, S.L., McConnell, S.R., & Peterson, C. (1990). *Combined intervention manual.* Unpublished manuscript, Vanderbilt-Minnesota Social Interaction Project, University of Minnesota, Minneapolis.

Ostrosky, M., Skellenger, A.C., Odom, S.L., McConnell, S.R., & Peterson, C.A. (1990). *The relationship between teachers' schedules and actual time spent in activities in preschool special education classes.* Manuscript submitted for publication.

Paine, S.C., Bellamy, G.T., & Wilcox, B. (Eds.). (1984). *Human services that work: From innovation to standard practice.* Baltimore: Paul H. Brookes Publishing Co.

Parten, M. (1932). Social participation among preschool children. *Journal of Abnormal and Social Psychology, 27,* 243–269.

Peterson, C.A. (1990). *Intervention integrity: Its relevance to translative research.* Unpublished manuscript, University of Minnesota.

Quilitch, H.R., & Risley, T.R. (1973). The effects of play materials on social play. *Journal of Applied Behavior Analysis, 6,* 575–578.

Sainato, D.M., Strain, P.S., Lefebvre, D., & Rapp, N. (1987). Facilitating transition times with handicapped preschool children: A comparison between peer-mediated and antecedent prompt procedures. *Journal of Applied Behavior Analysis, 20,* 285–292.

Strain, P.S. (1984). Social interactions of handicapped preschoolers in developmentally integrated and segregated settings: A study of generalization effects. In T. Field (Ed.), *Friendship between normally developing and handicapped children* (pp. 187–208). Chicago: Society for Research in Child Development.

Tremblay, A., Strain, P.S., Hendrickson, J.M., & Shores, R.E. (1981). Social interactions of normally developing preschool children: Using normative data for subject and target behavior selection. *Behavior Modification, 5,* 237–253.

Walker, H.M., Hops, H., & Greenwood, C.R. (1984). The CORBEH research and development model: Programmatic issues and strategies. In S.C. Paine, G.T. Bellamy, & B. Wilcox (Eds.), *Human services that work: From innovation to standard practice* (pp. 57–77). Baltimore: Paul H. Brookes Publishing Co.

Witt, J.C., & Elliot, S.N. (1985). Acceptability of classroom intervention strategies. In T.R. Kratochwill (Ed.), *Advances in school psychology* (pp. 251–288). Hillsdale, NJ: Lawrence Erlbaum Associates.

Witt, J.C., Martens, B.K., & Elliott, S.N. (1984). Factors affecting teachers' judgments of the acceptability of behavioral interventions: time involvement, behavior problem severity, and type of intervention. *Behavior Therapy, 15*, 204–209.

Yeaton, W.H., & Sechrest, L. (1981). Critical dimensions in the choice and maintenance of successful treatment: Strength, integrity, and effectiveness. *Journal of Consulting and Clinical Psychology, 49*, 156–167.

12

The Context of Social Competence

Relations, Relationships, and Generalization

Thomas G. Haring

$\mathbf{T}$here are three sources of confusion about the nature of social competence to consider in this concluding chapter. They are closely interrelated in the social competence construct: 1) defining social competence as a static catalog of skills and responses rather than as a dynamic relation between behavior and environment, 2) defining social competence as a set of responses that are abstracted and decontextualized from relationships with others, and 3) focusing on the acquisition of social skills rather than the generalization of social skills.

THE CONTEXT OF SOCIAL COMPETENCE ENCOMPASSES A RELATION

The idea that social competence and making friends can be broken into a series of discrete responses is counterproductive. Can social competence be defined merely in the scientific tradition of breaking it down atomistically into smaller and smaller sub-units, or is something lost when the whole is broken into parts? This chapter argues that something indeed is lost through this approach of reduction and that by looking more closely at contextualistic behavior analytic theory, one may find this missing element.

Contextualism as a Basis for Behavior Analysis

Contextualistic behavior analysis views events as part of the context in which they occur. It is from a complete event within an environmental context that the meaning of an event is derived. That is, the meaning of behavior is analyzed by consideration of the impact that the broad sequence of responses has on the physical environment and on others. For Berkeley philosopher, Stephen C. Pepper, "contextualism denies that there are absolute elements . . . that a whole is nothing but the sum of its parts" (1942, p. 238). Similarly, contextualistic behavior analysts view an event as a dynamic unit, and one cannot understand the event completely by breaking it down into its constituent elements and analyzing them separately. For behavior analysts, this view manifests itself in the basic unit of analysis: the interrelationship between behavior and environment (Skinner, 1953). The elements (i.e., behavior and its relationship to social antecedents and consequences) are not separable within a behavioral analysis. There is a similarity with the existentialist dilemma of deciding whether a tree falling in a forest makes a sound when there is no one present to hear it. To a behavior analyst, a response stripped of the environment, and the environment without an organism acting upon it, have no independent meaning. It is the dynamic interaction between behavior and environment, or more precisely, the functional relationships that are derived from the interaction, that a behavioral analysis focuses on.

Frequently, in this volume and in other literature, the construct of social competence is defined with a list of the socially desirable responses in which a child engages or should engage. The actions of social life are described with verbs such as greeting, sharing, following a teacher's verbal directions, or conversing with someone at a lunch counter. Several of the chapters of this book are excellent catalogs of the skills required to engage in social interaction in integrated preschools and of the differences in the social behavior of children with disabilities as compared with that of their nondisabled peers. Other chapters in this volume are well reasoned catalogs of response repertoires that students lack, this lack isolating them from efficiently learning socially competent behavior. Indeed, this performance-based conceptualization fits well with the idea of task analysis in the design of interventions. However, it is conceivable that many of the difficulties with current intervention efforts, such as limited generalization and maintenance, without fairly sophisticated additional strategies, may be due to failing to define social responses in relation to the motivational functions of behavior, and failing to understand the complexity of contextual stimulus control.

In contrast to the strategy of cataloging needed responses, a contextualistic behavior analysis views the response sequence within the larger social-cultural, environmental, and motivational context in which it occurs. The function of an event and its connection to the context are not necessarily served solely by the teaching of a specific skill to a learner (e.g., sharing a toy with a peer). The skill has to be understood in relation to the goals that a child has for her or his social behavior, the quality of support that the social behavior receives from others, and the power of the simple presence and responsiveness of others in the child's natural settings to increase occurrence of the behavior. In other words, a more contextualistic analysis considers the goals and functions of behavior from the child's perspective, as well as the social responses that the child receives in interaction with others, which reinforce social behavior.

Contextualistic analysis of behavior is related to, but different from, ecobehavioral analysis (e.g., Greenwood et al., 1984). It is related in the sense that both viewpoints are concerned with the relationship between the organization of an environment and aspects of human behavior. Both viewpoints focus on the interrelationship between behavior and the environment and on functional control as a means of understanding variables that control behavior. There are several differences. One important difference is that contextualistic analysis focuses on the purpose of behavior within and across settings or contexts. Getting into a car with the family, parking the car, going to a ticket window and waiting in line, and seeing animals can be described as individual response patterns. But the purpose of these individual responses makes the most sense when described within a context: a trip to the zoo. The meaning of an individual action is best seen in relation to the events that precede and follow it. There is a goal-directed aspect to contextualism that differs from aspects of ecobehavioral analysis. Contextualism describes the unfolding of events as they lead to a certain outcome. For example, if, in the car on the way to the zoo, a detour is encountered, the sequence of streets subsequently selected can be understood best in relation to the desired end point of the trip. Streets that may lead further from the zoo would be rejected in favor of streets that lead in the right direction. Also, in terms of social competence, the nature of the relationships between people is an important part of the social context. For example, nondisabled students who have been taught to view their role as helper, may interact differently with students with disabilities than may nondisabled students who view their role as playmate.

Social competence intervention cannot be the mechanistic imparting of knowledge, as in programming a computer, because instruction takes place within a social context and within a context of functional control. The social context concerns the nature of the social relationship between the child and the teacher, as well as the social usefulness of the content of instruction. A fuller understanding of social competence pedagogy must include not only the precise actions of the teacher in teaching the skill, but also the meaning (i.e., functional control) and interpretation of these actions derived for and experienced by the student and others in the student's life.

Efforts to establish a context for responding prior to instruction are an important outgrowth of this conceptualization. For example, embedding instructional trials within an ongoing flow of play is based on the idea that, from the perspective of a child who does not understand the teacher's perspective of the instructional purpose of the trials, instruction itself is a social interaction. Some social interactions (e.g., social play) are engaging and interesting events, while other interactions (e.g., discrete trial instruction) are unpleasant and uninteresting. One can analyze social contexts to identify those that elicit and support the more adaptive responding of the learner. Those that set the occasion for aversive interaction must be avoided because, not only are these unlikely to result in effective instruction, but they may also teach children that social interactions are unpleasant and are to be avoided.

A contextualistic approach to defining social competence includes a recognition of the broader and multi-level context within which response sequences are taught. For example, many interventionists now emphasize that the nature of activities within which specific skills are taught is critically important. Particular intervention goals are identified and embedded within activities and stable routines. Social skills become subgoals that are taught within the framework of the larger activity or context. Thus, if the goal of instruction is to learn a specific skill, such as more fluent expansion of conversational responses, this skill is taught within multiple, naturally occurring contexts. For example, a child could talk to peers while waiting for class to begin or a child could be prompted to ask a peer a question during a teacher-organized group activity. This type of approach stresses the broader context in which instruction occurs, so that skills are imparted within socially meaningful situations. This avoids a skill being taught in isolation and stripped of its context through the use of massed trials and other artificial instructional strategies.

Incidental teaching and other naturalistic language training techniques (e.g., Hart & Risley, 1975) are examples of contextualized skill training because these procedures embed instruction within the flow of events throughout a child's day. The instructional power of this strategy is probably due to its motivational aspect. That is, an instructional event is not successful until it is clear that a student wants to communicate.

A contextualistic behavior analyst, ever aware of the social context in which actions occur, should emphasize the social/interactive elements that are part of the sequences and activities of the school day. Even though social interactions may not be critical to completing a task, they should be taught and facilitated, within task analyses, because they are integral parts of the textures and strands that make up the overall quality of events that children experience. Embedding social prompting within ongoing activities also creates the basis for later social integration and community participation.

Social Motivation

As discussed, a major shortcoming of defining the construct of social competence by reducing it to solely a matter of skills used is that the interdependence of the behavior of the child and the characteristics of the social environment is not examined. For example, in understanding childhood behavior problems, there is increasing consensus that analyzing the motivational elements of problem behavior is critical. The Motivation Assessment Scale (e.g., Carr & Durand, 1985) focuses analysis on four potential types of functional control served by problem behaviors: 1) avoiding or escaping tasks and other undesirable events and interactions (i.e., the behavior is motivated by negative reinforcement); 2) gaining tangible rewards; 3) the intrinsic reinforcement of sensory stimulation (i.e., stereotypic behavior); and 4) gaining attention. Once a hypothesis as to the functional control of a behavior has been formed, the design of interventions that directly tie into the function can be developed and tested.

In his classic work, *Verbal Behavior* (1957), Skinner accounted for the development and use of language by analyzing the functional control of verbal operants. A *tact*, which in the language pragmatics literature would be called a comment, serves to bring the listener into contact with some aspect of the environment. For example, if two people share an interest in cars, and one points and says, "Lamborghini!", that utterance is serving to bring the other person into contact with what is probably a reinforcer for the speaker. A *mand*, called a request in the language of pragmatics literature, serves to bring tangible or intangible direct rewards. For example, if one says "Water please," within an appropriate context, one is highly likely to receive a glass of water. *Intraverbals*, the components of extended conversation interchanges, are utterances that are under the stimulus control of prior utterances. For example, in talking about the NBA playoffs, one might say, "The Lakers are going to win Friday night," and if the other person is a fan of the Lakers' opponents, the answer might be, "They don't have a chance." Clearly, the first statement exerted some degree of predictive control over the subsequent statement. The *audience* is defined as those listening to a statement. The nature of the audience exerts control over the composition of an utterance. For example, how one addresses one's department chair when requesting resources is different than how one addresses a friend after work. The point is that Skinner's analysis of language use stresses the functional relationship between behavior and its antecedents and consequences within the environment, just as the modern analysis of problem behavior entails examination of the relationship between behavior and its maintaining conditions.

It is necessary to develop similarly powerful conceptualizations of social competence that tie social responses to their inherent relation to the social environment. In many ways the outline for this more contextualistic or holistic analysis of social competence is clear. For example, the first level on which social competence can be understood can parallel similar analyses of problem behavior and verbal behavior. Some social responses serve to gain tangible rewards; avoid or escape certain social contexts, people or interactions; or gain attention or approval of others. As with the tact in Skinner's work, the vast majority of social interaction operants are under complex control that might best be described as *reciprocity*. A tact brings the listener's attention to something happening in the environment. Orienting the listener's behavior to an occurrence serves as the speaker's reinforcer, so it is clear that the listener's behavior comes under the speaker's functional control. The motivational control of the speaker is far less clear. He or she may be motivated by seeing the listener being reinforced in some vicarious process (i.e., seeing another person being reinforced may in and of itself operate as a reinforcer for the observer). More likely, however, the speaker is motivated by a reciprocal relationship with the listener in terms of the listener bringing the speaker into similar contact with reinforcers in the future. In one sense, this is the nature of reciprocity in that the behavior of one interactant occasions a quid-pro-quo in the behavior of another. In teaching children to share toys, for example, the reinforcement for the sharer is just as unclear as the motivational control of the tact is for the speaker above. In fact, it may even be a disadvantageous response—the sharer actually loses the toy. Building motivation to share in the absence of external rewards from the teacher must therefore be based on building an operant with motivational control similar to the tact. The sharer must engage in sharing with the generalized expectation that doing so will cause others to be more likely to share with him or her at some future time. Although interventionists are becoming skilled at defining responses and molding behavior to fit the definitions of social competence, they have only begun to understand the more complex natural functional and motivational control of social responding.

Examining social behavior in terms of the relation between the response and the social environment sheds light on perhaps the most critical problem in the social development of many children and infants with disabilities: developing basic forms of social-functional control. Developing the basic functional control of sharing in a fashion analogous to the functional control of the tact discussed above, is one source of social-functional control. Another source that requires intervention for development in many children with developmental disabilities is causing interaction with other people to be reinforcing in and of itself. For example, in autistic children many problem behaviors and stereotypic behaviors seem to serve the function of avoiding social contact, which to the child is not only not reinforcing, but punishing. Many children with developmental disabilities are tactilely defensive, withdrawn, or noncommunicative. For these children social contacts and attention patterns that seem to be naturally rewarding to the typically developing child have not yet acquired reinforcing properties.

Interventionists are only beginning to understand some of the variables and processes that control the development of motivational functions, including factors such as: 1) responsiveness to child-directed initiations, 2) pairing social reactions and approval within simple sensory-motor routines whose interruption and continuation become predictable to the child, and 3) setting the occasion for exploring the environment and manipulating objects in the environment, by interacting directly with the child and materials. Perhaps the practical problems of generalization and maintenance of the effects of social interventions are due to a failure to understand and build more basic motivational functions of social behavior.

Summary

Whether a child will actually initiate an interaction and open up to the possibility of making a new friend has to do with the strength of his or her motivation to engage in this social interaction. In a contextualistic behavior analysis, a response is analyzed as to its functional control. Simply listing and defining the steps is only half the task. Bypassing the analysis of this complex functional control, then, necessitates the use of rewards that are external to the process. While these rewards will work to teach and increase the behavior, the response class is still highly artificial because it is decontextualized from its natural source of functional control. Clearly then, it is likely that fading the external rewards will not result in the desired generalization and maintenance of responding.

THE CONTEXT OF SOCIAL COMPETENCE ENCOMPASSES A RELATIONSHIP

Interventionists are increasingly aware of the importance of not only increasing social competence, but supporting the development of relationships with others as the appropriate context for interaction. Sociometry is becoming an important means of understanding social competence more fully. Chapter 1 develops the rationale for broadening the perspective on social competence to include outcomes concerning peer perceptions and formation of social networks.

Friendships and Social Networks

As special education evolves with new values, the goals that are newly identified will provide a challenge to existing research strategies and interventions (e.g., Peck & Furman, 1990). One example of these new goals is friendship. Friendships, and the social networks that emerge from them, are now considered to be primary educational goals rather than hoped for side-effects of intervention and programming. However, the creation of friendships may not be amenable to simple sequences of responses (e.g., approach, greet, initiate play, and terminate). Instead, the development of friendships is based on an ongoing complex set of processes, such as creating opportunities for interaction; learning social skills that facilitate interactions; and generating organizational, emotional, and social support to maintain relationships.

Although social skill training can assist in some of these processes (e.g., learning to facilitate interaction by elaborating conversationally) it offers little guidance for other components. For example, the support of a relationship requires a set of interventions such as the seemingly mundane arrangement of times for opportunities for children to play together, or arranging for transportation to a friend's house after school or on the weekend. The adults in a child's environment, beyond the teaching of skills, engage in many support behaviors that facilitate friendship.

A Multi-Level Conceptualization of Social Competence A multi-level conceptualization of social competence is emerging. Each of the several distinct levels across which it views social competence has meaning and specific aspects that are not addressed when analyses are conducted at the other levels. Chapter 2 offers a useful hierarchical model for understanding social competence. Any model of social competence must incorporate not only the different levels and types of responding within the child's repertoire, but the hierarchical impact of social competence on the formation of relationships. The initial, most molecular focus of intervention concerns the *social interactions* and response patterns that occur between individuals. This area of research is already represented in a substantial body of literature (e.g., Haring & Lovinger, 1989) that has sought to understand the behavior of students with disabilities and nondisabled students at the level of social interactions and moment-to-moment changes that occur. Broadening the analysis changes the focus to the *contact patterns* among people and the *meaning of the contacts* to the interactants. At this level, the development, maintenance, and dissolution of social relationships are studied over several months or years providing analyses of, for example, how often individuals have opportunities for contact, how often contacts occur, how rates of contact change over time, and what variables influence contact patterns (Haring, Breen, Weiner, Laitinen, & Bernstein, 1991; Kennedy, Horner, & Newton, 1989). At another level, analyses focus upon the *social networks* of people (e.g., Yan et al., 1990). Social networks, or the individuals who are identified as socially important to a person, have been studied for a better understanding of the individuals who enter and become significant in a person's life.

Intervention   Intervention efforts to promote social competence increasingly must be directed toward building and maintaining social networks, not just teaching social skills. For older students in junior high school and high school settings interventions have been developed to address directly the building of more cohesive social interaction networks and friendships.

The intervention strategy developed is based on the operation of support groups to motivate and maintain attitude and behavioral change (Haring & Breen, 1991). This strategy enlists groups of same-age, nondisabled peers to provide ongoing social support during activities in nonstructured contexts throughout the school day, with the goal, as measured by greater participation and acceptance, being to integrate more fully individuals with disabilities into the social life of their school. These peer networks of a student with disabilities and nondisabled students meet weekly for problem-solving support, advocacy, and development of strategies for achieving the specific objectives of the group. In addition, the peer networks provide ongoing empirical data on their success through teaching nondisabled peers to monitor their own interactions with the student with disabilities in their network. Experimental analysis of the intervention indicates that students with disabilities who participated in peer networks had a greater number of: 1) opportunities for interaction with a stable group of peers, 2) interactions with members of the peer network, and 3) interactions with appropriate social responding within non-structured contexts throughout a school day. In addition, these results are substantiated by group members' increased satisfaction with aspects identified in specific program variables and improved attitudes and ratings of friendship toward the students with disabilities.

Anecdotal reports from peer group members, parents of members with and without disabilities, and teachers indicated that the intervention was successful in facilitating the inclusion of students with disabilities into larger social cliques made up of network members and their friends; the inclusion of the students in nontargeted contexts (e.g., activities after school and on weekends with group members); and shaping nontargeted social behavior (e.g., student initiations of social interaction with group members and peers outside of the group). Additionally, peer participants and their parents, both during and after intervention, remarked on the positive effects of their participation on their overall satisfaction with school life and feelings of ownership of the school experience. Following involvement in a peer support network, the majority of peers described their relationship with the student with disabilities as one of friendship. Within each of the networks, peer participants initiated interactions with the student that were not assigned by the adult facilitator or other members of the group. These interactions included spending time with the student between classes during nonscheduled times, and, at a higher level of commitment, spending time with the student away from school, after school, or on weekends.

A similar model can be extended to building stronger social relationships with younger children. Prior to developing interventions it is important to assess the existing social networks within the social ecology. Yan et al. (1990) offered a method of assessing social networks through analysis of social behaviors between individuals. This methodology has been extended to preschool settings and can provide an assessment of the nature of networks prior to intervention, as well as the changes in networks that result from interventions. The introduction of interventions can then be planned to include members of existing networks rather than attempting to mix students drawn from various networks.

Once the structures of networks within a group of children are clear, interventions can be designed around creating roles for children with disabilities to play within the types of play activities that the network members currently engage in. This strategy has been termed *creating social niches*. For example, in analyzing the social contact patterns of a kindergarten-age boy, it was found that he was attracted to a boisterous group of boys at recess who played a rough and tumble game on a playground slide. Interviewing some members of this group revealed that the game was called "slime monster," and the purpose of the game was for the boys at the bottom of the slide (the slime monsters) to pull boys at the top of the slide down. The boys were asked if the target student could be another slime monster with them during the free play period. For the next several days, the target student played with this group of boys without further need for intervention. Frequently, the integration of young children into extant peer group activities necessitates learning to play in a certain way that contributes to the overall functioning of the group (e.g., Haring & Lovinger, 1989).

Summary

In summary, friendship is a term not defined easily; there exist multiple levels of friendships from acquaintanceships, to friendships, to best friends. The nomination of friendships coupled with spontaneous, nondirected interactions within novel contexts, provides evidence of the development of friendship. Interventionists must be increasingly attentive to friendships as primary intervention outcomes. Social competence plays a critical role in the habilitation, participation, and inclusion of individuals with disabilities in school, neighborhood, and community settings. Friendships can be developed while the social competence of individuals within natural contexts is increased systematically. The use of peers as mediators of social relationships, for social support, and for instructional support is fast on the rise (see McEvoy, Odom, & McConnell, Chapter 5, this volume). Those specific variables that influence the effectiveness of peer network interventions to create circles of friends, and the application of such strategies, need a great deal more investigation.

THE CONTEXT OF SOCIAL COMPETENCE ENCOMPASSES GENERALIZATION

Generalization is the hallmark of socially competent behavior. It is somewhat easier to specify a sequence of responses for engaging in appropriate social behavior in a specific setting than it is to define the characteristics that make behavior generalizable across circumstances. Yet during the developmental period addressed by early child-hood special education, the latter should be the central concern.

As several chapters in this book indicate, there is a continuing need for applying empirically tested generalization strategies to ex-tend behavior across persons, places, and materials. Intervention must concentrate as much on extending performance of skills already in a child's repertoire as on building new skills. It can be argued that a major difference in social competence intervention at the early child-hood level as compared with later childhood and adolescence is this focus on building more generalized skills. As students age, the char-acteristics of their current and future living places, acquaintances, schools, and workplaces become progressively more determined, so the focus of intervention shifts more to supporting rather than build-ing basic generalizable behavior repertoires.

A variety of important generalizable skills have been discussed in several chapters of this book. These include building a basic imitative repertoire and using language as means of interacting. The basic so-cial interaction measures, such as social initiation and responding to the social initiations of others, can fit into an analysis of generalizable skills. For example, once a student learns a basic initiation strategy such as offering to share a toy, many other objects can be substituted into this basic response scheme. As described in Chapter 2, skills such as group entry, negotiating disputes, and assessing the current interests of others must be generalizable. Also, as discussed in several places in this book (e.g., the thorough review in Beckman & Lieber, Chapter 3, this volume), the ability to engage in pretend play, improv-isation of toy play, and forms of role-playing are critical to the development of social competence of young children.

These chapters encompass diverse literature across disability conditions and theoretical viewpoints. Though this material recog-nizes the importance of skill generalization, it shows up a lack of application of more theoretically-driven analytic and intervention sys-tems. For example, although recombinative generalization models have been applied in teaching language use (e.g., Mineo & Goldstein, 1990), there is a paucity of research demonstrating use of this impor-tant strategy to promote social competence. Clearly the types of gen-eralizable social skills listed above can be conceptualized within a recombinative model. Similarly, the developing technology of analyz-ing generalization across response classes, referred to as between-class generalization (e.g, Haring, 1985), has not been applied. Finally, general case programming (e.g., Horner, McDonnell, & Bellamy, 1986), one of the most proven, powerful, and effective means of creating complex generalized responding, has not been applied in teaching social competence to young children.

The strategies of recombinative generalization, between-class generalization, and general case programming can be used to teach complex generalizable repertoires. In fact, these strategies have been referred to as "breeder reactors" because the number of novel recombinations of responses increases exponentially in relation to the number of sequences and skills taught (cf. Haring, Breen, & Laitinen, 1989). The social competence of students with disabilities substantially lags behind that which would be predicted on the basis of other developmental indices such as cognitive development (see Odom, McConnell, & McEvoy, Chapter 1, and Guralnick, Chapter 2, this volume). This retardation in social competence relative to development argues that the students lack strategies and histories that promote the spontaneous and generalized use of responses that, in fact, may already be within their grasp. Clearly, the lack of social competence of many children should be characterized not as a deficit on their part, but as a failure on the part of interventionists to apply the most powerful intervention systems in promoting generalization.

CONCLUSION

The task at hand in understanding and intervening to build social competence encompasses: 1) understanding social competence as a dynamic relation within both situational and motivational contexts, 2) understanding social competence within the context of building human relationships and social networks, and 3) appreciating the developmental necessity of generalization in building social competence. Young children need to learn to play, interact, and communicate with others. These goals should remain critical for social support and intervention across the life span. The foundation laid in early childhood is essential, so it is imperative to understand the variables that control the development of this foundation.

REFERENCES

Carr, E.G., & Durand, V.M. (1985). Reducing problem behaviors through functional communication training. *Journal of Applied Behavior Analysis, 18,* 111–126.

Greenwood, C.R., Dinwiddie, G., Terry, B., Wade, L., Stanley, S.O., Thibadeau, S., & Delquadri, J.C. (1984). Teacher- versus peer-mediated instruction: An ecobehavioral analysis of achievement outcomes. *Journal of Applied Behavior Analysis, 17,* 521–538.

Haring, T.G. (1985). Teaching between-class generalization of toy play behavior to handicapped children. *Journal of Applied Behavior Analysis, 18*, 127–139.

Haring, T.G., & Breen, C. (1991). *A peer mediated social network intervention to enhance the social integration of persons with moderate and severe disabilities.* Manuscript submitted for publication.

Haring, T.G., Breen, C., & Laitinen, R.E. (1989). Stimulus class formation and concept learning: establishment of within- and between-set generalization and transitive relationships via conditional discrimination procedures. *Journal of the Experimental Analysis of Behavior, 52*, 13–25.

Haring, T.G., Breen, C.G., Weiner, J., Laitinen, R.E., & Bernstein, D.D. (1991). *Effects of contextual variation and teacher structure on social interaction across school, classroom, and community settings.* Manuscript submitted for publication.

Haring, T.G., & Lovinger, L. (1989). Promoting social interaction through teaching generalized play initiation responses to preschool children with autism. *Journal of The Association for Persons with Severe Handicaps, 14*(1), 58–67.

Hart, B.M., & Risley, T.R. (1975). Incidental teaching of language in a preschool. *Journal of Applied Behavior Analysis, 8*, 411–420.

Horner, R.H., McDonnell, J.J., & Bellamy, G.T. (1986). Teaching generalized skills: General case instruction in simulation and community settings. In R.H. Horner, L.H. Meyer, & H.D.B. Fredericks (Eds.), *Education of learners with severe handicaps: Exemplary service strategies* (pp. 289–314). Baltimore: Paul H. Brookes Publishing Co.

Kennedy, C.H., Horner, R.H., & Newton, J.S. (1989). Social contacts of adults with severe disabilities living in the community: A descriptive analysis of relationship patterns. *Journal of The Association for Persons with Severe Handicaps, 14*, 190–196.

Mineo, B., & Goldstein, H. (1990). Generalized learning of receptive and expressive action-object responses by language-delayed preschoolers. *Journal of Speech and Hearing Disorders, 55*, 665–678.

Peck, C.A., & Furman, G.C. (1990). Qualitative research in special education: An illustrative review. In R. Gaylord-Ross & J. Campoine (Eds.), *Research issues in special education.* San Diego: College-Hill.

Pepper, S.C. (1942). *World hypotheses: A study in evidence.* Berkeley: University of California Press.

Skinner, B.F. (1953). *Science and human behavior.* New York: Macmillan.

Skinner, B.F. (1957). *Verbal behavior.* New York: Appleton-Century-Crofts.

Yan, X., Storey, K., Rhodes, L., Sandow, D., Petherbridge, R., & Loewinger, H. (1990). Grouping patterns in a supported employment work setting: Clique analysis of interpersonal interaction. *Behavioral Assessment, 12*, 337–354.

Index

Academic/preacademic skills, so-
cial/survival skills and, transition planning and, 248–255,
273–274
Acceptance
social status and, 40
visual impairments and, 175
see also Inclusion; Peer rejection
Activities
affection, 124–125
classroom, 94
structure of, 94–96
time allocation for, 288–290, 298
types promoting peer interactions, 286–288
see also Play
Adaptive behaviors, specific language impairment and, 206
Adolescence, peer relationship development in, 194
Adult(s)
children's interaction with,
hearing impairments and,
137–143
involvement of, in interventions
with visual impairments, 182
prompting by, *see* Prompting
reduction of dependence on,
hearing impairments and,
155–156
see also Parent *entries*; Teacher *entries*
Adulthood, functioning in, early
intervention and, 19
Affection training procedures,
124–125
Age
at hearing loss onset, 137
initiations and, 76

of peers, 97–98
social strategies and, 49
transition and, 246–247
Aggression, crowding and, 100–101
American Association on Mental
Deficiency, mental retardation definition of, 6
Analogue settings, experimental
paradigms using, 38
peer group entry and, 50–51
Analysis
units of, 7, 228
see also Methodology
Appropriateness, 7, 39
of social strategies, *see* Social
strategies
social tasks and, 42
of utterances, 49–50
Assessment
behavioral, 12
see also Social behavior(s)
ecobehavioral, 281–282
see also Ecobehavioral *entries*
of information processing, 55
of intervention impact, 299–300.
multimethod, 17–18
performance-based, 16–18
of practice in ECSE
current, 282–297
earlier efforts in, 280–282
of social/communicative skills,
45–48
limitations of, 48–49
sociometric, *see* Sociometric assessment
techniques of, 39–40
timing of, sibling interaction and,
221–222
Assessment of Peer Relations, 45

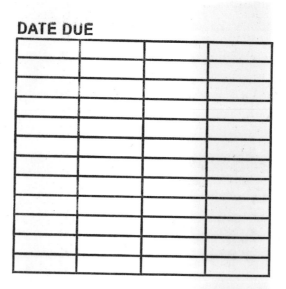

DATE DUE

DEMCO